INDIAN ESSENTIALS

INDIAN ESSENTIALS

PENGUIN BOOKS

PENGUIN BOOKS
Published by the Penguin Group
Penguin Books India Pvt. Ltd, 11 Community Centre, Panchsheel Park, New Delhi 110 017, India
Penguin Group (USA) Inc., 375 Hudson Street, New York, New York 10014, USA
Penguin Group (Canada), 90 Eglinton Avenue East, Suite 700, Toronto, Ontario, M4P 2Y3, Canada (a division of Pearson Penguin Canada Inc.)
Penguin Books Ltd, 80 Strand, London WC2R 0RL, England
Penguin, Ireland, 25 St Stephen's Green, Dublin 2, Ireland (a division of Penguin Books Ltd)
Penguin Group (Australia), 250 Camberwell Road, Camberwell, Victoria 3124, Australia (a division of Pearson Australia Group Pty Ltd)
Penguin Group (NZ), 67 Apollo Drive, North Shore 0632, New Zealand (a division of Pearson New Zealand Ltd)
Penguin Group (South Africa) (Pty) Ltd, 24 Sturdee Avenue, Rosebank, Johannesburg 2196, South Africa

Penguin Books Ltd, Registered Offices: 80 Strand, London WC2R 0RL, England

First published by Penguin Books India 2010

10 9 8 7 6 5 4 3 2 1

ISBN 9780143065265

Typeset in Adobe Garamond Pro by Inosoft Systems, Noida
Printed at Gopsons Papers Ltd, Noida

Contents

The Great Indian Family

. . . .

Geeta Doctor

It is the smile that you see on the faces of children by the wayside. It is the involuntary leap of a drummer boy who catapults into the air with a thump and a shout when he sees a stranger. It is the colour of life on the subcontinent. It spills onto the streets in an endless stream of people of every physical type and size and social difference. The Great Indian Family is a patchwork quilt of many bits and pieces that defines the way we live.

At one level it holds the whole of humanity in its embrace. It reaches out into the darkness of infinity and declares *vasudeva kutumber*—the world is my oyster. At another level, the Indian family is the most tightly run of corporations. If it's an oyster, it's a mean little oyster world that snaps itself shut the moment it senses an alien particle coming its way. It gobbles anyone who can serve its larger purpose. The intruder is hunted down in the name of caste, colour, community, fitness or anything else that might destroy the image of the unit. The family depends on a closed system of loyalties and allegiances. It feeds itself on its individual parts as intently and as ruthlessly as an oyster coats a particle of sand with layer upon layer of a nacreous substance and transforms it into a shining pearl. This is the precious pearl that every Indian yearns to possess in the name of identity.

The Great Indian Family stretches back into myth. It endorses images of legendary lusts and passions that even to this day find expression in dance, song and popular television serials that provoke equal amounts of anxiety and exhilaration about the Indian psyche from a dedicated viewership. It spills into the rituals and habits of everyday life. It weaves itself into the texture of fabrics, the cut and fall of a jacket; the invisible messages are embroidered into the patterns that adorn a veil, chunni, chador or dupatta; it insinuates itself into the pleats of a sari pallav—all the while reminding the person: this is where you belong. It stirs ancient secrets of spices and ingredients into items of food and decrees strict methods on how these should be preserved, prepared and partaken within members of a select community or household.

'Do not eat with your left hand, use only the right hand,' a child is admonished even before he or she learns to walk. It is just one amongst a myriad distinctions that are instilled into a person by family members. In south India, a marriage feast is traditionally served on a banana leaf, indeed at any important festival the *elai sappad* is an integral part of the celebration. Though they all seem the same, the way the food is served on the leaf presents a veritable identity kit, or map, made up of edible items. In some communities, when the leaf is placed before each guest, it is empty. The first thing that a person does is sprinkle some water on it and give it a sideways swipe using the edge of the palm of the right hand, before allowing the food to be served. In others, some items of food are already placed on the leaf. Even before you begin to eat you are judged on whether you are an insider or an outsider. A faux pas is immediately detected and commented upon: 'You are not one of us,' your neighbour will say, seemingly as a joke. It teaches you that people are always watching. In turn, you too grow up registering the minute play of differences. You learn a code that not only gives the individual a unique sense of belonging, it reaffirms the importance of the group.

In some ways every Indian is an outsider. Or to put it another way, every Indian is part of a minority. This is what makes being 'family' so important. As Nirad C. Chaudhuri put it so graphically in *The Continent of Circe*, our ancestors came across the harsh plains of Central Asia and the icy rock-strewn barriers of our northern frontiers as cattle herders. They came through the centuries in small groups in times of famine and war. They brought with them their martial traits, their alien gods, who in time made splendid marital adjustments with the original deities of the land whom they dubbed 'primitive' or 'feminine'. They absorbed them into their pantheon of charismatic male gods vibrantly alive with an irresistible abundance of energy and included them in their chants that extolled the masculine elements of fire and air as against the passive ones of water and earth.

As they settled in the lush tropical landscape of the Indian subcontinent, they succumbed to the torpor of the hot fertile Indo-Gangetic plain and, as the title of Chaudhuri's book suggests, they became fat, indolent and swinish in their turn. With each succeeding wave, the migrants became more dominant and dislodged the earlier settlers who were pushed further east and south with their cattle and their closely guarded obsessions with breeding and racial purity. They carried with them their nomadic instincts, keeping their memories alive through songs and histories told through the long winter night as they huddled under their quilts.

Like these itinerant family histories, the Indian quilt is made up of many such layers. It's called a *razai* and stitched together by the older women in the family out of the discarded material from worn-out clothes, each patch and layer carefully placed to cover a worn out place. The borders of saris are picked apart for their threads and each of these used to embroider motifs that carry forward tales and tokens that make up a family's history. In some communities these quilts are part of a girl's dowry, something that she would be expected to make long before her marriage, to carry with her to her new home. In other communities they are covered with symbols of fertility and used to decorate the marriage chamber to welcome a new bride or to wrap a newborn child. Most times, of course, a razai is just that—a wrap-around quilt that the family shares for comfort and warmth in the winter.

In nomadic communities, wealth is always of the portable kind. Jewellery, for instance, is of silver, mixed metals and, when possible, of gold and polished gemstones to make the glittering pieces of personal adornment that are the stuff of legends. As these communities settled down they tended to exchange their need for decorating their persons to adorning the image of a powerful deity residing in the temple of their choice and eventually, by extension, the personage of the local chieftain or ruler, whether as raja or nawab. The fabled gems that were discovered in the rich alluvial soils of the subcontinent became tokens of power between warring tribes in times of conflict. Notice, how even today the highlight of a marriage ceremony is marked by an exchange of gifts in gold and silver. The jewels brought by the bride are always scrutinized by the bridegroom's party and measured in exact amounts, as if she were indeed part of a cattle-herding culture.

Houses tended to be clustered in small fortified settlements. A traditional Indian home looks inwards into a courtyard or a series of them laid out in alternating sets of rooms that carefully designate, to a very precise ordering, which spaces are for general use and which for private audience, which areas are only for males, females, immediate family, guests, employees, servants and so on.

These are the survival strategies that held the promise of a future life. Some call this the powerful instinct of the 'selfish gene', which the Great Indian Family by its apparently altruistic impulses endorses. They ensure that it is the dominant group that wins the race. The family makes sure that its attributes are passed on to the next generation by defining its territory (what might be called 'branding' in marketing terminology). These are qualities that will enhance a kinship group while still being flexible enough to include in its gene bank the DNA of a spectacularly well-endowed individual favoured by the gods or by natural selection to add a rogue strain to the family line. Survival is the key. In an uncertain world where only chaos is a constant, the Indian family remains at the centre of the vortex contemplating its own navel. As depicted in Indian iconography, it is of course an exceptional navel, the navel of an enchanting god floating on the amniotic waters of the primal ocean, asleep upon a serpent. A smile plays upon his lips, while a lotus flower sprouts from the centre of his navel, a flowering umbilical cord as it were that connects him to the world; nature and nurture entwined in the most enigmatic of ways.

~

The onset of summer is when the Great Indian Family unfurls itself in all its triumphant glory. It stretches its limbs across the wide expanse of the subcontinent just as trees do against the incredible blue of the sky in that brief moment which marks the changing of one season to another. It's not quite yet summer. The mornings are still filled with the cool dampness of a winter night. The spring rains have come and gone. The sun has yet to begin its martial progress across the hemisphere wearing its helmet of burnished copper and methodically flattening the earth under its metallic tread.

In that brief interregnum, every tree and flowering plant worth its name bursts into colour, spilling its fragrance into the air. The branches of mango, guava, chikoo and tamarind bend down to offer the sticky-sweet sap of their tender fruit that attract fruit flies as regularly as they do the attentions of children on their way to school. It's a busy season, filled with the shrieks of nest-building creatures that scurry across the swollen network of fields and forest stocking up on their food reserves. Indian families reflect this bustle. This is when the planning begins and families consult their almanacs and carefully plot and plan their departures to family homes and estates, or villages and farms. It's almost as if the nomadic instinct is still alive and raring to go.

At railway stations and nowadays at airports the waiting rooms are filled with people waiting to go 'home'. They carry bundles of food. In the old days these were carried in 'tiffin carriers', food for the journey and special delicacies for those living back on the family estate. On the return trip, there are also vast amounts of freshly made food items. The pickles, the *podis*, the pappads, the preserves are all part of the process in which an individual is reminded that he or she does not exist by himself or herself—the family sustains every unit. In return, each unit is responsible for the welfare of the larger family group. With every sip and morsel that a person drinks and bites into, there is an unspoken reminder—this is who you are, this is who you are—as persistent as the hum of the wheels on the railway track. The more a person travels away from the family hearth, the more that individual becomes obsessed with a particular brand of coffee, or the taste and texture of a dosa, the manner in which a biryani is sealed into its container, or a bowl of sweetened milk and rice, lightly sprinkled with strands of pale gold saffron and slivers of golden fried almonds that he or she might have tasted many years back at the wedding of a cousin on his father's side, twice removed.

Memories of food are what bring families together. Every writer from the Indian diaspora who has dabbled in a summer course in writing will dip her ladle of memories into a cauldron of recipes from her grandmother's kitchen. The *tharawad*, the haveli, the *rasoi*, the *dastarkhana*, the tandoor, the tawa, the roadside dhaba and the even more mysterious *balti* have all become shorthand references for promoting a particular type of cooking which promises to be an authentic recreation of the flavours of a social group or community. Never mind that some of these terms refer to a form of architecture, others to a kitchen where the women of the house might have rarely entered, or to a type of kitchen utensil. It triggers an instant sense of belonging. Just as the moment you step into an Indian home or restaurant in any part of the world, even before you remove your overcoat, you feel as though you've been drugged and dragged into an underground cellar of memories fighting for fresh air. The atmosphere is thick with the aroma of oil and Indian spices. The coil of incense or scented candle that has been lit from a votive altar under the staircase impregnated with the fragrance of jasmine, rose or amber, depending on the community, curls up and clobbers you if you haven't succumbed already.

You feel you are at home, even though it might not be your home. It reminds you that amongst an older generation one of the ways of welcoming a person into the family fold was for the mother, granny or senior aunt to bend down and actually sniff the guest (of course, it was never actually a guest) as though to inhale that person's aura. 'Ummm!' the guardian of the family hearth would pronounce, 'you smell so different.' Or it could be: 'You smell so good, so foreign.' People in the extended family circle, the servants for instance, would generally comment on the individual's size. You were almost always too thin and too dark, and your hair looked like the proverbial crow's nest, that is to say not shining with oil, another sign of having left the family fold. Such inspections would invariably end with the words: 'Come, I will feed you properly.' In some families, placing the first morsel, or ball of mashed up rice with an accompaniment, either sweet, tart and sour, or buttery, in the mouth of an errant member is a privilege exercised by the matriarch which she insists on doing in front of everyone.

Or, if you are from Kerala, the injunction would usually be, 'Go and have a proper oil bath. The hot water is ready.' If not anything else, the person would be offered a gourd-shaped container (*lota*) or one with a spout at the side (*khindi*) with water to wash away the dust from his or her feet. The individual would immediately become a child again, as cherished and beloved as the stories told of the infant Krishna dallying amongst the milkmaids of Vrindavan.

It brings to mind the two giant blonde women guardians who used to stand at the entrance to the Rajneesh Ashram in Pune. As every visitor passed through the gates of the ashram, the two sniffer blondes would bend down and snort each person down. They were meant to check for any trace of soap, shampoo or deodorant with perfume to which the Bhagwan was said to be deeply allergic and thus had to be banned from anyone entering the portals of the ashram. It reinforces the idea that ashrams are an alternate family-type establishment, not built on bonds of blood but on another type of servitude: a negation of the self that is particularly attractive to the Indian mind. It promises the ideal of absolute freedom not just in this life but maybe when all the various surrenders are made in the next life and thereafter, as well as a sense of belonging to a special family unit with all its privileges and restrictions. It requires a one-time relinquishing of the individual self, that noxious buzzing of the ego or the 'I' that demands a special recognition and which has to be annihilated on the altar of whatever demands are made by a particular teacher or guru.

It goes without saying that the dispensation of food, whether as prasad or in the mass feeding of devotees that some ashrams still cook in pure ghee, is another aspect of the contract that endows these places with the caring outward face of the 'mother'. Some gurus claim rather that they are indeed the incarnation of the primal 'Mother' or Goddess. Ask them why they never feel inspired to give free food to a starving person or a cripple begging at their gates and their minders will answer that this is because they are not part of the family of this godperson or that guru. They have bad karma or, worse, the wrong genetic code. Only a 'real' mother can recognize her 'real' children.

Food is also what keeps families apart, as the various differences in their manner of procurement, preparation and dispensation are subject to every manner of debate and dissension. Even drinking a glass of water can be an immediate giveaway. The manner in which a person holds a glass or tumbler that has been given by a stranger with the tips of his middle finger and thumb two inches from his opened lips and levers it into his throat, with his eyes half-shut, is just one indication. If he is an adept he will just hold the glass by the rim and not spill a drop. When you travel in parts of interior Rajasthan, Uttar Pradesh or Gujarat, the casual way in which a tea vendor asks you where you are from, or more directly what your caste might be, will determine, even without your noticing it, whether he will serve you in a glass, a metal tumbler, a factory made tea-cup or a disposable container made of mud. Plastic containers are of course the great leveller.

When sitting in a railway compartment, you can identify the person camping next to you the moment he or she opens the tiffin carrier or sealed plastic container and the aroma of a particular oil or condiment that has been used for tempering (and thereby also preserving the food) wafts into the stale air of the train. The pungent, acrid smell of mustard oil in a north Indian paratha, the slow fermentation process by which the curd rice or tamarind rice that has been packed in banana leaf by a south Indian traveller ripens into the sour odour of one-day old towels, and the reek of asafoetida that is kneaded into the oily masala *theplas* packed by persons from Gujarat in stainless steel containers filled also by a peculiar form of crunchy savory fragment called *farsan* have a way of spreading into every crevice and corner of the compartment with a life of their own and are just some of the culinary treats that serve as points of reference. The more Westernized amongst the passengers, in the old days the Anglo-Indians and Parsis, travelled with sandwiches and cutlets, a tendency that survives in the institution of 'bread-butter-omelette' that some railway stations still provide during the morning hours.

As noted by the American travel writer Paul Theroux in *The Great Railway Bazaar*, his best-known book about the Indian subcontinent, these accompaniments to train travel invariably led to fellow travellers with a tendency to fart. It should not be seen as a social disgrace. Farting in trains is a perfectly companionable activity, caused by the rhythmic jolting of the wheels as much as by the need to start eating almost as soon as the train leaves the station. It's actually something of a salutation, a distant rumble let out usually by the paterfamilias to signal that he is now relaxed enough to start a conversation. The father, or uncle, may lean delicately, lifting the lower part of his torso to one side and then the other, to express himself in this manner. The women are usually more circumspect. They allow themselves, while bolt upright, to let out a series of small peeps, whistles and squeaks, rather like a junior officer onboard a naval vessel ceremoniously piping an admiral who is on a tour of duty.

This is a way of indicating that the family is now at ease, ready to open up to strangers and begin the process of discreetly establishing their position in the world, or as we would say today, revealing their identity. It signals, for instance, that the family has been well provided for by the host that they have just left, or the joint resources of the ancestral home. A person who has to fend for himself or herself by ordering the food that has been catered for by the railways immediately falls in the estimation of his or her fellow passengers. It's a sure sign that he is an individual without much family support. In earlier times, it was de rigueur that at every major railway station members of the extended family should come and provide fresh packets of food and water to the travellers. You never, ever ate anything that was not cooked at home. After all, what was family for?

~

Other civilizations might boast about their conquests, the rise and fall of empires, speak of heroes vanquishing the intruder with one mighty swipe of his antique axe that still hangs in the national museum. In India, mothers define the family, much as they do the Indian nation. 'Look at the outlines of the Indian subcontinent. The shape itself is like that of a beautiful woman.' These are people who believe that the country itself is a sacred land, *suvarna bhoomi*, a land of gold, literally, as it used to be in ancient times when the rivers ran with gold and diamonds, and, metaphorically, when the fertility of the soil made it a land of plenty. To these people 'Geography is Destiny'. Eternal India is always presented in the guise of a woman—her hair streaming behind her, her face radiant, goddess-like, with multiple arms ready to multi-task for the sake of the family or, in its extended form, the nation. She can be virgin, warrior woman and mother, a purveyor of nationalist imagery or, as is most often the case today, a delectable icon of consumerist fantasies from 'frigidaires to cellphones.

The idea of the land morphs into the ideal of the female principle, the woman who sustains the family. Both must be preserved, protected and at the same time kept under control by careful marshalling of natural resources. The ownership of a piece of Indian soil and of the Indian woman goes hand-in-hand. In 'The Santhal Family' by the Bengali sculptor Ramkinker Baij, one of the most poignant pieces of artistic imagination, the image of famine-stricken parents leading their two small children away from disaster, the woman carrying a headload of their belongings in a basket, symbolizes both the anguish and the hopes of the smallest of family units. They are refugees in their own country and yet they stride ahead with dignity. The basket is a sign that they can start their life again somewhere, on another piece of land. The husband has his woman and his family behind him.

Yet, whatever we may say about the persistence of the mother image and the worship of the mother goddess, it's the male principle that upholds and sustains every idea that we might have of the Great Indian Family. The images that come down to us from the two great epics of the subcontinent, the Mahabharata and the Ramayana, are not only of war and conquest and of families in conflict, but also the dominance of patriarchy, where women are trophies to be bought, conquered through acts of manly valour, or bartered. In a phallocentric society it's patriarchy that sets the rules.

Of all the aberrations that take place in the generally male-dominated Indian family (or patrilineal) system, the most interesting are those cases where women are on top, so to speak. The Nairs of Kerala are the best known, though there are certain hill tribes in the north-east of the country, such as the Khasis, who also follow the matrilineal system, or the inheritance of property through the women. In the case of the Khasis, it is the youngest daughter of the family who inherits the majority share of the family property. It is the bridegroom who moves into the wife's house after marriage.

Amongst the Nairs of Kerala the tradition of women ruling the roost probably evolved on account of the Nair men being members of the warrior caste. Their need to be continually involved in feudal fights amongst the various noblemen seeking to establish their rights made it necessary for the women to take a martial stance themselves. Not only were the Nair women of those times supposed to be trained in the famous methods of combat that come under the name of Kalaripayattu, they were fiercely independent householders. They kept their family homes, or tharawads, running without their men and accepted a system of 'visiting husbands' who could cross their thresholds at night as long as they left their chappals or sandals and spears or swords at the front door. (Today, it would probably be an injunction to leave their cellphones and laptops on the doorstep.) This also indicated to any possible real husband or rival that the lady of the house was otherwise occupied.

'Take your chappals and leave!' has become a phrase by which a woman from this part of the country traditionally gets rid of an unwanted mate. The positive side of the arrangement is that it recognizes the children born into the household and they are nurtured by the mother's family, regardless of whether the father is around or not. The inheritance is through the maternal line, hence the term matriliny. An added feature is that it's the older brother of the senior woman in the family who performs the role of the male head of the family, which is why it can't really be described as a matriarchy or a woman-dominated system either.

A constantly repeated refrain in Indian society is about the threat to the honour of the woman from abduction and rape, or defilement. These conflicts cannot but suggest the deep fear of the 'other' that lurks in the Indian psyche. Even as there are many examples of gods that take on the anthropomorphic forms of animals with human qualities who display superhuman instincts on behalf of those who seek their help—the wise monkey, the kind elephant, the magical horse, the golden swan, the all-seeing eagle—the opposite is also true. It suggests equally that within the safety of the Great Indian Family, there are un-named desires that threaten to destroy its harmony. Even though in every community there is a complex range of titles that spell out the relationship between the different members of the family that implies a code of conduct between them, the unspoken fear, the hidden secret is of incestuous longings and feelings that are most often repressed or buried away in the silent recesses of family history.

It also suggests that in a hostile environment women are to be protected or nurtured. When you travel through the harsh desert countryside of Rajasthan and notice how the women are covered from head to toe-ringed feet in vibrantly coloured cloths and heavy silver jewellery, you may surmise that some of it is for protection against the fierce heat and the abrasive wind. Even the men wear turbans and sturdy clothing. The women work in the fields just as hard. They carry pots of water on their heads and forage for firewood over long distances. They smoke both tobacco and opium. On a surface level, there is some degree of independence.

For all the outward appearances, they are ruled by strict taboos that do not permit them to uncover their faces, technically, even in front of their mothers-in-law. They are drilled into showing respect in a strictly observed hierarchy of obligation. The higher up the women are on the social ladder, the more constrained they are to follow the rules. It's not just the veil that cuts them off from the world, but the beautifully chiselled stone *jalis* or screens, the embroidered curtains and drapes that were used to cover the *dolis* or palanquins when they travelled, the very architecture of the now famous havelis and mansions of the merchant and princely classes—everything conspired to suggest that women had to be sheltered from the gaze of the outsider, but equally insistently kept behind gilded bars.

The birth of a son is the prime need and requirement of the wife. Almost all rites of passage within the Hindu way of life suggest that without a male heir there can be no hope of achieving any degree of freedom in this life or even the next couple of lives. The edicts of Manu, an ancient law-giver, are explicit on this point and, however grotesque or absurdly anti-woman his precepts might sound, they are so ingrained within the Indian psyche that no matter what the subsequent thinking on the subject might have been the woman is defined by the men in her life—her father, her husband, her son.

Of all the myths, the one in the Mahabharata concerning the continuation of the bloodline of the Kuru dynasty is one of the most fascinating. Satyavati, who went on to become the Queen Mother of the royal house of Kurus, was the daughter of a fisherman. As a young woman, she was as beautiful as a fresh blade of grass in the early morning, but she had a terrible problem. She smelt of fish. So powerful was the odour (notice the obsession with body odours even in these early times) that she was known as Matsyagandha or the One with the Fishy Smell. One morning she had to row a holy man across the river, since her father was not around. The holy man was attracted to her youth and charm and did not remark upon her pungent body odour. It's not unusual to find sages and other holy men equipped with advanced libidos, then as now. He told her that if she rowed him to the middle of the lake and allowed him to make love to her, he would give her a gift that she could not refuse. He would make her body full of an enchanting fragrance. They made love on the boat and when the fish-maiden returned she became Satyavati. As the sage predicted, her beauty was now complete. The fragrance of Satyavati's body attracted the attention of the king of the country. Her life was transformed. She became his wife, the beauteous Queen Satyavati, she of the fragrant charm.

She did not tell anyone that her first sexual adventure with the sage had produced a son named Vyasa. She had given him up for adoption to a group of holy men. He disappeared into the forests and became known for his austerities as a holy man living without any thought to the needs of his body.

Many years later, his mother called him with a strange request. Her two legitimate sons had been killed in battle. Their widows, the princesses Ambalika and Amba, were childless. Would he impregnate them, she asked, so that the line of the Kurus could continue? They were, after all, the wives of his half-brothers, all said and done his *family*. How could he refuse? He agreed to perform his duty.

Vyasa was covered with ash, his hair matted, his body unwashed, even stinking perhaps. When he entered Ambalika's bedchamber, she was so horrified by his appearance she closed her eyes during the whole process. It was a kind of rape. Her son was born blind. He became Dritharashtra, the blind king, head of the Kauravas.

The queen ordered Ambalika to try again with Vyasa. This time, Ambalika sent her maid. The child born of this union was called Vidura. In his time, he was wise and kind, but as the son of a servant girl, who remains un-named, he lacked status. What's interesting is that the offspring of such unions are generally described as exceptionally clever. At moments of crisis, these are the sons or daughters who come forward to save the honour of the family. Vidura never wavered in his duty as a person who guarded the dharma of the clan.

Queen Satyavati wanted yet another grandson. This time she asked Princess Amba to receive Vyasa. Notice how it is the mother-in-law who calls the shots and decides with whom and when a prospective mate should enter the marital chamber. This is still a feature of traditional joint families in some communities. When he came into her bed, Amba grew pale at the prospect of being impregnated by such a man. Her child was called Pandu, the white one. Perhaps he was an albino. He became the father of the Pandava clan. Along with the Kauravas, the Pandavas represent the two main branches of the Kurus who wage war through the stormy episodes of the Mahabharata.

In a sense these stories track the kind of disputes that exist in every large Indian family despite the apparent sense of solidarity that they are meant to represent. It's usually a case of filial dispute over land and power between the male members of the family, even if in popular lore it manifests itself as intense rivalry between the competing daughters-in-law who are in conflict with the older women in the family, most often their mother-in-law. The case of the servant woman who bears a child is also a strand that appears in many families, as the dominant male finds ways of using the girl who has been brought as part of the bride's dowry. Such a child lives in a parallel universe, both part of the family as a companion to the legitimate son, or daughter, and yet without any rights.

In some cases, the servant girl, the peasant woman or tribal woman who accompanies a bride to her husband's house also acts as the wet nurse, giving rise to the term 'milk brothers'—babies who share the same breast of the woman who may well have the more abundant supply of breast milk, as convention dictates. Again the offering of a strange woman's breast as an act of female bonding gets a strange twist in the case of baby Krishna, who is offered the breast of Puttanna, who pretends that she would like to feed the lovely boy child. She is of course a demoness, the quintessential other, and though she has anointed her nipples with poison, it is the infant who sucks the life-blood out of her with his supernatural powers.

The ideas of the purity of the bloodline and the importance of family are reinforced in the stories depicted in the Ramayana. No matter the different types of interpretation that might be given today to Sita's treatment by her husband Rama, the main image is of a couple who remain faithful to each other no matter what the terrible ordeals fate has in store for them in their stormy life together. Sita will always be seen as the chaste wife. Rama never marries again, though as king and ruler of a prosperous kingdom, he has every right to do so. Again, the underlying message is that no matter what their individual feelings, individuals represent the family bloodline, which is more important than any personal desires or feelings of love and longing for each other. Such concerns simply do not matter as long as dharma—the inviolable sense of duty to the family and the clan—is kept sacred.

It trundles across the Indian imagination with all the weight of a juggernaut. The towering wooden chariot or *rath* with its two massive wooden wheels that carries the grandly decorated gods and goddesses on their annual walkabout around their temples has often been likened to Indian society itself. The two wheels represent the two partners of this enterprise, a man and a woman, a husband and a wife, both of whom are required for a stable way of life, for the well-being of a society and a family.

~

It may not be a palatable truth. The individual does not count. In the long run it is the tribe that must survive even if it is at the expense of the other or others. It is a belief that is so deeply bred into the bone and blood of the Great Indian Family that it seems to be part of the rhythms of the Indian soil itself. The group lives on the body of the individual, just as the god Shiva danced on the supine form of a dwarf or demon. This is why we have compared the Great Indian Family to the most tightly run of corporations. It lumbers down the Indian subcontinent with mergers and acquisitions that are as carefully assimilated in its capacious genetic portfolio as any corporate raider. They might take the form of migrant tribes looking for greener pastures. Or of waves of ferocious invaders seeking to expand their territory. Or even of argosies of merchant adventurers seeking to fill their coffers with the fabled splendours of the East. Each one of them has left a genetic imprint on the land that is carefully graded and calibrated in an invisible social register that is called caste.

Caste consciousness, or an obsession with purity, is the sinister element that lurks underneath the facade of the family. The inviolable mother fixation is only one of its more benign manifestations. The so-called four major castes that are routinely held up for debate and inspection are just the superstructure of a system so elaborate that even within its smallest recognizable unit, the family, there are minute distinctions of hierarchy that will assign a place within it to every individual at a certain time of his or her lifespan.

Families function not just as a social register but also as a primary filter for social differences.

'I remember a time when I brought a complete outsider to my family house in Kerala,' reflects a very well educated doctor, who was telling me a story from his college days. 'You will forgive me when I say that he was from Nigeria, a black man. My grandmother received him with all the courtesy that she would extend to a guest, but when he left she insisted on washing the floor of the entire house down to the front steps with milk. Herself. It was not that she was a racist. Such terms did not exist at that time, but such was the preoccupation with purity in those days.' Even today, some temples in Kerala insist on a ritual purification with milk and other propitiatory fluids if they imagine that the place might have been defiled by the presence of a person of the wrong gender or religious affiliation.

Festivals are a time when traditionally the different communities (and families) welcome others into their midst. The barriers are lifted, even if they happen only once a year. During the festival of Holi, which marks the vernal equinox, there is a sudden explosion of group energy as families gather to celebrate a ritual that is almost pagan in its manifestation. The first day starts with a ritual burning of rubbish, a clearing up as it were of the year's accumulation of detritus. This is followed by a day of revelry where the normal restraints of carefully observed social hierarchies are thrown to the winds and even strangers are allowed to smear each other in the streets with the symbolic red powder. The division between the sexes and the invisible barriers that protect the members of a joint family are suddenly dissolved in a mutual orgy of throwing of coloured powders and coloured water at each other. It's almost as if the festival sanctions contact between persons who may not be permitted to do so as a means of defusing the sexual attraction that must be there in so many hidden forms when different members of a family share an intimate space together. At night, the sky is filled with tiny bobbing lanterns of paper filled with light as kite fliers send up their hopes and wishes on the slender strings of their wind borne creations. The Great Indian Family is something like that—an intricately made kite filled with light floating through the dark, tied to the earth by a string called tradition.

Weddings, births, deaths, festivals, celebrations of the passage of time in the lifespan of the elders of a community (as when the head of a family, the dominant male, attains what is known as 'a thousand moons' or the age of eighty)—all these are occasions when the invisible network of blood and kinship draws the Great Indian Family into its fold, with reminders of past obligations and bonds that have to be periodically strengthened to make sure that not just the present but even the future is assured. It's a question of loyalty. It's a matter of survival. It's a reminder that when all else fails, there is still the family.

Chalta Hai

. . . .

Bachi Karkaria

ANYTHING GOES

In a sweetmeat shop in a swanky Delhi 'colony market', the confections are all kept in a spotless glass case, but there's a swarm of insects inside it as well. 'Why are there so many flies on the *mithai*?' asks the aghast customer. The salesman replies, 'If there aren't flies on mithai, what will there be? Elephants?'

The intersection near Mumbai's Mahalakshmi local train station is one of the busiest. Taxi drivers think nothing of stopping in the middle of traffic to pick up and disgorge passengers. The cabbie may be a rustic lout who has paid his way to a licence, but none of the well-heeled passengers ask him to take his vehicle to the side either; instead they take their own time getting on or off, and counting out the fare.

The plumber says he'll come at 9.30 a.m. You keep waiting, missing that important meeting at work. He doesn't show up till noon. '*Kayko boom marta hai, bai*? What's there to get so het up about, madam? I'm only a few hours late,' he says insouciantly.

You finally reach the railway ticket counter, after an hour's crawl in a queue. Several people appear from nowhere and elbow you from all sides. 'We just want to ask one thing,' they say, taking up another fifteen minutes of your time, instead of waiting their turn. 'So what? We are not taking away your ticket are we?'

The queue gets longer and more restive. The man at the counter couldn't care less as he exchanges pleasantries with his colleague, looks around the room as if he were a tourist at a cathedral, or wanders off without explanation.

School children are expected to do projects as part of their board exams. But their parents outsource these to professionals. The board knows about this, but does nothing. These things happen.

Don't let your blood pressure rise. Learn to live in mad, exasperating, irrational India. Go with the flow. Restore your inner equilibrium by chanting the mantra that keeps a billion Indians going: *Sab chalta hai, yaar. Om shanti, shanti.*

~

We are a one billion kilometre walkathon. A nation not quite on the move but certainly on the amble. We stroll, arm in arm, with our casualness, waltz dreamily to a karmic que sera sera. No sweat, please adjust, *theek hai, jaane do*. It is Gandhian pacificism in all its great, glorious, exasperating travesty. But turn the other cheek? Of course not, what audacity! When we should let a slight altercation or an impatient car simply pass, we thrust out our scrawny chests, roll up our kurta sleeves, and plunge into a slanging match. If we live in Delhi or its belligerent environs, we will proclaim who our father is, question the paternity of our antagonist, and pummel the fellow to a slow death. Or make short work of it by whipping out a gun and shooting him in hot blood. Then we will walk away. No one will intervene. Chalta hai.

Chalta hai. These things happen, let it go. Don't deliver, don't demand, don't strain at the oars or rock the boat. This is our defining attitude, the mantra which we live—and occasionally swear—by. It helps us explain our past, deal with our present, and it enables us to sashay into our next birth. We came on this earth with a pre-calibrated speed of attitudinal ambulation. We will pass on to our next avatar as ordained by the divine Master Plan. There's no point in our tightening up our own development rules, zoning our neighbours or segregating our stinking officials in separate garbage bags. If the Almighty has ordained that we will dwell in the Great Sewer of Indifference, who are we—mere mortals—to question it, step on the gas or call for our own autonomous recycling unit? Whatever will be, will be. Chalta hai.

This has been the wisdom of the sages. Didn't Krishna preach detachment to Arjuna on the battlefield of Kurukshetra? So must we distance ourselves from getting involved in corrective action. Or any action that seems like hard work.

This has been the wisdom of the ages, passed down from father to son, as much a part of oral tradition as spitting. Why is this lout expectorating great big globules of germ laden spittle on the street as if it were his *baap ka rasta.* No one questions it. We simply walk on, or express our disgust of it with a similar hawk and splat. *Et thoo Brute*!

It's passed down too from mother to daughter. Why is this lout expecting me to do all the housework when I've been slogging at the office all day and would like some rest at home? Why is he beating me up for my pains? Why are the neighbours burning up their bahu? Why is the upstairs lady thrashing her little maid servant to death for daring to try on her lipstick? Ask no questions, and you'll be able to lie in peace. Chalta hai.

This has been the wisdom of our stages. In Ram Rajya, someone else provides food and fairness in ample measure, so everyone can sit back and never have to strain for perfection or against injustice. In Kalyug, our destiny is fraught by bombs, deluge, paedophiles, serial rapists, organ rackets and popcorn at forty bucks a tub, but everyone shrugs helplessness, and walks on. *Chalta aa raha hai, chalta jayega, chalta hai.*

Globalization, try your damnedest to turn our tide. N.R. Narayana Murthy thinks bad infrastructure is the enemy; the Central government, the Confederation of Indian Industry (CII) and most sane people think the enemy is Marxist pigheadedness or Mamata Banerjee. They are all mistaken. These are but a conjunctural problem, a little pimple on the face of progress, a speed bump easily levelled. A far bigger obstruction lurks at every corner, insidiously sneaks out of the woodwork. It is that seemingly innocuous shrug which will topple our Atlas ambitions. We should put our nose to the grind? Develop a work ethic? Fulfil targets? Respect deadlines?

Be punctilious about quality? Forget it. *Paakalam. Parvah nahin. Ki pharak painda? Chalse. Chalta hai.*

~

With the number of chickens coming home to roost, we should be praying for another outbreak of bird flu. So we can cull them all in one full swoop. Bury the carcasses in pits, incinerate them, vaporize them in a zap of nuclear lightning. Destroy any which way we can the centuries of the Great Indian Malaise. For too long we've followed the slow 'n' easy rhythm of chalta hai, how the hell are we now going to quicken the pace and break into a trot, readying ourselves for the race with the world? We'll be at the finished line even before you can say 'Chindia'.

Baba, why we got into all this global competitiveness? You know how much *work-shirk* it will take. We aren't used to work, we've got by well enough on shirk. Yaar, our chalta hai was so much easier than all this *run-shun*. Who wants to be an emerging economy? Better to crawl back under the cosy *kambal-wambal* and snooze a little more. We don't want to be the sunrise sector.

No need for son to rise either. Let him bunk school today also. What they will teach anyway? No books, no blackboards, no lessons, no masterji. No, no, masterji is there, sleeping, stretched out, *lamba ho kar* on the bench, and telling the class, '*Chalo ladkon,* gather around me. Sit up straight, fully at attention. Ready? Now begin. Begin, begin. Mother did not give you roti or what this morning? *Josh lagao.* Go at it with vigour. *Hanh*! Very good. *Shabhash* Lallooah. That's the way. Finally you have learnt. You are No.1 in class. What a good *maalish* you are giving. My old legs are ready again.' Ready for the chalta hai approach to education.

We've had a commitment to universal education for fifty-six years; the University Grants Commission was set up soon after Independence. We have only 350 universities when there should have been 1500 according to the chairman of the latterly established Knowledge Commission. Sam Pitroda also says their churn out rate is just 7 per cent of the eligible population, half that of the Asian average. Even when we seem to be cranking out graduates like impecunious poets spinning out ghazals, like Mumbai locals disgorging peak hour commuters, they remain unemployed. Till fifteen years ago, we despaired that they were underemployed. The sweeper with the BA degree. The M.Phil measuring out his learning in the rice scoops of the corner *bania.* The engineer hawking export rejects on heartless city pavements.

Now, the IT czars say they are unemployable. The *Times of India*'s lead story on 18 December 2006 was headlined, 'India Inc floats own edu system', and spoke of how burgeoning businesses simply could not find appropriately trained manpower among a billion strong population, and so were trying to grow their own. Ernst & Young was chasing graduates to join its tax academy, the software giant TCS was about to launch its own science academy, and the juggernaut Infosys had provided facilities on its $300 million Mysore campus to lodge a record 13,500 trainees. Even the retail major Pantaloon has seeded MBA programmes in seven business schools whose graduates would be absorbed into this sponsor company.

Decades of the slapdash, *chalta hai* attitude to higher learning have ensured that no one from the routine system is worthy of hire in a truly competitive economy. Nearly sixty years of Indianizing, saffronizing, patronizing the education system we inherited, we're in trouble. We haven't given our kids the skills, let alone the nerves to take on the destiny which is suddenly ours. So, serious players are now forced to set up dedicated institutes to provide the raw material for the demands of a global power-in-waiting, trained in IT, investment banking, insurance, in biotech, patent laws, and all the complexities that have arisen along with India.

Yes, we need to put our shoulder to the wheel of destiny, gird our loins, get our act together. We need to pull out our Excel sheets and excel. Fortune beckons, and so does the *Fortune* cover. It is potentially the hour of The Brilliant Indian, programmed with the right cyber circuitry, cognitive powers in place, right brain-left brain clicking at equally frenetic pace. But will it be like the clicking needles of Madame Defarge, counting the heads that roll off the guillotine, dreams all lying in a bloody heap? Will this be the denouement because, at the critical moment, we failed to muster that mass of energy to grab the trophy? Because we could not deliver, get things done to Six Sigma perfection, meet quality control parameters? Because we could not stay the course? How will we be able to run, when for as many generations as can be counted on a goddess's hands, we have been calibrated to one pace? That of chalta hai.

~

Chalta hai is our most popular deity, and like our gods, it has many avatars. Scandalous neglect, the gesture rather than the act, hypocrisy, social and civic irresponsibility, all spring from its sluggish font. And, as a pantheon or individually, they all leave their cosmic imprint on each of the parameters of development—health, gender equality, equitable urban growth and socialized living.

It's not just our chalta hai attitude to education that's smudging our report card at a juncture when our ranking in the world demands straight As. One billion can be a gargantuan human resource, or it can be a staggering burden. No prizes for guessing which is our lot, our slot, our blot. Among the most terrifying visages of the seemingly cute excuse of chalta hai is official apathy, worsened by corruption. In the battle between accountability and indifference, the latter has always stolen the honours—and public resources. It's a victory that could defeat our new win-win plans.

The declaration of 'Health for all by 2000' at the global conference on primary health at Alma Ata in 1978 proved to be a chimera for all the countries of the underprivileged South, and even in pockets of the over-indulged North. India's lofty socialism didn't help the situation on the ground. The beguiling ads of bright-faced children running carefree in sun-dappled fields don't reflect the real picture. The infant mortality rate may be down to 54.6, but compare that to China's 23.1, or Sri Lanka's 14. Prime Minister Rajiv Gandhi bravely and belatedly set up six technology missions in the 1980s—universal immunization, literacy, drinking water supply, telecommunications, dairy and oilseeds. Of these, immunization was declared a success and a can-do beacon for other development agendas. We congratulated ourselves from platforms political, media and zilla parishad, boasting that a project seriously undertaken and sincerely implemented could deliver results; that if we set our minds to it, we were not the blundering bunch of inepts that we were made to believe we were. We could do it.

But polio, which we had 'eradicated', has come limping back to taunt our smug complacency. In 2006, there were 614 reported cases, up from sixty-four the previous year. That old cur had slunk in with its rabid bite: our chalta hai attitude to health care. It has attacked us from the top and from below. The authorities were not vigilant enough to ensure the essential herd immunity; parents did not care enough—or know enough—to take their babies on the designated day for those vital drops of the Pulse Polio campaign. Both happened—or did not—despite the high-profile publicity featuring the prime minister and an array of chief ministers.

The main culprit is Uttar Pradesh, long part of the development defaulters aptly acronymed BIMARU (the others being Bihar, Madhya Pradesh and Rajasthan). Ninety per cent of cases emanate from here, and have spread to other states by the migrant population. If the showpiece polio is now causing such concern, what of other health programmes whose names never blazed from fluttering banners? The chalta hai of chronic-laggard states resulted in local populations not demanding that their local primary health centres be adequately stocked with supplies and qualified staff; by contrast, in highly aware Kerala, mothers marched in procession to the district authorities whenever these were found wanting.

We are now a food surplus nation, but even when we were not, granaries fed rats more than they did people. Malnutrition, or under-nutrition, still stares us with the dull, accusing eyes of children with straw-like hair, patchy skin and pot bellies. It's not only that they aren't a pretty sight. Deficiency diseases blind and cripple them, and their digestions make them unable to retain what they eat. The water they drink is sludgy with bacteria. But like a Nero with poor priorities, we seem to find all the energy needed to make a huge cry about pesticides in colas. If it weren't so tragic, it would be a laugh—going after the soft drink target, when milk and plain, simple water are equally suspect.

We haven't licked (if that be the word) our waterborne diseases which are responsible for our gastrointestinal ailments. One out of 250 Indian children dies of diahorrea every year. Forget the remote tribal belts of Gadchiroli, even in swaggering Mumbai people are laid low by jaundice, or even die of it.

Malaria has remained a stagnant pool, into which similar afflictions have drained their deadly impact. Dengue, chikungunya, Japanese encephalitis and, as was tragically manifest after Mumbai's Biblical-grade flood, leptospirosis. How easily these words trip off even the tongues of little children. As easily as accountability slips off the conscience of those entrusted with our civic administrations.

Thus, while our business emperors continue to seize global companies and international magazine covers with entirely creditable and awesome regularity, while the mighty USA has bowed to the purchasing power of our market and our nuclear need to fuel this, while Indian scientists deliver horizon-shifting research, we ironically have not been able to reduce correspondingly our list of dubious toppers, from Vitamin A deficiency blindness to diabetes. The first can easily be prevented by cheaply available food sources. In the second, independent WHO sources say India already has the highest number of cases; the official estimate is 19.4 million. And, now, at 5.7 million, we have the largest number of people on the planet living with HIV-AIDS. Which would be bad enough even without the fact that it has frighteningly complicated our TB situation allowing the bacillus to rampage opportunistically over a compromised immune system. Our 1.8 million new cases a year are the highest in the world.

This Human Immuno-Deficiency Virus is a master of disguise. And it has been helped by that other quick-change artist, chalta hai. Its guise of hypocrisy is the one which allowed HIV to slip in and lay siege to our health—and our economy, to say nothing of the terrible social cost of stigma. 'AIDS is a disease of the decadent, promiscuous West,' we proclaimed with sanctimonious smugness in the early years. 'We don't have to worry about it because we are all upright, monogamous men. If anything, it's the problem of sex workers who deserve this divine retribution for their disgusting morals,' we said, as if the poor women had a choice, or were having sex with themselves. Thailand as poor a nation and with an economy dependent on the sex industry has seriously tackled its HIV epidemic. Brazil overcame poverty and the resistance of the predominant Catholic Church to condoms; it got plaudits at global AIDS conferences even before world economic forums sat up in admiration of this once-straggler country.

Irresponsibility, that other avatar of chalta hai, revealed its hideous form in the refusal of men to use the precaution of safe sex. They lustily bought the commodities of the garish, squalid sex bazaars, and took their free gift of HIV home. Our vaunted 'moral rectitude' has created a situation where marital sex constitutes high risk behaviour for the hapless wife. For the past eight years, sentinel surveys keep presenting disturbingly high HIV incidence in truly monogamous women and, as cruelly, in the children fathered by their uncaring, uncondomed husbands. Women are hit hardest by HIV, thanks to both biology and skewed gender equations; with true *arya nari* selflessness, they are the ones putting the brakes on the epidemic. Unlike their African sisters, our women are not typically promiscuous, and so do not take up the baton to relay the infection to another set of males. The F**K Stops Here.

This has in no way shamed us into tempering our blasé indifference to gender violence. It's the same demonic shrug which permits the foeticide or early neglect of the girl child which has pushed us to the bottom of the world on sex ratios. At a national average of 927 girls for every 1000 boys, the equation is skewed in all but three states—Kerala, Pondicherry and Lakshadweep; rich Punjab is the cruelest defaulter.

Poverty and overpopulation, ignorance, poor access, global warming, Page 3 flippancies—you can find any number of reasons, real and absurd, for our abysmal health record, but at the end of the line, or even right in front of it, is that familiar enemy, chalta hai. A slipshod formulation of plans, slapdash implementation, a blithe indifference to using a simple prophylactic, a holier-than-thou smugness, and a frightening lack of accountability/responsibility—this is our slippery ground, the resounding slap to the healthy country we should have been by now.

~

The bullock cart pace of chalta hai can somehow be explained in our slow and ancient villages. What's the excuse of our cities rushing frenetically into a paradise of plate glass and penthouses? They talk of 'can-do', but continue to shortchange their future by saying 'will do' to the second rate and the unacceptable. Nandan Nilekani is an IT czar programmed with the software of social responsibility. He says, 'Our global ambitions are posited on how quickly and effectively we urbanize.' Effectively is the operative word, but it is also the one with the ugliest post-operative complications.

Our cities are not places in which you want to live or work, forget about play. As with health, the blame game has many names, but only one big sponsor. You can point a finger here too at the usual suspects—poverty, overpopulation and municipal laziness, ineptitude, indifference, corruption or bad breath. You can rant about the land mafia and the builder–politician nexus. But, once again, at the cold and blocked heart of the problem lies that familiar lout, Mr C. Hai.

Civic sense and pride are sacrificed on his altar, we tolerate hawkers and spitters and people who hold up traffic while they unfurl leisurely out of their cars. Encroachment is as endemic as E-coli. Our newly anointed cities, no less than old ones, have, like Topsy in Uncle Tom's Cabin, 'just growed' without any conceptual integrity, as if the master plan has slipped off for a besotted afternoon assignation with its mistress. Zoning laws, where they exist, are blithely violated. Sometimes, when this lapse comes close to sealing the city's fate, sealing drives swing into action, creating urban aneurisms of their own, as we saw in Delhi in the dying months of 2006.

In Mumbai, the misuse of spaces earmarked—and subsidized—for IT parks is merely the latest avatar of the encroachment deity which has been worshipped for as long as Indian cities have been inhabited. Like the diversion of great rivers, or some grand experiment in urban grafting, shops flourish where children should have played, and municipal schools mysteriously make way for the newest exterior-decorating feature, mall-to-mall carpeting. Ours is not to question why, ours is just to go and buy, or simply add dirty footfalls to the stampede. Only the manifestations of the urban destroyer change, the *tandava* remains the same. It is a frenetic dance choreographed to the slow and lazy beat of *chalta aa raha hai, chalta hai, chalta rahega*. Like Brahma, our indifference to civic despoliation is endless, infinite, omnipresent, omnipotent.

In 2005, Mumbai's Biblical-grade flood turned India's proudest city into a marooned Bihar village look alike for three days, killed 1058 people in the city, suburbs and affected districts of Thane and Raigad, caused a loss of Rs 65,560 million, gave us our own date of catastrophe, 26/7, and wrote off a fleet of BMWs and Mercedeses in the bargain. At its core, this deluge too was the gargantuan result of urban chalta hai, a languid anarchy under which every environmental principle was savaged along with draining pools, open spaces, mangroves and the entire Mithi river. The juggernaut of unregulated, irresponsible construction trampled every outlet of natural drainage under its relentless concretization. Each new violation added its lethal layer to the past disregard for development control rules. Each was allowed to continue unchecked, or with the most perfunctory of questioning. Why bother with questions when we already know that money is the omnibus answer?

In the end, 'What can we do? This is the way it's always going to be' becomes a self-fulfiling prophecy. Because of this mass shrug, the people of Mumbai lost a large chunk of expected public space when Development Control Rule 58 was surreptitiously changed. With this sleight of hand, only the unbuilt-up part of mill land was allotted for public housing and open spaces instead of the presumed one-third of the entire 400 acres available for redevelopment. For the same reason, the Ahmedabad–Sarkhej highway has become a raucous destination instead of a route, the entire stretch now a tangle of unregulated malls and traffic.

The same chalta hai has allowed industrial units to spew their noxious waste into the residential air and water supply of all our cities and towns. The same attitudinal yawn allows licences to be given to untrained truck drivers who then turn roads into killing fields. Cars, taxis, auto-rickshaws and two-wheelers routinely come to a sweating, swearing, time-and-money-squandering standstill because of a total disdain for maintaining lanes and compulsory maintenance. Stick to the rules and you will be glowered at and rammed off the road.

This karmic casualness has added up to the bigger metropolitan mess, a higgledy-piggeldy vertical and horizontal nightmare with a shortage of everything except people and pestilence. This is the gloved punch of chalta hai. As we said earlier, the concept is about being laid back; its consequence is dynamic, aggressive, no-holds-barred. '*Theek hai*' said often enough with other-worldly detachment from the rules of organized living leads to a situation distinctly NOT theek hai.

'Antiquated system' we say; 'pressure of population' we shrug; 'corrupt officials' we despair. But we don't muster our potent people power to stop that drain water from seeping into the network which brings water purified at great cost from our state-of-the-art filtration plants. BRISTOWAD, the Brihanmumbai Storm Water and Drainage project remained in epic exile for fourteen years thanks to this same lethargic attitude.

Calcuttans belligerently, readily marched in procession, shouting '*Cholbe na*' to US imperialism in distant Nicaragua, but accepted without a whimper the mountains of garbage colonizing their own backyard. Or the debris, destruction, disruption and diversions which piled up as the Metro Railway took a slow twenty years to be constructed.

This contradiction is of a piece with the Indian reality. Slums sprawl at the foot of our skyscrapers. Sub-human Third World conditions coexist in an easy peace with the sybaritic indulgences of the First World. One ought to be revolting, the other revolted. Both should rage, rage against the dying of the right, instead of going gently into the urban blight.

~

At one level chalta hai is the manifestation of our karmic fatalism, our belief that the wheel will turn whether or not we put our shoulder to it, so why exert ourselves? Why stress yourself driving through life's traffic snarls when you can simply ride pillion?

But there's a less easygoing interpretation to our national languor. It isn't uniformly applied. Don't we jump up with exemplary energy to protest when someone does unto us what we so cavalierly do unto them, and to public spaces, property and interest? We don't mind what gets messed up, as long as our own hands, houses and happiness remain shiny clean. Therefore, chalta hai may have less to do with lofty karma and more to do with base selfishness.

Cast the most cursory look around. We are as meticulous about our surroundings as we are casual about anyone else's. To use the most obvious and cited example, see how we spit on and litter our streets, in complete contrast to the sparkling insides of even the poorest of our homes. You cannot miss it as the local train brushes past the slums that lie along the tracks. The shanty colony may be a squalid tangle of rags and cardboard packing, of open drains and fly-haloed excrement, but each little hovel is a sparkle with lovingly burnished pots, the stamped-down floor is meticulously swept, the pathetic belongings are neatly stacked in a corner. And mothers hold down slippery toddlers to scrub them within an inch of their lives regardless of the fact that, within minutes, they'll be lolling in the filth outside.

The poor cannot help the ambient atrocities, but what's the excuse of the middle and upper classes? It's no exaggeration that the fancier the car, the greater the certainty of a gush of betel-nut juice expectorated from the suddenly opened door. To be hit by both is the pedestrian version of adding insult to injury.

It seems as if our 5000 years of civilization have bestowed upon us the ultimate in philosophical, spiritual, intellectual and cultural attainment, but left us socially challenged. We are a collection of highly individualized beings without any consciousness of the collective good. The centrifuge of life sucks us into any number of vortexes, pleasurable, creditable or abominable, but it simply does not make us stick together in caring co-existence. Any self-respecting hive would be stung by a comparison with the Indian attitude to communal living.

Go to any housing colony. Squeeze past the cars parked exactly where it says, 'No Parking at Gate'. Survey the balconies festooned with laundry dripping on passersby, the façades mural-ed with the streaks of brown from balcony flower pots watered not wisely but too well. Edge gingerly upstairs decorated with paan-Indian art. Don't bother to ring for the lift; someone has left its door open, so it's stuck on the seventh floor.

Televison sets blare from every flat, no need really to switch on your own. Kitchen taps run like they were practising for the marathon. *Achha*? There's a water shortage in the city? *Hoga, honay do.* It's 2 p.m., but the upstairs neighbour has chosen exactly the snooze hour to start grinding her week's supply of masala, or getting nails hammered into her wall with the ferocity of a crucifixion. So what if there are babies and grannies who need the rest? I'm free only now. Why you are making so much fuss, you were born in England or what? Here, sab chalta hai. We are like that only.

You go for dinner to an expensive restaurant. You look forward to an evening of quiet, candlelit conversation. You can have one—if the brats haven't blown out the tapers in addition to tearing up and down the passages, pulling apart the flower arrangements and shaking their dandruff into your soup as they jump manically on the banquette behind you. *Chalta hai, bachcha hai.* And no point expecting their accompanying adults to discipline them, because they are too busy laughing and shouting at top pitch themselves.

A plane journey is fraught with much of the same, more even than on a train, because the sounds are amplified in the constricted space. Papa shaking his rattle with demented vigour is more nerve-wracking than bawling baby he is trying to pacify. And no one, but no one, would dream of stopping the child in the seat behind you steadily kicking the small of your back to smithereens.

Don't even think of using the toilet in a resort. Go, pee in the pool because you would have to wade through the bathroom floor; the picnickers have had almost a full bath at the sink. Toilet paper? It lies in a crumpled heap like a ravished maiden after having been yanked off the roller. It's for public use, no? We are public, no? We can use it as we like, no. Yes, yes, yes. Sab chalta hai.

Our ambulatory attitude creates the awesome force of a multitude of anarchic armies. We are a billion mutinies now.

~

The 1960s' slogan was 'Do Your Own Thing'. It was hip and cool and all of us growing up then aspired to it. It was the way out, and somewhat stoned, culmination of an economic principle created two centuries earlier by French thinkers: laissez faire, or to spell it out in full, *laissez faire, laissez aller, laissez passer*—let do, let go, let pass. It told government to keep its hands off trade, and soon came to be synonymous with the free market. This non-interventionist policy was later expanded to promote every shade of social liberalism. It arrived in the English language in 1774 courtesy George Whatley, who used it in his book, *Principles of Trade*, co-authored by Benjamin Franklin.

The 1960s' flower children wilted (or went to pot). The hippies regrettably gave way to Yuppies (young upwardly mobile people) who were also willing to do their own thing as long as it was what all their peers were doing. But laissez faire continued and flourishes, despite the many attempts to make it apply for an operating licence, in triplicate. On it was founded the might of the US; it was the Holy Grail sought by nations chafing under state-controlled regimes; and it was the dream of private industry dominated by the commanding heights of the public sector. In India, good sense and an IMF ultimatum finally brought in the economic reforms of 1992. Our netas learnt not only to spell laissez faire, but also to pronounce it worthy of adoption.

Wait a minute. Before the descendants of the French thinkers or the hippies start charging us a patent fee, let me point out that the transfer of know-how is really in the reverse direction. We came up with it first, and they followed. What is laissez faire if not chalta hai, the easy going slouch which is our contribution to free thought and anti-social behaviour? For as long as anyone can take the trouble to remember, Indians had realized the underlying principle of the French theory and cast it in their own nonchalant image. For us, it is not so much laissez faire which fits our DNA as the other two parts, *laissez aller* and *laissez passé*. Of course, it is our own, distinctive interpretation of 'Let go, let pass'. Our version is 'It's okay, why bother, don't get your knickers in a twist about doing things the way they should be done.' This lies at the lazy core of chalta hai.

We have a native genius for maladroit adaptation. We are always taking an idea or object which is a global totem of desirability and distorting it into something uniquely our own. This may be best reflected in chalta hai vis-à-vis classical laissez faire, but it is not the only example. We make a habit of *not* letting alone or accepting anything in its original form, however much the rest of the world may covet it.

Take the McBurger. Globally everyone and his Pomeranian wants exactly the kind that you'd get in New York. McDonald's goes to great lengths and expense to ensure this consistency and customer delight. The poundage, the number of additives in the patty, the scatter of sesame seeds on the bun, the same glisten, the exact angle of the overhang of the cheese slice, even the expression of the boy sliding the carton to you. But in India, we aren't impressed by all those millions of dollars that have gone into creating this uniformity. So, the global conqueror is forced to doff its cap to us, and make the one exception. It creates the McAloo Tikki, and it drops the quintessential beef. Mark my words, one day it will keel over completely and start serving a McJain, with *sab cheez—pudina chutney aur aigless mayoneez.*

This maladaptation is a recurring pattern on the cultural tapestry. Take design. The Dior dress has worked assiduously to achieve the correct degree of discreet embellishment, but when we jump on this bandwagon, chalta hai kicks in. We go over the top with jing-jang beads and baubles and Swarovski crystals. We've done the same to the classical paisley on a jamevar. With scant respect for its pedigreed lineage and lines, we tart it up with zari and sequins. Who cares if the old purist elegance is sacrificed on the altar of excess? We have bhangra-fied design like we have done to western music. Chalta hai's to-hell-with-the-rules rampage has ravaged the shape and form of a skirt, shawl or a song in the same way as it has pulverized the paradigms of civilized social living.

Just as we have mutated laissez faire, we have provided our own convenient interpretation of that other globally toasted form, minimalism. In our case 'less is more' translates as 'less effort is more preferable'. Get by by saying bye-bye to conscientiousness.

And mock or murder anyone who tries to do an honest day's job. Satyendra Dubey, the Bihar engineer who blew the whistle on institutionalized corruption, was killed for his conscience. Remember what would happen to the old-time steno who made typing a letter into a work of art, getting the margins just so, ripping the paper off the roller should a wrong key be banged, choreographing spaces like a dancer on a stage? Her colleagues ridiculed her out of court and office picnics. It was very uncool to 'ruin the system', set a wrong precedent and force everybody else to strive for perfection. Chalta hai was the unwritten rule. And, very often, written into trade union rules. Which is why today's performance-linked pay is like drink—the new curse of the working classes.

Let's face it. Socialism's safety net was as much about protecting the laidback as about safeguarding the vulnerable. When it began to get dismantled, even the private sector, which had chafed under it, made a fuss. The old 'Bombay Club' of industrial houses wanted to eat the liberalized cake and have protectionism too. Who cares for the undiluted quality of an economic principle? Chalta hai. We can distort it as long as it suits our self-centred purpose. But now liberalization has drawn the lines, erased the blur. It's the end of endless chai breaks, and civilization as we've known it. Such dangerous notions as transparency, accountability and variable pay have sabotaged the workplace. Corporate governance is trying to overthrow the old corporate anarchy in a paperless putsch. Will another call go out just in time to save the somnolent satraps, the bumbling bureaucracies from extinction and exit policies? Babus of the world unite, you have everything to lose, starting with your claims to the chalta hai operating standards.

Not only do we distort what the world upholds as the gold standard in desirability, we perversely uphold what has globally been rejected as obsolete. Marxian economics has fallen as unceremoniously as a Lenin statue and designer-apparelled chicks have replaced apparatchiks in Red Square. The other communist giant, China has turned into the world's market economy model,

Coca-colonizing every mall and pavement stall in every corner of the globe. But our own Comrade Canutes assume they can call back the tide.

The Karats & Co. continue to debate issues that were resolved into irrelevance years ago. They may not actually exhume phrases such as 'capitalist roaders' or 'running dogs of imperialism', but their divorce from reality is embarrassing. Ironically, in CPM-led West Bengal, Chief Minister Buddhadeb Bhattacharya woos industry with the zeal of the convert, or the pragmatist. Why are Delhi commies allowed to stymie progress? Why don't we show up the contradictions which should rightly be carrying within them the seeds of their own destruction? It's because we shrug our shoulders, and say, 'Netas can say anything. In politics, sab chalta hai.'

Our familiar friend and his disfigured cousin, *desified* laissez faire, are as ubiquitous as Udupi cafes. Like dosas they spread and sizzle across the whole griddle of our culture, from food to fashion to office dynamics. Not surprisingly, they play the lead role in our biggest cultural extravaganza, Bollywood. In Hindi *fillums*, anything goes. Which means everything goes for a six—consistency, plot, logic. For decades the industry flourished without ever feeling the need for a script. The director made up the story, such as it was, as he went along. Its prevailing shape depended on what he'd had for breakfast, the tantrum of his stars, the credit status of his producer, or the diktat of his astrologer. As long as the heroine was gorgeous and had an equally riveting wardrobe, as long as you could keep the audience distracted with lightning fists and thundering dialogue, anything went. And went. Sab chalta hai, yaar. It's only now that we've begun making films for the Oscars that directors worry about such inconveniences as a plausible script and the styling of scenes, not just of the stars.

The world of flash can get away with superficialities, but surely the groves of academe would never submit to such despoliation. Isn't 'research' always prefixed with 'painstaking'? Ho-hum. You could fill a library with theses on the prevalence of lazy research—or rigorous plagiarism. The academic world is as mired in the debt trap as the most indigent farmer. Lifting is so easy, why exert the mind? With a little luck no one will find out, because examiners are too armchaired themselves to bother. And even if they do realize the uncredited borrowing, you can rest assured that they are also too lazy to make a fuss about it. Let it go, let it pass.

Okay, you might argue that hamburgers and heroes, designer tops, state bottom-lines, even PhD theses are all luxuries of different degrees and genres. It's all right for them to have chalta hai as long as the rot stops there and does not invade the basics, namely, our home—in the same way that different litter standards apply to the street and to our flats. But thresholds have already been crossed, and lowered. Take our most magnificent obsession—marriage. For centuries it drove us to distraction and debt. Whole families were engaged in the finding of a suitable boy; industries and ancillaries were built up around the compelling need to prevent horoscopes from becoming horrorscopes; newspaper fortunes were made on the strength of matrimonial columns. But the creeping paralysis of effort has sidled in here too. Just find an NRI, yaar, and live consumerist-ly ever after.

Sometimes even that bother isn't necessary. Find the right event manager, pay the right price, and everything will be taken care of. Not just planning the Gobi Shashlik, but also skewering a groom.

~

It's easy to laugh over chalta hai, but it's not a harmless buffoon. Even literal matters of life and death such as crime and punishment don't escape our lassi-fied version of laissez faire. Jessica Lall, a model, is shot dead because she doesn't serve a drink to a well-connected brat high on single malt and multiple machismo. A party leader organizes the abduction and jungle killing of Shashi Nath Jha, his secretary who knew too much—and demanded more. A top cop's son stalks, rapes and strangles Priyadarshini Mattoo, a pretty, young law student. Manu Sharma, Shibu Soren and Santosh Kumar Singh were all allowed to get away with these murders because they used political clout to clobber justice. The year 2006 marked a turning point because public outrage finally flexed a stronger muscle. But inquiries into gruesome pogroms, terrorist bombs or negligent accidents still drag on interminably. Faceless undertrials languish in prison for periods longer than their sentences would be. The goons who tore off a woman's skirt and pawed her in the middle of a New Year's eve animal crowd at the Gateway of India are booked only for the theft of her mobile phone. This is still the reality of life in both Bharat and India.

No we cannot afford to dismiss chalta hai as just a negative lapse. It's worse. Often it is actually the front of an attitude positively sinister. It hides a visceral disdain for those deemed beneath our own norms of security and justice. Which means the vulnerable are doubly exposed. The brother of Mulayam Singh, ex-chief minister of Uttar Pradesh, dismissed an unprecedented and unthinkable series of crimes as '*chhoti-moti ghatnaein*, minor incidents, which keep happening'. He was referring to twenty-two kids and one woman subjected to hacking and alleged necrophilia, even cannibalism, not by some prehistoric tribe in a remote forest but involving a public school educated industrialist and his psychopath servant in the heart of the national capital region. The police couldn't be bothered to register cases when they were reported, let alone see the macabre pattern. These were only poor kids after all, and plenty more would be bred even if they were dumped in drains, or worse.

Only politicians dressed as crocodiles shed tears when tribal children die of diarrhea or Dalits are massacred. No one weeps over the lost generation of babies, because they were only burdensome girls. But no one said chalta hai when the son of the Adobe CEO was kidnapped.

In yet another way, chalta hai may be laidback, but its ambit is not.

~

Why do we walk on the mild side? I have explored the different dances which choreograph our indifference. The Que Sera Sera Waltz, the Selfishness Salsa, the Laissez Faire Lambada. In the first, we take the easy way out, and accept the unacceptable by shrugging karmically—it is thus fated and nothing we do will make it bated. The second reveals us as a bunch of egocentric individuals who spit uncaringly on the norms of socialized living. And the third brands us as a people too lazy to demand perfection, or deliver it.

But are these the only numbers on our programme? Are we wholly to blame? And for which we should rightly be whipped, crucified and denied a second helping of blueberry cheesecake? Or is there yet another dance, one that will let us off the hook? Yes, there is.

It is the Helplessness Hip-Hop. We do things in chalta hai fashion because we genuinely have no control over our lives; we are at the mercy of a higher power. This manipulative entity is not the vague Unseen Hand That Rules the Universe, but the Visible, Palpable, Un-shake-off-able Hand That Rules the Local Ward Office. There's always some institution, functionary or individual authorized to screw up our happiness or our kitchen plumbing.

We may be the world's most populous functioning democracy. On occasion we may even be marvelled at for being the world's greatest functioning anarchy. But the truth is that our free will is indeed an illusion, as philosophers and bloggers never fail to tell us. We are only the 'monkey riding the tiger and frantically making up stories about being in control'. In ways macro and micro, we must always defer to the powers that be. They operate from both public and private forums.

The licence-permit raj and the excruciating delay in police investigations have lost some of their stranglehold in the age of transparency, but systems are still not as see-through as a feckless fashionista's shirt. Yes, we have the Election Commission's code of conduct, but the ballot box isn't always there on demand. The wheels of democracy may grind exceedingly fine, but they aren't an instant idli powder. Vested interests will always drag their feet to keep us from voting with the same extremity.

Flat seekers must make do with cubby-holes that cost the earth and have every pestilence on the planet, from damp walls to dry rot; they have to say chalta hai to rapacious land sharks and greedy, corner-cutting builders. Conversely, landlords of old, high-maintenance buildings are at the mercy of the rent act, and thereby of tenants who pay a pittance for sprawling homes in the heart of town, but refuse to shell out a paisa for repairs. The sick poor have to grimace and bear overflowing wards and a shortage of bandages at public hospitals, because if they smash up the place in protesting exasperation, they'd only be pissing on their own scarce beds.

We let pass without doing anything about it simply because there's nothing we can do—about a petty official who holds up our small payment, or the callous bureaucrat whose lack of efficiency, responsibility and ethics squanders public money.

~

Is this a dance without end? Happily, no. The long-reigning, slowly destructive chalta hai might soon be quick-stepped off the floor. A cool new couple has sashayed into the scene—Big Business in his sharp suit and the Empowered Individual in her coat of many causes. Both are chafing to seize control of their trophy-destiny. They can change the rules and tempo of the way we work, shop and react.

India Inc. is already pirouetting all over the stage, cheered on by venture capitalists, private fund managers, and the BRIC Report. Reliance, Infosys, Wipro, the Tatas, Mahindras and Kiran Mazumdars not only have their moves planned out, they are swiftly moving according to plan. No one wants to look back in frustration; everyone's looking forward to their progress in awe. They have watched the world's nifty dancers and want to be as sensexy as the best.

We have seen that the go-getters of the world get there only with a can-do spirit. The Asian Tigers did it between the 1960s and the 1990s, and the newly lionized countries display the same attitudinal horse-power. No one trots out the old pulling-back excuses of poverty, traditionalism and torpor-inducing tropical climate. India Inc. has also learnt that it's going to get very competitive, and no one's going to give us grace marks because we have the Taj Mahal, Iyengar Yoga or Mallika Sherawat. China is not the only story. Indonesia, even Vietnam, have preened into the spotlight, feet tapping impatiently. The heat in the global kitchen is going to intensify. And our corporate cooks are fully aware that that we can no longer deal with it by pulling up our *ganjis*, fanning ourselves lazily, and dozing off in the hope that the temperature will have fallen by the time we stir ourselves awake.

The Big Player of whatever stripe knows that the grand gesture is no longer enough; it will have to be followed up by worshipping the God of Small Details. It's not going to be enough to set up state-of-the-art institutions, they will have to have high-tech handlers. We can no longer import crores worth of diagnostic machinery and have it become a showpiece of the spider's art simply because no one knew how to use it correctly, or bothered to replace a faulty 100-rupee part. We can no longer say chalta hai.

The small individual is equally poised for the dance with destiny. She is empowered by knowledge and choice. Now armed with the Right To Information Act, people are demanding to know the who, how and why when a plot reserved for a playground gets handed over instead to a Gangster's Mall. Spurred by activists, citizens are getting a slew of rights, from clean water to clean municipal election candidates. Lit by the incandescence of a hundred candles—to say nothing of the flash of a thousand smses—justice is being seen to be done to once-powerless victims of rape and murder. And thanks to a freed market, the consumer can pick and choose in contrast to the old, chalta hai regime where the only choice was Take It or Leave It.

Our time is now, as the *Times of India*'s 'India Poised' campaign confidently declared at the start of 2007. Will we maintain our newly seized lead or will we drop behind, or even drop out altogether because we slowed down to our customary amble? Who will triumph? Rocking 'n' rolling globalized ambition, or the slow languid shuffle of chalta hai? For the first time, the answer is not a forlorn, foregone conclusion. We are happy to report that the jury is still out. We really, truly, adrenalin-pumpingly could shake off our loser label. And tell chalta hai to go take a walk.

Hum Log, the Sex Log

. . . .

Samrat

Sex in India is about saving the species. We are very interested in conservation. We believe strongly in ensuring that we humans, especially we Indians, and especially people from our state, and more especially people from *our* corner of our state who speak our language and eat our food and worship our gods in exactly the way we do and hold similar views on Kashmir and Himesh Reshammiya, and who are not much poorer or much richer than us, should continue to thrive. This is the only reason why all of us think of sex.

In fact, we think about it a lot, and are often very imaginative. In our epics, for example, procreation happens when the gods send down well-aimed bolts of lightning from their palms direct to people's wombs (women's wombs, usually, but mishaps must have occurred, for there is mention of an unfortunate man or two becoming pregnant). As responsible adults, typically post marriage and motherhood/fatherhood, we still wish such a miracle or some variant of it were possible. This is true; don't let the pulp fiction in twenty-five languages, bi-annual sex surveys in the English weeklies and the breathtakingly risqué ads for condoms (plain, ribbed, scented) fool you. If only we could procreate like the gods! Or like amoeba. Or vegetation! Imagine waiting lovingly, in eager anticipation, for the wind or a stray bird or bee to carry the sperm from keen, exposed, upraised penises to fertile, receptive, exposed vaginas somewhere. This was our deepest national desire for decades and was reflected in our cinema by flowers, which are the botanical equivalents of penises and vaginas, swaying suggestively in the breeze every time the hero and heroine got within a hand's distance of each other. In our country, a few million people learn about life from cinema, so this raised their hopes and penises. But alas, it was not to be. God and evolution have conspired otherwise, and so, fuck we must.

As we are a deeply traditional, highly patriotic society, we take this duty seriously. Men, naturally, take on the greater share of the burden. For evidence, ask any woman who must walk on our streets after dark or take a public bus or stand alone, waiting, anywhere outside her home or a ladies' toilet with security at the door. Every man wants to do what he threatens to do for god, country and clan; he's only doing his duty. Those who don't want to do it are administered rough justice by their families who gather into vigilante mobs and tie them up in holy matrimony.

Families stop at nothing to achieve their objective, which is to ensure that all among them, male or female, marry and procreate. If blandishments in the form of photos of suitable girls/boys fail to awaken the procreator in young unmarried members of the family, the elders turn to blackmail and threat. 'Wanted' photos of the recalcitrant person are printed in newspapers. Simultaneously, they are circulated at kitty parties and marriage venues and the aunty gang, which is the hit squad of the family mafia, swings into action. After that, it's all over, bar the shouting. The subject will be caught, married off and must procreate on demand.

This is provided the poor fools know how to do it. We don't have any form of sex education because sex is a Dirty Thing and we can't officially talk about it. Our education in the science and art of procreation, also known as fucking, is therefore unofficial. We all know it takes forever to do anything the official way, and bribes must be paid, and forms filled in triplicate. To have sex education in schools officially, it would be even more complicated: a whole bunch of legal luminaries would have to make a law on what about the fuck should legally be taught, and Parliament would have to meet to pass the law, and then state assemblies would have to meet to pass the same or similar laws, and the President and sundry governors would have to sign it, numerous boards of education would have to meet innumerable times to decide whether it is okay to let the kids know what a penis or a vagina looks like, and purple-faced teachers would then have to be persuaded to talk about these vile things and figure out how exam questions in the subject should be phrased. At the end of it, they would all receive MMS clips of students doing the entire *Kama Sutra* in the school loo during tiffin break.

The students get their awesome knowledge from the informal education system run by non-governmental organizations (NGOs) comprising friends, older cousins, video CD pirates and the Internet. The pirates, who are actually sex educationists in deep disguise, have their little NGOs in every major market in every major town and city. The educational matter distributed by these friendly neighbourhood pirates can, however, be slightly confusing to the new student. If everyone you see in the video is either white or black, and all the men are hung like donkeys, please do not feel left out and small. You can get there too, in your next life, if you are reincarnated as a donkey.

Sex education was a lot harder to come by when I was a student, before India liberalized. There was no Internet, and not everyone had a video cassette player (VCP), so we had to come together as a community and rent a VCP and instructional videos to take care of our educational needs. Things got a little easier once we reached college. The town I was studying in had a cinema hall which screened a new film every day. The hall consisted of stone benches apparently stolen from municipal parks, a VCP and a projector. Shows were advertised through handwritten signs stuck on walls, etc. at random places. The one-eyed man who was king of this hall had his own system of certification. Every movie had an 'A' certificate of variable size, depending on how adult it was. In addition, it could also be 'Sexy' or 'Superhit Sexy'. The hall had no lights or air conditioning. In fact, it had no roof. However, most patrons did not notice these deficiencies. There were regulars who, after months of watching 'Superhit Sexy' movies in the hall, would be astounded to discover one night that the water falling on their heads was from the sky above.

This was still a whole sight easier and better than how our parents and grandparents had it. A hundred years ago, when the aunty gangs were even more powerful, young people had to get married at fourteen or sixteen and find out things for themselves. It was all 'do and learn' education. There were many trials and errors, especially in Bengal, where the errors gave rise to the term *boka choda* or stupid fucker. Now we are more advanced and don't officially acknowledge sex till we are officially twenty-one, when we can officially do it but still cannot talk about it, unless we are Khushwant Singh.

Advances in technology have clearly made things simpler over the ages. Back in the bad old days when there was no electricity, they couldn't show movies. So sculpture, painting and literature had to shoulder the whole burden. I'm afraid theatre was way behind, as usual. Literature and painting, however, did a sterling job and deserve medals with pictures of Shakeela on them. Remember those old cave paintings of men with spears chasing unarmed woolly mammoths from the last Ice Age? And of the mammoths chasing them back? The sequence would occasionally move on to a picture of a man and woman fornicating. Scholars are divided over whether this means the man went home and had a good time or whether it is a pictographic depiction of the words 'Oh fuck!' In any case, cave painters and miniaturists have been contributing to procreation education since prehistory.

About 10,000 years after the mammoths lost their sex drive and became extinct, a sage in India, a man called Vatsyayan, who had been meditating for many years, got up from his meditation and wrote the *Kama Sutra*. That should tell you what he was meditating about. Therefore, don't worry if dirty thoughts run amok through your head when you are in a temple, a church or wherever. Remember, it's for god and country. Besides, you can always come out and write an all-time best-seller like the *Kama Sutra*, which has never gone out of print since about AD 100.

Some 2000 years after Vatsyayan, we have many who aspire to his status. More and more people are now becoming amateur sex educationists, in the spirit of 'each one, teach one'. So, while earlier you'd have to go to the street-side bookseller and wink at him until he gave you a fucking book or a tight slap, now you only have to go to the Internet, which is full of many horny men and women from our great country trying to contribute to procreation education. It's all very democratic; anyone can upload a story or read it for free. This is great for education, and for artists and writers. All the usual variations are freely available. There are stories of people doing it with their friends, teachers, uncles, aunts, cousins, sisters-in-law, brothers-in-law. Characters, too, have moved beyond the legendary fucker Mast Ram. There's Savita bhabhi now, the horny unsatisfied housewife. Some of the stories merge popular themes. A fine example of this is found in a story called '*Kavita aur Savita ki chudai*' or 'The fucking of Kavita and Savita'. This is a different Savita, not the straight toon porn character. The story is about what Kavita and Savita do to each other using brinjals. Before getting to this act, however, Kavita gives Savita an Ayurvedic oil massage and a shave. The passage reads:

> *Khar-khar ki halki aawaaz ke saath razor ne Savita ki c*** ke aas paas uga jhaanton ka badaa jungle saaf kar chikna maidaan banaa diya jiske beech mein uski patli c*** ek cricket pitch ki tarah nazar aa rahi thi. Kavita boli, 'Jaan, stadium taiyar hai, pitch bhi ready hai, match khelne waala khilaadi kahan hai?'*

This is very hard to translate, but roughly it would be:

> With a light khar-khar sound, the razor shaved the big jungle of pubic hair around Savita's c*** and made a smooth field of it, in the middle of which her narrow c*** appeared like a cricket pitch. Kavita said, 'Darling, the stadium is ready, the pitch too is ready, where's the player who'll play the match?'

The player, in the form of a fresh brinjal, is then produced, legs are spread 'like the gates of a dharamshala' and the game begins.

This is an example of true democracy. Any pervert, anywhere can now give shape to his wet dreams. Earlier, only sages and kings could do it. Thus, for example, Khajuraho was built. Clearly, anything went in those good old days. The temples of Khajuraho have images carved in stone of twosomes, threesomes, foursomes, fivesomes at it like gymnasts or circus artistes. There are sculptures of men buggering rather surprised-looking horses out there. Those brave men were also doing it for the human species. Sometimes it was for domination, sometimes jealous possession, but often it was out of love or syphilis. A royal doctor had apparently decided that doing it with a horse was a cure for syphilis, so male patients were advised to do it with horses thrice daily before meals. (It takes a lot of courage and considerable expertise to approach a horse from the rear. Don't try this at home or at the races.)

To this day, if you go to Khajuraho, you will be accosted by descendants of the royal doctor who now sell mementos. They will take a quick look at you and instantly diagnose your syphilis and innermost desire. Then they will sell you a key-ring depicting a threesome, or an aroused horse. In rare cases, they even offer threesomes involving horses. (Therefore you should never show anyone what key-ring you bought in Khajuraho.)

It seems our honourable ancestors also shagged other domestic animals, like buffaloes and sheep, though this, sadly, is not celebrated in temple architecture. The evidence for this tradition can be found in occasional newspaper reports saying so-and-so was arrested for having sex with a buffalo. For the arrests, we must thank the British, who love sheep and justice equally. They considered it mighty unfair for people to be buggering buffaloes without so much as a by-your-leave and so in 1861 they passed a law that says, 'Whoever voluntarily has carnal intercourse against the order of nature with any man, woman or animal shall be punished with imprisonment for life, or with imprisonment of either description for a term which may extend to ten years and shall also be liable to fine.' God alone knows what 'order of nature' really means, but a lot of gay people seem to think it means 'no gay sex'. I think it only means 'no doing it with buffaloes unless you are a buffalo'. But I could be wrong, and maybe nature did mean for some humans to be attracted to buffaloes but not to other humans of the same sex.

This is a topic of hot debate. The health ministry shares my view, but the law ministry doesn't, so they're having conferences about it.

Everyone in India has conferences all the time. All this talking makes people either habitually loud and gregarious—so they come and ask you questions about your wife, marital status, buffaloes and sex life—or it makes them defensive—so they think you are asking *them* about their wives, marital status, buffaloes and sex lives. So, for example, you might ask 'How do you do?' and get a frosty 'Better than you' in response. Or you might get a very detailed description of the person's life and times. Among friends, however, conversation flows easily, with no inhibitions or second-guessing. Among adult males in every square inch of the Indian landmass, every sentence typically begins or ends with the conversationalists affectionately calling each other sister-fucker or mother-fucker. As they age, the term of endearment changes to daughter-fucker. In parts of central, east and north-east India, friends express their affection towards each other by calling them arse-born or simply penis. Some creative types add their own signature touches to these words. For example, a bright spark may see something special in you and honour you with the title 'barber of pussies'. If you are a man, you will know you are among friends only if you are called these names at least once in three sentences.

Foreigners may think these are insults, but let me clarify once more that they are nothing of the sort. Making out with cousins, for example, is a worldwide tradition as old as making out with horses. Therefore, sister-fucker is often nothing more than a statement of fact. If you truly want to insult a man, say, 'Your penis is a peanut.' For women, say, 'Your vagina is a vast cave.'

Of course, it is possible that even these intended insults may only be mere truth. I base this considered opinion on my extensive reading of the 'Ask the Sexpert' pages of magazines. No problem that the depraved, barely human mind can conceive is too outlandish for these pages. And the experts can solve them all. So, for instance, you might find someone writing in with a problem like:

> My penis is blue, bent like a banana, and rises sideways instead of vertical so that I can only have sex with someone to the left of me. This is causing great difficulties for me because I have two wives, and the one to the right always feels neglected. Please help. Signed: Sidewinder Yadav, Patiala.

At this, the doctor or agony aunt pretending to be one is likely to say:

> Dear Sidewinder from Patiala, your problem is a common one—2.5% of the Indian population, that is 250 million people, suffer from it. Don't worry; it can be cured by yoga and good diet. Avoid masturbation with your left hand, which is the general cause for this condition, and every morning after surya namaskar stand on your erect penis for ten seconds. Your body must be at ninety degrees to the ground. It will be difficult at first, but if at first you don't succeed, try and try again. Remember, practice makes perfect, and also remember that man is never given a wish without being given the power to make it true.

To this, Sidewinder is likely to reply with profuse thanks but say there's only one problem: he can stand on his penis for ten minutes, but the angle is a problem and makes balance difficult. He will get no response this time.

Men are not the only ones with sexual problems. Women have them too, but usually these stem from relationship issues. They ask questions like, 'I am deeply attracted to my best friend, her husband, and their pet Alsatian, but I love my husband and his brother too. Please advise. Confused Kumari.'

At this, Dr Sexpert or Aunty Pervert will tut-tut sagely and say something very logical, such as, 'Only a saint can love all of creation. You are not a saint. Therefore be a good girl, you naughty girl!' This is true, as everyone knows. God, and by extension godmen, does love all of creation.

Sometimes, though, the Confused Kumari won't heed these words of wisdom and therefore reappears as a case study in *Crime & Detective*, 'the premier magazine on true crime stories'. This typically has stories about the terrible things that happen to people who do terrible things. 'The Wounded Lover's Inhuman Revenge' is a favourite theme. So, in these stories, a Confused Kumari who does it with half of creation finally winds up with her carved butt on a platter. We learn that there is depravity, wild animal sex and justice in this world and put down the magazine reassured that, while we are missing out on the wild animal sex, we are also being spared the terrible justice that follows.

Our movies tried to teach us similar moral lessons for a long time. Thus, while the hero and the virginal heroine would be in deep romantic love and feel the desire to procreate like flowers through cross-pollination by birds and bees, the evil villain would want to have sex with pretty girls, including the heroine. He would woo her first by looking her up and down with tongue and eyes hanging out, then by whistling at her and calling her names of fruits and vegetables and explosives. 'Your cheeks are like apples! Your lips like tomatoes! *Hai* [an expression of sweet pain] my Diwali cracker!' he would say. When the charm offensive failed, he would be most upset and try to chase her down and take off her clothes. This would mean a bit of free-running for both. In the end, he would meet the hero instead, and have a good punch-up as a substitute for hot sex.

Apart from India, this morality is also largely true for Pakistan, Bangladesh and Nepal. We are all moral folks, unlike the immoral

West. Those villains actually *want* to have sex and shamelessly say so. Thanks for capitalism and democracy and Bo Derek, but surely we can't openly accept men—*and* women!—wanting to have sex. In our part of the world, the official position is, WE DO NOT HAVE SEX. This is also known as the '*sarkari* position' or 'ostrich position'—head buried in sand, arse waving in air.

However, though we subcontinentals are all unlike the Westerners, the Indian fucker is also vastly different from his fellow fuckers in Pakistan and Bangladesh. Those gents fuck like rabbits; if you don't believe me ask Praveen Togadia or anyone from any Hindu outfit. Everyone except caste Hindus, especially Muslims and tribals, fucks like a rabbit, they will tell you. The caste Hindu (no relation of the Pope) is a good person and only performs his or her duty. Of course, not all caste Hindu fuckers are the same. They differ in the vigour with which they perform their duties. Up in the mountains and in Punjab they are reputed to be very energetic and enthusiastic. In Gujarat they apparently get enthusiastic during the Navaratri festival. In Bengal they are secretly enthusiastic with the neighbourhood sisters-in-law a.k.a. *boudis*. In Uttar Pradesh, Maharashtra and Bihar they are never enthusiastic. These are also, mysteriously, the three most populous states in India. Someone there is doing it, but we don't know who. Could it be the neighbours? Or is it the gods sending down those lethal bolts?

The tools with which procreation is done are divine. Representations of Lord Shiva and his wife Shakti are widely worshipped. The tools of non-gods, however, are awful things and must be hidden from view at all times, including while having sex. We fuck with our clothes on and lights off. It's too embarrassing to see all that nudity. The embarrassment has nothing to do with the results of a 2006 study by the Indian Council of Medical Research which found that international condoms don't fit Indian men because the average size of the penis here is too small. While the international condom comes in standard sizes of between 6 and 7 inches, the average Indian penis was found to be 5.33 inches.

(However, in a 1996 study by the *American Journal of Urology*, the average American penis was found to be 5 inches. This indicates that international condoms are made to fit big liars.) Indian men can take comfort in a 1993 study published in the *American Journal of Obstetrics & Gynecology* which found the average depth of the human vagina to be 3.63 inches. It was also found to be 100 per cent stretchable. This indicates that any penis over 7.3 inches is a waste of meat. Indian men, take heart.

Measuring the erect penis for study purposes, by the way, is a somewhat complicated procedure. In the beginning, scientists used to break into bedrooms in the middle of the night, rulers and measuring tape in hand. However, this was found to have adverse effects on most erections. Then the scientists made a computer program which would enable a computer to take a picture of the penis when placed in a certain position and infer length from it. For this, the study subject had to go to bed with a woman on one side and a computer on the other, and try and make both happy. This was very complicated too, so finally scientists, this time from India, decided to train lab rats to sneak into people's beds in the dark with measuring tapes and do the measuring. The training is likely to be over by AD 2508.

Till then, you can rely on experts like me and magazines wrapped in yellow cellophane for answers to all your libidinous queries. If you have more money to shed, buy *Debonair* or *Cosmopolitan*. *Debonair* is part of the informal procreation education material and has stories with lines like 'He placed the tip of his manhood at her opening as her legs wrapped around him tightly.' *Cosmo*—and now *Femina* (yes, indeed, times *have* changed)—tell every 'fun fearless female' at least seventy-eight ways (in each issue) in which they and their men can turn into little jets of bodily fluids.

This is the kind of stuff some adventurous couples attempt to do in parks, fields and beaches, except in Mumbai, where they do it on the rocks by the sea while keeping one eye out for crabs and another for relatives and/or spouses. Need drives them to it. Most youngsters have nowhere to go to do their sex education practicals because there are parents and grandparents and siblings and visiting aunts and uncles at home, which is often a one-bedroom space. No one can have sex with anyone in that space unless they can do it silently, without moving. This skill takes a while to master, since it involves not breathing as well. Till then, the learners must take their procreational instincts onto the rocks. Sometimes there are accidents and unintended consequences out there, like strangers or the police popping by to take part in the fun. I've also heard of a chap who was conceived on one of those rocks in Bandra and named Rocky. His mother even showed him the rock to which he owes his existence. In Kolkata, some budding capitalists with party links have brought order to this difficult situation. Thus, in the park surrounding the lake in Lake Town, couples can rent out mattresses by the hour. The service is only available after dark. If you want sponge mattress, dada, you will have to pay double. What you do on the mattress is your business. And if you have trouble doing your business on the mattress, the mattress man can refer you to a sex doctor, hakim or vaid for help.

Hakims are people who can fix all problems for all people for a fee. The legendary Hakim Harkishan Lal of Lahore and Delhi claimed to have received accolades from both Lord Mountbatten and Jawaharlal Nehru for fixing the problems of mankind. More recently, the legendary Ayurvedic sex doctor P.K. Jain of Lucknow, who has 'treated 74,000 patients since 1975', claimed in advertisements to have received accolades from the governor of Uttar Pradesh for *his* services to mankind. He was arrested after the governor complained. This led him to claim in advertisements that he had received accolades from the Indo-American Friends Group. A second case of fraud was lodged against him in August 2008 after the Indo-American Friends Group complained.

Most such specialists, however, do not feel the need to carry any endorsements in their promotional literature. Simply telling us men all that can go wrong with our penises, brains and sexual chemistry—all of which the said doctor can fix—is enough. Here's the text from the visiting card of a 'V.D. SEX SPECIALIST' from Bombay:

> *Mardaana taakat, josh dobaara praapt karein!*
>
> *Bachpan ki galatiyan ya umra ki adhikta, indree mein poori tarah se shakti na aati ho, sambhog karte samay indree ki nasein dheeli padti ho, aur sheeghra patan ho jaata ho, khoon ke sahi na chalne se chhotaapan, patlaapan, tedhaapan, swapnadosh...kitaanu ki kami se santaan ka na hona, garmi...ghabraein nahin, swayam aakar milein. Bawaasir tathaa auraton ke gupt rogon ka bhi ilaaj hota hai.*

Again, this is impossible to translate without losing much of its persuasive power. Nevertheless, here's an attempt.

> Regain your virility and masculine vigour!
>
> The mistakes of adolescence or advanced age; lack of adequate strength in your member; weakness in the muscles of the member while copulating; premature ejaculation; small size due to faulty blood circulation; thinness; crookedness; nightfall...childlessness due to low sperm count; heat...There's no cause for worry. Come and meet in person. Piles and secret diseases of women are also cured here.

(That piles should be mentioned together with venereal disease and sexual dysfunction is revealing about us Indians, us sex log. More revealing is our vocabulary for the unmentionables. In the specialist's ad copy reproduced above, *swapnadosh*, or nightfall, translates literally as 'the fault of a dream' or 'dream-sin'; *sheeghra patan* [premature ejaculation] is 'a fall too soon'. And the word used for sperm—*kitaanu*—is, literally, 'germ'.)

The website of a certain Dr Jain is slightly more professional-sounding. It has 'Medical FAQs' with answers to questions like 'What is masturbation?' and 'What is night discharge?' These are both common diseases, and if you suffer from either, you can contact Dr Jain. Sorry if you're annoyed by this suggestion. According to Dr Jain, one effect of excessive masturbation is that 'the person turns hot tempered and unfriendly'. Night discharge is a more serious problem.

> An ejaculation which happens during sleep while having a sexy dream and without the desire of a person is called nightfall or night discharge. In case such a discharge in sleep occurs three to four times in a month, the person concerned should immediately consult some sexologist because the aggravated disease may cause complete sleeplessness. Others symptoms are weakness, disappearance of beauty and brightness on the face, giddiness, darkness in sight, tiredness even after light work, failing memory, etc. The person may even become impotent if the disease takes deep roots. Hence early treatment by a specialist is advised.

Please check in the mirror to see if your face is glowing. If it isn't, you can confirm the diagnosis by testing your memory. Try and remember something simple, like the names of all the twenty-eight states in India. In case of inability to do so, please call an ambulance and rush to Dr Jain's clinic.

Elsewhere, Dr Jain defines woman: 'A woman is like a metre to gauge the potency of a man.' I hope you know how to get a metre reading. Otherwise, call an ambulance and rush to Dr Jain.

Dr Jain does not dispense any of his medical advice for free, but the Sablok Clinic is more generous. 'To prevent frequent nightfall young men should not indulge in vulgar talk, see nude photographs and should not read sexual literature which arouses their sexual feelings. Do not take hot milk at night. Walking barefoot in the morning on the green grass is very helpful for the patients,' it says.

All our *akhada* wrestlers try to follow this advice. Only very few among them are actually able to do so. Most fall prey to temptation and drink hot milk at night and therefore we have only two medals in wrestling in all of Olympic history. Had they been more like the god they worship, Bajrang Bali a.k.a. Hanuman, we would be carting our medals back in sackfuls like the abstemious Chinese. Hanuman the monkey-god who had the strength to move mountains was a celebrated *brahmachari*, a celibate. It is believed that brahmacharis have enormous strength because they do not fritter away their life force through masturbation or sex or nightfall.

The Hindu vaid is not the only one who advises against masturbation and related 'bad habits'. Even the Muslim hakim has similar advice for men. The hakim also has simple, non-medicinal cures for problems of a sexual nature. For example, if you suffer from premature ejaculation, the famous Hashmi Dawakhana advises you to:

1. Think very hard about something totally unconcerned with sex (like tax)
2. Pinch yourself hard
3. Bite the pillow

Your startled partner may inquire why you are pinching yourself and biting the pillow in the middle of sex, but don't worry about that. She will get used to it. If she doesn't, and leaves, you still have yourself and the pillow, so you won't miss her much.

More serious treatments like penis and breast enlargement require medication. For breast enlargement, there are herbal remedies and massages. Penis enlargement can be done with the help of the Mughal-e-penis patch. 'The patch should be placed on the dry, hairless area of the lower abdomen or buttocks...Rubbing alcohol is recommended to ensure optimum cleanliness. Replace the patch after the third day with a new one.' This wonder of ancient medicine is available from Doctoradvice International of Amroha, district J.P. Nagar, Uttar Pradesh.

Do not doubt any of this, my country-people. Please remember the famous saying: 'Never be sceptical about love and sexual medicine.' Of course the patch works; otherwise why would people buy it? Or sell it? The risks are too high for the sex doctors. They all remember the case of the young patient who shot his sexologist dead on a busy road in Delhi in May 2006.

I did tell you we take our sex very seriously. No one in the whole country laughs when they're at it. It's about family, god and country, after all.

Matrimonial Nation

. . . .

Namita Gokhale

Marriage in India is not a private bond of commitment between two individuals. It involves one's family, society, economy and the gods with an intensity and enthusiasm unusual in the rest of the modern world. An Indian marriage is a display of kinship, caste and community status. It is an affirmation of financial standing and social and political hierarchy. It is also a cure for a host of tragedies and misfortunes: waywardness, impotence, unemployment, sleepwalking, chronic indigestion, loneliness, drug abuse, extreme idealism, love, communism, alcoholism, homosexuality, bankruptcy, low self-esteem, epilepsy, bed-wetting, insomnia, general confusion, low and high blood pressure, a tendency to gamble or give in charity, insanity, lassitude, solo sex, kleptomania, shyness in men and too much ambition in women.

There are many among us who make a relatively modest claim for the institution—that, at its best, it is a moving and deeply human sacrament. Some others, a lot not to be taken seriously, disagree. They point out that, at its worst, the Indian marriage is an unequal union (read the laws of Manu, they say) and an inhuman transaction that spawns cruelties like dowry and bride-burning.

But all that—the good, the bad and the ugly—comes after, when it isn't about marriage anymore but procreation and parenthood. Marriage in India is in fact the wedding, the search for the suitable boy/girl, the invitations, the *baraat*, the wedding feast, the rituals. The incredible enterprise that keeps us loud, robust and endlessly inventive about the preservation of family, clan, race, morals, self and humanity (in that order).

There is proof of our passion every winter: In cities across India, traffic comes to a halt on the most auspicious days when 10 million families enter into matrimonial alliances and the roads are given over to 10 million baraats—processions of the bridegrooms' families, friends, neighbours, retainers and gatecrashers.

~

CLASSIFIED INFORMATION

> SM for Agarwal 31/165 b'ful IIT MS USA wkg. Engr USA good salary looks younger holds USGC first brief marriage BHP happymrg@gmail.com
>
> PQM 4 a Mglk slim Smart B'ful, M.F.C. 26/5 ½ Bhardwaj Non-Punjabi Brahmin Religious wkg girl: contact . . .
>
> Respectable Punjabi Kapoor business family well settled in UK. Seeks alliance from a cultured Prof. B'ful girl (can adjust in joint family) for their H'some son/ Nov, 82/ 5'10/ UK Born Master in Law, working for Int'l Solicitor firm. G. Father presently in India.

Open the matrimonial supplement of the *Hindustan Times*, the *Times of India* or any of the other bastions of the free press in the world's most populous democracy, and you will find a vital, throbbing, pragmatic, segmented matrimonial market, orchestrated by dense insider jargon that can appear impenetrable to first timers.

'SM', in the advertisements above, for instance, is an acronym for Suitable Match, and 'PQM' for Professionally Qualified Match. 'Mglk' is Manglik, a person with a strong Mars in the horoscope, an unfortunate astrological hurdle on the road to matrimonial bliss. USGC, of course, is the Holy Grail: a US Green Card. A BHP, as far as I can conjecture, is a request for Biodata, Horoscope and Photo. As I write these words, I still haven't figured out what MFC is.

Every waking hour, and in dreams at night, grooms are wanted—urgently—for Agarwal, Arora, Iyer, Brahmin, Khatri, Punjabi, Kayastha, Rajput, Jain, SC/ST, Tyagi, Yadav, Gujjar, Jat Sikh, Ramgarhia, Khandelwal, Vaish, Himachali, Malayali, Tamil/Telugu, Sindhi, Oriya, Garhwali/Kumaoni, Catholic, Shia, Sunni, Syrian Christian and Jewish girls. Also for 'Innocent divorcee/Widow', 'MBA/Professional', 'IAS/Allied Services', 'Handicapped/Disabled' and 'Cosmopolitan working girl'.

Brides are requisitioned too for 'handsome' men of various castes from 'well-settled' families, among them doctors, pilots, 'high status' businessmen, professionals with 'six-figure' salaries and H1B Visas, 'well-cultured' industrialists, Radhaswami teetotalers, risk analysts and young-looking divorcees.

In today's IT-defined society, the old game has been updated. Marriageable singles spend a lot of time conducting an extended online search for soul mates with compatible social status, commensurate salary bands and matching height, weight and colour parameters. The click-for-compatibility databases reveal a new generation weaning itself away from the limitations of parental choice into a fecund virtual environment of matrimonial quests. Till the 1980s, anxious Indian mothers searched for a Suitable Boy for their daughters. In the 1990s, the middle classes dreamt only of a Professional Match. Today's urban bride, usually a professional woman herself, places a premium on an employee of a multinational company (MNC).

A recent study forecast a 50 per cent growth in the matrimonial sites segment, driven largely by the need for a convenient matchmaking mechanism in our busy times, the increasing Internet penetration across the country and the demographic profile of a market where 65 per cent of the population is under thirty-five years of age. The geographical break-up is fascinating too. A quarter of online metro-marry hopefuls are located in Maharashtra (of them, 17 per cent in Maximum City Mumbai), 12 per cent are from Tamil Nadu and 7 per cent from Karnataka. The largest and most populated state in India, Uttar Pradesh, has just 6 per cent, as does West Bengal. And an eye-opening statistic: 30 per cent of the metro-marry seekers are from small-town India.

I made further discoveries of my own. Researching this piece on the Internet led me, inevitably, to the incredible universe of matrimonial sites where I saw the following onsite commentary:

> Through a marriage two families come into mutual relationship, and both families together try to work out the marriage if problems arise in the marriage.

This was followed by an alluring flash:

> You can find your life partner in next 10 minutes. Search-chat today! SimplyMarry.com/REGISTER FREE-NOW! On India's only Metro-monial site!

And so I did. With a virtual might-have-been-me-profile: a widowed journalist, fifty-two years old, living in New Delhi, with an unpredictable bank balance and a sometimes foul temper. I didn't expect to hear from anyone, but the Web astonished me. Within seven minutes I had the details of willing Hindu males from California to Kanpur, aged fifty-two to fifty-six, with their dreams and aspirations laid bare. There were passport-size photos too—fierce frontal stares; not a smile in sight. Well, I could have changed my life then and married one of them, but I didn't. Not just yet. But there really were some good men out there. There was, for instance, a 'Confident Truthful, Non Cheater and Honest Man, doing Bio movements of grip research in Tennis game. Searching for Enlightenment and spirituality.' Hmmm . . . On this evidence he could have been from Silicon Valley, Tikamgarh or Hyderabad. He didn't tell, and I couldn't.

Matrimonial advertisements, whether in the newspapers or on the Web, define India in all her diversity and contradictions and weirdness. They decrypt the bewildering codes of caste, community, region, religion and social class that are the markers of a complex and layered society. Added to all this is pan-Indian cultural codes. An experienced eye can interpret the small print in the advertisements. 'Early decent marriage' indicates an eager negotiation of dowry figures. A 'wheatish complexion' implies a dark skin that no amount of Fair & Lovely cream has lightened. 'Innocent divorcee' asks for the near impossible in a once-married woman. (Progressive—or realistic—men will settle for an 'issueless divorcee/widow'. As for women with imperfections that deny them a previously unmarried man, they can only pray that the 'issues' are no more than a couple and preferably college-going, or at least toilet-trained.)

As ancient marriage customs are accommodated by new technology and reinterpreted in step with changing times, the tradition of the *swayamvara* or self-choice has also been revved up. In myth and legend, the swayamvara involved a public arena where women of high birth chose their mates from among men of matching caste and status who participated in public demonstrations of valour. The wildly successful matrimonials have introduced a new form of swayamvara, where an IT-enabled generation trawls the Net in search of the perfect mate. These virtual romances culminate in marriage ceremonies where hi-tech priests and pundits officiate from Hardwar over nuptials in Houston.

But the old ways are not all lost. The Gud-Gadheda fair in Gujarat's Dahod district is held in the village of Jesawada every March. As potential grooms clamber up a 40-foot wooden pole, unmarried girls holding sticks in their hands dance to the beat of drums, playfully lashing out at the young men intent on scaling the pole. Thus do the maidens choose their men.

FINDING THE SUITABLE

'You too will marry a boy I choose,' said Mrs Rupa Mehra firmly to her younger daughter.

Lata avoided the maternal imperative by looking around the great lamp-lit garden of Prem Nivas. The wedding guests were gathered on the lawn.

'Hmm,' she said. This annoyed her mother further.

'I know what your hmms mean, young lady, and I can tell you I will not stand for hmms in this matter. I know what is best. I am doing it all for you . . .'

—A Suitable Boy *by Vikram Seth*

Since the assumption in an Indian marriage includes a lasting alliance between families, it's no surprise that prospective matchmaking is a highly skilled social activity for a certain generation of aunties. Indians will understand this immediately. The non-Indians can turn to Vikram Seth's monumental novel *A Suitable Boy*, which first introduced international audiences to the labyrinthine minds and psyches of matchmakers, mothers, aunts and cousins.

Kamadeva, the Indian god of love, like his Western counterpart, aims floral arrows of sudden passion at gods and mortals alike. But nothing he can do will cause a large-scale revolution. According to the famous psychoanalyst Sudhir Kakar, the concept of romantic love, which the Western world acknowledges as a birthright, 'is recognized as a fantasy by most Indians, a fantasy that, however, does not lose all its magnetic power by being acknowledged as such'. This fantasy—'of love unimpeded by the shackles of family obligations and duties toward the old and all the other keepers of society's traditions'—plays itself out at a safe remove in the shared dreaming of popular cinema. In life, all but the brave and mad few choose order over subversion.

Our society has evolved a neat way to accommodate Kamadeva's mischief. 'Arranged or Love?' is the question that often follows the announcement of urban marriage plans. But it is often neither and a bit of both: 'Arranged Love' is the hold-all compromise that has worked its way into consensus matrimony. In this script, boy meets girl via eager relative or friend (in our part of the world the two are interchangeable); failing that, they meet via advertisements, BharatMatrimony.com, or *deus ex machina*—and then the two, assisted by their families, assess each other in a subtle mating dance of DNA suitability, credit-card rating, hormonal excitement and social snobbery. Love, in a pragmatic culture, follows marriage, rather than the other way round.

Arranged marriages are not only a pan-Indian norm cutting across divides in education, class, region and religion but, more importantly, they are rarely seen as an imposition by the young people concerned who overwhelmingly endorse them over the love marriages typical of contemporary Western society. Naturally, then, the matchmaking industry in India is a serious enterprise, straddling both the organized and non-organized sectors. It productively employs priests, astrologers, matrimonial bureaus, barbers, massage and beauty parlours, maids, *halwai*s, bangle-sellers, jewellers, tent-walas, henna-artists, fake-jewellery-for-hire shops, courier companies, band-walas, eunuchs, dress designers, garland weavers, fake-currency-into-garland weavers, florists, abortionists, belly dancers, traffic policemen, horses, elephants, elephant poop cleaners, photographers, qawwali singers, shehnai players, goldsmiths, caterers, food adulterers and many, many others.

Despite the above, however, and despite the great speed and spread of the Internet, the task of finding brides and grooms is still largely the work of *bua*s, *masi*s, *mami*s, *chachi*s and other female relatives of a certain age. These aunties and their breed crunch data about eligible boys and girls—academic and domestic qualifications; skin colour and salaries; personal 'bad habits'; and morals of ancestors. They frequent weddings and funerals to sniff out possible alliances. In this sense, they play a pivotal role in facilitating arranged love and keep the human race going. One-sixth of it, anyway.

In the new world, when the Indian small town is spread across the shrinking globe, the aunty brigade is in even greater demand. The new internationalism has created a globalized arranged marriage marketplace. Apache Indian gave voice to the deepest desire of the Non-resident Indian (NRI) male post adolescence: '*Me wan' girl from Jalandhar City/ Me wan' girl say a sooni kudi . . ./ Me wan' girl sweet like jalebee . . ./ Me wan' girl to make me roti.*' If he did find one, there must be an aunty somewhere to thank for it.

The NRI types tend to return in seasonal migratory patterns from Canada, the US and the UK to shop for brides in their homeland. They advertise and trade in visas and work permits. In the pre-recession era, the marriage market was overrun by rosy dreams of dollar brides and visa grooms. The chimera of the Foreign Match, however, can prove expensive in the long run, as the network of social sanction and scrutiny that keeps arranged marriages going isn't really operational in 'modern' countries. Sometimes, fraud, deceit and incompatibility are only the smaller problems. Ask the South Asian women transported to the desi ghettos of the first world and they will tell you, if they can dare, stories of beatings, house arrest, murder and suicide.

Yet the seasonal migrations continue. The dollar and pound NRIs keep coming to the great tent house that is the land of their birth or of their parents or grandparents. They can hold up traffic here, litter the streets, make the penthouses and hovels tremble to the sound of music and firecrackers, hire a Bollywood item girl or boy to entertain the guests. None of the things they can do in their adopted homeland, unless they are Lakshmi Mittal. And what's an Indian wedding without any of this?

Even post-recession they will find a way. Visiting Chandigarh recently, a friend walked past a surprising number of cycle-rickshaws to reach his hotel, and blundered into a designer-wear crowd speaking in a mix of English accents and expensive Punjabi. Later that evening he caught the *mohalla* news on a local TV channel. A son of Punjab was down from London to get his grandson married. The family had hired half of Chandigarh's rickshaws, decorated with marigolds and zari, to transport the baraat from the city's oldest hotel to its largest gurudwara and back.

SUTRAS FOR THE HOUSEHOLDER

In a culture obsessed by ritual, matrimony is the most important sacrament of life. It marks entry into the *grihasta ashram*, the phase of the householder. In the ancient concept of Samskaras, or ritual life phases, the passage embodied by marriage is the most transformative one. Both the Rig Veda and the Atharva Veda have extensive romantic, philosophical and literary allusions to marriage. It is not only a social necessity towards the propagation and perpetuation of family and community, but a sacrifice and religious duty through which the individual pays off his ancestral debt. 'He is indeed without sacrifice who has not got himself a wife,' proclaims the Taittiriya Brahmana.

Eight types of marriage were recognized in the Hindu world view. These were the Brahma, Daiva, Arsa, Prajapatya, Asura, Gandharva, Rakshasa and Paisacha vivaha. These eight ancient classifications pretty much sum up the range of motives and situations for human coupling even today.

The Paisacha vivaha was considered the basest and most barbarous of the eight forms of marriage. The definition that Manu (of the sometimes problematic *Manusmriti* fame) gives it is: 'When a man co-habits with a girl in a lonely spot when she is sleepy, mad or intoxicated, it is called the Paisacha mode.' This, and a far less peaceful version of such manipulated union, happens every few minutes in today's India, as indeed it does in every other part of the world.

The rakshasa form of marriage treated women as booty or spoils of war. 'Capture of a woman/girl by force after having killed, scattered and injured her relatives is called Rakshasa vivaha.' Some commentators feel that the format of the North Indian marriage, where the bridegroom arrives on horseback or seated on an elephant and in a procession to take the bride away derives from the practice of marriage by capture.

The Gandharva vivaha is the most spontaneous form of natural selection, proceeding from instinct and love. In the Mahabharata, the sage Kanva, father of Shakuntala, says, 'The marriage of a desiring woman with a desiring man, though without religious ceremonies, is the best marriage.' Naturally, the law givers discouraged the Gandharva marriage on moral grounds. While enough young people still elope, and some of them are pursued and killed in the name of family honour, the moral strictures are easing a little. To everyone's astonishment, the Maharashtra government recently passed a bill recognizing the rights of women in live-in relationships. (The central law ministry, however, is squeamish about following the example.)

The Asura form of marriage, also referred to as the Manusha, treated marriage as a transaction. 'Where the husband after having paid money to the relatives of the bride and the bride herself accepts her out of free will, it is called an Asura marriage.' In times when women were treated as chattel and family property, this seemed pragmatic. As it does today in parts of Haryana and Punjab where the sex ratio is heavily skewed after years of female foeticide. There aren't enough young women around, so the men pay to get brides from as far as Kerala and Assam.

The Prajapatya mode of marriage treated the institution as a contractual exchange and duty. 'That form of marriage where the commandment "you should both perform your duties together" is given is called Prajapatya,' say the scriptures. Ninety per cent of modern Indian marriages will qualify as Prajapatya, as long as the duties are properly divided and not gender neutral. (With the boon of affordable round-the-clock domestic help in our country, well-to-do progressives can legitimately claim that there *is* gender-neutral sharing of duties. Till, of course, the female of the pair gets pregnant and goes into labour.)

In the Arsa mode of marriage, the father of the bride was given cattle as a gift. The Daiva form of marriage decreed that the daughter be given by the father to a priest who performed sacrificial prayers for him. In the Brahma marriage, the girl was given by her father, 'with such ornaments as he can afford, to a man of character and learning whom he invites voluntarily and receives respectfully without receiving anything in return.'

Marriage as contract. And always, the girl will be given away. If she's lucky, she'll find a man who will respect the moving invocation to which the man and woman, in a Hindu marriage, walk the seven steps round the sacred fire: 'One step for sap, two for juice, three for the prospering of wealth, four steps for wellbeing, five for cattle, and six for the changing seasons. And with the seventh, friend—with this step—be united with me, be devoted to me.'

Amen to that.

Yet, whatever the nature of the marriage, in essence the wedding ceremony is almost always an atavistic ritual of kinship, hierarchy and the bowing order. It is a marker and index of wealth, power and beauty. A perpetuation of family, clan and social order.

OF WEDDING PLANNERS AND MEGA WEDDINGS

Great Indian Weddings don't just drop out of the sky. They come to be through Wedding Planners and the Great Indian Wedding Industry.

Conservative estimates assess the worth of the Indian wedding industry at over Rs 1.25 billion. It's a seasonal industry, spiking during the auspicious months, and growing at an average rate of about 25 per cent per annum. It's an aspirational industry, bringing together the Indian love of ritual, pageantry, glamour and plain demo-effect showing off.

The mega-media impact of the Mittal vows transformed the fundamentals of the Indian wedding industry. This was in June 2004, and all the world and its matchmaking aunts watched in awed fascination. Declared the grandest wedding of the century, steel king L.N. Mittal's six-day bash for his daughter's wedding made it to the Forbes list of billionaire weddings, leaving other rich dads like Donald Trump and the Russian Andrei Melnichenko way behind. A thousand guests were flown in from around the world to Paris and lodged in five-star hotels. Five thousand bottles of Mouton Rothschild were consumed in the festivities (the wine tab alone was $1.25 million). Half of Bollywood and Kylie Minogue performed for the guests. And the ladies among the guests went back with little bags of jewels as gifts.

In February 2006, Vikram Chatwal, American hotelier of Indian descent, married Priya Sachdev in what was breathlessly described as 'The wedding that had them talking from Manhattan to Mumbai'. The wedding ceremony was spread over a week and three Indian cities with a fleet of private jets and three 737s to transport the seriously rich and famous from across the world, and 50,000 kilos of fresh flowers from Holland, Bangkok and Calcutta. The wedding even made it to the Discovery Travel and Living channel as 'The Great Indian Wedding'.

And then there were the Liz Hurley–Arun Nayyar nuptials—not as blindingly rich, but rich enough, and with mountains of glamour. Fights between reporters and security guards, and media friendly slanging matches between family members gave the celebrations an authentic local flavour.

These, of course, are the extreme high-end examples. But they certainly are a reflection of the great Indian marriage tamasha that we Indians—those of some means, at least—appear to have perfected. Carved, gold-painted thrones for the bride and the bridegroom; garlands of currency (usually Indian); band-walas in red-and-white uniforms (with smart caps) playing Bollywood hits; acres of lehnga or silk sari; firecrackers and occasional gunfire—all this has been part of our wedding day aesthetics for decades. Recent additions have included DJs, cheer leaders and television and cinema stars. The growing numbers joining the middle class club use marriages as photo-ops to showcase their newfound status and disposable incomes, and to win friends and influence people. One social observer rated demonstration-effect show-off weddings as equivalent to 'an Ivy League education in the US'.

It is serious business, the show-off wedding. And afterwards there's the honeymoon in New Zealand for the couple and the detox clinic for the partied-out guests. (Some years later come the divorce courts and alimony settlements.)

And only some six decades ago, Mahatma Gandhi, the father of our nation, sent a wedding gift for the then Princess Elizabeth.

It was a 'rectangular, deeply-fringed piece of cloth' of no discernible purpose. It is said that the Dowager Queen Mary misunderstood its purpose, and thought it to be a loin cloth, like the one Gandhi wore. She described it as 'rather vulgar'. How times change!

BOLLYWOOD VIA LUDHIANA

In the triangular map of India, Ludhiana in the state of Punjab wins the most points and ratings for seven- to nine-star weddings. Hologramed invitations, 'invitation gifts' of silver trays laden with Swiss chocolates, tulips flown in from Belgium, a buffet table with at least a hundred dishes—all these 'exclusive' event markers push the one-upmanship that drives the Ludhiana business community.

Ludhiana wedding negotiators wager a 'wedding budget' figure, and only when this is approved by the family finance committee is the alliance finalized. Then the full nine yards roll out for the Hindu/Sikh wedding cards (with add-on tassels), *mehndi* cards, *sangeet* cards, rice grains, gold foil, *kundan* drops, royal scrolls and *firmans*, all soaked in wedding mood.

After this begins the tedious process of the wedding itself: slimming clinics, etiquette coaching classes, trousseaus of silk and brocade, bed and table linen, engagement *thaals*, *shagun* envelopes, suit lengths, saris and shoes, 'His' and 'Her' watch holders, *mujras*, mehndis, stag nights, exclusive silk shamianas, laser light shows and more. The wedding industry grinds along with its invisible baraat of tailors, jewellers, beauticians, designers, dance masters, dancers, DJs, bodyguards, prompters, an army of cameramen and another of caterers, waiters and idlers. And on the wedding day descend squads of young relatives and friends of the families—hormone-inflamed boys and girls; gold-digger boys and girls. They come from as far away as Mumbai, London, Lahore and Vancouver. For Indian, and certainly Punjabi, weddings are no longer contained by the shorelines of the subcontinent. Indian theme weddings are the stuff of romance and legend wherever the curry and butter chicken culture has triumphed.

Bollywood, naturally, has a lot to do with *this* as well. At home and abroad. The Great Bollywood Wedding—the climactic scene of so many Indian films—is the primal cultural fantasy that continues to inspire millionaires, politicians, fixers, cricketers, NRIs, eloping teenagers, small-town seth sahebs and gutka kings with children of marriageable age. The sets, costumes, jewellery and music that predicate the culmination of arranged love are sourced straight from celluloid.

India may be the world's largest democracy, but it has an enormous obsession with royalty and status. Bollywood aspirations ride on the glittering dream of the 'King and Queen for a Night' theme. An Indian wedding is the ultimate leveller, where everyone can feel as royal as any blue-blooded plutocrat for a few hours. Every Indian girl and her mother have been subjected to intense social pressure for the day when the gods will bless them with the pomp and paraphernalia of royalty. Every girl and her family want a wedding; they want lehngas, saris, *shaadi ka joda* and glittering jewels. For the extended family, it's their chance to meet, eat, celebrate and squabble, to play at Bollywood Royalty, record it on camera and replay it when dull daily life reasserts itself.

So the bride gets a wedding and the family gets a marriage. Then stage two of the family drama sets in, with mothers-in-law, power plays, dowry demands and all the other vile stuff of Indian saas-bahu tele-serials simulating life and the other way around.

POST SCRIPT

I have lunch with a school friend. She is a UP Brahmin, married into similar circumstances. Her son works with a major American firm. He wants to marry a suitable Indian girl, and has left the choice to his mom. 'You know any nice girls?' she asks, screwing up her eyes to focus on the immediacy of the problem. 'You know, similar background, someone who will fit into the family.'

'I know of this girl,' I tell her, 'living in London. She has a PhD in gender and development . . .'

'Caste?' she checks. 'Not that it matters, but . . .'

'The same as yours,' I assure her.

Height, skin colour and family background are next on the checklist. 'Ask her mother to send me her Date of Birth, please,' my friend says. 'If the stars match we can take it forward.'

And so it goes on, the matrimonial game, with another international Indian wedding.

Pilgrimagetirtha.com

. . . .

Devdutt Pattanaik

A young girl wanted to go to Shirdi, a popular pilgrimage destination near Mumbai dedicated to the saint Sai Baba, with her friends, unaccompanied by adults. 'We girls just want to have some fun,' she told her father. Not wanting to appear 'uncool', the father agreed, hoping the more traditional mother would say no. To his surprise, she did not. 'How could I say no?' explained the mother. 'She said she felt Sai Baba was calling her.' Till date, the parents are unsure about the real reason for their daughter's trip. Was it a spiritual calling? Or just an excuse for fun? So it is with any Indian pilgrimage. The reason for the trip is a bit of both, or perhaps neither.

The young girl may never have heard of Shirdi and Sai Baba had it not been for the film *Amar Akbar Anthony* starring Amitabh Bachchan made in the 1970s that made the Sufi saint a household name. Pilgrimages are a recurring theme in Bollywood because the producers, sensitive to the pulse of the masses, have realized the crucial role pilgrimage plays in the lives of most Indians. Little wonder then that when a superstar gets arrested for aiding terrorist activities he ensures the media follows him when he travels to each and every pilgrim shrine of repute in India. That is how he gets the sympathy of the masses. That is how he also ensures divine intervention for his judicial problems. Sincerity and strategy have always been part of the great Indian pilgrimage.

THE ORIGINS

The idea of travelling to a sacred place is not unique to India. What we find in India is a unique cultural expression of a universal practice. Hindus refer to a holy place as *tirtha*, which means a ford, the shallow part of a water body that can easily be crossed. Perhaps the earliest tirtha refers to the River Ganga, the most sacred river in India, believed to have descended from the heavens to help man conquer death and cope with life—when ashes of the dead are scattered in its waters, it offers the option of another life; and when the living bathe in its waters, it holds the promise of release from the wheel of rebirths. Perhaps the earliest pilgrimage was the *yatra* or journey made by people to this river to scatter the ashes of their ancestors or it was the final journey to be taken after completing all worldly duties. The river in a sense bridges the land of the dead and the land of the living—a spiritual bridge that prevents man from sinking and drowning in the material. Since then, all such places where there seemed a connection between the transcendental and the mundane became tirthas, a pilgrimage to which every Indian was, and is, encouraged to take.

Most people do not realize that it is the pilgrim routes of India that created the notion of India in the first place. The routes connected rivers and lakes and mountain springs through various trails, identified by wandering monks, who were forbidden to stay in one place for too long—a rigid rule that helped them experience detachment and indifference to all things worldly. According to Jain chronicles, in the latter part of his life, Chandragupta Maurya, founder of the Mauryan dynasty in the third century BCE, renounced the throne, became a Jain monk and travelled to what is today Sravanbelgola in Karnataka with his guru. Hermits travelled all the time, except during *chatur-maas* or four months of the rainy season when they were sequestered in a monastery or in the house of a charitable patron. The average householder accompanied them sometimes, to some places.

Generally speaking, Indians have never been a very mobile people. Women spent the early years of their life in their father's house and the rest of their life in their husband's. Other than monks, the only people who travelled outside the village were traders, performers and soldiers. The tirtha yatra offered everyone an opportunity to see the world and taste the wonders of what lay beyond the village frontier. Naturally, they were seen as threats if undertaken by young unmarried men. It was feared that men who went on such trips would never return—either seduced by the charms of a foreign land or by the freedom offered by a mendicant's existence. In south Indian Brahmin weddings, there is a ritual in which the groom goes on a Kashi yatra, suggesting he is renouncing married life. He is coaxed by the family of the bride to return and sit with his wife on a swing, which is the symbol of conjugal harmony. Marriage was thus seen as an anchor that rooted a man; pilgrimages were permitted, so long as it did not threaten the household, either with wife and family or when one was old, having performed all their duties in life. Since travelling was fraught with danger (foul weather, dacoits, wild animals, no guarantee of either food or shelter), return to the village was no guarantee. Those who returned were hailed as heroes. Their feet were washed and their bodies touched because it was believed that the sacredness of the sites they visited was transmitted through their person.

While the idea of a sacred journey is alluded to in the Rig Veda, conservatively said to have been composed around 1500 BCE, it is explicitly elaborated in the Mahabharata, an epic that was, after centuries of oral transmission, put down in writing between 300 BCE and 300 CE by various writers. In the Aranyaka Parva, which describes the exile of the Pandavas, there is an entire section devoted to pilgrimage. In it, various sages, like Lomasha and Narada, inform the Pandavas of various sacred sites located in the north, south, east and west and advise them to visit all of them. By doing so, they are told they will earn spiritual merit which will turn luck in their favour. They are also told it will offer them an opportunity to grow emotionally and intellectually. The Pandavas take this advice and make these journeys, often accompanied by sages. During the trip, they hear stories, learn about rituals, encounter demons, have adventures, experience spiritual epiphanies and secure the blessings of many celestial beings. When they finally reach the Himalayas, the climb becomes very strenuous and so they are helped by other creatures of the wilderness (rakshasas and yakshas) who carry them on their backs, much like mountain tribes today carry burdens. At the end of the exile, the Pandavas are shown to be wiser and stronger and more humble, thereby reinforcing the value of the pilgrimage to all those who hear this tale.

THE MOTIVATION

Every sacred scripture written after the Mahabharata continues the practice of referring to sacred sites, narrating the reason why a site is sacred and the benefits of visiting the place. Some of these sites are real, others imaginary. But through them the ancient seers encouraged travel. What was the strategic intent one wonders? Trade, say some scholars, since most pilgrim spots like Pushkar in Rajasthan were also famous for their bazaars and fairs. The people who travelled needed to be housed and fed and so pilgrimages fuelled commercialization. But not all sites have commercial value; some are located at extremely inaccessible places atop cold, icy mountains. So why did sages encourage people to go to these spots? Was it because this was one way of encouraging a highly rooted agricultural population to break free from the limited perspective offered by the comforts of the village? Some say, the rise of pilgrim sites and pilgrim routes ensured the cultural unity of India. But was this the political agenda of the sages? These explanations are perhaps attempts to rationalize, and hence legitimize, pilgrim destinations. The real answer lies in the realm of belief—these were sites that offered the holy men of India an experience that was greater than the mundane and the material; it was something they wished to share with the rest of humanity.

For Muslims, making a trip to Mecca (the Haj pilgrimage) is an obligatory sacred duty. There is no such obligation for Hindus,

Jains, Buddhists, Zoroastrians or Christians. But a good son is expected to show his parents the sacred spots of India before they die. The image of young Shravan Kumar who took his blind parents on a pilgrimage, carrying them on baskets hanging from two ends of a stick that he held on his shoulders, is imprinted in the minds of most Indians. The archer who accidentally shot Shravan Kumar dead was cursed that he would die of heartbreak at the loss of his own son. To prevent a son from taking his parents on a pilgrimage has therefore been seen as *paap*, an act that brings bad luck. In the sixteenth century, even Akbar, the great Mughal emperor, organized for his mother to make a trip to Mecca.

Pilgrimages are prescribed to harness good luck. A pilgrimage generates good karma, helping to improve one's lot in life. Tirtha yatras are sometimes undertaken by people to fulfil a religious vow. Many families take the vow to visit their village deity or family god on getting jobs, getting married, or getting children. Sometimes, parents are advised to take their children to specific holy places such as Rameshwaram in Tamil Nadu or Gaya in Bihar to perform rituals in order to appease malevolent astrological or ancestral spirits that have a negative impact on their fate. Pilgrimages are also advised to cure one from any affliction. Many pilgrim sites are especially popular because the sites are said to possess curative powers. Stories of miracles, documented in local prayer books or the Sthal Puranas, enhance the sacredness of a shrine. Thus, the shrine of Bahucharji in Gujarat is popular in the local region because she helps women conceive sons. Tirupati Balaji is famous for bestowing wealth. This is restricted not just to Hindus shrines. Two hundred kilometres south of Chennai is the shrine of Our Lady of Good Health, popularly called Our Lady of Vailankanni, that was built by Portuguese sailors in the sixteenth century. It draws vast crowds of Catholic and non-Catholic pilgrims seeking cure from various ailments. In Ajmer, Rajasthan, is the dargah of the Sufi saint Hazrat Muinuddin Chisti. Ever since his blessings led to Emperor Akbar becoming a father, his final resting place has become the refuge of thousands of childless couples belonging to all faiths.

Pilgrim spots are also places where various rites of passage are performed. People get married here because it is faster and cheaper. Exchange of garlands before the deity is enough to ensure you are married. This *gandharva* form of marriage is popular amongst devotees, not least because expenses of the great Indian wedding are spared. And it is coupled with direct blessings of the divine. Many temples provide services for performing other rites of passage—the first shaving of the head, the first feeding of rice. In Kollur, Karnataka, in the temple of the goddess, who is the patron of writers and poets, many children perform the ritual of first learning, writing the first alphabet on a bed of grain or on a piece of paper, which initiates them into education. In Chidambaram, Tamil Nadu, students of dance present their graduation performance before the lord of dance.

Until recent times, Indians never travelled for fun. Holidays meant either a visit to one's native place or it meant visiting a place of worship. This is reflected in all online travel portals where there are more pilgrimage tours than leisure trips. The yatra provides a goal post to the trip. Merely travelling for fun induced guilt and did not justify the expenses of the trip to the middle class self-employed man. Travel to pilgrim towns usually takes place in groups with the extended family. This keeps expenses down but it also helps families bond with each other, especially now when the joint family has given way to the nuclear family. Trips such as these reaffirm family ties and ensure children do not drift away from their cultural roots. It is also a time to break away from the monotony of family life and get away from the routine problems that plague marriage. Trips such as these clear the mind, help one develop a fresh perspective towards life, and in the process gather some good karma.

CHOICE OF DESTINATION

India has thousands of pilgrimage sites. Some are parochial, known only to people living in a particular city or town. Others are pan-

Indian. Most belong to a particular religious denomination or sect, and many open their gates to people of all faiths. So where does one go?

Choice depends on the intention of the pilgrimage. If it is about rediscovering cultural roots, then the trip will be to the hermitage of the family guru or the temple of the village deity. If it is about seeking good luck, a site famous for delivering results is selected. Those for whom pilgrimages double up as vacations use this opportunity to see all of India, for there is a pilgrimage site in every corner of India; if it is the northern pilgrim route this year then it is the southern pilgrim route next year.

Buddhists like to travel to places associated with the Buddha such as Bodh Gaya in Bihar where Buddha attained enlightenment or Sarnath where he gave his first sermon. Jains prefer sites associated with their spiritual masters, such as Shikhaji, a hill in Jharkhand state, where twenty of the twenty-four *tirthankaras* or ford-finders who revealed their faith attained *kaivalya* or liberation. Zoroastrians, who migrated to India around the tenth century CE, are keen to visit the oldest fire temple located at Udvada in Gujarat following the thread ceremony (*navjot*) of their children.

The rise of Muslim kingdoms after the eleventh century CE saw the building of grand mosques such as Jama Masjid in Delhi and Imam Bara in Lucknow, which have become famous as architectural marvels as well as pilgrim spots. Churches doubling up as healing shrines are especially common along the coasts of India which, since the sixteenth century, were centres of European trade. In the city of Mumbai are two such churches—one at Mahim where people go every Wednesday and another in Bandra atop a hill where people go during the annual fair, offering clay effigies of hands and legs and other body parts that need curing. The Basilica of Bom Jesus in Goa is also associated with healing; it houses the mortal remains of the seventh-century Saint Xavier: the body has miraculously not decomposed over the years.

With the rise of the Sikh religion in Punjab 400 years ago came the gurdwaras, or 'doorways to the guru', where Sikhs hear words of their spiritual masters documented in the Granth Sahib. Some of these gurdwaras, such as the Golden Temple at Amritsar and Anandpur Sahib, have become pilgrimage sites due to their historic importance. As in Muslim places of worship, one enters the gurdwara with a covered head and, as in Hindu places of worship, one bathes in the pond there and eats in the communal dining hall.

Over time, pilgrimages have also evolved around sites associated with holy men—the sants of Hinduism, the saints of Christianity and the sufis of Islam. There is the shrine of Haji Ali located on an island next to Mumbai and of Sai Baba located in Shirdi in Maharashtra. In modern India, sites associated with the life of political leaders such as Shakti Sthal in Delhi where former prime minister Indira Gandhi was cremated and the ashrams of political preachers such as Sabarmati Ashram of Mahatma Gandhi have also become part of the pilgrim trail.

Hindus by far undertake the most pilgrimages, testimony to the fact that the religion evolved in the subcontinent over 5000 years and that it is followed by of over 70 per cent of the population. The earliest sacred sites were just rivers such as the Ganga, sources of rivers such as Gomukh in the Himalayas, confluence of rivers such as Prayag at Allahabad in Uttar Pradesh, lakes such as Pushkar, hills such as Palni in Tamil Nadu or caves such as Amarnath in Jammu. At Kashi, now called Varanasi, the River Ganga flows northwards rather than southwards towards the delta, a peculiarity that made it sacred long before the gods came. Scholars are convinced that sites were sacred long before they were associated with sectarian deities, which explains why Mount Kailas in Tibet is sacred not just to Hindus but also to followers of Bon, the pre-Buddhist Tibetan faith. As time passed, the Badrinath caves became associated with the guardian-god Vishnu; Kedarnath with the ascetic-god Shiva; the Vaishno Devi caves in Jammu with the goddess; the peaks of Palni with the divine warlord, Murugan; the hills of Simhachalam in Andhra Pradesh with Narasimha, the man-lion incarnation of

Vishnu. Often the rivalry between religious sects to claim a holy site is fairly evident. Thus, what is Hari-dwar in Uttaranchal or the gateway to Vishnu to Vaishnavas becomes Hara-dwar or the gateway to Shiva for Shaivas.

Adi Shankaracharya, the great Vedanta scholar, who travelled across India in the eighth century CE as he tried to reaffirm the Hindu faith, is credited with connecting the pilgrimages of the north and the south. He is said to have listed and popularized the twelve jyotir-lingas and the 108 shakti-peethas. He even established his matts or missions in the four corners of India which became the Char Dhams, or four essential pilgrim spots of India. These are Puri in the east where Vishnu is said to eat his meals each day in the form of Krishna, Rameshwaram in the south where he bathes in the form of Rama, Dwarka in the west where he rules in the form of Krishna and Badrinath in the north where he meditates in the form of Nara and Narayana.

Vedanta teachers who followed Shankara continued the practice of establishing or at least associating themselves with temples. Thus Ramanuja who lived around tenth century CE is closely linked with the Srirangam temple of Tamil Nadu. The Udupi Krishna temple in Karnataka was established by Madhavacharya in the thirteenth century CE and is the focal point of the Madhava Brahmin community, while Srinathji temple established by Vallabhacharya in the fifteenth century CE, relocated to Nathdvara in Rajasthan following Mughal excesses in Vrindavan, is the most favoured pilgrimage destination of the followers of Pushti Marga.

Although many Indian shrines are open to people of all faiths, there are temples which are restricted to Hindus. At one time, temples were restricted to members of the higher caste but this practice has stopped with the increasing unpopularity of the caste system in modern India. The Jagannath Puri temple in Orissa allows only Hindus: but how does one recognize a Hindu? This means people who do not look conventionally Indian, who may be practising Hindus, can be stopped at the gates. Muslims and

Christians, with Indian features, accompanying Hindu pilgrims, however, can and do manage to enter comfortably, encouraged by their friends who reject this 'Hindu only' policy. In such subversion is inclusion, for the deity is Jagannath, lord of the world. There are temples in India which are open only to men. Women, especially menstruating women, are expected to stay out. This men-only policy of Ayyappa temple at Sabarimalai in Kerala is currently being challenged by social reformers. Those who believe in the Hindu-only and men-only policy argue that they do not want sacred shrines to become tourist attractions. Temples, they say, are where the gods reside, not museum pieces for secular historians, and every house has its rules.

SOURCE OF SACREDNESS

Sites believed to be especially sacred are ones where the divine presence made itself known without human intervention. These are *swayambhu* sites or self-created sites. A story that is typically associated with these sites is that a cowherd found his cow releasing milk over a termite hill. On investigation, under the termite hill was found an image of a deity that was then enshrined. Sites such as these have to be distinguished from non-swayambhu sites established by man. The latter is considered of lower rank. Of course, no one admits to a shrine being non-swayambhu.

Sometimes a shrine becomes famous at a particular time. For example, depending on the movement of the planet Jupiter across the zodiac over a twelve year period, the cities of Haridwar, Allahabad, Nashik and Ujjain become sites of the grand Kumbha Mela or the gathering of millions of Hindus who bathe in the local waters at the prescribed hour. Stories add to the sacredness of the gathering: it is said that when the gods churned the ocean for the nectar of immortality, four drops from the pot (*kumbha*) of elixir fell on these four spots when the stars were aligned so. That is why bathing in the local waters during the Kumbha Mela guarantees good karma which manifests in luck, health, wealth, children and even moksha.

Geographical sites associated with Hindu deities typically are located in the north. Shiva lives on the Himalayas with the goddess while the cities of Vishnu's avatars are located north of the Vindhya Mountains. To accommodate people who lived far away from traditional sacred sites, new sites sprang up in the south claiming to have the same spiritual potency as the original ones. Thus, the River Godavari came to be known as the Ganga of the south. And both the River Kaveri and the hills of Palni were said to have been brought down from the Himalayas by the sage Agastya who was advised by Shiva to move south to serve his devotees living far away from his mountainous abode. There are stories of how the rakshasa king Ravana tried to carry Shiva southwards and how his brother, Vibhishana, tried to carry Vishnu southwards, and how they were made to place the deities on the ground midway by Shiva's son who induced in them a frantic call of nature.

Grand temple complexes housing the three great deities of Hinduism—Shiva (Nataraj temple of Chidambaram), Vishnu (Sriranga temples on three islands on the River Kaveri) and Devi (Meenakshi temple of Madurai)—are most frequently located in south India. The one at Thiruvananthapuram in Kerala anchors a city which has now been declared the capital of the state. It is suggested that realizing that the north was famous for pilgrim sites associated with natural formations, kings in the south were encouraged by local priests to build grand temple complexes which would redirect pilgrim traffic southwards, which explains why there are more temple complexes in the south than in the north. Others offer a different explanation: that the temple complexes of the north were razed to the ground by Muslim invaders and they never rose to their former glory.

Certain shrines are of parochial importance—the eight shrines of Ganesha, the Ashta-Vinayak, are popular especially amongst Brahmins in and around Maharashtra while the shrine of Khandoba located in a citadel in Jejuri, also in Maharashtra, is the pilgrim spot favoured by the Marathas. Some, like Vaishno Devi in Jammu, which were once parochial, have now become pan-Indian. The rising popularity has led not only to a large influx of pilgrims but also of wealth. Sabarimalai, which had a few thousand pilgrims and an income of around Rs 2 million in the 1970s, now has over a million pilgrims each year with an income crossing a billion rupees. Naturally, it makes business sense to become a pilgrim centre.

UNDERTAKING THE YATRA

Temples constantly seek uniqueness to attract pilgrim traffic. So on the coast of Andhra Pradesh is the only temple dedicated to Kurma, the turtle incarnation of Vishnu, essentially an ancient sacred rock which is equated with the shell of the sacred turtle. In Pushkar is said to be the only temple dedicated to Brahma, the creator of the Hindu world.

While nowadays even the most inaccessible places are connected by road, rail and air, there are many who still believe that merits of a pilgrimage are enhanced if the journey involves great physical strain. The journey to a shrine is made difficult by walking barefoot or rolling to the shrine or crawling or walking on one's knees or lying flat, arising, walking only up the distance equal to the length of the body, and then lying flat again. This has been institutionalized in many places. Men who visit the shrine of the warrior-god Ayyappa at Sabarimalai prepare themselves by enduring forty days of extreme austerity, wearing black clothes, bathing in cold water, eating vegetarian food, sleeping on the floor and practising celibacy. In Maharashtra, hundreds of Varkaris, comprising simple farmers and herdsmen, have for hundreds of years walked to the sacred shrine of Vithal at Pandharpur with women carrying on their heads the sacred tulsi plant and men singing hymns composed by the sixteenth century poet-saint Tukaram. In the north, thousands of young men known as Kavadiyas collect the holy water of the

Ganga in *kavads*, which is basically two pots hanging from the ends of a bamboo stick carried on the shoulder, and take it either to the Shiva temple of their village or to the Augharnath temple of Shiva at Meerut, never once placing the pots carrying the holy water on the ground.

Stories abound of people who have lost their way during pilgrimages being helped by mysterious children who disappear once the destination is reached. Everyone concludes these were gods who accompany pilgrims on their journey. Likewise there are stories of sinners who despite all their attempts are unable to reach a shrine until they beg for forgiveness or return home and complete certain household responsibilities that they had shunned.

On reaching the pilgrim site one has to stay somewhere. Many take sanctuary in the houses of local priests who in exchange for a small fee offer them a bed and meals. Hotels are a recent phenomenon. Most pilgrims still cannot afford the rentals and prefer staying free at dharmashalas or charitable guest houses built by affluent businessmen who seek to earn good karma by serving pilgrims. These places provide free room and water. People can cook in the common kitchen. Everyone is advised to carry their own food and a lock for their luggage.

The point of going to a pilgrim site is to have *darshan* of the presiding deity. In Nathdvara in Rajasthan one has to flow with vast crowds to get a glimpse or *jhanki* of Srinathji, the lord with bow-shaped eyes. By just looking at the deity, a glimpse that lasts for less than a moment, one is said to be blessed for a lifetime. In Shiva temples, especially in north India, one is allowed to touch the image and pour water over it. In India, it is considered bad manners to visit anyone without gifts. Since the temple is the house of a god or a goddess, one is expected to carry offerings—flowers, fruits, sweets, incense, cloth and even money. A whole line of shops cater to this need of the pilgrim. They offer a safe place where the pilgrims can leave their shoes, bags and even belts, since many Hindu shrines do not allow a person wearing leather to enter.

Often when one visits a shrine, one is advised to visit a satellite town and pay one's respects to a different deity there, or to visit an ancillary shrine. Unless we do so, we are told that our pilgrimage is incomplete and we will not get the full merit of the pilgrimage. At each shrine, one is informed of another nearby temple. Thus a chain of pilgrim sites is created, one that benefits the various families of priests, linked by marriage, serving different temples. Thus the wealth of the pilgrim is distributed over more people. This practice also attempts to create peace between rival religious sects.

If one is visiting the Vishnu shrine of Tirupati Balaji, one is advised to visit the Shiva shrine of Sri Kalahasti or to visit the shrine of his consort, Padmavati, at the foothills. Likewise, as one makes a journey to the shrine of Ayyappa, the son of Shiva and Vishnu, one is perforce made to stop at the shrine of Vavar-swami, the Muslim companion of Ayyappa. There are temples devoted to the consort of the main deity or his mother (Rukmini temple in Dwarka) or her guardian (Bhairo temple in Vaishno Devi).

Also located around the temple are sacred trees and tanks. One goes around the trees and bathes in the tank.

In Buddhist shrines, the point is to circumambulate the stupa. In Vraja, the sacred land of Krishna, there is a pilgrim trail that takes one around the holy land. In places associated with a water body, say a river or a pond, the point is to bathe and so wash away one's bad karma and earn good karma. After seeing the deity, going around the shrine, bathing in the sacred waters, it is necessary to feed the poor and the priests. In the temple of Jagannath Puri, there are priests who, in order to serve pilgrims, do not mind eating three or four meals for lunch.

Pilgrims visiting holy places are often terrorized by local priests known in the Gangetic plains as *pandas*. These priests serve as guides and bully pilgrims into giving them exorbitant service fees or *dakshina*, cursing them with bad karma if their demands are not met. They argue that this is their only source of income, that the pilgrimage being performed is like a mother who feeds them and so pilgrims have to give them money. In recent times, eager to promote tourism and prevent such harassment, the temple authorities and government are regulating the activities of these pandas. Now, one can visit any shrine after buying tickets at special counters, without the menace of sacred middle men.

All pilgrim spots are filled with amusing stories of travellers and resident priests. In Puri, one pilgrim suddenly found a panda grabbing his right hand, placing few grains of cooked rice on it, licking it, and saying, 'There, you have fed a Brahmin. Now pay me dakshina for helping you earn your good karma.' In Varanasi, a generous pilgrim found the priests being very friendly and tying a red thread round his wrist, which they claimed was a rare privilege. Shortly thereafter, the pilgrim noticed that even before he entered the next temple, he was accosted by priests. He realized the red thread round his wrist gave him away as a wealthy, generous pilgrim.

There is the folktale of a miser who went secretly to the Ganga to take a dip in the waters; he did not want any priest to know he was going there for then he would be obliged to give them gifts. Unfortunately for him, he was recognized by a local priest. The priest picked up sand from the river bank and smeared it on the miser's forehead, saying, 'This is the sand of the Ganga which is more valuable than the sandal paste of any temple. I have applied this on your head, now give me dakshina; a cow would be most welcome as it befits your stature as the richest man in the village.' The quick-thinking miser looked around and saw a frog. He caught hold of the frog and gave it to the priest saying, 'This is a frog of the Ganga. Take it as my gift as it is more valuable than any cow from a rich man's shed.'

Pilgrimages are especially popular during the festival seasons. These festivals may be pan-Indian such as Navratri or Dussera or Holi, or may be specific to the temple such as the marriage of Meenakshi in Madurai. During this time the number of pilgrims swells a hundred-fold. Many pilgrimages are associated with stories of stampedes as a result of crowds running amuck and children getting lost. The story of brothers separated during a pilgrimage was once a recurring theme in Bollywood cinema. A story goes that a child slipped and fell into the *daan-hundi* or charity box of a temple. The temple authorities immediately claimed the child belonged to them. The parents pleaded and explained it was an accident but the temple refused to budge. As the parents returned home determined to contact the police and authorities, their bus met with an accident and they died. The devotees concluded this was god's way of saving the young child.

When it is time to leave, everyone wants to leave a bit of themselves at the holy place. Those who are rich either unfurl a flag atop the temple spire or leave a stone slab on the temple wall or floor with their name on it, hoping to earn blessings of the deity for all eternity. In Jain shrines atop Mount Abu in Rajasthan one finds images of temple patrons shown saluting the images of the resident tirthankara. In Kanchi, Tamil Nadu, everyone is advised to make a small pile of rocks under a sacred tree in the temple of Varadarajaswami for Vishnu to bestow a boon. In Sufi shrines, as in Ajmer, people tie threads to the window lattice in the hope that the saint will listen to their prayers and give them children. In ancient pilgrimage centres like Varanasi and Gaya, one is asked to enter one's name in a roster. The priests there claim that they have been maintaining rosters of pilgrims for thousands of years and on getting the family name and village of any visitor can trace their family tree and inform them of earlier forefathers who visited the shrine.

For centuries, pilgrimage centres were also dumping grounds for those rejected by mainstream society. Widows who found no place in their family homes found refuge in pilgrim spots such as Mathura and Varanasi. It was also the spiritually ordained home for the old, the orphaned, the crippled and the illegitimate. One often hears stories of how, terrified by social stigma, young unmarried girls were whisked off to temple towns where their children were delivered and abandoned. In many temples one hears stories of saints who were foundlings, raised in the temple as children of the deity.

With many unattached young men visiting pilgrim towns, and with commerce rising, it was but a matter of time before these centres also attracted the world's oldest profession. Varanasi became famous as much for the gods as for the courtesans who sang and danced in the by-lanes not far from the temples. The Puranas tell many stories of incest in pilgrim spots. There is the story of a woman who following widowhood became a prostitute in a temple town and ended up, unknowingly, having sex with her own brother, who was much younger than her. Perhaps these stories were meant to deter people from succumbing to the pleasures of the flesh while travelling to holy places. It has been suggested, but violently refuted, that the practice of devadasis or women who were married to the gods and hence were free to sexually serve any man began to attract tourists in medieval times. It has also been suggested that the erotic art of temples advertised their skills. There have been news reports of how some of these temple towns have become nodes of HIV transmission due to the rising flesh trade in and around the bus stations that cater to pilgrims.

POWER OF THE YATRA

The cultural power of pilgrimage is best realized when one hears the story of Radha, the consort of the Hindu god Krishna. There is no mention of Radha in India prior to the twelfth century CE. There were stray references to her in folk literature. But a poet called Jayadev composed the *Gita Govinda* describing Krishna's affection for one milkmaid called Radha. The work in ornamental Sanskrit fuses erotic content layered with sophisticated metaphysics. It fired the imagination of the priests who sang it every evening in the temple of Jagannath Puri, inspiring devadasis to choreograph dances around it. Pilgrims who came to the great temple saw the dance, heard the song and carried the lore of Radha all across India.

Before long, Radha became the consort of Krishna, his beloved, in popular belief. Worship of Krishna was considered incomplete without mentioning Radha, this despite the fact that most Krishna temples, except those in the Gangetic plains, do not enshrine the image of Radha next to Krishna.

Vedanta scholars like Adi Shankaracharya, Vallabhacharya and Chaitanya Mahaprabhu took their doctrine across India through pilgrim trails. Every holy place has a matt that can be equated with a monastery or a mission. It was here, through debate and discussion, that the wisdom of India was articulated and harnessed. From the matts and mandirs, these doctrines eventually reached the villages of India and gradually seeped into the soul of India.

Realizing the power of pilgrim trails across India, politicians have been keen to exploit them. All politicians ensure that they visit local holy shrines and photos are clicked showing them making offerings to the resident deity. In recent times, yatras like the Kavadiya yatra have taken on a distinctly fundamentalist overtone. New pilgrim fairs are being organized like the Sabari Kumbha Mela by Hindu hardliners in Gujarat to stifle the activities of Christian missionaries bent on bringing the vast and grossly neglected Dalit and tribal population into their fold.

Politics has made many pilgrimages hotbeds of political activity. Most infamous of these is Ayodhya where a disused mosque called Babri Masjid was demolished on grounds that it stood where there was once a temple marking the birthplace of Lord Rama. Now the agitation has spread to other cities like Mathura where attempts are being made to reclaim mosques and even churches by politicians claiming to serve Hindu sentiments. Not to be left behind, politicians claiming to serve Muslim sentiments are fighting back. Thus, transferring land to make way for a resting place for pilgrims on their way to the shrine of Amarnath in Jammu led to widespread protests and riots. Not long ago, Tibetan Buddhists were prevented from entering the shrine at Bodh Gaya by Indian Buddhists on grounds they were wearing footwear, not accepting the argument that the Indian practice of removing shoes before entering a shrine was not part of Tibetan rituals since the climate did not allow for it. It is known that in the days of the Delhi Sultanate and Mughal empire many temples were destroyed to make way for mosques. It is also known that old Buddhist centres made way for Hindu temples. Such has been the political way—to use force and transform a holy place into a centre of power. And this hunger for power spreads across religious denominations. The city of Kashi, for example, is holy for Hindus and Jains and Buddhists—then who does it belong to? The city of Gaya is holy for Hindus and Buddhists—whose is it actually? The shrine of Shirdi is being increasingly stripped of its Sufi roots and being overwhelmed by Hindu rituals—who calls the shots finally?

The twentieth century has seen many pilgrim centres being targetted by terrorists. As mysterious e-mails are sent threatening one shrine or the other, many temples and mosques are turning into fortresses with armed guards, scanners, police frisking and barricades, eroding the ambience of piety associated with a sacred spot. The Siddhi Vinayak temple in Mumbai now looks more like a jail from a distance as the shadow of bomb attacks by fundamentalists looms large.

Modern technology is also claiming its piece of the pilgrimage pie. At one time, you had to make arduous trips to reach a holy shrine. Now, all you have to do is sit in the comfort of your house and click on a particular TV channel which, for a small fee, will give you darshan, 24×7, never mind the belief that the potency of a shrine falls if the deity is continuously exposed to devotees. There are mobile phones which promote themselves by appealing to the desire for pilgrimage among Indians—the advertisement shows you can send the sound of bells of the holiest shrines, as you ring it, through your mobile phone to your loved ones who could not make the trip. Mountains are being broken for helipads and rivers are being polluted by the waste created by the very pilgrims who worship its waters. On the positive side, political treaties are being signed to allow Sikhs to visit gurdwaras in Pakistan and Hindus to visit sacred peaks in China.

As more and more pilgrims rush to sacred spots, natural ecosystems are being destroyed by increasing urbanization and commercialization. Many temples have broken old structures and built new ones using granite, marble and even bathroom tiles, have provided air conditioning, and blare sacred music on loudspeakers. One has to take all this philosophically. There is a folk saying: 'That which creates a holy place also destroys it.' Pilgrims make pilgrimages; they also destroy it, spreading chaos and mayhem and garbage as they rush to earn karmic points.

Like all things in life, a holy place waxes and wanes in commerce, crowd and sacredness. This modernization is but one event in the long history of the tirtha. People and priests, politicians and philosophers will come and go but the ford that allows man to wade across the river of worldly trials will always remain.

Gold's Fools

. . . .

Srividya Natarajan

To Nigel, who wouldn't know a gold bar if it came up and goosed him in Panagal Park. Unless he could get a whiskey-soda and two gin-and-limes off it.

Gold? Yellow, glittering, precious gold?...
This yellow slave
Will knit and break religions, bless th' accursed,
Make the hoar leprosy adored, place thieves,
And give them title, knee and approbation
With senators on the bench.

—Shakespeare, *Timon of Athens*, 4.3.

JEWEL-CASE DISCOVERED STAGE RIGHT

I have always thought that Timon was basically sound on the subject of gold. Asked to take gold or leave it, I generally choose to leave it. In fact, my mother did ask me several times, from when I was sixteen onwards, to take it, and every time she asked me I reacted with a consternation and outrage quite disproportionate to the simple request.

The mid-to-late teens can be a pleasant phase. The scabs on a girl's knees, once assumed to be a permanent anatomical feature, have disappeared; she has finally found a bra that fits, and can ask for it by name and size instead of yammering incoherently at the smirking saleswoman. Teeth have straightened out, the brow is smooth and untroubled, the intellect shows signs of ripening.

Then comes the rite of passage, familiar to most middle-class Indian families, involving a girl, or girls, a conscientious mother and a jewel-case. When the curtain rises, the jewel-case is discovered, stage right, on the bed. Enter mother, stage left, followed by her two daughters. Mother opens the jewel-case with a solemn flourish—it is one of those ugly tin contraptions with a marbled finish, and the girls can see their faces in the spotty mirror on the inside of the lid—and extracts two identical pairs of earrings from its navy velvet interior.

'This is for you,' she says to Sister Number One. To Sister Two, 'And this is for you.' The delicate chain with the lotus pendant, for which the older girl had a mild affection, is given to the younger girl, and the rather assertive mango-pattern necklace, which the younger girl has secretly coveted for years, is part of the older girl's destiny. The process of sorting is repeated with bangles, rings, anklets, belts, until all the carefully hoarded knick-knacks, down to diaper-pins, are lying in two glittering heaps among the repulsive printed roses of the Bombay Dyeing bedsheets.

In sexually liberated societies, mothers mark the end of the idyll of their daughters' adolescence with the Talk about Contraception. In countries that haven't heard of Kinsey or the G-spot, they suggest that the future bride Shut Her Eyes and Think of... (insert name of country or sovereign). In India, the duty-conscious mother parcels out the family gold.

There is a subtle menace in the gesture.

Any girl perceptive enough to know her own relations can see that it has something to do with the fact that that social pestilence Kamala Maami—she of the green pocket-diary and pencil, she of the telephone numbers of bachelors from the ends of the earth—paid her mother a visit last week. Every Indian family has a Kamala Maami whose singular nose relentlessly sniffs its way through all the hedges that a desire for privacy erects, hot on the scent of the young and the marriageable. When Kamala Maami's nostrils flare with excitement, when her nose-hairs quiver, when she makes ecstatic baying noises, girls who can read the signs run for their lives. Because soon the postman will arrive at the door staggering under the weight of unsolicited horoscopes and fuzzy pictures of non-resident Indian supergeeks with rimless glasses and salaries that make parents salivate. 'It wouldn't be a bad idea to get our Valli married off right away—after all, she can finish her BA in the US later. An opportunity like this...'

At the time my mother enacted the jewel-case scene, I had no clearly formed opinions whatsoever on gold. I wore a pair of gold studs in my ears all the time, and at weddings obediently wore any other pieces of jewellery I was given. But something about the drama of being Prepared for Marriage made me feel baulky, so I said sharply, 'I don't want those *jimikkis*.'

I didn't want earrings any more than I wanted earwigs; I didn't want a pair of bracelets any more than I wanted a pair of handcuffs. To my eyes, that gold chain seemed a likely thing to dangle a puppet by. Besides, it would make my neck itch.

'Nonsense,' my mother said. 'You'll soon be wanting pretty things to wear.'

'Never. I won't *ever* wear or buy anything gold. I *hate* gold. It's stupid to walk around wearing it all over your body. Stoo-pid, stoop-id, stoo...'

My mother got in such a snit about the scene going off-script that she gave the earrings to my cousin. I didn't feel the slightest pang. In fact, as I grew older, the hissy fit became a settled antipathy. With a few lapses, I more or less stuck to the resolution not to buy the jaundiced mineral myself.

Then I found the medal.

A TOUCH OF GOLD FEVER

'Tell me where all past years are,' the poet John Donne demanded, in a song cleverly titled 'Song'. If he'd been writing after the invention of modern furniture he'd have found the missing years, along with all their detritus, in that gap between the blocky foam-cushion and the back-panel of the living-room sofa. When I was visiting my grandmother this summer, I stuck my hand down behind the sofa cushions, and I found—

I'd better begin at the beginning. Five years ago, a Chennai cultural organization hung a medal around my neck in recognition of my dancing. Since there are dancers all over Chennai, some as young as ten years old, walking around positively clanking with medals, and since any solvent grandfather can launch his own personal cultural organization and fondly honour his spavined granddaughter with a title and an imitation Tanjore plate with a Nataraja embossed on it, this honour was nothing to boast of. The medal, the usual pathetic brass disc trying its damnedest to look like gold, was thinner than the plotline of a Tamil soap. I took it to show my grandmother, lost it, and thought no more about it. Soon afterwards I left the country, and it was four years before I could save enough money to pay for flight tickets to India and a holiday.

This summer, spending that long-awaited holiday at my grandmother's, I stuck my hand in that spongy graveyard of vanished things, and there, among the salted peanuts and the dusty Gems, the toffee-wrappers and pens, the cat's hairballs and the spectacle-case, was that medal. It was indecently shiny for a brass disc that had been exposed to the humid Chennai air for five years, even allowing for the fact that the crack of a sofa is not generally remarkable for its air circulation.

It occurred to me that the medal was not brass at all. I might be holding about ten grams worth of gold in my hand. I studied the disc with a wild surmise. The Mittals would probably have had their servants grind it down into the Unani tonic that preserved the sexual vigour of the pet aardvark; the Birlas would have just used it as a coaster for a liqueur glass or something. To me, however, ten grams of gold seemed like a good deal of gold.

Until this point, my thoughts on gold could have been written down on a postage stamp. It doesn't take a lot of space to write 'Pshaw!' or 'Crock of shit!' I might also have hawked and spat, before or after writing 'Pshaw!' I'd have spoken of the uselessness of the metal. True, it does very well as tooth-filling, a fact that both dentists and Nazis turned to their advantage, but now that we have other substances which do the job better and don't make you coruscate every time you yawn (I would have said), there isn't a single reason why we Indians should continue to consume a fifth part of the world's annual supply of gold when our GDP accounts for 1.6 per cent of the world total.

John Maynard Keynes arrived (by an independent route) at the same opinion. He thought it was regrettable that the citizens of a country as poor as ours could find no better way of investing their scant savings than buying mango-pattern chokers and zigzag bangles by the gross. Capital ought to be mobilized to create more wealth, he argued; people ought to buy stocks and shares. But as I turned that medal round and round in my hand, letting its pure and stainless surface catch the light from this angle and from that, my eyes grew a little glazed. Didn't full-fledged capitalist societies merely fetishize mobility instead of fetishizing gold, and turn built-in obsolescence into a virtue? The chi-chi Gucci pointy shoes that torture the *beau monde*'s feet one season can't possibly be recycled the next. Hadn't Indians, for centuries, blown gigantic raspberries at the prosaic utilitarianism of well-channelled investment, preferring the poetry of glowing things, even if their footwear was last decade's Hawaii chappals? Had they not flipped Keynes the bird, Balaji-shaped rings winking among the curling hairs on the back of the middle-finger? Had they not said, in many different dialects, 'Stocks and shares, pshaw!'

As far back as the first century AD, our ancestors were saying it. The Roman historian Pliny the Elder (AD 23–79) grumbled about the Indian hunger for gold in Book VI of his thirty-seven volume *Natural History*: '...in no year does India absorb less than 55 million sesterces of our Empire's wealth, sending back merchandise to be sold to us at one hundred times its prime cost.' The merchandise exchanged for gold was pepper and ginger and cloth; Kerala's coastal towns were key ports on the trade routes. Farmers ploughing their fields in Kerala have occasionally dug up entire potfuls of Roman gold coins, relics of transactions in happier days, when the balance of payments was actually in our favour.

And we are still saying it. There isn't that much gold in the world, when you compare its quantity with that of other metals, but we Indians, producing almost no gold at all in our own country (even the Kolar fields have been shut down) shovelled 700 tonnes of it into our safes and jewel-cases in 2005.

One might even say, I thought, looking at the yellow disc in my hand, that it is positively unpatriotic to knock the old mineral. Yes, the whole question deserved some thought, even if only of the free-associative kind represented in this essay.

Economists suggest that gold is one of the few investments that shows no signs of losing its value, or even of ceasing to appreciate, because it has always been and will always be scarce. Indians, they suggest, especially those who live far away from modern banking services, or don't want to keep their money in a sock, tend to accumulate wealth in the form of gold.

Wait a minute. Ninety per cent of the gold that Indians consume is turned into jewellery. Jewellery, according to experts, typically costs *four* times the value of the gold it contains (presumably for the workmanship and that item beloved of goldsmiths: 'wastage'). So why jewellery? Why not, say, ingots, if investment is the objective?

Because ingots are less portable, say the experts. Say you keep your ingots in a box, and your house catches fire or starts to slide seawards in a major flood. Wouldn't you be better off if you could save your life and your property at one stroke, getting out of bed in all your finery and running, or climbing a sturdy tree?

But then, look at any of the accident or disaster statistics from around the country. Where women and children are involved, they are always the casualties, suggesting the existence of a healthy instinct for self-preservation in the Indian male. If wearable wealth is easier to save, it should, ideally, be worn by the most physically active members of the family, and the ones most likely to survive a calamity—the menfolk.

Any painting of a king or landlord will prove that Indian men, until about a century ago, did their gold-flaunting on their own persons. The Nizam's jewellery collection, on display at the Public Gardens in Hyderabad, includes about 326 pieces and is worth, they say, approximately Rs 1 billion. The singer G.N. Balasubramaniam's diamond earrings made my grandmother's heart go pit-a-pat. The flash 'minor' chain still gleams among the chest hairs of the affluent young stud-about-town. But somewhere near the beginning of the twentieth century, the Indian male learnt from the white man (who had himself reached this position only about a century earlier) that male flamboyance was vulgar. He took to wearing the sober uniform of bourgeois masculinity, while women became more and more the bearers of social status. This obliges women to hang the family wealth about their persons the way vegetable shopkeepers hang bunches of bananas and gourds about their shops, while men restrict themselves to a ring or two, and perhaps a watch or cufflinks. Most non-professional gold transactions tend to be women's responsibility. The big fat Indian wedding is the ultimate locus of conspicuous consumption. Display is everything. If you've got it, you must strut it.

The wife in a Hindu household is often identified as Lakshmi-in-the-flesh, bringer of prosperity. Raja Ravi Varma has pictured Lakshmi for all ages as a plump, fair, smug housewife in a pink sari. Lakshmi's body is golden; gold coins are stamped with Lakshmi-images, allowing earthly greed to dovetail perfectly with other-worldly spirituality. Gold is rarely worn as anklets or toe-rings: the careful Hindu woman does not want to lose the goddess's favour by stomping on her symbolic form. The collapsing of the wife into Lakshmi and Lakshmi into gold might explain why Indians prefer their female flesh to be as close to gold-coloured as possible. Until a few years ago, south Indian women plastered their faces with turmeric in their quest for a gamboge radiance.

Having turned into portable wealth depositories, Indian women need protection from the personalities the papers love to call 'miscreants'. I never travel in ladies' coupés, because at least one of the passengers will be a substantial and self-opinionated lady, the clashing of whose ornaments drowns out the clattering of the train itself. Her third cousin six times removed will have had both her ears cut off for her gold earrings in 1937, somewhere between Salem and Erode, on the Rameswaram Express, when she was sleeping with her head under the window. 'The way *you* want to sleep,' the lady will say, with a grim prophetic look at my ears, before decisively slamming down both the glass shutter and the metal one, thus condemning her fellow passengers to suffocation. The lady who brings down the windows will also break abysmal amounts of wind in the night.

It won't occur to the flatulent lady that she might leave her ornaments behind when she travels. There is something irreducibly irrational and excessive about the Indian hankering for gold. The baby is welcomed into the world with gold; a gold grain is placed in the mouth of the dear departed, while the heirs engage in unseemly squabbles over who gets the jewellery on the lady's body. Thangam and Swarnam, Kanak and Sona, Kanchana and Aishwarya are names that are still common around the country. A generous person has, in Tamil, a *thangamaana manasu* or a golden heart; really well-behaved children are golden children or golden pitchers. The Banaras brocade and the Kanchipuram silk transform silver and gold into cloth. You can't buy a Bengal cotton sari with the traditional threadwork any more, at least not in the south: now it comes with a gold border.

While not all Indians spiritualize gold the way the Hindus do, no social group in the country is completely untouched by the love of gold. Even the tenets of relatively ascetic religions like Islam (under some versions of which men are prohibited from wearing gold) and Jainism are no proof against gold-fever. People of all classes and all political persuasions buy and hoard the stuff as if their lives depended on it.

Millionaires see gold as providing an opportunity for obscene ostentation. Fortune 500's darlings sip single-malt Scotch with gold dust sprinkled on it. On the persons and in the bank-vaults of the upper middle class, gold represents the complacent glow of achieved security; among the poor, gold is the colour of aspiration. The poorest citizens will grub away at menial jobs half their lives in order to put a thin chain around the neck of a beloved daughter. The genteel poor harbour an ever-present atavistic terror of having the rungs of the class ladder snap under their feet. Gilding the rungs somehow seems to make them less prone to rot.

Sitting on his balcony and scratching his chest, every Indian gent of a certain ripeness and conservatism will demonstrate the metaphoric uses of gold. 'Old is gold,' he will declare, with a certain finality (or, if he is a Tamil, 'Wold is gold'), thus justifying whatever piece of casteist or religious or customary obscurantism is being debated at the moment. Every now and then the papers will report a burglary—twenty lakhs worth of gold jewellery (twenty *lakhs*?)—in the house of some fierce unbending revolutionary. A man of the people, an exemplar of voluntary simplicity, a friend of the poor: what, is he falsifying the monetary value of his loss so that he can claim insurance? Ten to one he has a wife who is in the habit of saying, 'After all...all this liberal thinking is all very well, but one can't very well go around looking poverty-stricken—I mean, one has a duty to oneself...'

THE SEVEN AGES OF WOMAN

Since men don't wear gold in large quantities any more, we come to the symbiosis—archaic, yet reproduced with endless variations, Ganjam hand-crafted for the matronly housewife, Tanishq updated for her career-woman daughter—between the Indian woman and gold. Her life's stages are defined in terms of the yellow metal, in ways that are, alas, mostly unpleasant.

The Baby: Mewling, Puking, but Gilded

Visitors who come to see a new baby in the Syrian Christian community, bring, along with the usual rattle or the nubbly hand-knitted blanket, a little honey and gold dust to mix and smear on the baby's tongue. The gesture represents a wish for both happiness and prosperity. For many Hindu children in the south (for both boys and girls at one time, but mostly only for girls now), the naming ceremony coincides with the ear-piercing ceremony. This, if the doting parents have not already put little bangles on the pudgy wrists or a waist-chain that starts a rash on the belly, is the little cherub's introduction to gold ownership.

In some parts of the country, like Usilampatti in Tamil Nadu, babies who don't come up to standard barely make it to the naming ceremony. Their natural enemies are not pneumonia germs or poor nutrition, but tough old village harpies: a grandmother with a good line in suffocation techniques and the will to use them, or a midwife as expert in the art of helping infants out of this world as in the art of helping them into it. Baby girls, of course, are the ones Returned to Sender in this way. What makes them substandard is that their maintenance adds figures all down the debit side of the family ledger, whereas the projected long-term returns from their existence are negligible.

If baby girls are by definition in the red, it is because their value is determined in relation to the value of gold. As M. Jevamani expressed it, 'Whenever gold prices rise, the value of a girl child goes down because gold is viewed as...synonymous with marriage' (*The Hindu*, Madurai, 28 October 2006). Ms Jevamani was explaining why she and a group of her friends started a grocery store in Usilampatti just so they could will its profits and shares to their granddaughters, thus upgrading them from little Grade B squirts who can be put down painlessly (it hurts grandma more than it hurts the baby) to Grade A babies, worth keeping.

As to why a baby girl's value is measured against gold, the question leads us naturally to the issue of dowry and lavish weddings. But we will simply refuse to follow that question, moving on, instead to—

The Girl: A True Story

The girl—call her Anu—is in the twelfth standard. She was rather bright at one point, and excelled at mathematics, but is now marking time. She knows that she is to be married at the end of the school year to an obese cousin who runs a textile showroom in Guduvancheri. Her grandfather is the village landlord and moneylender. He converts the fruits of his usury into gold coins; when he has collected an auspicious number, he has the goldsmith make them into a coin-necklace and puts it on his granddaughter, his pride and joy.

My grandmother used to recite a Tamil nursery rhyme that went:

Little golden girl, listen to me,
Stay away from the goldsmith's house.
For if you go to the goldsmith's house,
On his scales he will put you and weigh you.

I think something dire happened to the little girl in subsequent verses, but I can't remember them. Anyway, the weight of the gold that encrusted Anu on festival days was so nearly equal to her body weight that she sounded like lots of metal buttons rolling round in a tumble-dryer every time she took a tottering step, and had to pass on the hopscotch game, since there was no question of her hopping on one overburdened pin.

Lately Anu has taken to standing by the window of her room and gazing besottedly at a local Romeo called Jayaseelan who sits with his friends every evening on the compound wall across from her house. Her parents think of Jayaseelan as an unsuitable rowdy. Jayaseelan and his fellow yobs ignore her at first, except to point at her window and laugh immoderately, a development that puzzles Anu until her classmate, visiting her and being treated to a sight of the adored one, points out that Anu's room is lit up like Deepavali, and the whole street can see her making cow-eyes. As her grandfather puts more and more jewellery on Anu's neck and wrists, in preparation for Anu's wedding, lover-boy sits up and takes a more passionate sort of notice. Shortly before Anu's wedding, she puts on every scrap of gold she owns and streaks like a comet into the night. Jayaseelan vanishes from sight at the same time. One week later Anu is returned, but her jewellery is not.

The Bride: She Who Tried and Failed

The bride—call her Sadia—is of mixed parentage. Her mother was a Muslim, her father a Hindu. Her early life was one long free-thinking Marxist *adda*. After bringing her up to value her intellect and abilities, her parents died in an accident. Working as an underpaid assistant librarian and underpaid shop-girl, Sadia put herself through college, and registered for an MA. In her MA history class she met Harish—personable, intellectually gifted and, presently, in love with her.

When they discussed marriage, Sadia made it very clear that it was going to be a simple affair: 'After all, it's nobody's business but our own,' she pointed out. Harish laughed genially. His family was so liberal—almost shockingly so, in fact—that there would be nothing but approval for such a move.

'My mother is a social analyst specializing in poverty studies, for god's sake,' he said. 'My father is an active member of a civil liberties group and a fiery radical journo. There won't be any fuss.'

Sadia was nervous in the beginning, partly because she had always been so independent, but was rather pleasantly surprised by the warmth with which she was received as future daughter-in-law and the passion with which lavish weddings were denounced.

Three days before the wedding—the simple wedding at the registrar's office—Sadia sees a couple of delivery men wrestling a dung-brown Godrej cupboard into the flat she and Harish have rented.

'What's that for?' she asks in a startled voice.

'You'll need a cupboard for your valuables—we've paid for it already, don't worry,' her almost-mother-in-law says.

'But I *have* no valuables.'

'Just a couple of things we want to give you—with all our *love*—you're our daughter now—you're not going to say no, are you? We'd like you to wear them to the reception.'

'What reception?'

'Oh, just a couple of elderly relatives who'd be terribly hurt if they weren't asked to Harish's wedding.'

The Mother-in-law

The shockingly liberal mother-in-law, for the last couple of days, has been starting her statements with 'After all is said and done...'

They really are progressive, Harish assures Sadia. They are not measuring her worth in gold or anything.

'I mean,' he says, trying to cheer her up, 'just read what's being written on those really extravagant weddings—the Mittals spending millions of pounds, Amitabh giving Aishwariya 100 kilos of gold, Bombay ganglords gold-plating their toilet seats before their son's weddings so the guests will feel good about widdling in them...'

Come the wedding day in the progressive household, our Sadia finds herself shanghaied into being part of a full-blown ritual affair and into wearing a gold chain or two, a gold bangle or ten, rings on her fingers, bells on her toes. Liberal mother-in-law qualifies an already wishy-washy progressiveness with a watery concern for the feelings of elderly relatives (entire battalions of elderly relatives have to be eliminated from the face of the earth before her type can put its money where its mouth is) and comes up with the perfect Indian nostrum for maintaining status quo. Take a spoonful morning and night, and perpetuate timeless idiocies in the name of custom.

Indian rites of passage are still bound up with the warmth of family feeling, and we can never ever test the goodwill of those platoons of maamis. We may speak ad nauseum about the foolishness of buying gold for the new bride instead of giving her, say, enough cash for a down payment on a flat. But when it comes to the crunch, it is never within our *own* power to cease and desist. There is a strange poltergeist called Wotwilltherelativesay who wanders around, peering into keyholes, upsetting thrifty plans, poisoning the minds of in-laws, replacing frugal hospitality with wild potlatch, clubbing deviants with a second-hand rolling-pin and, of course, turning the modest jewellery needs of one young woman into a Midasian hunger for the precious mineral.

The Wife

Yellamma, who does the dishes and washes clothes in Kamala maami's house, used to have a jolly good cry when that emotional moment came up in the Tamil melodramas she watched: the moment at which the lady of the house is forced to put her *thali* up the spout. Only, now, she is on the verge of losing her own thali. Her husband is a hard-working, affectionate man, but he has sisters who have to be married off. Yellamma was used to the idea of gold coming and going in her mother's home. A medical emergency, for instance, would require a visit to the pawnshop, and a Deepavali bonus would redeem the pawned bangle, the grime of years of labour still caught in its knotted crevices. But while she was expecting to part with her gold on a rainy day, Yellamma was not quite prepared to have fortune piss on her parade without let.

As she is thinking, Yellamma's eyes drift to Kamala maami's earrings—one pair among dozens—soaking in soap on the dresser. Kamala maami immediately seizes the earrings and locks them in her Godrej cupboard.

'Servants are so greedy and disloyal these days,' Kamala maami says to no one in particular.

In the calendar picture that hangs in Yellamma's tiny tenement, ochre coins, added by some literal-minded minor artist, tumble from the Ravi Varma Lakshmi's right hand. Yellamma, with her chocolate skin, looks nothing like that calendar oleograph; Kamala maami does.

The Mother and Maami

Kamala maami is a moralist. Goldiness, in her book, is next to godliness (she thinks it is no coincidence that the words are anagrams). Maami thinks it is more culpable to come to a wedding without earrings the size of small cauliflowers than, say, to kick a dog or pay an orphan child a pittance to do tasks that are much too heavy for her. She is no slouch, though. Since she sings Carnatic music for a living, she often travels outside India. Singapore is her favourite place to visit, because there's gold in them thar big markets on Serangoon Road.

Maami is never so happy as when lost in the dazzle of Mustafa's or any other gold bazaar. She goes out every year with some old plastic beads around her neck and glass bangles on her wrist; she comes back, triumphant, with twisted chains that look like fat earthworms enjoying unspeakable sexual acts, her flesh bulging grotesquely on either side of the new bangles she has bought in her daughter's size and forced onto her wrist with soap. An aggressive and knowledgeable shopper, she doesn't need the reassurance of the old-fashioned reliable name or the solid trust that the family jeweller guarantees. She liked being ahead of her stay-at-home contemporaries in the bling rat-race, and is a bit disconcerted that retailers in Chennai have cottoned on to Singapore supermarket strategies.

The Grandmother

Across religions, places of worship are gilded. The Sikh community has painstakingly gold-plated the walls of the Harmandir Sahib at Amritsar, which the world knows as the Golden Temple. As soon as a Hindu temple becomes wealthy, it gilds some part of its architecture: the entire *vimaanam* at Tirumala/Tirupati; the roof of the sanctum at Chidambaram. God's status, no less than man's, has to be maintained with oodles of yellow mineral.

The grandmother is going from gilded temple to gilded temple to make offerings and to pray for grandchildren. In the sanctum at Tirumala, she strains to see the stone Balaji that is familiar to her from a picture in her shrine at home, but all she can see is gold ornaments. The priest claps a gold-and-diamond crown on her head for a moment, and she feels grandchildren sprouting in her future.

She remembers that Balaji himself—setting a fine mythological example to all his earthly subjects who are up to their ears in debt to the local landlord—took a loan from Kubera to finance his wedding, and can't repay it without the help of his devotees. An opportunistic myth, but she doesn't see it that way. She puts an extra couple of her own bangles in the temple's *hundial* on her way out.

THE ARTS

On her way home, the grandmother picks up a Thanjavur painting. It catches her eye at once in the handicraft store, standing out among the paintings of Kerala boats in silhouette against sunsets with palm trees, and batiks of Rajput princesses. There is a gargantuan mutant babe sitting in a welter of bas-relief scrolls and curlicues all covered in gold-leaf, looking like a perfect subject for a future coronary, and the shop assistant calls it a 'Butter Krishna'. It is just the thing for her daughter-in-law. Women these days need to be reminded to make babies.

THE QUESTION OF DOWRY

Long ago, in the mists of prehistory, one of our ancestors was taking a primeval dump by the side of a river—excreting right beside one's water source is one of the few ancient traditions we still respect—when he noticed a gleaming piece of rock. He took it home and showed it to his missus.

'What's it called?' she said, looking up from her cooking.

'Lump,' he said. 'It's a Lump.'

'What's it good for?' she sniffed.

'Damned if I know,' he said, absently taking a louse out of his beard and squashing it.

She lost it. 'Meat! You promised this time you'd bring home a mammoth. Nothing for days and days, not even rabbit! I'm sick of eating masala-grass and masala-deerskin-sandals! Here—that's what I think of your Lump!'

And she took up the prehistoric piece of rock that she used to mash down mammoth meat for her babes and brought it down on the Lump.

The rock flattened the Lump out.

The next day, when the woman came out, she noticed how the Lump shone in the sun. She punched a hole in it and began to wear it on a thong around her neck. She showed it to the neighbour.

'That slut next door—she's got a Lump,' the neighbour chuntered away to her husband everyday. 'Why can't you get me one too?'

Her husband tried for a year and a day, but found no Lumps, because he took his dumps next to a different river. Meanwhile the first woman's husband found more Lumps.

'Well, if I can't find Lumps, I can't,' the neighbour's husband said.

His wife bit her nails and thought vicious thoughts.

The years passed. The lady with the Lump waited for one of the neighbour's boys to drag one of her daughters away by her hair, but no one came.

'What's the matter with my girls, they got overbite or what?' she asked her neighbour at last.

'Here's the position,' said the neighbour. 'If you want my sons to club your daughters, you have to give me your Lumps.'

The Lump-owning couple tried to think of a way around the difficulty, but finally succumbed. The girls were getting pretty long in the tooth by then.

The Lumps changed hands.

And so it has been ever since, in this great and glorious land, with the families of girls giving away Lumps so that their girls can get clubbed by their husbands and dragged away by the hair.

And so it is, even today, that parents of future brides are always in the middle of selling off a field to raise the money for a ten-sovereign choker or melting down great-grandmother's bun-ornament into earrings, even though the statistics suggest that the number of dowry murders increases steadily year by year. But the funny thing about dowry is that it's only given, never taken—no one will admit to wanting it. Demanding it is never the groom's own doing, for instance. 'It's mother,' he will say if challenged, his eyes wandering shiftily around the room. 'I don't want any of it, but you know how old people are—she's always thought of me as a fifty-five sovereign boy.'

Suppose you ask the bride's father, 'Well, who's forcing *you* to give a dowry anyway? Who's holding a gun to your head and insisting that you foot the bill for the wedding?'

Father, clucking impatiently, 'No one will marry the girl if there is no dowry. Are you suggesting that we let dear Valli be an old maid?'

'Well, there's John Thamburaj…' you say before you can stop yourself. 'John wanted to marry her, didn't he? Nice man, steady, handsome…'

Father, drawing himself up: 'John Thamburaj! A *Christian* boy, earning a *clerk*'s salary, and of a *different caste*!'

Oh well. If Father wants a son-in-law who's exactly the right caste and the right religion and in the right income bracket, I guess he'll have to fork out.

AKSHAYA TRITIYA AND OTHER SCAMS

I was telling you about finding that medal. I broke my lifelong habit of despising gold and everything it stood for, and went off to get it assayed. Since my grandmother's flat is in Panagal Park, I only had to go around the corner. But I took my life in my hands. Panagal Park, once a place where you could get downmarket plastic toys for two rupees and Tiruppur knitted cotton underwear, has been established as the yellow-metal district of Chennai. In the four years I had been away, gold shops—no, gold *supermarkets*, floor upon gaudy floor of them—had mushroomed all around the pathetic dehydrated park and the vegetable market. There were no parking spaces. The shops blocked the pavements with giant palm and banana trees made of some kind of shiny material, gigantic Mickey Mouse inflatables and even, in one case, twelve damsels dressed in white-and-gold, palms folded, plastic smiles pinned to their mugs, lined up idiotically in front of the doorway. Customers milled about, their ache for gold undiminished by the discomforts of walking on the overcrowded street, into chill streams of air-conditioning that emanated from entrances and then into the blasts of blazing heat produced by the air-conditioners themselves.

Turfed off the pavement, but still doing their precarious business on the road, reassuringly and miraculously, were the old pushcarts with gooseberries and sliced mango, *naaval* fruit, sugarcane juice, peanuts roasting in a *dekchi* and dancing to the heavy-metal ringing of the peanut lady's spoon. The prices were all through the roof, though. The customers were a new demographic—they were rich beyond the dreams of the old working-class clientele that once patronized these carts.

The new gold supermarkets are a great improvement on the old humble goldsmith shops, and are in fact putting the latter out of business in many parts of India. Which goldsmith on a small scale can put up the capital to cover acres of display space with swathes and festoons of the yellow mineral, exactly as if he was putting up paper streamers? Time was when the local goldsmith was so hard up he used brass pattern necklaces and bangles, the way tailors use pattern-books, buying the gold after the customer had ordered the piece of jewellery. Time was when an aspiring criminal had to nick one or two small things, find a fence. Now, he can operate on a grand scale. He can take the stuff away in a sack.

The last time I did buy gold, ten years ago—one of the exceptions to my gold rule—I went to the smallest of the small shops, so afraid was I of making an ass of myself. At the time, I was the sort of person who thought a carat was a misspelt root vegetable. In my purse I had a couple of odds and ends my mother had given me—earrings without screws, screws without earrings—and the two gold rings my husband and I had exchanged outside the registrar's office after we had signed our marriage papers. My husband and I had been extremely broke and had bought extremely thin rings which had turned into oblongs after a couple of years. I was going to add the gold from the odds and ends and see if I could get the rings made thicker.

I spent about an hour in the little shop, trying on rings and dithering, not knowing how to broach the subject of my odds and ends. I got it off my chest at last, and the goldsmith examined my offerings, did tricky things with his scales and used words like 'wastage' and 'making charges', which might have rolled trippingly off Kamala maami's tongue, but meant nothing to me. The upshot was that I was going to have to pay a great deal more money than I could afford to get the rings made thick enough not to bend into lozenges.

I looked around the shop desperately for something I could buy, in return for wasting so much of the owner's time. I settled on a tiny nose-stud, paid in cash, and prepared to flee from the goldsmith's scorn. But he, old-fashioned salesman that he was, put my nose-stud in a small box, dusted the box with a kerchief, placed a jasmine bud on it, and handed it to me with a flourish that would have satisfied the buyer of a 200-gram necklace with the Koh-i-noor for a pendant.

Ten years later there were no small shops left. The day I set out to have the medal assayed, traffic conditions were far worse than usual between my grandmother's flat and Panagal Park. Cars were parked all the way along my grandmother's street; one, in fact, was parked right against the gate of the flat and while I was trying to squeeze my way past it without leaving a scrape, a lady inside was trying to get out without being cut in half. People were jammed so close together that the whole locality looked like a Mumbai commuter-train during peak hours.

'What's going on?' I said.

The woman in the car looked up in amazement. 'You mean you don't know it's Akshaya Tritiyai today?'

'Er…no. What's that?'

'Maybe you know it as Akha Teej,' a younger woman piped up, adjusting her white-gold necklace.

'No. What *is* it?'

'It's a festival—very auspicious day to buy gold,' a third lady, very stout, informed me. 'Are you Christian?' she demanded.

'No madam,' I replied with dignity. 'I've just never heard of the festival before. And would you mind getting off my foot?'

A gold-hunter could have been run over anywhere between Pondy Bazaar and the north end of Usman Road, or could have croaked of asphyxiation from all the carbon monoxide curling upwards from idling vehicles, and people would have just calmly tramped on towards their gold, not even noticing the corpse underfoot.

'Akshaya Tritiyai,' said the woman in the car, 'is Parasurama's birthday.'

'Excuse me,' said the young woman. 'It's the day Draupadi received the Akshaya Paatram from Surya. I read it on the Web.'

'Web-sheb,' said the stout matron. 'It's the day Adi Sankara composed the Kanakadhara Stotram.'

'Piffle,' said another by-stander. 'It's the day Kuchela was rewarded by Krishna.' She turned to the younger woman. 'How come all your jewellery is white?'

'Oh, I read an ad that said it was even more auspicious to buy platinum and white gold, because white is the best colour for Akshaya Tritiyai.'

Something doesn't smell quite right here: how is it I have never heard of this damn festival all the time I grew up in a fairly traditional Hindu family? How come all these accounts of the origin of this festival conflict so violently with each other? Me, I'd be mighty suspicious about the fortuitous coincidence between the arrival of the gold Wal-Marts and the celebration of a festival that compels devout Indians to go out and buy thirty to thirty-five tonnes of the blinking substance in a single week. These figures, by the way, are courtesy of the World Gold Council (WGC), which ought to know, since one of its raisons d'etre is to unload as much gold on Indian consumers as possible. This may have something to do with the fact that the rest of the world is going off gold, partly in favour of other consumer goods, but partly in response to campaigns, like the No Dirty Gold drive spearheaded by Oxfam America and Earthworks, that make people aware of how environmentally destructive gold mining is. I wouldn't be too surprised if the WGC had a think-tank sitting on the enormous cyanide-soaked tailings of some mine in Australia or South Africa, working on new Akshaya Tritiyai myths. As in: 'Let's hook the Malayalis by bringing in that Parasurama guy—the legendary founder of Kerala. Hey, Adi Sankara fetches the Tambrahms every time. What about the Buddhists? Let's say it's the day Maya Devi conceived Siddharta—no, forget the Buddhists, the south Indians are the biggest suckers for gold anyway, not many Buddhists among them. You got a yarn for the Draupadi-worshippers?'

Akshaya Tritiyai comes up in April/May, in time for the wedding season, which always inaugurates an orgy of gold buying and exchanging. Too many coincidences, wouldn't you agree? Which is why I conclude that the whole thing is a splendidly orchestrated piece of baloney. It is an offshoot of the bullshit industry that supports the gold industry. It is the invention of gold dealers, just as Valentine's Day is the retroactive mythicization of a perfectly harmless Catholic saint by Hallmark Cards CEOs, stuffed teddy-bear tycoons and candy magnates.

We swallow the myth because the aurum reflex is deeply embedded in the national psyche. We are so genetically programmed to hanker after gold that some advertising genius only has to cook up a festival that rewards jewellery-buying for the whole nation and its wife to rush out like demented lemmings heading for the sea. Our neurons start firing, Pavlovian drool collects in the corners of our mouths, we paw the ground, snort, snatch up our purses and head out towards places like the Prasanth Real Gold Tower, which is coming up in Panagal Park and is the world's first supermarket *entirely* devoted to gold. And if the jeweller has run out of gold, no worries: he just puts out an advertisement suggesting that what we really need to maximize our blessings on Akshaya Tritiyai day is—isn't it lucky we have this alternative—platinum.

HOW TO ACQUIRE GOLD IN SIX EASY LESSONS

If these random meditations haven't diminished the mystique of gold for you, then you have truly been bitten by the gold bug. Gold, as the jeweller's advertisement says, makes you feel radiant, sensual and sensational. You want to acquire more of it. Which is why I conclude this essay with the following do-it-yourself section on how to acquire gold.

Chain-snatch

A popular pastime in dark urban alleys, this takes a certain degree of skill, first of all to gauge whether a chain is thin enough to snap and, secondly, to assess the snatchees and home in on the ones who won't squawk too loudly. Pick on old ladies. Practice on tailor's dummies with nylon rope or thick metal wire. If the dummy's head keeps falling off, consider an alternative career in the *matka* cutthroat industry. If you're going to spend time in the cooler for petty larceny, you may as well stay there indefinitely for murder. Another method is to use a pair of metal cutters and operate in crowded places like commuter trains and temple melas. With practice, provided you haven't gone directly to jail without passing go, you should be able to whisk away a heavy chain with a feathery touch.

Take the Chit-fund Route

Join a chit-fund scheme that promotes gold jewellery, but don't touch either the capital or the interest until you have enough money saved up to finance your daughter's dowry. Two hours before your fund matures and you redeem your savings in the form of a ten-sovereign chain, eight-sovereign bangles and other gew-gaws, the crook who runs it will stuff your money into a sack and disappear to the Bahamas. Avoid this calamity in the only way possible: *be* the crook who runs the chit fund. Then you can buy plenty of gold with your ill-gotten gains or start a chit-fund business in the Bahamas.

Win an Olympic Medal

Bear in mind the fact that Indians have actually won, in all the years since the Games began, only about half-a-dozen golds. Your chances will be improved considerably if you get the Olympic Committee to officially recognize one of our national pastimes. Something like betel-juice spitting contests, for instance, or *gilli-danda*, or grabbing the breasts of women on moving suburban trains.

Track the Himalayan Mountain-ant to Its Lair

Herodotus, in his *Histories* (3.102–105) mentions 'ants that are of bigness lesser than dogs but larger than foxes' that live in burrows. 'The sand that they dig out has gold in it,' he observes. The correct technique for getting the gold is to take with you a male camel and a female camel that has just calved. Plunder the burrows when the mid-afternoon heat drives the ants underground, load the female camel with the gold, jump on its back and head like the dickens for home (the thought of its calf will make the female camel go faster). The male camel will be eaten, meanwhile, by the ants. The trouble is, no one knows where these ants and their burrows are; Herodotus's directions ('Eastward of India') are not much help.

Recent research suggests that the ants are marmots, and live on the Indo-Pak border. If you don't mind the shelling, have a go.

Snuggle Up to a Smuggler

If you travel on an airplane from Dubai or Singapore with a gent who is wearing a strange quilted vest, slit the lining of the vest with your plastic airline cutlery. If a somewhat shiny biscuit-like object falls out, eat it, chewing twenty times before you swallow. This is a Ten Tola bar—a TT bar, exactly 116.64 grams. It will taste slightly better than airplane food, but will be slightly less digestible, which means you can recover it at leisure. Remember, no pain, no gain. If you cut your doctor in on a small share of the profits, he will make the recovery painless by prescribing an appropriate laxative.

Your chances of striking it rich this way would have been much better before 1992, when smuggling was big money. The deregulation of gold in that year has meant that there isn't that much difference between gold prices elsewhere and gold prices in India, and to some smugglers there's just no zip and excitement in it any more. Many stalwarts of the old hawala brotherhood have lost their enthusiasm and have made mid-life career changes. They now go in for better rackets like match-fixing, terrorism and extortion.

Become a Biscuit Bandit

During the wedding season, bake home-made biscuits with a couple of valiums or any other sleep-inducing drug mixed in the dough, and buy yourself a ticket for an overnight railway journey. When the average mark comes along—she's likely to tell everybody, over her dinner of curd-rice and lime-pickle, that she's going to her niece Vatsala's wedding—take note of the bag on which she involuntarily rests her eyes every two seconds. Share your biscuits with the mark. When she is asleep, get off quietly at a small station with her bag.

Try to make sure your victim is a non-Brahmin if you don't want to be spending all the fruits of your banditry on manicurists. Somewhere in Manu, who can always be relied upon to produce bizarre strictures that urge the righteous Hindu to fatten up the Brahmin, and warn him of evils that will beset him if he fails in this duty, I came across this gem: 'He who steals the gold (of a Brahmana) has diseased nails.'

CODA

The medal turned out to be worthless. All that glistens is not gold. Some of it is metallized plastic.

I thought you'd like to know.

We, the Babalog

. . . .

Anand K. Sahay

The Nobel warrior of public causes in India, Amartya Sen, has reflected on the 'prolixity' of his compatriots—their penchant for ceaseless debate and disputations around issues of politics and governance. Not for nothing is India the world's largest—and possibly the most truculent—democracy, with an assertive, even pugilistic electorate in excess of 600 million that frequently trips up the high and mighty. The range of political parties is bewildering. Socialism of every stripe has found nurture in India, bewitching at various times the upstairs and downstairs of society, to say nothing of the mezzanine level. And yet, who can gainsay that Indians are inexorably drawn to the aura of dynasticism?

Indians revel in the idea of counting in their midst 'great' families and clans of distinction; they love to flaunt connections with these—connections that may be real, remote, or nearly imagined. The link may be too distant to be obvious, and seeking to state it is possibly no more than an exercise in making the tenuous real, but it is the perception that is pertinent. Such perceptions constitute an element of self-identity and refurbish self-esteem. For the upper-middle classes even an acquaintance with the grand families is a mark of distinction. 'The daughter of my maternal uncle's wife's cousin is married into the raja saheb's family. We are *khandani log* (people with a pedigree)...' This is not an unfamiliar refrain in India. And 'raja saheb' here is no more than a measure of value. It could just as well be the leading lawyer, intellectual, politician, artist, social reformer or business figure, someone who has established the kind of name and influence—preferably spread over more than a single generation—that feudal grandees once commanded.

In a highly diverse and hierarchical society, basking in vicarious pride helps to assert status as well as remoteness from the ordinary, no matter how mundane the life conditions of those making the claim. More, with the relatively rapid expansion of segments of the Indian middle class in recent years and their fast-rising incomes, the formerly dominant upper-end of middle-spectrum India perceives a challenge to its status. Swimmers in this social pool find particular solace in dredging out contacts with prominent families as a signal that they are still special. In a universe where new economic peers have emerged and others may be fast catching up, prominence through association is still deemed to be of value even if does not necessarily add to substance. Name dropping may have its limits but it is unquestionably an Indian art form with a life of its own.

The notion of being even in symbolic proximity to 'greatness' tends to appeal to Indians. For the humbler folk who may do no more than toil for the great, this is a value in itself, traceable to the awe with which the upper echelons have traditionally been held, although some of this may be changing, especially in metropolitan settings. For those with prospects, dynasties and exalted families are something to look up to because they also describe an arc of aspiration even if replication is beyond one's power or means.

Clearly, the 'elders' in the system are deemed worthy of emulation and respect, for have they not accumulated power, influence, wealth or grandeur in this world which is more than can be said of most? The word denotes not only seniors in the family who merit deference on account of their being older than the others, but also important people in the community, the region in which one lives, or the country—the Urdu and Persian word *buzurg* perfectly catches the sense. From this it is a small jump to hold in esteem dynasties, leading families and successful clans that become buzurg manufactories.

Sacred Hindu texts buttress the attitude of according respect to the leading lights of the social system. In the Bhagavad Gita, Krishna speaks of the 'best' (*shreshtha*) in the community: 'Whatever the best do, others follow.' A similar outlook was evidently extant in an earlier period, approximately 3000 years ago, in the age of the Upanishads, the learned works of commentary, speculation, interpretation and debate in post-Vedic India. In the Taittiriya, in the course of the famous instructions or *shiksha*, the teacher tells the pupil: 'In case of doubt about the propriety of your actions, look around and observe how the best in the community behave in the circumstances. Take their actions as examples.'

In a cultural universe arising from such a milieu, the Kennedy clan or dynasty, for example, would have been lapped up with avidity in India. This, although President Kennedy's talks in New Delhi with Prime Minister Jawaharlal Nehru (himself modern India's most enduring icon after Mahatma Gandhi and from whom contemporary India's most famous dynasty is descended), were a clear failure and India–US ties were hardly boosted in the Kennedy years. Yet JFK had by then romanced his country and the world.

The president was held in wide regard and considerable affection across India. Not yet a teenager in a small town in poor and chaotic Bihar, I recall being saddened to tears when a transistor radio announced the news of his assassination. My friends and I closed our badminton game prematurely and trooped back home with a heavy heart that evening. Middle-class children had naturally soaked up the aura of the Kennedy dynasty from the adult world. Apart from the glamour, JFK's personal life before he became America's leader was seen as being one of achievements, with a succession of high points including authoring a book relatively early in life. Traditionally, possessors of knowledge have commanded a high premium in Indian society.

Without the ingredient of achievement thrown in, the Kennedy story would have meant little in faraway India. The Bushes have given America two presidents and clearly have serious money, for they are oil-men, but they are an unlikely clan for an Indian to hold in awe. There is something missing, and it is not necessarily glamour. It may be pertinent to keep in view that while contemporary

Indians are predisposed as perhaps no other people in the world to an adulation of dynasties, a successful Indian dynasty of today is primarily about influence, wealth or glamour built on the bedrock of attainment. Therein lies the fundamental attraction or the soft power it exudes; without this, it is nothing.

In the absence of that glow it is futile to speak of influential families, clans or dynasties in the age of democracy. In this essay we include dynasties and great families that have held sway in the era since India's independence from colonial rule in 1947 in which sovereign growth and development—and flowing from this the flowering of talents in diverse fields—became possible; but we exclude from consideration business dynasties as these are legally grounded in inheritable wealth, much as temporal power was in a bygone age. In pre-modern times, dynasts—acting within systems of unquestioned power for the power-wielder—had unfettered freedom to choose or name their successor if they so wished (in the event of primogeniture being bypassed), and power was automatically handed down from one generation to the next unless it was forcibly annexed. The present-day counterparts of such arrangements, typically to be found among our business empires, are outside the scope of the treatment here.

Dynasties of modern India being looked at here do not have the luxury to preordain succession in any meaningful sense. This signifies a great transformation in India's social psychology that has only become more pronounced as the years have rolled by since independence. Dynastic or clan influence must today be earned or it will be scorned. The sun has truly set on the age of maharajas, rajas, sultans and nawabs, giving way to the time of the sturdy electorate. No one now desires a return to the feudal order, although many cultural traits of the past have abided, such as the deference accorded to the buzurg.

To remain as contenders in the public domain, former feudal houses now typically choose the electoral route and canvass the votes of their erstwhile subjects on a party platform. Most come a cropper, though there have been outstanding successes as well, such as the Scindias of Gwalior. The third generation of this former royal house is now in Parliament and a daughter of the dynasty, Vasundhara Raje, is a chief minister of Rajasthan in northern India. Madhav Rao Scindia, the leading light of the feudal family, was a prominent federal cabinet minister until his untimely death in an air crash in 2001.

Dictated by their individual ideological leanings and given the demands of competitive politics, members of the Scindia family have chosen different parties at different times to be their vehicle for forward propulsion. Nor have they omitted to switch constituencies to maximize the chances of winning elections (they have also lost), indicating that they are shrewd enough to want to be in step with the popular mood in changed circumstances. As such, the Scindias today are as much a political dynasty as they were a feudal one in another age.

Of late, members of well-known business families too have begun to take a direct interest in political affairs and have entered Parliament, but at present none can lay claim to represent a political dynasty. Remarkably, in contrast with some of the former royals, the members of leading business or industrial houses on view in Parliament have avoided direct elections and have chosen the Rajya Sabha route of indirect election or nomination instead. Interestingly, in the early phase after independence, representatives of prominent business families did seek to contest elections for Parliament but did not exactly shine in the electoral arena. They were apparently out of sync with popular aspirations and style. Unlike the former royals, they could not invoke nostalgia either as the emergence of industrial houses was a relatively new phenomenon in the country.

In pre-democratic times dynasties were tolerated as a necessity but were not necessarily loved. Present-day dynasties and great families that are perceived as having made good are esteemed or held in affection but are in no way seen as being essential to existence. Contemporary India does not have to cope with its dynasties any more. Rather, it enjoys having them around for their glamour, status and achievement value—somewhat akin to the interest in celebrities. When they get too overbearing, as sometimes they do, it simply dumps them (especially if they are operating in the political field) for a time.

The success of modern-day dynasties in India is predicated on their being of some worth to the system, in tangible or intangible ways. In the end, it really boils down to a perception that dynasties are rather fun—they radiate achievement and prestige—and cost nothing to behold and have around. Were it otherwise, they will doubtless be resisted, as was the case in the mid-1970s when it was widely perceived that Prime Minister Indira Gandhi was seeking to impose her younger son on the country. It is noteworthy that in popular perception Mrs Gandhi was at fault on two counts: first, for imposing a state of national emergency in order to advance her own political agenda by sacrificing the country's. And, second—and this is remarkable—for not living up to her father Jawaharlal Nehru's democratic vision and elan; in other words, of not being true to her dynastic legacy! Nehru's daughter took the hint, revoked emergency rule, called elections and was roundly defeated. But she stormed back to power not much later, regaining her place in popular affection.

Dynastic formations are common even in small-town India; as such, dynasties that take the national stage convey little in the social sphere that is new in essence, although they are naturally more famous, more envied and more copied. No matter where one travels in the country, one is apt to find families of two or more generations of professionals in the middle-level towns and even in the mofussil—district or sub-district towns in the states, administrative and political units just below the federal level. These 'little' or sub-national dynasties are local families of a region that have gained distinction on account of their work and with whom others are only too eager to associate. Some may have wealth (though not necessarily glamour), but most have undoubted intangible influence and that very evocative Indian term for influence—'pull'.

Given luck, or the sheer magnitude of their achievement, some of these families may well transcend the outback life and rise to national prominence, travelling up the social and economic scale. The film star, Amitabh Bachchan, is an example. In a popular Hindi film song he calls himself '*Chhora, Ganga kinare wala*' (the boy from the banks of the Ganga), referring to his home town, Allahabad. His father, Harivansh Rai Bachchan, gained iconic status as a Hindi poet. The senior Bachchan's literary stature helped the young Amitabh gain his first break with a director who was also a well-known writer. Amitabh would rise to great heights in Bombay (now Mumbai) cinema and found a film dynasty—his son is now firmly established as an actor. But he came of regional stock in that his father had shot to fame in the world of Hindi poetry and was not a familiar figure outside the confines of the Hindi belt.

Sub-national dynasties often tend to be those of doctors and lawyers. This is a legacy of British colonial policy in India that imparted education only of a general nature, specialized degrees being mostly confined to medicine and the law in keeping with the broad requirements of the time. During the freedom movement individuals inclined toward the anti-colonial struggle found it expedient to become lawyers and doctors, particularly the former, rather than government officials (school and college teachers were then employees of the state) who could be penalized more easily for agitational politics.

Besides, the law course at university was shorter than medicine. The study of law also bestowed other benefits. Lawyers probably made more money than other professionals on account of rising litigation in British India flowing from policies that allowed for the alienation of land; moreover, politically minded lawyers could render useful service to freedom fighters in their court battles. Some of the best known leaders of the national movement against colonial rule were lawyers. For a long time after independence not much changed in India in terms of education policy. Specializations remained confined to only a few fields. This accounts for the continuing preponderance of dynasties of doctors and lawyers in small-town India.

Dynasty is treated with reverence by Very Important Persons (VIPs) and Very Very Important Persons (VVIPs)—such sobriquets are common ways of indicating government officials of high rank, typically ministers and higher; this strange (though widespread) usage being a testimony to the exaltation of hierarchies in India. I recall President R. Venkataraman swearing in a clutch of ministers at Rashtrapati Bhavan in New Delhi. Among them was Rangarajan Kumaramangalam (who passed away prematurely in 2000). After the ministers had taken the oath, I overheard the president tell Kumaramangalam (he seemed to have known the family): 'First your grandfather, then your father, and now you!' He was referring to three generations of ministers.

Curiously, India's capital city, Delhi, has lacked the dynasty spirit in the modern era which has found such liberal spread in other metros and smaller towns. The last dynasty it hosted (not counting today's political class) was the Mughal dynasty, and they petered out in the nineteenth century after ruling the subcontinent since the sixteenth. Their remnants are not people of note and probably count among the city's poor if occasional newspaper reports are to be relied on.

The influx of millions of refugees into Delhi after the partition of India in 1947 radically transformed the imperial city's character, leaving little room for its autonomous development in the manner of other cities in which existing communities expanded and accommodated gradual change. Delhi was traditionally the emperor's city. The professional classes did not grow here with the same naturalness as in India's other great cities and their hinterland where the coming of British rule was felt much earlier.

Delhi, of course, did have its leading families that serviced the imperial court in diverse ways, but many were in the business field which is excluded from consideration here. The lawyers, officials and other professionals simply got scattered as the city began to expand physically without the cement of cultural affinity that binds communities.

For a dynasty to be deemed one, there must be a natural community that savours it, which the dynasty in turn serves with its achievements. Such communities were missing in Delhi, especially after 1947. Delhi very rapidly turned into a city of outsiders as it became firmly entrenched as the political and administrative centre of independent India to which populations began to gravitate from other parts of the country. Important leading families became submerged in the rush. In this melee perhaps stands out the Ansari dynasty of old Delhi. A scion of this distinguished family is Hamid Ansari, a retired professional diplomat who is now the vice-president of India. The family had made significant contributions to the freedom movement and to the cause of education. The Ansaris contributed significantly to nurturing the institution that would later become the Jamia Millia Islamia university in Delhi, a centre of modern and liberal learning. The way Delhi's rhythm has developed, however, it is unlikely that many in the capital city would know that the vice-president comes from a leading local family.

In considering the question of dynasty here we do not reject cases of what economists call product differentiation, or minor differences within a genus. Thus we might have a dynasty of politicians, lawyers, doctors or cinema personalities, that is, successive generations in which representatives of the family make a name in the same line of work. Or we might have a dynasty that has thrown up prominent individuals in different fields in successive generations. In both cases, the merit of individuals helps enhance the dynasty's brand value and public appeal. We treat both variants on an equal basis as exemplifying the dynasty type.

One more consideration needs to be stated. In this essay there is no privileging of the male—a daughter carries as much weight as being part of a dynasty as a son, or we would not have the Nehru–Gandhi dynasty, the country's most pre-eminent.

Before we take a look at dynasties that have followed the same field of activity over generations, it might be convenient to first regard the genus in which one family or dynasty has produced men and women of distinction in more than one field—there are fewer of this kind.

It is hard to think of Mohandas Karamchand Gandhi, or Mahatma Gandhi (no relation of Indira Gandhi) as he is better remembered, as the begetter of a dynasty. But since the dynasties we speak of are essentially built on personal commitment and achievement, it should be noted for the record that one of the Mahatma's sons, Devdas Gandhi, was the editor of *Hindustan Times*, a leading English language daily, and two of Devdas's sons (that is, the Mahatma's grandsons) are prominent figures today—Rajmohan Gandhi has been an editor and a member of Parliament and is a well-regarded biographer of some of the stalwarts of the freedom movement. His younger brother, Gopal, a former civil servant and diplomat, is the governor of the state of West Bengal and held high in public esteem. He is also a novelist. Rajmohan and Gopal Gandhi also happen to be maternal grandsons of C. Rajgopalachari, a towering figure of the Indian freedom movement from Chennai.

An outstanding example in this category—where members of a dynasty make a notable contribution to more than one sphere—is that of the Sarabhais of Gujarat. They were an important business and industrial family of the region, specializing in chemicals. They extended support not only to Gandhi in the course of the freedom movement, but sections of the clan also backed the communists for a time in the early years, an unlikely preference for members of an industrial house. In the years since independence, individual Sarabhais have made important contributions to India's space programme, education and the arts. This would probably make them the most versatile dynasty in India.

The Tatas, India's most prestigious industrial family and one of its largest and most solid, just miss the cut in this group. Although their contribution to a very wide field of activities—covering vital spheres of national life—is impressive and in some cases special, this is essentially an institutional achievement of that famous business dynasty. In fairness it should be said, however, that continuing support to causes for public benefit would hardly have been possible without the endorsement of successive generations of Tatas. It is also pertinent to recall that India's first aviator, J.R.D. Tata, was a distinguished member of this dynasty who also set the tone for a sense of ethics in his business enterprises that is the envy of corporate India.

While there is no shortage of dynasties in small-town India and in the bigger cities, each looked up to in a given area, there are only a few dynasties that catch national attention. In recent times—the age of pervasive mass media—these have tended to belong to the realm of politics and cinema, a testament to the levels of media interest in these fields of activity, though there is representation from other fields as well.

The fragmentation of political parties in India is due to both the resurgence of dormant social forces as well as the creation of new ones. Moreover, the regions have come into their own. These elements have combined to establish parties that owe their existence to a central figure or regional satrap. Several of these run their parties as little fiefdoms and have sought to spawn dynasties. Among them may be mentioned M. Karunanidhi in Tamil Nadu in southern India, Mulayam Singh Yadav in Uttar Pradesh and Bal Thackeray and Sharad Pawar in Maharashtra in the west. Their children have now taken centre stage in their respective parties and exert influence in the regions they come from. It is far from certain, however, if such dynasties can sustain themselves once their founders have departed the scene.

The Patnaik legacy in Orissa in eastern India has proved more enduring, however. Biju Patnaik, the founder of this dynasty, was a colourful personality and a federal cabinet minister. He became the chief minister of his state and established a short-lived airline and an industrial plant. By all accounts a dashing young man in the 1940s, Biju created a sensation when he quit the air force, where he was a pilot, to jump into the anti-colonial struggle as a courier for revolutionary elements who ran an underground movement. Later, Prime Minister Nehru would despatch him to Indonesia to fly out a beleaguered Sukarno. After Biju's death, his son Navin received urgent summons to help bail out the regional party his father had set up. The younger Patnaik was uniquely unqualified for the job. He could not even handle the local language well, having grown up in elite surroundings speaking nothing but English. However, Navin, who was known as a party animal on Delhi's social circuit and given to 'esoteric' pursuits such as the conservation of monuments, has proved remarkably successful as a regional political leader and state chief minister, surprising his friends most of all.

It is reasonably clear that but for the mystique his father's name evokes in Orissa, Navin is unlikely to have had a shot at power. But it is just as clear that he has made the most of the opportunity. Navin's sister, Gita Mehta, writes with assurance and made a name a quarter century ago with her novel *Karma Cola*. The Patnaik dynasty has clearly proved both resilient and versatile.

But modern India's most illustrious and enduring dynasty known throughout the world, which has on occasion attracted political controversy, is the Nehru–Gandhi lineage. It has produced three prime ministers in successive generations. The clan narrowly missed a fourth prime minister when Rajiv Gandhi's widow, Sonia Gandhi, the Italian-born, naturalized Indian, whom sections of Indian opinion insist on calling a foreigner, deemed it politic to pass up the opportunity of being the leader of government when the position was offered to her on a platter by her party and its allies in 2004.

The first famous Nehru was Motilal, father of India's first prime minister, Jawaharlal Nehru. But Motilal did not live to see free India though he had gained a place of prominence in the Congress party, India's principal vehicle of struggle against colonial rule. In his day Motilal was probably the wealthiest lawyer in the country and a self-made aristocrat who could afford to send his son Jawaharlal to study in England at Harrow and Cambridge more than a hundred years ago. On his return, the young Jawaharlal would shed his aristocrat's skin and become Mahatma Gandhi's favourite disciple and, later, with Gandhi's open endorsement, emerge as the first prime minister of free India. He also wrote resonant, captivating, English prose and penned two books while serving long jail terms in British India that continue to impress succeeding generations. Nehru was a western-style liberal, a republican and a socialist in his political beliefs, and an idealist who strove to embed the template of democracy in the fabric of India.

Nehru's daughter Indira became a Gandhi after her marriage to Feroze Gandhi (no relation of the Mahatma), who would emerge as a forthright and dynamic left-leaning Congress parliamentarian sometimes described by the ruling party benches as a one-man opposition to his father-in-law Jawaharlal Nehru's government. Indira did not succeed her father as prime minister and there was no 'dynastic succession' as her critics sometimes allege. She was not even a cabinet minister in her father's government but was for a time the head of the party organization. When he died Nehru could not have known that his daughter would one day be the national leader.

Lal Bahadur Shastri succeeded Nehru as prime minister but after his sudden demise Indira Gandhi was led to the prime minister's chair as a compromise candidate by squabbling party stalwarts who perceived her as being too weak to establish herself as leader. The heavyweights were wrong. Indira emerged as a leader with an iron will. In the domestic arena no Indian prime minister has courted as much controversy and attracted as much violent criticism as Indira Gandhi did when she suspended constitutional rights for a time. But she was also an admired figure. She conducted India's first nuclear test and was instrumental in the creation of Bangladesh following Pakistan's rout in its war with India in 1971. In Indian eyes these were historic achievements, though the western world was riled, as was India's powerful neighbour China.

Indira Gandhi met a violent death in a hail of gunfire discharged by her Sikh bodyguards disaffected by her decision to assault Amritsar's Golden Temple, Sikhdom's holiest shrine, in a bid to put down terrorist activities of a religio-political Sikh group. In the aftermath of her assassination the Congress party chose her son, Rajiv Gandhi, to be their leader—in effect the country's next prime minister—though he was only a junior member of Parliament. Subsequently Rajiv would win the national election with a landslide margin due to what then came to be described as the 'sympathy vote'. It was the Congress party that calculatedly pitchforked him into the leadership in the hope of invoking dynasty to win an election in a moment of national grief.

Did he have to accept? That is not an easy question to answer, but it appears fairly certain that he accepted against the will of his wife, Sonia Gandhi. Probably Rajiv succumbed to the burden of expectations and felt he would be letting the party down after his mother's death if he declined to shoulder the responsibility. He was certainly deeply conscious of his family's historical association with the Congress party and its role in shaping the course of the country for well over half a century. An experience such as this is naturally alien to most of us. In a family that is not a dynasty, expectations are not exogenously driven and built up by extra-family considerations.

It is possible that any Congress leader could have stepped in to fill the void after Indira's assassination and would have won the election, especially when the grief element was likely to work to the party's advantage. But the Congress was not taking chances. It preferred to put its faith in the country's penchant for dynasty, especially one so well established.

Rajiv's widow Sonia Gandhi, who currently heads the Congress party and whose nominee Manmohan Singh is the country's prime minister, has brought her son Rahul into Parliament (of course, he won his election very creditably) and has even made him a party general secretary, a top position. Is this preparation for a bigger role? Does she have dynastic ambitions for him? Does he himself harbour such ambitions? We cannot know. But Sonia has gone on record to suggest that family connections can give a person a leg up but the beneficiary would eventually have to prove himself. The statement was made in a broad context but its proximate political meaning will elude no one. In any case, it is a fair observation to make. Dynasties in India rely on achievement; without achievement they are nothing. Family name goes only thus far.

In Sonia's own case, it went a long way in making her Italian origin quite irrelevant, (which she has also demonstrated by winning Parliament elections repeatedly, and in different parts of the country. After her husband Rajiv Gandhi's assassination at the hands of a Sri Lankan Tamil woman suicide bomber of the LTTE during an election campaign near Chennai, she resolutely turned down suggestions from the Congress leadership to head the party—this was not an invitation to be prime minister as the Congress had then gone into Opposition. But the urgings underscored once again the importance the party attached to the dynasty factor: no other national party—as distinct from regional ones—is subject to this tendency as none has been home to a dynasty.

The Congress went into the election battle under another leader and analysts noted that it was the first time in decades that the party was on its own, without the crutch of dynasty. As it turned out, it did not fare well at the hustings. Sonia campaigned but she was not a candidate, indicating that she was not in the running for prime minister.

The Congress's relatively poor showing could have been on account of more serious, underlying causes that were reshaping the country's political and electoral map. But in the popular imagination, not least within the party, the less than solid performance was ascribed to the Nehru–Gandhis missing from the scene.

Subsequently, Sonia was importuned once again to head the Congress. This time she accepted. Did she, like her late husband earlier, feel the impact of popular and party expectations from the family in a moment of crisis for the party? Again, we cannot know. But with Sonia's arrival on the scene the dynasty magic was turned on. Though the Congress performance was still somewhat weak in the general election of 2004, it was the best it had been in the recent past; at any rate, it was better than that of its principal rival, the Hindu-nationalist Bharatiya Janata Party (BJP), which was defeated and obliged to relinquish power. The Congress came to lead the federal government at the head of a coalition. It was widely believed it had Sonia Gandhi to thank for the upturn in its fortunes.

While the impact of the Nehru–Gandhi dynasty on India's political life is all too evident, the contribution of the Nehrus is not confined to politics. Jawaharlal Nehru was also a writer of substance. His sister, Vijayalakshmi Pandit, was India's ambassador to the USSR and later president of the UN General Assembly. Her daughter, Nayantara Sahgal, is an accomplished novelist. The wider Nehru clan has also produced ranking officials and diplomats.

Like politics in India, cinema is a field in which dynasties have proliferated. This is most evident in Mumbai's Hindi cinema which is also known by the imitative and unfortunate appellation of Bollywood, after Hollywood, though it turns out a greater number of films each year than its American counterpart. Regional Tamil and Telugu cinemas, based in Chennai and Hyderabad respectively in south India, which produce more films than Mumbai on a year-to-year basis, have also given rise to many dynasties, though probably fewer than Hindi cinema.

Since the spread of regional cinema is confined to a linguistic territory, its dynasties are less familiar to trans-India audiences than those of Hindi cinema which is viewed across the country and also everywhere in the world where people of south Asian—Pakistani and Bangladeshi, besides Indian—origin live (which means pretty much in all continents with the possible exception of South America). Hindi cinema is truly magnum. It is seen by and affects millions.

Politics is real; cinema make-believe, surreal. Therefore, successful political dynasties project and enjoy real power while their cinema counterparts cast a spell through the soft power they command. In both cases, however, it is the numbers of people influenced by the actions of the principal cast that matter. If these numbers were to be small, dynasties of one kind or another would not be worth paying attention to. This is why it is useful to keep the numbers in view.

The actions of political dynasties in India, national and regional, have a bearing on the lives of hundreds of millions as they are often at the helm of policy making; the cinema dynasties do not lag behind much. They can be money-making machines, given the sums stars command, especially in Mumbai. There are also dynasties of film producers, directors and playback singers though they do not command the same premium with the viewing public.

Since there is so much money to be made in Hindi cinema on account of its reach, it is not uncommon for sons and daughters of famous male and female actors to follow the family occupation. In general, the Indian cinema experience is not an artistic experience and the potential to act is the last question posed, though many young actors are beginning to get 'trained' at mini courses of a few months' duration that have sprung up in Mumbai. For the audiences, and therefore for the producers, the family name counts since it provides the recognition factor. If the progeny of the famous stars are able to fit themselves into the formulaic acting that Hindi cinema generally calls for (or in the melodramas of Tamil and Telugu cinema), so much the better. The main concern is that their films should not bomb at the box office.

Abhishek Bachchan, son of Amitabh Bachchan, the all-time superstar of Indian cinema, and his equally famous former actor wife Jaya Bhaduri, is now a popular actor and has recently married the female star Aishwarya Rai. This is perhaps the dynasty with the greatest glamour-power in Mumbai. Amitabh is a former elected member of Parliament and has powerful political friends in regional politics; they have helped his wife Jaya secure a Rajya Sabha berth. This cinema-politics constellation does make the Bachchans a powerful dynasty.

In terms of star power, perhaps no less striking are Saif and Soha Ali Khan, the son and daughter respectively of Sharmila Tagore, a descendant of Bengal's illustrious Tagore dynasty made famous by literature Nobel-winning Rabindranath nearly a century ago, and Bhopal nawab Mansur Ali Khan Pataudi, the filmstar-handsome former Indian Test cricket captain, whose father Nawab Iftikhar Ali Khan Pataudi also led the Indian cricket team and played for England before India's independence.

Well-established Mumbai actor dynasties include the Deols—the former film hero Dharmendra and his two sons and daughter; the Khannas—the former film star-turned-member of Parliament Vinod Khanna (who had also become well-known for becoming a Osho groupie) and his versatile actor-sons Akshaye and Rahul. There are also dynasties of producer-directors in Hindi cinema such as Basu Bhattacharya and his son Aditya; Yash Chopra and his son Aditya; and Yash Johar and his son, Karan Johar; the Sippys are well-known film producers.

But the 'dean' of the Mumbai film industry and unquestionably its most glittering and abiding dynasty is the one that issued from Prithviraj Kapoor who straddled the silent era and the talkies in Indian cinema (covering a remarkable three decades in celluloid), set up Mumbai's Prithvi Theatres which he would subsidize with his ample cinema earnings as the actor of actors of his generation, and left behind children, grandchildren and great-grandchildren who have animated three generations of the Mumbai film scene as actors.

Each one of Prithviraj's three sons—Raj, Shammi and Shashi—shone in Hindi cinema for the space of two generations—Raj as producer and director as well—and each began his life on the stage under the tutelage of their formidable father whose ultimate passion was theatre, though as a cinema character-actor he was without equal in his day.

The Kapoors can be said to be a film as well as theatre dynasty, given the institution of Prithvi Theatres their patriarch established and the wide influence that institution was able to command among the generation of Indians after independence. Prithvi Theatres shut down in the 1960s as it could not muster the finances needed for its survival. Shashi Kapoor and his English stage-actor wife Jennifer Kendall would resuscitate it later. For several years now it is being run by their daughter Sanjana who has succeeded in putting Prithvi on the map of contemporary Indian theatre. Sanjana belongs to a theatre dynasty from both sides of her family, her maternal grandfather and grandmother, the Kendalls, also being theatre-wallahs. She has done a film as well.

The tendency among Mumbai film children is to jump into cinema. Anecdotal evidence suggests that they are encouraged by producers to do so. A young Kapoor was not so interested in doing films for a living. When approached by a producer he quoted what he thought might be an outrageous price in the hope that the producer would be fobbed off. But the producer did not turn away. The young man was then left with no choice but to act in that film. Such can be the power of the dynasty factor in Hindi cinema.

There have also been cases of children of film actors seeking other avenues but returning to cinema. The sums to be made in Hindi cinema cannot ordinarily be matched by any other profession. Unlike, say, in Tamil cinema, in Mumbai, sons and daughters of those in the industry, especially if they are successful, are expected to join the industry—inbreeding is thus far from uncommon.

In Chennai, the home of Tamil cinema, the children of successful film stars and directors tend to enter the trade if they have not picked up a good degree and entered a profession or business, though there are exceptions. Nevertheless, dynasties are not lacking. The great actor of Tamil cinema, Sivaji Ganesan, has an actor son in Prabhu whose nephew, Dushyant, is a producer and director. Kamal Hassan, who is something of a current acting sensation in Tamil cinema, had two older brothers who were actors. His son and daughter and a clutch of nieces have been associated with cinema acting and playing television host. The formidable Tamil Nadu politician Jayalalitha, a former chief minister, comes from a line of actors—her mother, Sandhya, as well as an aunt were in films.

Politics and cinema, associated with power and money, have thrown up more dynasties than, say, sports or music—also very much in the public eye through the mass media—where good money can be made if one is good and successful. The difference between them is that in sports or music a performer is constantly being tested before top slots are annexed. A degree of talent is a necessary condition and it must be honed through years of training under expert guidance and long hours of practice. This is particularly the case with classical music which has a wide audience throughout the country (although not as much as popular music).

The rigours of the regimen inhibit all but the committed in these fields. Also, and this is especially the case with classical music, the audiences are discriminating, critical and discerning. The baton cannot simply be passed on from one generation to the next as in politics or cinema where what matters most are family name and the useful connections that come with it.

In sports there are too few families of note. None of them can really lay claim to dynastic status even when there is a father and son combination that made a name, as the Pataudis in cricket, easily the most glamorous of the sports in India where earnings at the top can be considerable. But the cricketing Pataudis were around too long ago to be in contention now. Pataudi's children are in Hindi cinema rather than in cricket, having followed in their mother's footsteps. From cricket again, there is the example of the Amarnath clan, but they can hardly be termed a dynasty. Besides, they also operated a long time ago. Sunil Gavaskar, the world-beating batsman known as the 'Little Master', continues to be a presence in the cricketing world and his son Rohan has played cricket at a high level but he continues to hover on the periphery of India's national team. Vijay Manjrekar and Sanjay Manjrekar, father and son, also come to mind as leading batsmen of their day, but that hardly makes them a dynasty.

Perhaps the pertinent point in respect of sports in general, not just cricket, is that no sporting family has enjoyed power or soft power, though as individuals the top names noted above (and many others) have been lionised at various times. Without influence and power, there can hardly be a dynasty. Glamour and charisma alone do not suffice to make a dynasty. Power and influence can accrue, and dynasty strike root, only when father and son or daughter overlap in time as players. This is impossible given the nature of sports where people must call it a day when—quite unlike politics or cinema and other fields—their children have not grown up.

Moving away from cricket, the story is even more dismal. In hockey, in which India was once a world leader, a man who commanded awe wherever hockey was played in the world was the wizard Dhyanchand. He alone, among all the top sportspeople in India one may think of, was considered glorious and enjoyed far-reaching soft power. His name had been heard even in villages though he was playing before the age of television in India and at a time when literacy rates were abysmal. Dhyanchand's son Ashok Kumar also played hockey for the national team, but there is nothing more to add to the story. As for other sports, there is even less to say.

Many more dynasties—still current—can be discerned in classical music. North Indian classical music is in any case centred on the gharana system, the Hindi word for dynasty, except that the gharanas were not named after maestros but usually after the ruling feudal principalities in the regions that patronized them. In effect, they were schools of music even if they followed a common grammar. The gharana system did not typify Carnatic or south Indian classical music in less feudalism-bound southern India.

Among the music dynasties or families most fans would doubtless recall straightaway the sitar spellbinder Ravi Shankar and his daughter Anoushka; the tabla genius Alla Rakha and his charismatic tabla-player son Zakir Hussain; the vocalist Pandit Jasraj and his daughter Durga; the santoor player Shiv Kumar Sharma and his son Rahul, who has followed in his father's footsteps; the Dagar dynasty—today the Dagar brothers are noted classical singers. Kishori Amonkar, whose voice emerges from the land of dreams, is the daughter of a classical singer who is better known in her own region of western India.

There are other modern dynasties as well, such as the well-regarded Indian novelist in English, Anita Desai, and her novelist daughter Kiran Desai; the Menons of the diplomatic service, three generations of whom have headed the foreign office, or the Cariappas—the father was the first Indian head of the Indian Army (after the end of the British era) and his son an air marshal. Unlike political and cinema dynasties whose recognition and therefore influence spreads wide, or dynasties of professionals in small-town India who are known across classes and categories of people, the dynasties of writers, musicians, artists or civil servants typically enjoy only niche appeal.

Two more integrated points help us understand the dynasty phenomenon better in the Indian context—one concerns caste, the other relates to class. Caste is a discriminatory system of socio-economic categorization, broadly corresponding to occupational structures, that has held India in its grip for about 3000 years. This scourge of the traditional Hindu order has rigid characteristics of heredity and hierarchy, and strata of caste or *jati* reproduce themselves by a socially enforced, within-the-community marriage regime from which there was no escape until fairly recently.

Such a system, which marked out the 'high' and the 'low' and even the 'untouchable' (typically those who performed 'polluting' tasks), was sanctified by *varna*, the religion-endorsed older ideology. Varna arose in early Vedic times, about 4000 years ago, to privilege the priest and the warrior classes, subordinating all others to them in a strict, not-to-be-trifled-with, social hierarchy.

The caste system has loosened considerably, especially in the social realm on two counts. First, on account of intense social and political struggles conducted against it in the last hundred years or so; second, because of industrialization and urbanization which threw the 'high' and the 'low' castes together on shop floors and in cheek-by-jowl slum tenements in the emerging metropolises from about the 1920s. But caste has not ceased to be relevant. The perpetuation of caste-based occupational structures, which society had assimilated and internalized over such an extended period, in some ways made it 'natural' for dynasties of upper-caste professionals to emerge in the smaller towns and the mofussil. This was really the first tier of the dynasty phenomenon. The situation was accepted by all, not only without murmur, but with approval and admiration since dynasties—on account of their achievements—brought prestige to a locality or community. The division of society into fixed status groups was already an accepted feature of society and dynasties are, after all, all about status in the end.

Typically, most dynasties in India, save those of a few backward-caste regional political leaders who have gained traction in recent decades, are composed of upper-caste men and women. The emergence of local dynasties was due to the unequal access that different caste groups had to economic assets—the access depended on their position in the caste hierarchy. In a more equitable social universe, in which anyone with a certain talent would have as much of a chance of bagging achievements as the next person, dynasties—signifying concentration of money, education and exploitable talent in a few hands—may not have come up at all, or if they did they might not be objects of admiration since they would not symbolize unattainability for the majority.

It bears pointing out that although the caste system is Hindu of provenance, its pernicious impact spilled beyond religious boundaries in the subcontinent and informed Muslim attitudes as well, although Islam celebrates equality. Professor Imtiaz Ahmad, a noted scholar of social, cultural and political dynamics of Indian

Muslims, has observed, 'The presence of a caste-like system of social stratification among Muslims of India, Pakistan and Bangladesh has been recognized for a long time.'

It is evident that the attitude of Indians to the question of dynasties has been religion-neutral. On account of being infected by the caste-like virus in the Indian setting, Muslim communities in India have displayed an attitude to dynasties that is hardly different from those of the Hindu majority. The same can be said of other religious groups as well.

Other than the caste factor which predisposes Indians to dynasty adoration by inuring them to hierarchies, in seeking to understand dynasties in India (other than industrial and business dynasties) it is well to remember that they are essentially a middle-class phenomenon. Odd as it may seem, this makes dynasties a modern-day feature in India since the evolution of the middle-class is a process that can be traced not much further back than about a hundred years. Also, the fields of activity in which dynasties are the most visible belong very much to our own era.

Approximately 300 million Indians are said to form the middle class whose definition is somewhat loose and flexible: it broadly takes in those who might still be riding bicycles in the mofussil to jet-setters steering luxury cars. This class is high on aspiration and is a conscious consumer of education. It avidly seizes opportunities in order to climb social and economic ladders. Naturally, it adores glamour, power and also dynasties which, in fact, arise from it. It is not far-fetched to suggest that India might not have its dynasties if it did not have an established and large-sized middle class. Loving dynasties is thus self-love for the middle classes.

The origins of the middle class lie in British policy in India. In time its spread came to be crucially linked to the establishment of the rule of law and dispersal of democratic freedoms in the system as a whole. Along with the proliferation of science and technology, this had the effect of allowing activity to flower in a wide array of fields from which would arise contemporary India's many dynasties. Without the existence of a democratic space, and the spread of education and science, modern-day democracies would have been unthinkable in India. Achin Vinayak, an Indian political commentator, has noted in Pavan Varma's *The Great Indian Middle Class* that in no other (European) colony did there develop 'such a large stratum of urban professionals steeped for the most part in the values of bourgeois liberalism.' The late Professor B.B. Misra noted in his classic study, *The Indian Middle Classes*, that it was the 'gradual substitution of custom by law' that led to the growth of the middle classes in India.

If British education policy (at the core of which was the teaching of English language, literature, history and philosophy) was designed to *create* a class to assist the colonial authorities in administration and to help with the development of internal resources necessary to pay for increasing imports of British manufactures, it is the progeny of that class, now commanding a much broader range of activities, that are now in the business of dynasties, establishing them and exalting them. This, of course, could hardly have been foreseeable in the late 1870s or the 1880s when the first adumbrations of middle-class life in India became visible.

The caste system and the rise of the middle classes are placed in a state of paradoxical tension in the context of dynasty-making. If the caste system had remained as rigid as in the past, or if there had been no 'gradual substitution of custom by law', it is hard to see how the middle classes could have developed in India. The middle classes themselves are made up of castes (typically the upper castes) and have not fully broken from their caste consciousness to this day, but they have come a long way, especially in the principal urban centres. With their achievements, the middle classes have created India's modern-day dynasties, but in order to 'enjoy' them as a harmless pleasure, society relies on the hierarchical mode of thought ingrained through the philosophy of the caste order.

ACKNOWLEDGEMENTS

The references to the ancient texts are from S.K. Ramachandra Rao, *Social Institutions Among the Hindus*, Rao and Raghavan Publishers, Mysore, 1969.

On Hindi cinema, I have benefited from a discussion with Sanjana Kapoor, a scion of the illustrious Kapoor family, whose contribution to Mumbai cinema and theatre is a pioneering one.

I am grateful to Archana Ramaswamy, the Mumbai-based stage actor and dancer, for sharing with me her understanding of Tamil cinema.

Tradition in Six Yards

. . . .

Seema Goswami

It hadn't really struck me till I travelled to the Far East. No matter where I went—Thailand, Singapore, China, Japan—there were always reminders of the local culture amidst the gleaming skyscrapers and the flashy cars.

In Thailand, men and women would greet each other with the *wai*, a gesture similar to our namaste but accompanied with a deep bow. In the compounds of fancy apartment buildings you would find small spirit houses, built like a doll's house, a home for the local spirits. In Singapore, I came across a tall, gleaming building that had been built four years ago but was still unoccupied. 'There's a problem, la,' my guide told me. 'The feng shui is not right.'

And yet, despite these reminders of ancient traditions, something didn't seem quite right with the picture. I would stare out of the window of my taxi, take in the street scenes and try and put my finger on it.

What was wrong with these images flashing by me?

It took me a couple of trips to work it out. The women were usually well-dressed, well-groomed and well put-together. Many were young, most were thin, and nearly all had fashionable haircuts.

But hardly ever did I see a woman wearing what could be described as the local dress.

The only times I saw women in cheongsams, kimonos or other traditional attire was when I went to a hotel or a restaurant or travelled on the national airline. Local dress was no longer something that these women put on as a matter of course. Instead, it had been transformed into a costume worn either to play a role or to entertain tourists.

Each evening, when they finished work, the women would slip out of their silken outfits and change into jeans and skirts. With that one gesture, they seemed to be abandoning centuries of tradition and embracing the new era of globalization.

I knew then that I had worked out what puzzled me—what was so different about these pictures.

Wherever you go in India, you still find women wearing the sari. For us, it is not a costume or an outfit for show. It is part of our lives and few of us would ever question why we wear it.

We may sometimes find it a drag to put it on first thing every morning, we may crib about how difficult it is to run around while managing six yards of fabric. But for all our carping and complaints, we would never dream of disowning the sari—or relegating it to costume wear, for that matter.

Even today, to be an Indian woman means to identify with the sari.

~

And I do mean Indian woman in a specific sense. In Pakistan, where our cultural traditions should be similar, there has been a conscious and deliberate rejection of the sari.

Across the border, the sari is increasingly seen as an Indian (read Hindu) garment and treated with suspicion and derision while the salwar kameez—imbued with a glorious Muslim tradition—has been adopted as the new nationalist dress.

Strange, isn't it? Given our shared heritage, one would have thought that the sari would be just as popular in Pakistan. And certainly, that was the case immediately following Partition. In fact, when Pakistan got its independence, Muhammad Ali Jinnah's sister, Fatima Begum, was photographed wearing a sari for the occasion. It is perhaps an indicator of how rapidly things went downhill between the two neighbours that Fatima Begum—now awarded the honorific title Madr-e-Millat or Mother of the Nation—was later credited with denouncing the sari as a Hindu dress, which Pakistani women, as good Muslims, must abjure.

Fifty years on, Pakistani women are faithfully following her lead. In 2005, when Sehba Musharraf, wife of then President of Pakistan, Pervez Musharraf, arrived on a state visit to India, she wasted no time in pronouncing a strong, unequivocal repudiation of the sari. As is customary on such occasions, Mrs Musharraf was taken shopping by a delegation of Indian ladies. The group arrived at Delhi's Cottage Industries Emporium and the First Lady of Pakistan was duly presented with a sari as a goodwill gesture. Mrs Musharaff declined the gift. 'We don't wear saris in Pakistan,' she said firmly, denouncing centuries of our common history and heritage in one fell swoop.

At one level, it was a display of extraordinary boorishness. At another, it was an indicator of how hard the Mohajirs—Indian Muslims like the Musharrafs who went over after the creation of Pakistan—have to try and play down their Indian origins.

It wasn't always like this, of course. In the early years of Pakistan's history, the streets of Karachi and Lahore were full of sari-clad women. Zulfikar Ali Bhutto's wife, Nusrat Begum, often wore a sari to official functions (and she wasn't even Pakistani—her roots lay in Iran). Her daughter Benazir was also pictured in a sari several times, as were the wives and daughters of other prominent Pakistani leaders.

But that was before Pakistan resolutely turned its back on its South Asian heritage and began searching self-consciously for a faux-Arabic, pan-Islamic identity. And with this denial of its subcontinental roots, came the rejection of the sari.

~

But this Hindu–Muslim divide between the sari and the salwar kameez is really an artificial construct. In the days before India was divided in the name of religion, wearing a sari or salwar kameez wasn't a function of which God you worshipped. What you wore pretty much depended on where you lived. In the Punjab, women wore the salwar kameez irrespective of whether they were Hindu or Muslim. And in Uttar Pradesh and Bihar, they wore the sari, whatever their religious persuasion.

My mother, for instance, who grew up in pre-Partition Punjab, wore salwars throughout her childhood and adolescence. And yes, she wore one at her wedding too, like most teenage Punjabi brides of her generation.

When I look at pictures of my parents' wedding now—those carefully-posed studio portraits typical of that age—I can see the story of the sari and the salwar kameez reflected there as well.

My mother's youthful frame is lost within the voluminous folds of her salwar kameez and her red, brocade-bordered, zari-encrusted dupatta, as she sits shyly by my suit-clad father. Standing behind her is that formidable matriarch, my future grandmother, resplendent in a sari worn *seedha pallav* style (with the pallav draped across the right shoulder rather than the left).

But it wasn't religion that was the marker of the difference between the two. It was just a question of their personal histories: where they grew up and where they went on to live—captured on camera in that frozen moment.

Growing up in Lahore, my mother did not even know how to drape a sari when she got married at eighteen. And while my grandmother had grown up wearing the salwar in the North Western Frontier Province where she was born, she had switched to the sari after living in middle India for many decades.

When she moved to Calcutta after her wedding, my mother had to make the same switch. Salwars really didn't cut it in Bengal—well, not for conservative married women anyway. So, while her unmarried sister-in-law ran around enjoying the relative freedom of the salwar, my mother was pressed into sari-draping lessons by her mother-in-law.

Yes, wearing the sari was a function of where you lived in those days.

But it was also a rite of passage. Lissome young things wore salwars, respectable married matrons wore saris. Once you got married, it was expected that you would move on to saris, which were as much a marker of your marital status as the mangalsutra or streak of sindoor.

Today, as India becomes part of the global village, things have changed. Now married women are not expected to spend the rest of their lives in saris. And it is not uncommon to see newly-married girls flaunting their *chura*—the red and white bangles by which you recognize the new North Indian bride—in jeans and skirts.

But even the girls who are most comfortable in shorts can never quite abandon the sari. When it comes to special occasions, family weddings—hell, even their own—it is to the sari they turn.

~

In many ways the story of the sari is the story of India itself.

Like the country, the sari can trace its story back to the very beginning of civilization. Artefacts recovered from the Indus Valley Civilization have shown both men and women dressed in a long strip of cloth draped around them. Called the *sattika* in Prakrit, this gradually evolved to become the sari (and the dhoti for men).

But despite their pre-historic origins, both India and the sari have evolved over the centuries to relaunch themselves in fresh new avatars in every age. While in the Vedic age, both men and women dressed in loosely-draped fabric, by the time the middle ages came around, women were required to dress more modestly. They were at risk from the marauding gangs raiding India from the west, and needed to cover up. And the sari came in handy for that.

The Muslim invaders brought with them the concept of the purdah, and the pallav became a device to hide behind. And legend has it that the blouse and petticoat were pressed into service only after the prudery of the British missionaries and the Victorian values of the Raj began affecting Indian society.

By the time India emerged as an independent state, after a long and protracted struggle for freedom from the British, the sari was showing a fresh new face as well. The various regional draping styles were abandoned in favour of a more modern version—based on the Nivi style of the South—which was judged most convenient for the exigencies of twentieth-century life.

Soon, the statue of Bharat Mata came to be depicted in this drape, which was not identified with any one region and thus had a certain neutrality. It was a symbol of unity in diversity. And once it was adopted by most women, it became a symbol of a newly resurgent India as well.

But then, that's the thing about both India and the sari. No matter how much things change, they still remain essentially the same.

So, just as India has evolved from an ancient civilization into a vibrant nation state, the sari has metamorphosed from a simple unstitched piece of cloth to a statement of both style and identity for a newly self-confident people. But the spirit of both endures no matter how great the changes.

The parallels between India and the sari don't end there.

India has many faces; the sari has many versions as well. And while each of the many faces of India represents an essential truth about the country, the many versions of the sari showcase its versatility as a garment of choice for millions of Indian women.

Never mind all that politically correct nonsense about the 'Real India'—that it lives in villages, well below the poverty line, with no education and no drinking water. About how the India of the prosperous middle and upper classes is an urban myth that obscures the reality of the Indian experience.

I'm sorry but I don't buy that.

The India of the gleaming metropolises of Delhi and Mumbai, the brand-new shopping malls, the luxury brands, the shining new cars is as real as the India of the dusty villages, the suicidal farmers, the impoverished factory workers, the ragged slum dwellers and all those who struggle to make enough for two meals a day.

And the sari has a place in both these Indias.

In the villages, women use it to cover their threadbare blouses, take shelter beneath it from the harsh, relentless sun, and when it gets too ragged to wear, stitch its many layers together to make soft quilts for the kids to snuggle under during cold winter nights.

In the gleaming social circles of the cities, the sari has taken on a designer hue. It may have lost its appeal as everyday wear as far as the younger generation is concerned, but it has become a wardrobe staple for special occasions. The mother may wear it to go to work, but her daughter will yearn to put one on for a Diwali celebration.

Blue jeans may have become the standard uniform for the urban young. But wearing a sari for the first time is still an important rite of passage for an Indian girl. Draping it around her quickly becomes a communal activity with everyone pitching in with comments and directions. Fond aunts and grandmoms fuss around the pleats and pin anything that could come undone. And Mom tends to get a little bit teary through the entire process.

As for the girl in question? She starts to feel like a woman for the first time ever as the sari enfolds her within its feminine grasp.

The truth is that no matter how much we veer away into wearing western clothes, the pull of the sari remains irresistible. We may whine about how cumbersome it is to put on, we may moan about the fact that it's not exactly practical to jump on and off buses in it, we may even drone on about the difficulties of keeping it well starched and ironed.

But all these practical considerations come to nought when weighed against the insidious appeal of the sari to our inner glamazon. There's something so sensuous about the way it swishes around you, caressing every curve, the way it shows off your best features while masking the worst, the way it brings out the woman in you.

When you wear a sari you don't just look different, you feel different as well. Your walk takes on a more sinuous quality as you sway your hips gently to negotiate walking within its loosely-draped folds. You hold yourself a little bit straighter, emphasizing the curve of your bosom and your bottom. And you certainly feel different: more feminine, more alluring, more pulled together.

To put it simply, you feel more of a woman when you wear a sari. So, how could you possibly resist its appeal?

And that's exactly how it is with India.

However much we may love Hollywood films, hip-hop music or the latest episodes of *Entourage*, at the end of the day it is Indian popular culture that really gets our juices flowing. Our reference points are still Shah Rukh Khan and Karan Johar rather than Brad Pitt and Angelina Jolie. On television, the saas-bahu serials and talent shows are far more popular than foreign programming. And of course, on the dance floor we'd much rather jive to bhangra beats than trance music.

However Westernized we may become, we can't really resist the appeal of Indian popular culture. And that's how India reels us right back into her embrace no matter how far we might have strayed.

And that's exactly why the sari will never become like the kimono or cheongsam—costume rather than everyday wear.

~

The real sameness of India comes from a sense of difference. Never is this more apparent than when you travel across the country. The landscape is never quite the same, the food is markedly different, as is the language.

And as it is with India, so it is with the sari. Not only does it vary markedly from one state to another, it is even worn differently in every region. If Gujarat takes pride in its *patan ki patola* and its *bandhani* style, then Bengal swears by its *tangails* and *jamdanis.* If South India is the favoured home of the *pochampalli* and the *kanjeevaram*, then Orissa makes the most of its *ikat* weave. In Madhya Pradesh you can sample the delicate delights of the Chanderi and the Maheshwari while the region of Kota has its own eponymous style.

Banaras is best known for its zari weaves while Lucknow uses its chikanwork—the art of shadow embroidery—to great effect. In Maharashtra, the *paithani* has pride of place while legend has it that the *tanchoi* was so named because the weaving technique was brought over by three Chinese brothers called Choi (tan for three in Gujarati and Choi) and adapted by the locals to make an indigenous style of their own.

In a sense, the sari is the fabric upon which the best artisanal talent of India showcases its work, the stage on which it performs.

The many different weaves, the vibrant colours, patterns and prints, the different embroidery techniques—that's how the depth and variety of talent in India makes its presence felt. Whether it is a soothing cream and gold of the Kerala sari or a colourful *baluchari* from Bengal, it is just another expression of the rich textile heritage of India.

No wonder then that the sari has even won over those who aren't native to India. The Zoarastrians, who came over to seek refuge in the Gujarati kingdom of Surat, adopted the sari as their own. Today, the Parsi community takes pride in its *gara*s, the elaborately embroidered saris which they wear with a seedha pallav to best show off the beauty of the work on it.

But then, every region, every community in India has developed its own special way of wearing the sari.

Gujarati women—from whom the Parsis evidently took their stylistic cues—favour the seedha pallav. This had gone out of vogue over the years, being seen as a fuddy-duddy way of wearing a sari. But it has now been given a fresh lease of life by some of the saas-bahu serials on television, in which the ladies invariably favour this drape.

In Rajasthan, the influence of the royal ladies of the former princely states is apparent in the popularity of slinky chiffon saris, with either *leheriya* prints or flowery designs. More often than not, the pallav is taken across the shoulders to cover the head in keeping with feudal tradition, while the sari itself is accessorized with pearls and glass bangles.

Maharashtrian women down the ages have worn the sari in the masculine way, tucking it dhoti-style between the legs, a nod to some of the Maratha warrior queens who took to the field in this style. This drape has gone into disuse of late, being revived only on festive occasions or as performance wear. Lavani dancers in Maharashtra, for example, still wear the sari in this style.

In Bengal, too, the traditional way of draping a sari has been abandoned by most women. The generation of grandmothers who kept the tradition alive, complete with key chain at the end of the pallav, have passed on. And the style made familiar to us through so many Satyajit Ray movies is now only seen on the most eccentric dressers.

Though the salwar kameez has made a considerable dent in the sari bastion of South India, the sari is still the outfit of choice of the older woman, who prefers traditional woven cottons and rustling silks with larger borders and elaborate pallavs.

But despite its rapidly changing look, the sari still remains identifiably a sari. Just as however different things may look as you travel through India, the essential spirit of the country shines through.

To use that hoary old cliché there is certain unity in diversity both in India and the sari. And what's more, there is a certain joy and beauty in the diversity as well.

Only in India can you go to the beach, ski in the mountains, scuba-dive, go white-water rafting, visit historical monuments, sail on the backwaters, go on the pilgrim trail, soak in the chaos of cities. In India, you can choose what best pleases you.

And so it is with the sari. It has infinite varieties and you can pick the one that appeals to you the most.

~

On the whole, though, the sari has proved to be resistant to too much change. International labels like Zandra Rhodes and Hermès have experimented with the sari but without much success. Jerry Hall was famously seen in a Hermès chiffon sari, but for the most part, such experiments have been both short-lived and less than triumphant.

The experiments of Indian designers, on the other hand, have worked better because they have respected the traditional parameters of the sari and worked within it.

The most successful of the lot has been Ritu Kumar, who revived traditional crafts in her sari designs. Back in the 1960s, Ritu set up her own-name label in Calcutta, using such age-old techniques as block printing, *mukaish* embroidery and *zardozi* to embellish her fabrics. More than forty years later, her brand is still going strong, riding on the wave of her trademark prints, patterns and embroideries.

In some ways, her success is based on the consistent appeal of the sari itself and the strength of the Indian design tradition that adapts itself to the demands of every age and all kinds of consumers. Even today, modern brides want a couple of Ritu Kumar saris in their trousseau, a nod both to Ritu's talent and to the perennial appeal of the sari.

But while Ritu stayed well within the traditional boundaries of sari design, those who came after her have pushed the envelope just a little bit further. Fabrics like chiffon and georgette were brought into the mix along with the more traditional silks, cottons and zaris. And the embellishments went beyond the usual zardozi and *ari* work to take in Swarovski crystals and the like.

The sari was being updated for a new lease of life on the party circuit. Hell, it even had a new name: the cocktail sari. Not because you wore it while drinking a Cosmopolitan (though you could do that too) but because it was worn while working the cocktail party circuit.

Hindi cinema played a crucial role in this changing face of the sari. Back in the day, heroines were always modestly clad in voluminous silks and prim cottons, which covered every inch of exposed flesh. Then came the era of sleeveless blouses and the diaphanous chiffon sari, worn well below the waist. Stars like Asha Parekh, Mumtaz, Sharmila Tagore and Zeenat Aman in the 1960s and 1970s showed off their hourglass figures—all the rage in that era—in these styles, draped tightly around the bum and bosom to make the most of their curves.

The 1980s saw the sari getting a bit saucier. The blouses were now tinier, the saris even more transparent, and as if that weren't enough, the heroines were routinely given a good hosing down in the course of one song sequence or the other to make their charms even more apparent. Sridevi made the wet sari dance her own in countless films and Madhuri Dixit took the (sodden) blouse from her and ran with it through her chequered career in the movies.

But it was only in the 1990s that the sari took on a completely designer hue in the movies. And the credit for that goes entirely to Manish Malhotra. He was the pioneer of the new, improved, filmi sari—all crystals, sequins and soothing pastel shades, worn with a barely-there spaghetti-strap blouse. He wrought his makeover magic with this new-look sari on almost every leading lady you could think of. Everyone from Urmila Matondkar, Karisma and Kareena Kapoor to Rani Mukherjee, Kajol and now Deepika Padukone have had the Manish Malhotra sari work its magic on them.

Soon enough, the trend started by Bollywood trickled down to the bazaars of India. Suddenly, high street shops and the little markets of small-town India were flooded with faux Manish Malhotra saris. Indian women, young and old, thin and fat, were tripping over one another to buy one of these for their wardrobes.

But while Manish Malhotra was the first to make such an impact on high street fashion, Indian designers had been working their magic on the sari for decades before him. And some of the more innovative work can be credited to the design duo of Abu Jani and Sandeep Khosla. To them goes the honour of designing the sari with the double pallav, the first of which fell gracefully across the shoulder while the second was draped any which way you wanted. As is usual with most such innovations in Indian design—and they are few and far between—there are many claimants for this honour. But by now it is well documented that this honour, at least, belongs to Abu-Sandeep.

But more than these little touches, what Indian designers did most for the sari was to revive the traditional arts and crafts that went into its making—and were fast dying out.

Chikankari, for instance, the traditional shadow-work embroidery native to Lucknow, had fallen on hard times. Traditional hand-embroidered pieces were too expensive for most people to afford. And the master craftsmen who worked on it could barely make a living because of the rising popularity of machine work.

Enter the Indian designer fraternity. Both Tarun Tahiliani and Abu-Sandeep used the chikankari style of embroidery extensively in their saris and salwar kurtas, giving both the craft and the craftsmen a new lease of life. So, just as a generation earlier Ritu Kumar had revived the block-print tradition, Tarun and Abu-Sandeep gave chikan a new incarnation in which it could captivate people. Since then such designers as the husband-wife duo of Muzaffar and Meera Ali have made chikankari the leitmotif of their collections, ensuring that the craft lives on in the twenty-first century.

Other designers have concentrated their attention on fabric, reviving weaves and patterns that were in danger of extinction. Martand Singh, the cultural czar of India, put up an exhibition of the sari in the late 1980s, taking it across the world, reviving weaving traditions that were in danger of becoming extinct. Since then, Rakesh Thakore and David Abraham of the Abraham & Thakore label have done their bit for rejuvenating long-forgotten weaves, updating patterns and designs to suit our modern sensibilities and designing saris around them.

But while Abraham and Thakore still remain rooted in the traditional sari tradition, some of the younger designers have adopted a more iconoclastic attitude. Take Sabyasachi Mukherjee, for instance, the archetypal Bengali boy made good. His saris are traditional enough in terms of fabric, weave and pattern. And he displays them on the ramp in a style reminiscent of old Satyajit Ray movies, but with a twist. Thus, the high-necked, ruffled blouses with long balloon sleeves are accessorized with oversized peacoats, black-rimmed glasses and jumbo jholas to add a Left Bank intellectual edge to the otherwise old-style look.

Sabyasachi gives an old look a brilliant new feel by mixing and matching startling shades that we would never put on the same palette; he contrasts shiny brocade with dull handlooms, using embellishment in the most unexpected ways. In the best tradition of India, he marries the conventional with a certain edginess to create an element of surprise, bringing a completely different sensibility to the fore.

And then you have the uncomplicated, unabashedly new-fangled designs of the Satya Paul saris. The label has been revived recently with its new-look saris and with Shobhaa Dé as brand ambassador. And with its modern styles—in which geometric patterns and animal prints jostle one another cheerfully—and easy-to-maintain fabrics, the label has found many fans in the working Indian woman.

~

What makes the sari the most versatile garment ever, though, is that you wear it to show as much or as little as you like.

You can pull the pallav over your head to show respect in a temple or in front of family elders (or to establish your credentials as a Rajasthan royal). Or you can let it drop discreetly to create an erotic riff with the occasional glimpse of your bosom. You can wear it high up on the waist to keep all your flab under wraps or let it slide down low on your hips to reveal your perfectly toned midriff. You can go for maximum coverage in your choice of blouse or get as daring as you choose.

My first glimpse of the erotic possibilities of the sari, though, came as a child—bizarrely enough, through the pages of the Amar

Chitra Katha comics that I used to devour so hungrily in those days. All those lissome ladies in their skimpy little boob-tube type blouses and diaphanous pallavs bore little resemblance to the sari-clad women I saw around me. Even my naïve childish eyes could see that these women were sexy and inviting in a way that my mother and aunts were not.

Nor did the saris themselves have much in common with the kind that the women of the day wore. The saris worn by the heroines of Amar Chitra Katha comics rode treacherously low on their slim waists, their blouses were held together with a precarious knot and will power alone, and their pallavs swayed and sashayed around them instead of demurely covering their pert little embonpoints.

Looking at these images today, you almost immediately make the connection with Sridevi and her wet chiffon saris, Madhuri and her heaving bosom, Kareena and her barely-there blouses. Or even with the Kama Sutra-type blouses made fashionable by Abu-Sandeep and Rohit Bal and accessorized with the shimmering saris of the kind that Adarsh Gill and Manish Malhotra trade in.

More recently, another image has come to exemplify the sexy, sari-clad Indian seductress: that of India's first toon porn queen. Her name is Savita Bhabhi and she lives on the Internet, where you can follow her sexual adventures as she slithers in and out of her sari at the drop of a pallav, her luscious breasts forever escaping the confines of her too-tight blouse.

But when I was growing up, there were no such reference points. So, the sensual (if tame by Savitha Bhabhi standards) images I saw in the Amar Chitra Katha comics had a heady exoticism to them as I drank them in. Gazing upon them with a longing that I barely understood, all I knew for sure was that I couldn't wait to grow up and wear a sari myself.

Wear it for real, that is. As a child, like most other Indian girls, I did my share of playing grown-up in a sari belonging to my mother. My grandmother, in fact, took a particular delight in draping a sari around me, majestically ignoring the fact that its width far exceeded my height. And my elder sister enjoyed playing dress-up with me as well, treating me like a real-life doll provided for her own personal amusement.

Soon enough, I got into the spirit of things as well. On quiet afternoons, when the rest of the family was enjoying a siesta, I would creep into my mother's dressing room, sneak out one of her prettier saris and drape it around myself as best I could. Then, standing on tip-toe, I would peer at my reflection in the mirror to see how I looked. And that's invariably how my mother caught me in the act—gazing admiringly at my own image.

So, the sari and I already had a personal history of sorts by the time I got to wear it for real. As first times go, mine was rather mundane. The convent school that I attended decided, in a sudden flurry of Indian pride, that from now all the girls in the senior school would be required to wear a sari uniform a couple of days a week.

The sari in question was boring as hell—as most uniforms tend to be. It was light blue in colour, made of a georgette-type fabric, and we were expected to wear it primly pinned up and with a blouse with half-sleeves and a modest neckline.

Of course, we did no such thing. Just as we had cheerfully flouted the usual uniform rule by hitching up our skirts to mid-thigh level when we left the schoolyard, we put our wits to work on making the sari sexier as well.

As you can imagine, it was the easiest thing ever. While in school, we wore our saris like proper little ladies. Once off the premises, it was another matter. Petticoats rode lower down the waist to display slender midriffs of the kind only teenagers can boast of, the first few buttons of the blouse were undone to show a glimpse of budding cleavage, and the pallav itself was left unpinned to go its own jaunty way.

It wasn't quite the Amar Chitra Katha image that I had nurtured in my heart for so many years. But given the circumstances, it was as close as I could possibly get.

My attempts to sex up the sari, surreptitious and otherwise, continued apace. All through college and my early years as a young professional, it was the sari I always fell back on when it came to glamming things up. It helped that my early adulthood coincided with the revival of the sari as a high fashion garment by Indian designers. And that meant it was no longer enough to just drape a sari around a standard issue blouse. You had to accessorize your sari with a designer *choli*.

The corset blouse rapidly became the most popular choice, where your bosom was trussed up in layers of fabric so that it pointed proudly upwards even without the benefit of a push-up bra. But the Kama Sutra blouse—cut so punishingly that your breasts spilled over from both the top and the bottom—had its own fans as well. (Of course, in the days of the Kama Sutra, the ladies didn't wear any blouses—but that, as they say, is another story.)

All this attention to the blouse was rather ironic, given that it came to the party rather late. Historians have it that women didn't really wear blouses—or petticoats—with their saris until the British Raj, when the missionaries infected the sartorial choices of India with their own prudery.

Until then, the cholis that women had worn resembled bras more than anything else: sexy little numbers that revealed about as much as they concealed. In Rajasthan and Gujarat, for instance, the cholis were cut deep at the bosom, held together with strings at the back, heavily embellished with mirrorwork and kept hidden behind voluminous pallavs.

But then, in the nineteenth and early twentieth centuries, women stayed in purdah for the most part, so there was no occasion for any nods to modesty. It was when the brown sahibs starting bringing their women into polite society, the blouse and the petticoat became essential to the wearing of a sari.

~

But however much the sari may have changed over the years, taking on a new face with every twist and turn in the evolution of India, it still remains a mark of being Indian.

I don't quite know why, but you have to be an Indian to carry it off. Foreign women may wear the sari on occasion to play dress-up, the wives of global leaders may put them on as a nod to Indian culture, but no matter how hard they try, the sari never looks quite right on them. Somehow when the sari is seen on these women, it ceases to look like an outfit—it looks like a costume instead. You know, like the kimonos and cheongsams that women in the Far East put on in an attempt at role-play.

I've always been intrigued as to why this should be so. It's not as if all these women don't drape it properly—most of them manage quite perfectly. Nor is it because they haven't mastered a feminine enough walk that would do justice to the sari.

So, why does the sari look wrong on these women, no matter how hard they try?

Take Elizabeth Hurley, for instance, possibly the most famous Western woman to wear the sari quite often (as a nod to the heritage of her half-Indian husband). Nobody could accuse La Hurley of being less that 100 per cent feminine, even girlie when the mood takes her. She is undeniably graceful when she wears a sari, she handles it beautifully, hell, she even looks like a billion bucks.

Yet, there's something just a little bit off about the picture. For all her efforts, she never quite looks the part. Instead it seems as if she is playing a part: foreign wife of Indian man trying to fit in with the desis. Or worse, posh totty going native for the annual fancy dress ball.

And when even Elizabeth Hurley can't quite pull this off, what hope does poor, misguided Cherie Blair have? The wife of the former British prime minister, Tony Blair, has never been known for her deft sartorial choices. But rarely has she looked as silly as she did when she got all togged up in a sari for events hosted by the British Indian community.

The cliché goes that the sari can hide a thousand flaws. Alas, it didn't quite work like that for dear old Cherie. Her hips looked wider than ever, her torso even broader than before, and her face was a study in misery as she tried to ensure that the sari did not unravel around her in public. So graceless was the picture she presented that the kindest thing to do would be to draw a discreet veil over it for all time. Suffice to say that she has since sworn off the sari and adopted the long kurta, which frankly is a much more flattering look on her Amazon-like frame.

That's not to say that nobody who is of foreign origin can carry off the sari. Of course, they can. But there's a catch. Before you can make the sari your own, you have to make India your own. Or to put it another way, India has to make you her own.

It's only when you feel Indian, immerse yourself in India, become one with it, that the sari begins to look good on you. You have to become a part of India before the sari starts to become you.

It certainly worked that way with Annie Besant, an Irishwoman who was brought up in England but ended up in India, where she was one of the founder members of the Theosophical Society and mentor to the young J. Krishnamurti. Besant adopted both India and the sari as her own, playing a leading role in our freedom struggle, marching alongside the other stalwarts of the Congress—clad always in a simple homespun sari. Today, she is always portrayed in a sari, even though she spent a major part of her life wearing Western gowns with frills and ruffles all the way up to her neck. But in India, that's not how we remember her. In our minds, it is her sari-clad figure that lives on.

So it was with another foreign woman who made India her own: Mother Teresa. She arrived in India as part of an Irish missionary order, and taught at the Loreto School in Calcutta, wearing a habit like all nuns did in that day and age. But when she decided to move away from the cloistered environs of the nunnery and go work in the city's slums, where she felt she was needed the most, it was the sari that the young Teresa adopted as the garment that would help her fit in.

Today, the light blue sari with striped border that she wore is forever associated with the Missionaries of Charity, an order that she founded. And Mother Teresa, clad in a sari with her own distinctive drape, has become an iconic figure in modern India, her image frozen forever in a series of paintings by M.F. Husain.

There is a reason why these women have been immortalized in a sari—and why the sari looks so right on them. It's because the spirit of India is imbued in their very bones. And that spirit always looks best draped in a sari.

In a sense, that's exactly what accounts for Sonia Gandhi's success in politics. Think about it. How did an Italian-born woman who had no interest in politics for the better part of her life manage to win over the hearts and minds of the Indian people? It's because she presented the image of everyone's ideal daughter-in-law: always draped demurely in a sari, looking suitably decorous and respectful.

One reason why Sonia Gandhi is regarded as being indubitably Indian by all of us is because she wears the sari so well. It doesn't look foreign on her; nor does she look foreign in it. The sari becomes her; it has, in fact, become part of her persona. It's hard to think of her in anything other than the sari—even the occasional picture of her in a salwar kameez seems a trifle jarring.

In fact, I often wonder how Indian politics may have played out if Sonia Gandhi hadn't looked quite so right in a sari. Would the Indian people still have taken to her? Would she still have been the Congress' star election campaigner? Would there have been the same clamour to make her Prime Minister of India?

Somehow I think not.

Part of Sonia's appeal has always been that she seems like the torch-bearer of the Gandhi–Nehru tradition. And part of the charm is that she has inherited her mother-in-law's gift of using the sari as a political tool. Just as Indira Gandhi had the knack of pulling out the right sari for the right region—a tangail in Bengal, a kanjeevaram in Tamil Nadu, an ikat in Orissa, a Maheshwari in Madhya Pradesh—Sonia also displays a rare sensitivity to regional pride in her choice of sari. It helps, no doubt, that she has inherited her mother-in-law's formidable collection of saris, including the famous pink handloom one—woven by Pandit Jawaharlal Nehru himself—in which both Indira and Sonia got married. But more than that, she has inherited Indira's style and panache when it comes to draping a sari. There is a certain no-nonsense air to how both the Gandhi women throw a sari around themselves, the way they tuck the pallav into their waist when tramping through rural areas, the way they cover their heads when visiting temples and other religious places, the way they don't let the folds of the sari restrict their long, almost-masculine strides.

If there is one important lesson that Sonia learnt from her famous mother-in-law it is this: if you want India to make you her own, you first have to make the sari your own.

Because at its very core, the story of India is the story of the sari itself.

City of Clay

. . . .

Arvind Krishna Mehrotra

For Palash

CITY OF CLAY

He has a handlebar moustache, side-parted hair, and is dressed in a shiny black suit. She wears a pleated pink skirt with matching blouse. They have red *tikas* on their foreheads and look newly married. From their features, they look Bengali. Standing against a Honda motorcycle, they are staring at me when it ought to be the other way round. *I* should be staring at them, which I am, because his left hand is nowhere near where you expect it to be but cupping her right breast.

This is Diwali time. With crowds of shoppers at every stall, it is not easy to catch the toy-seller's eye. When at last I do, I point out the motorcycle couple and ask the price. Twelve rupees, he says, then goes back to attend to the other customers, one of whom is bargaining for a clay weightlifter and the other for clay images of Ganesha and Lakshmi. It's a while before I am able to catch his eye again and pay for the toy, which his wife hands over to me, wrapped in a piece of newspaper.

The trunk in the living room, its tin painted brown to make it look like wood, is stuffed with quilts, blankets, woollens, mosquito nets and army surplus kitbags. Some of the bags, going by the stencilled markings on them, are of World War II vintage; some of the woollens, like my grandfather's *achkan*, go back to the Great War. Kept on the trunk, in no particular order, is an assortment of toys from previous Diwali melas. Seen together, the toys make a city of clay, a clay city that is overcrowded and bursting at the seams. Here you will find a motor car, colourfully painted; a pair of street lights, one with its light smashed; four loudspeakers fixed on a pole; a vase with two green leaves and two pink flowers; a battle tank in camouflage colours, with a piece of stiff wire for cannon; a woman carrying two pots, one on her head and the other tucked under her arm; a coiled snake whose springy hood goes back and forth when tapped; a cock with a red cockscomb; a blue-winged fairy with a parrot sitting on her shoulder; a schoolboy, neatly dressed; a caparisoned horse; an old man with white cotton wool stuck on his chin; a traffic policeman, the position of his arms making him look like a Bharatanatyam dancer; a tiger on the prowl; a tiger resting, as though after a meal; a six-member brass band in green uniform; and a prison which I was told is Naini Jail. But, as in a real city, there is room on the trunk, despite the overcrowding, for one more family. With a little shifting around, between the cock with the red cockscomb and the fairy with blue wings, I accommodate the motorcycle couple.

ALLAHABAD LIVE

I've harboured the illusion, from the time I was seventeen years old, that I do not live in Uttar Pradesh but New York, and, to keep the illusion from shattering, I have, instead of the local rag, always subscribed to a Delhi paper. Delivered a day late and useless as news, I read it to keep myself abreast of cultural events in the nation's capital, like the film show at the Hungarian Centre or the exhibition at Art Heritage. But two years ago, after a visit to my GP, all this changed.

The GP fancies himself as a wildlife photographer, and whenever I've gone to him he's given me the impression that he'd rather I talk about the elephant or antelope herd he's put up on the clinic wall than about any ailment I might have. On this occasion though, seeing me come in, even before I could sit down on the revolving stool next to his revolving chair and fake my interest in his expensive hobby, he threw up his hands and gave me the news that Allahabad was in the grip of a JE epidemic. The nursing home he was attached to was full up, he said, and he had been advising his patients who needed hospitalization to go to the district hospital or the medical college. Many of the patients were from Rajapur, an area close to where I live.

'JE?' I asked.

'Japanese encephalitis. It's the only story in the papers these days. Don't you read them?'

The charade of living not in Allahabad but New York (or even Delhi) I realized, had to end, and it had to end very soon if I didn't want it to cost me my life. The next day I changed my paper; I started reading *Allahabad Live*.

Along with reports of murders, dacoities and the latest epidemic, *Allahabad Live* gives you the reminiscences of distinguished local octogenarians ('When Indira Gandhi chastised a Congress leader') and on page 3, under 'Around Town', information on birthday celebrations ('Habib Tanvir's birthday celebrated'), yoga camps ('Yoga training camp organized'), probes ('CM urged to order probe'), meets ('Women astrologers meet today'), and melas ('Dadhikando mela').

I did not need 'Around Town' to tell me about Dadhikando. Year after year, the mela was brought live to me at night, when hundreds of loudspeakers played Bollywood music at full blast. The music would pound the air as though the air were the coast and the music the sea at high tide. The relentless pounding, against which one was powerless in the same way that one is powerless against the sea, would catch me unawares. Rudely shaken out of sleep, I would stay awake until daybreak, pacing the small bedroom as though I were an animal in a cage, all the while composing in my head a lengthy petition to the senior superintendent of police, with a copy marked to the President of India, complaining about the loudspeaker menace. But not any more, not since I changed my newspaper and started to get, through the local rag, advance news of the annual musical onslaught. With a supply of sleeping pills and cotton wool by my side, I was now ready to take on the mela, just as I was the no less fatal JE epidemic.

Muir Road is a long straight road, and one stretch of it passes through Rajapur, where the mela is held. Rajapur used to be a working-class area, supplying the neighbourhood with domestics, carpenters, plumbers, masons, house painters and electricians, and most of it still is. To its south are narrow lanes, paved with brick. They branch off the main road and end in the *kachchar*, rich alluvial land bordering the Ganges where watermelons are grown in summer. To its north is Rajapur Cemetery, which has existed since colonial times. There isn't a single 'wine shop' in Rajapur, but right by the popular Hanuman temple, the dado of whose interior wall is faced with white bathroom tiles, the old country liquor bar still flourishes.

It was getting towards noon and too hot to walk. Arriving there on my bicycle, I saw on either side of the road, at a distance of every few metres, wooden poles fixed into the ground. Between the poles were stretched three strings of fairy lights, one below the other and each of a different colour, yellow, red and green. The electricians installing the lights were young lads in trousers and body-hugging singlets. With pliers in their hands and rubber flip-flops on their feet, their dark skin glistening with sweat, they moved from pole to pole on wooden stepladders placed on bicycle-trolleys, making sure that when the lights were activated, every one of them twinkled. Each pole had, in addition, attached to it near the top, a fluorescent light whose glass strip was coated with transparent blue paint; and in the centre between two poles, between the first string of fairy lights and the second, were lights in the shape of a heart. To the left and to the right of the heart were more lights, diamond-shaped. The heart lights were red and, compared the mini bulbs used in the strings, their bulbs were of a larger diameter. The diamond shapes had lights of a deep yellow colour.

On the pavement, wherever room could be found, makeshift open stalls had sprung up. A length of nylon cord tied to a metal railing served as the poster stall. Posters hung from the cord, attached to it with clothes pegs. One of the posters said 'Everyone loves me'. It showed five golden-haired toddlers playing with plastic toys and learning blocks. Another said 'Welcome' in big letters. Tired-looking men and women sat on the pavement, under a fierce sun, their goods covered with grimy plastic sheets. They did not need to set up stalls, even makeshift ones, and were only waiting for the sunset to unpack their goods. These they would spread out on the ground, on the same sheet that was covering them. They were all waiting for the mela to begin.

Week after week, the forecast had said 'thundery weather' but the sky had remained clear. The monsoon had failed once again. As I cycled down Muir Road, the air on the skin felt like flames, like bicycling through fire. Men, both young and old, sat on the front steps of houses, fanning themselves with anything that came to hand, an envelope, a piece of cardboard, a newspaper, a handkerchief. I was looking for a place with some shade, where I could stop awhile and find out where the 'office-bearers' of the Shree Krishna Dadhikando Samiti, Rajapur, lived. Their names, followed, if they were advocates by their profession, had appeared in 'Around Town' and I thought I would talk to some of them. But places with shade are hard to find in Rajapur. When I finally stopped, it was not under a tree but in front of a packing-case kept beside a pavement paan shop. There was a man sitting on the packing case. He was Bankey Lal; profession: plumber. The packing case was his office. I said I was a journalist, and in my eagerness to break the ice told him how knowledgeable I was about the insides of toilet cisterns. I told him that I fixed my own. He probably thought I was off my head, but offered to help all the same.

'Pradeep Srivastava is not going to be at home,' Bankey Lal said. 'Not today, when all the mela organizers are out collecting funds. But I can show you where he lives. You may have to come back later.'

We had not gone very far when he pointed to a short, thickset man with a small paunch standing outside a paint shop.

'That's him,' Bankey Lal said. I wanted to thank him for escorting me, but before I could do so, he had vanished and probably returned to his perch on the packing case.

Srivastava was the secretary of the Dadhikando Samiti and, like many Samiti members, he, too was an advocate. He said he was busy with the arrangements and still had many things to see to, but all the same was eager to talk.

'Though Dadhikando melas are also held at other places in Allahabad,' he said, 'they are nothing compared with the show we put up in Rajapur. Our light decoration extends for two kilometres, the longest for any mela in Allahabad, and we draw the biggest crowds. The float parade will start after midnight. If you come around 9, you'll be able to see one of the floats right here, parked outside the shop. Allahabad's Dusshera is famous all over the country and it is time its Dadhikando became famous too. Last year a television channel from Lucknow covered us in the news.'

I asked him if he knew how old the mela was.

'It's very old and goes back to British times. I have papers at home to prove this, if you're interested.'

He gave me his telephone number and hopping on to his motor scooter sped off in the direction of Sadar Bazaar. I thought I would call him but never did.

Before leaving, Srivastava introduced me to the owner of the paint shop. A busy-looking man in his mid-twenties, he was also the person who had put up the money for the float that Srivastava had wanted me to see. We shook hands but he did not tell me his name, nor did I ask.

He said, 'Dadhikando, which celebrates the childhood of Lord Krishna, is one of the many melas of Allahabad. We hold them with great enthusiasm here, and everyone participates, regardless of age and rank. Even the poorest man will make a small donation towards the expenses. If the city's been spared natural disasters and epidemics, it's because the people here are deeply religious.'

A delivery van carrying Berger paints drew alongside. He went up to the driver and signed a piece of paper that the driver handed him. He then called out to his shop assistant to unload the cans of paint.

Paint wasn't the only thing being unloaded in Rajapur that afternoon. Bicycling back, I saw loudspeakers being unloaded too. Big conical loudspeakers, the name of the loudspeaker company stencilled along the rim, were stacked beside every lamp post I passed.

In the evening, Muir Road looked like fairyland. The lights on either side of the road faded and flashed, and for the first time I saw that there were strings of lights above as well. They were chasing lights, placed 10 inches apart, and formed a kind of low canopy. The loudspeakers played Bollywood hits, but the music wasn't ear-splitting yet. A sound like that of twenty motor cars, their engines revved up, came from the light controllers, one of them installed near the Hanuman temple. Bunches of thin electrical wires connected the controllers to the lights, making them flash or fade or give the chasing effect. Dressed in their best clothes and wearing their gayest footwear, women and children, some accompanied by a husband or brother, gathered round stalls selling traditional mela goods: plastic xylophones and rattles, toy kitchen sets and doctor sets, baba suits, glass bangles, powders and fairness creams that faked popular brands. Lodged between the stalls were food and ice cream carts. I stopped by a tattooist and watched him at work.

He sat on the pavement, a sheet of handmade paper filled with tattoo signs in front of him. On the sheet, meticulously drawn in black ink and arranged in rows, in each row the same sign repeated five or six times, was a half moon, a half moon and cross, a coiled snake, a swastika, a flower vase with a single flower, an OM sign, a dagger, three dots arranged in the form of a triangle, a lotus, a peacock, a scorpion, a turtle, Hanuman, a heart pierced with an arrow and the word *dil* written inside it in Hindi, and another with *dil* written inside it in English. Hidden away in a rectangular tin box, the size of a biscuit tin, were his instruments of torture.

A young man wanted his name tattooed. From his close-cropped hair and strong physique he looked like an army cadet, and very likely was one. He asked how much the tattoo would cost. Two rupees for every letter of the Hindi alphabet and double that for English, he was told. He had one other question: would it hurt? 'About as much as an ant bite,' said the tattooist.

The young man sat down on his haunches and stretched out his arm, his fist closed. He had a broad forearm, with space on it for a lot more tattoos than just the name. The tattooist wet a piece of rag with transparent liquid from a bottle and cleaned a small area of the skin. He then took out a small battery-operated drill from the tin box. Two wires connected the drill to the batteries. After dipping the bit into a bottle filled with a black liquid, he gently pressed it into the skin. The man winced for a second and, regaining his composure, watched the letter R form on his arm. The letter was still wet and smudgy when the tattooist lifted the drill and wrote out the next letter, A, and then the third, M. The three indistinct letters ran into each other until the tattooist wiped them with the same rag, making them stand clean in the skin. The letters were of the same size and the spacing between them was equal, as though a computer had printed them.

It was past nine and there was no sign of the float. I made enquiries at the paint shop, but the owner I had spoken to earlier was not there and the others seemed not to know. I started to make my way back, out of Rajapur. At the Hanuman temple was a TV cameraman, standing very still in the middle of Muir Road, shooting the crowds streaming past and the twinkling fairy lights.

JEJURI—BANDRA—JEJURI

On a visit to Pune in September 2004 to see Arun Kolatkar, who had been seriously ill and who died that week, I read in the *Times of India* a report on the changing face of Jejuri. Until then, although I knew that Jejuri was a town in western Maharashtra,

I had not seen it in this way. For me, as for many others, it had always been associated with a book of that name. It came as a shock, then, to read that Jejuri also existed outside the imagination of its readers, that like any other place on the map it had ordinary people walking about its ordinary streets and living their day-to-day lives. This 'real' Jejuri, which city newspapers reported on and information technology was transforming, had seemed unreal and abstract to me at the time; it still does.

The main attraction of Jejuri is the temple dedicated to Khandoba, a folk god popular with the nomadic and pastoral communities of Maharashtra and north Karnataka. Arun Kolatkar's *Jejuri* is a record of a visit to the town. Here are the opening verses:

> The tarpaulin flaps are buttoned down
> on the windows of the state transport bus
> all the way up to Jejuri.
>
> A cold wind keeps whipping
> and slapping a corner of the tarpaulin
> at your elbow.
>
> You look down the roaring road.
> You search for signs of daybreak in
> What little light spills out of the bus.
>
> ('The Bus')

After 'a bumpy ride' when 'all the countryside you get to see' is 'Your own divided face in a pair of glasses / on an old man's nose', the bus comes to a halt 'in front of the priest' who has been patiently waiting for it all morning. And here is why: 'purring softly', the bus has

> A catgrin on its face
> and a live, ready to eat pilgrim
> held between its teeth.
>
> ('The Priest')

Only incidentally is *Jejuri* about a temple town or matters of faith. At its heart, and at the heart of all of Kolatkar's work, lies a moral vision, whose basis is the things of this world, precisely, rapturously observed. So, a common doorstep is revealed to be a pillar on its side, 'Yes. / That's what it is'; the eight-arm-goddess, once you begin to count, has eighteen arms; and the rundown Maruti temple, where nobody comes to worship but is home to a mongrel bitch and her puppies, is, for that reason, 'nothing less than the house of god'. The matter of fact tone is easy to get wrong, and Kolatkar's Marathi critics got it badly wrong, finding it to be cold, flippant, at best sceptical. They were forgetting, of course, that the clarity of Kolatkar's observations would not be possible unless he had abundant sympathy for the person or animal (or even inanimate object) being observed; forgetting too, that without abundant sympathy for what was being observed, the poems would not be the acts of attention they are. The last poem in the book is 'The Railway Station'. In it, from the stationmaster to 'the young novice at the tea stall', no one is prepared to tell the narrator 'when the next train is due'. The book had opened with daybreak; it closes with sunset:

> the setting sun
> large as a wheel

Apart from a 'young woman' who arranges 'A Little Pile of Stones' in the belief that if the pile does not topple over she will have a long and happily married life and a 'teenage bride on her knees' who performs a ritual under the watchful eyes of a smiling priest, ready-to-eat pilgrims are absent from Jejuri. The opposite was true on the day I visited the Bandra Fair in Bombay. Held every September for one week to coincide with the feast that follows the nativity of the Blessed Virgin Mary, I had gone there on the evening of the last day, which explained the rush of pilgrims on the roads that led to Mount Mary Church. The BEST bus I was in kept getting stuck in the traffic and it seemed quicker to walk the rest of the way. The crowd that had looked like a mass of slow moving ants from my window seat in the upper deck felt more like a swiftly flowing river once I was part of it. Stalls lined the pavement, and I had to push hard against the current to get to them. They were selling candles and what, to me, looked like toys: motor cars, houses, doll-like figures, all made of wax. Some of the toys, unlike any other toys I'd seen, were body parts: wax models of dentures, hands, arms, legs, eyes and breasts. Also on sale were wax-covered photocopies of hundred rupee banknotes and a wax sheet with a row of tiny protuberances down the middle, which I could not immediately identify. It was a model of the spine and the tiny protuberances were the cartilage discs.

The models corresponded to specific boons the pilgrims sought. For the childless was the doll, for those who wanted money, the banknote, for those anxious to own property, the house, for those who wished to avoid a trip to the dentist, the set of teeth, and for those looking for relief from back pain, the spine. It had started to drizzle. The pilgrims continued to arrive, unmindful of the rain that was now falling steadily. They stood around the stalls, made their purchase, and continued on their way to Mount Mary. I hesitated for a bit, then crossed the road to join the stream of people who had lit their candles and made their offerings and were now headed in the opposite direction, towards Bandra Station. But before doing so I bought, out of an old collecting habit, a banknote and a few body parts.

Our Blessed Virgin's counterpart in *Jejuri* is Yeshwant Rao. Called 'only a second class god', he is not much to look at:

Yeshwant Rao,
mass of basalt,
bright as any post box,
the shape of protoplasm
or a king size lava pie
thrown against the wall,
without an arm, a leg

or even a single head.

('Yeshwant Rao')

While he cannot 'double your money', 'triple your land holdings', or 'put a child inside your wife', in some things the 'mass of basalt' is as effective as Our Lady of the Mount:

Yeshwant Rao.
He's the god you've got to meet.
If you're short of a limb,
Yeshwant Rao will lend you a hand
and get you back on your feet.

In Dilip Chitre's short film on Kolatkar, made for the Sahitya Akademi in 2004, there are shots of Jejuri, including one of Yeshwant Rao. He looks exactly how Kolatkar has described him, a rock 'the shape of protoplasm' and daubed with red paint. Another shot shows the replicas of the limbs—a crudely made arm, a leg—that pilgrims have offered at the shrine. Fittingly for a god in rural Maharashtra, the replicas are life-size and fashioned from wood.

STONE CARVERS' LANE

A friend tells me about the Kartik Mela at Baluaghat. Situated on the Jamuna, Baluaghat is about 5 kilometres, or thirty minutes by rickshaw, from where I live. Having spent my life in those parts of Allahabad from where the Ganges was never more than a short walk away, going to Baluaghat was a bit like going to a foreign country. But a foreign country, as I knew only too well, that in the end would turn out to be a mirror image of the native one.

Located in the old part of town, to get there from Civil Lines involved negotiating the lanes of Johnstonganj and Bansmandi, the latter a specialized bazaar dealing in all things related to wood, from sawn logs, planks and boards to dowry furniture (armchairs and sofa sets upholstered in printed velvet, chaise-longues, dining tables with Formica tops). There is never a time of year when Bansmandi is not crowded, and since I'd decided to make the trip on the day before Diwali, which also happened to be the last Friday of Ramadan, I expected it to be even more so. Surprisingly, perhaps because it was three in the afternoon and everyone was taking their siesta, the roads had little traffic. The only time the rickshaw I was travelling in slowed down was when it neared its destination, and then too because of the condition of the road, which was full of crater-sized potholes when it was there at all. On either side were cowsheds and, whenever I passed what looked like a house, it had a cow or calf tied to a stake outside. Occasionally, an advocate's nameplate was tacked on a door, the letters indistinct and the door paint peeling. Behind the door, which was firmly shut, it seemed unlikely that any human activity, let alone legal activity, took place. A tacky metal sign advertising a PCO, a public call office, tilted into the road and, while a grunting pig ran alongside the rickshaw before finally overtaking it, the rickshaw swerved to avoid another pothole. A girl stood in a doorway, a thick science textbook in her hand but her eyes focused elsewhere; a woman sat by an open drain, weaving a basket. The afternoon light weakened, the gold turning to a pale grimy yellow, and I wondered why I was making this trip to Baluaghat.

It came to me then, as it had earlier too, that the urban face of Allahabad, created during colonial times, was only a mask. The wide roads, the crenellated houses, the gravelled drives, were as a piece of theatre on which the curtain had long been drawn. In the sixty years since independence, most of the public and domestic buildings of the Raj had collapsed through age and neglect or had been torn down and, as the stones of empire turned to dust, they laid bare Allahabad's essentially rural features. This deathly fact, I realized, I had concealed from myself by surrounding myself with a large number of books and a handful of friends, all of whom lived in other cities. In one of these books, which I had taken down at random from my shelves, I once came across a passage I had been looking for without knowing that I was looking for it. It put in perspective what I now saw around me. 'The life of the dynasty is the life of the town,' wrote the great fourteenth century Arab historian Ibn Khaldun in *The Muqaddimah*. 'If the dynasty is of short duration, life in the town will stop at the end of the dynasty. Its civilization will recede, and the town will fall into ruins.'

The link that Ibn Khaldun saw between cities and dynasties (or empires) has continued into our own time. Nirad C. Chaudhuri's oft-quoted dedication of *An Autobiography of an Unknown Indian*, in which he says that 'All that was good and living / within us / was made, shaped, and quickened' by British rule, if applied less to the subject population and more to cities like Allahabad, conceals an important truth.

The unofficial name of the road leading from the Baluaghat crossing to the Jamuna, a distance of about hundred metres, is Patthar Wali Galli, or Stone Carvers' Lane. This is where the mela is supposed to be held, but except for a few stalls selling cheap crockery (cups and saucers, mugs, dinner plates) or cheap plastic goods ('All items Rs 5'), there was no sign of the mela. For a moment, I even wondered if I had come to the wrong place. Little by little, as a tourist might, I gathered that the mela proper would begin after Diwali and continue for the next fourteen days, concluding on Kartik Purnima. On that day, I learnt, people in large numbers would take a ritual bath in the Jamuna at Baluaghat, just as they would in rivers and tanks all across the country, in the Ganges in Haridwar, in the Mahanadi in Cuttack, in the Gandak in Sonepur, in Pushkar in Ajmer. This larger significance of Kartik Purnima I understood not by talking to the sullen stall-keepers of Baluaghat but, later, by Googling the phrase.

By the side of the road, at the head of Stone Carvers' Lane, stood a row of idols, carved in relief. In front of them sat a young boy, chipping away at a fresh block, teasing out the figure in the grey stone. I could make out some of the gods—Hanuman, Ganesh, the more obvious ones—but certainly not all. The goddesses particularly were difficult to identify, and I sought the boy's help.

He looked up and pointed to an elderly man, wearing a lungi and vest, who was busy talking to someone.

'Could you help me with the names of these gods?' I asked him.

'Which one do you want to buy?'

'Well actually I just wanted to . . . '

I had not completed the sentence when he turned his back and resumed the conversation I had interrupted. Clearly, Baluaghat was not the place to come to if you wanted a quick lesson in Hindu iconography.

A few steps away was a stall selling clay toys. After my encounter with the idols, or more precisely with the idol maker, I turned to the toys with a sense of relief, knowing that I was on home territory here, that the toys would not show up my ignorance in the same way the gods had. The stall, arranged in tiers, stepladder fashion, had all the usual mela favourites—motor cars, flowerpots, hens, policemen, yogis, guavas—but then came something that, in all my years of mela going, I had not seen before, something that left me completely stumped. This was a standing figure, about the height of a man's palm, with a pointed mouse-like face, coloured electric blue. Its slit eyes were outlined in red, with black eyelashes, and there was a triangular silvery mark on its forehead. It wore a yellow gown with an attached hood. The gown covered it from head to toe, so that except the hands, which were of the same electric blue colour as the face, no other part of the figure was visible. I asked the stall keeper what this strange object represented and he said it was an 'alien', using the English word. I later learnt that the 'alien' was based on a character in a Bollywood film starring Hrithik Roshan and Preity Zinta.

Stone Carvers' Lane ended at the river. With boats idling in the water, as if they were waiting for someone to arrive, it appeared to be an idyllic scene. It looked desolate as well, in the way idyllic scenes often do.

At the bottom of the lane was a stone carver's shack, outside which sat a well-built young man covered in grey dust, gently tapping a stone with a hammer and chisel. Once bitten, I hesitated before putting my question to him.

'What are you carving?'

'Jagadamba,' he said, after a long silence, and then shot back a question of his own.

'You from Allahabad?'

'Yes. From near Rajapur, in Civil Lines.'

'It doesn't look so to me, not from your appearance.'

'Well, Rajapur is a long way off from Baluaghat, which is why people look different there.'

'Why don't you speak the truth?'.

We continued in this fashion for a while. The conversation was getting nowhere and I did not know how to extricate myself from it. There were flat chisels and point chisels lying around and I picked up a flat chisel, feeling the blade with my thumb.

'Where do you get these from?'

'Why do you want to know?'

'I am interested in tools generally. You could say that I collect them.'

'We have our suppliers. The tools come mostly from Rajasthan.'

He had continued to work on the stone, on one of Jagadamba's four arms, as we talked. Stone dust filled the grooves and he removed it with a brush. For the first time I noticed that the idol had paint on it, streaks of yellow, red and black. He was removing the paint bit by bit, by tapping the painted area with a chisel, which he held at a 30-degree angle to the stone.

'You're taking off the paint,' I said. It was an unnecessary remark and I regretted making it.

'I could even take the skin off your flesh,' he replied, giving the paint another tap.

Often, putting my eye to the peephole, if it's the courier, the milkman, the vegetable seller or the dhobi who's rung the bell, I find him studying the poster pasted on the front door. He's seen the poster before, on previous visits to the house, but still looks at it as though he were seeing it for the first time.

Based on the Hindu belief that the dead, after departing from this life, have to cross the Vaitarani, the shit-filled river of hell, before the infernal regions can be entered, the poster shows a young, fair-complexioned woman, her eyes chastely lowered, crossing the river, holding the tail of a cow. Also in the water are two fire-breathing dragon-like creatures and a drowning man. While the woman is reaping the rewards of good karma—she may have, for instance, donated a cow to a Brahmin in her lifetime—the man suffers for lack of it. As the other panels in the poster show, his ordeal, without a cow to guide him across Shit River, has only just begun.

There is a story told about the Suprematist painter Kasimir Malevich and his model for a statue of Lenin:

> Malevich who, like all other Bolshevik artists, has been working to express the greatness of Lenin in a model for his monument, proudly exhibited a huge pedestal composed of a mass of agricultural and industrial tools and machinery. On top of the pile was the 'figure' of Lenin—a simple cube without insignia.
>
> 'But where's Lenin?' the artist was asked. With an injured air he pointed to the cube. Anybody could see that if they had a soul, he added. But the judges without hesitation turned down the work of art. There must be a real figure of Lenin, they reason, if the single-minded peasant is to be inspired.*

*T.J. Clark, *Farewell to an Idea: Episodes from a History of Modernism* (New Haven, 1999), 225.

Whoever made the poster (it is unsigned), the bazaar artist needed no Soviet judge to tell him about inspirational art or how best to get his message across to 'the single-minded peasant'. Crudely drawn and brightly coloured, the figures in it are 'real' in the way that comic-book stereotypes are real. The carter who overloads the cart, the grocer who sells you short, the woman who goes in for an abortion, the cat burglar who breaks into your house, the profiteer who deals in the black market, the butcher who sells meat are, in separate panels, shown committing the ill deed, the bad karma. The panels below them show its terrible consequences.

The person is tied to a pole or stuffed in a vat, and as flames leap up from below, a burly two-horned demon figure, spear in hand, disembowels him or, in the case of the abortionist, her. Some of the punishments are an attempt at humour, of the rustic sort. The carter's punishment for overloading is that, harnessed to the cart, he is made to do the work of the bullock. His load is a smiling giant. Two panels show the crimes of bribery and adultery. In these cases, both the bribe-giver and the bribe-taker, both the adulterer and the adulteress, are punished. Though unlike her partner in crime who is punished in the usual way, by being tied to a pole and disembowelled, the adulteress is lying on the floor and has a pole sticking out from her thighs. While she undergoes her torture, the two-horned devil sticks out his long tongue at her.

I had bought the poster at a local mela, as an example of modern bazaar art, except that there was nothing modern about it. Early Jaina literature of the third century AD has references to a *mankha*, a kind of mendicant 'whose hands were occupied by a picture board'. Wherever a small crowd could be gathered, at a mela or shrine, you would find, among the fortune tellers, wrestlers, acrobats and mimes, a *mankha* or more often a picture-showman, who, combining a display of gruesome visual images with the art of storytelling, would tell his listeners about good karma and bad karma, about Shit River and the way across it. Ironically, these depicters and narrators of hell punishments could on occasion be thieves themselves. A tenth century collection of Jaina stories in Kannada tells of a picture-showman who was hanged for stealing. While he kept his listeners enthralled by telling them punishment stories (the horned demons and boiling vats of my poster), other members of his gang made off with the bags of paddy belonging to the paddy merchants sitting in the audience. In the oral tradition of the Garodas, a community of picture-showmen in Gujarat, there existed until thirty years ago a description of a member of their profession: 'He moves around with a painted scroll. He wears a sacred mark on his forehead and a turban on his head. On his shoulder he carries a bag and there is a stick in his hand'.*

The middle-aged man I bought the poster from did not have a stick in his hand nor a turban on his head. He was wearing a shirt and trousers, and before giving me the poster had rolled it up and secured it with a rubber band. But he could have been a Garoda of Gujarat or a third-century Jaina mendicant, just as I could have been sitting in the attentive crowd, among the believers.

My other mela poster, similarly printed on cheap paper and priced at one rupee, is a map. Though it says 'Tirthraj Prayag Map' in English and 'Tirthraj Prayag ka naksha' in Hindi at the top, it's not a map in the traditional sense. On three sides, forming a border, are pictures of gods, goddesses and rishis: Vishnu, Shankar, Siddhanatha, Mahavira, Balmukunda, Lalita Devi, Gorakhnath, Kuber, Dharmaraj, Shesha, Markandeya, Vedavyas, Yama, Garuda, Dattareya, Bharadwaj, Kalabhairava, Narasimha, Satyanarayana, and Rama, Lakshmana and Sita. In the foreground are the rivers, sky blue in colour, with tiny figures taking a holy dip in them, the bathers' heads no bigger than the letter O. There are boats in the water, a swimmer and images of three river deities: Yamunaji (sitting on a turtle), Gangaji (sitting on a crocodile) and Saraswatiji (sitting on a swan). Bridges cross the river. On one bridge are pedestrians,

*Jyotindra Jain, 'The Painted Scrolls of the Garoda Picture-showmen of Gujarat', *NCPA Quarterly Journal*, Vol. IX, No. 3 (1980), 3–23.

on the other a railway train, a squiggle of smoke coming out the front. Across the bridge, against a background of bright yellow, is the city of Allahabad.

As in tourist maps, Tirthraj Prayag Map shows places that are of interest to visitors. The places are not marked with a dot or circle but a small picture. There are pictures of the clock tower, the museum, the Kamala Nehru Hospital, the university, Muir College, Khusrau Bagh, the railway station, Anand Bhavan and the fort. Allahabad is not a city of temples, and the map has pictures of the few there are. Except for the fort and the clock tower, the buildings, arranged in straight lines and equidistant from each other, look the same. It matters little that they do, or that there is on the map only one unnamed road, shown snaking past the railway station. Meant for ordinary pilgrims, who will treat it as a divine object to put up with the other framed gods on their walls, it does not aim to represent things objectively in space. The map is purely imaginary with the names of some real buildings on it.

In a Henri Cartier-Bresson photograph, taken at the Allahabad Kumbh in 1966, we get more versions of it.* The photograph shows a woman sitting on the ground with pilgrim maps spread out around her. Some of the maps are stuffed inside a plastic shopping basket, next to which is a small, unsteady pile of religious books. The woman's bangled right arm is stretched over the maps to receive a glinting coin which a man is about to place in her open palm. The man, except for his hand, is not in the picture, but other people are, crowding round the woman.

They are rural folk, all of whom, from the clothes they are wearing, especially the identically tied turbans, seem to come from the same village. Some of the men are standing, looking at the maps, others are sitting on the ground, among them a young man with a shaven head and grinning from ear to ear; yet others are bending over those who are sitting on the ground to get a better

**Henri Cartier-Bresson in India* (New York, 1987), 18.

view of what the woman is selling. One of the maps she is selling is similar to the one I have, with the buildings shown in a straight line. The other map is without any buildings. In fact, nothing on it corresponds to any feature you might associate with a city map, even an imaginary one. It shows, in four rows, images of Hindu gods, the entire pantheon as it were, and that is all. No buildings. No bridges. No river even. This version, preserved only in Henri Cartier-Bresson's photograph, for I haven't seen it anywhere else, comes closest to the truth of that imagined reality called Tirthraj Prayag, the Lord of Pilgrim Places.

UNCLE MULK

Everyone dies, but some people, writers particularly, get a second life. This second life takes many forms: biography, memoir, a volume of uncollected work, selections of letters, a public archive that preserves, for future researchers, the writer's papers. Not in India though. Here, whether writer or not, you live only once.

About ten years ago, I was in Bombay researching illustrations for a history of Indian literature in English. An obvious source for illustrative material, like frontispieces and amply worded title pages, were books published in the nineteenth century and I was mainly looking at them, but also at later titles. One of the books I couldn't find, and which none of Bombay's public libraries seemed to have in their catalogue, was Mulk Raj Anand's *The Lost Child*, published in 1934. Illustrated by the English sculptor and typographer Eric Gill, it appeared in a limited edition and was Anand's first book. If anyone had a copy, I reasoned, he would.

Anand's house in Cuffe Parade, with its gravel drive, cupolas, porte-cochere and rose windows, was among the few remaining colonial houses on that road. The others had been pulled down to make way for high-rise buildings. Surrounded by them, the house, in comparison, looked Lilliputian. I had gone past it many times, but I did not know Anand and had never been inside. The chance came when the poet Adil Jussawalla, who was a friend and neighbour of his, was visiting him and asked me if I'd like to come along.

Anand, who was in his nineties, answered the door himself. He was a short man with large, protruding eyes, and was dressed in a loose khadi kurta and pyjamas. His voice, gently authoritarian in tone, was the voice of someone who, in his time, had been a dandy and heavy smoker, though I'm not sure if he had been either. He pointed to two cushioned easy chairs, which we took, while he sat on the one beside a standard lamp, a side table next to it.

The room in which Anand received us was more like an antechamber and had a larger room attached to it, which was probably Anand's study. Parts of the study, where the light of the standard lamp didn't reach, were in darkness. I scanned the bookshelves but, disappointingly, they were crammed with papers rather than books. Presently, from the shadows, a servant emerged, carrying a bottle of rum, three glasses and warm water in a jug. Anand's longtime companion, Dolly Sahiar, hovered about.

Those who knew Anand in his last decades say that he had a repertoire of stories which he repeated to all visitors. The stories, from the days when Anand was a young writer, were all about his encounters with the Bloomsbury set in London and his meetings with Gandhi in Sabarmati Ashram. He would hold forth and the others would listen. Unfortunately, I recall little of what he said that evening. At some point, I asked him about *The Lost Child*, hoping he would walk up to a bookshelf and get me the book. He said he did not have the edition I wanted, nor did he know anyone who might, but as we were leaving he went inside and came back with something which, from a distance, with its glossy red cover, looked like an Indian wedding card. It was of the same thickness too. On the cover, in gold letters, it said *The Lost Child and Two Lyrical Tales* by Mulk Raj Anand. Anand pulled his chair closer to the lamp and, sitting down, inscribed the book before giving it to me, signing himself 'Uncle Mulk'. One of Anand's Indian publishers had brought it out as a gift on his ninetieth birthday, which partly explained its celebratory get-up. Printed on cream-coloured paper with the text printed in a light shade of brown, the book was designed by Dolly Sahiar.

'The Lost Child' is about a little boy's visit to a village fair with his parents. There, he looks longingly at jugglers, balloon sellers, sweetmeat stalls and the roundabout, knowing what his parents' response will be if he makes a demand. They'll say that the bauble is too expensive or he too old for it and drag him away. At some point, he gets separated from them, and when he realizes what has happened begins to sob. A kind man, seeing him crying, takes him round the mela again. He offers to buy him anything he wants, but the child is inconsolable. All he says is, 'I want my mother, I want my father.'

As Anand explains in a brief afterword, the story both draws on a childhood experience and is an allegory. He also dwells on the circumstances of its first publication. In transcribing the extract below, I have corrected a few obvious errors:

> The story 'The Lost Child' was written in the early hours of a morning in a room in Cambridge, from persistent recall in my subconscious, of a poem by Guru Nanak: 'We are all children lost in the world's fair.'
>
> This memory brought back the panic I had felt when I had myself got lost, at the age of six, in a fair in Kaleshwar village, on the banks of the river Beas in Kangra valley of the Punjab Himalayas. The story was sent to seven magazines, and all sent it back with the usual editor's rejection slip.
>
> The artist Eric Gill read the story and graciously offered to print it, with two other lyric tales of mine, 'The Eternal Why' and 'The Conqueror', as a little book decorated with an engraving, on his press at Piggots, High Wycombe, Buckinghamshire, as a consolation for a budding author.

Few today would remember 'The Lost Child'; fewer still would be interested in its publication history or in the fate of Anand's papers. His first published story, like the papers he left behind when he died, have all vanished into the thin Indian air, much as the announcement I once heard over the crackling public-address system at a mela did. It was about a boy who had gone missing. The boy's name, the announcer said, was Aman. He was six years old. When last seen, he was wearing a blue shirt and grey shorts and carrying a balloon in his hand.

The Great Indian Election

. . . .

Vidya Subrahmaniam

My car was stuck on the outskirts of Ramnagar in the Meja Assembly constituency in Allahabad. I was on the campaign trail of Uttar Pradesh (UP) chief minister Vir Bahadur Singh and I was impatient to catch up with his cavalcade. Yet here I was, immobile and held prisoner by a bunch of youths. As I watched, as much in delight as in exasperation, they clambered atop the bonnet, dancing and shouting, 'Vir Bahadur *vapas jao, kiraye ko tattoo vapas jao*' (Vir Bahadur, you hireling, go back, go back).

The boys, all fans of Vir Bahadur's rival, Vishwanath Pratap Singh, had been on the lookout for the chief minister's white Ambassador. Instead they pounced on my deceptive replica, unaware that the official entourage had sped ahead.

It was June 1988, and I was in Allahabad to cover a parliamentary by-election that posterity would record as a turning point in Indian politics. The previous summer, V.P. Singh, finance minister in the Rajiv Gandhi government, had finally broken with the ruling Congress party, though, typically, he would have to be coaxed and cajoled (he hated being seen as coveting power) into taking the next step—fight an election and position himself as a challenger to Rajiv Gandhi. V.P. Singh trounced the Congress's Sunil Shastri in that by-election.

Sixteen months later, he dethroned Rajiv Gandhi at the Centre, when the coalition he led—the Janata Dal—won the general election. However, his government fell prematurely, a victim of internal Janata Dal politics.

But 1988 held a bigger significance. It marked the start of the Congress' long-term decline, till its slow recovery in the mid 2000s (through it is yet early to declare the process complete). At the time of the Allahabad by-election, the Congress held an incredible 414 out of 541 Lok Sabha seats, a vote share of 49 per cent. This was brute Congress power. Yet, from here on, the party, the principal pivot of Indian politics for close to four decades, steadily lost seats and votes, and though the Congress formed governments in 1991, and again successively in 2004 and 2009, the party has not been able to claim a majority in Parliament and its vote share since 1996 has remained under 30 per cent.

It is a measure of the extent to which the polity has fragmented in the past decade that in the much acclaimed 'comeback' election of 2009, the Congress won 206 seats with a vote share of 28.52 per cent. Compare this with the verdict in 1989, widely interpreted as a humiliating defeat for Rajiv Gandhi because the Congress crashed in the election from 414 seats to 196 seats. Yet even in this decimation, the party held a vote share of 36 per cent. Over the years I would learn more about the quirks of the first-past-the-post system: that from the same number of votes a victory could be conjured as easily as a defeat.

The 1988 by-election, my first serious assignment as a journalist, was a heady experience. I revelled in the colour and the spectacle that has no equal anywhere else in the world, but by Indian standards, the elections would soon become unrecognizably tame. In 1991, a man called Tirunellai Narayana Iyer Seshan became the chief election commissioner (CEC) and cracked the whip on India's proudest in-house production, stripping it of its unique character. Soaring cut-outs, irreverent graffiti, catchy slogans, competing party colours, buntings and loudspeakers at their loudest—elements that gave Indian elections their drama and made them a living, throbbing experiment in popular participation—would be brought under the scanner of the Seshan-inspired Model Code of Conduct.

The CEC's men trailed the candidates, captured footage of walls defaced, inducements offered and booths captured. The new regulations certainly brought much-needed order to a system that was endearingly chaotic but also undeniably flawed. The celebrated Indian election was free and fair more in theory than in practice.

Over the next two decades, Seshan's successors would improve on the model, holding elections in phases, placing the polling process on surveillance and virtually eliminating the rigging and manipulation that had been rampant earlier.

The May 2007 Assembly election in UP would show just how much elections had changed in the nineteen years since my first election experience in 1988. Back then violence was considered integral to the election process. Stories of rigging and booth-capturing were legion, especially in the badlands of UP and Bihar.

In the 1989 Lok Sabha election in UP, violence spread to even the high-profile constituency of Amethi where the sitting prime minister, Rajiv Gandhi, was pitted against his Janata Dal opponent, Rajmohan Gandhi. Hooligans stormed polling booths, scared away voters and damaged vehicles—all in full view of the international media, which predictably lapped up the sensational turn to the Gandhi versus Gandhi fight. My own car was battered, and as I took in the destruction, news came that Sanjay Singh, Rajiv Gandhi's former buddy and now a member of V.P. Singh's inner circle, had been shot and wounded.

Travelling in UP just under two decades later in 2007, however, I was struck by the calm and quiet of the Assembly election. The state completed this election in seven phases, reporting not even a stray instance of violence. The transformation was the greater for the near silent political revolution accompanying it. This election would witness UP—once the unquestioned bastion of the Congress, and then of the Bharatiya Janata Party (BJP)—handing out a clear majority to Mayawati, the self-described '*Dalit ki beti*' (daughter of the Dalits), a leader of the Bahujan Samaj Party (BSP) founded by her mentor Kanshi Ram just over two decades earlier.

In the 1980s and the early 1990s, the intimidation of Dalits by higher-caste Hindus was commonplace. In 2007, with the Election Commission on guard and Mayawati's victory on the anvil, Dalits would vote en masse for the Bahujan Samaj Party (BSP); for some Dalits, this would be the first time they had voted since India gained independence. A superlative achievement by any yardstick.

Nonetheless, for all the refinement of elections today, I was lucky to have witnessed the classic, untrammelled version in the 1988 by-election and in the 1989 and 1991 general elections. Each brought a new shade of colour and a new message. In 1988 it was pink, the colour of V.P. Singh's flag. In 1989 it was the Janata Dal's green. And in 1991 it was the BJP's saffron. The high point of V.P. Singh's brief reign was the Mandal Commission's recommendations on reserved quotas for the Other Backward Classes (OBCs) in government jobs and educational institutions. This, in turn, triggered the Mandir backlash—when the Babri mosque at Ayodhya in UP was brought down by members of Hindu religious groups who wanted to build a temple to Ram on that site. If Mandal spelt the end of upper-caste dominance of politics, Mandir made religious sectarianism acceptable, in some quarters even fashionable.

Indeed by 1991, saffron was in fierce ascendant, blazing through UP and searing its way into the collective Indian consciousness. For the Congress, the grim symbolism of this would be hard to miss. From the Congress tricolour of green, white and saffron, the green (later to became the chosen flag of left wing–minority–backward caste politics) and saffron (to become the favoured hue for right wing–majority–Hindu politics) would seem to have torn themselves away, leaving the party clutching at the barren middle. The white in the tricolour signified peace and stability; on their own, the green and the saffron could assume virulent forms, and by itself the white recalled the peace and stability of the graveyard.

The by-election of 1988 was a teaser-trailer in other ways too. I met Kanshi Ram for the first time during this campaign. No sooner was the election announced than Allahabad's walls were plastered with the BSP's elephant symbol and the party's blue flag was fluttering everywhere. At that point, hardly anyone knew what these represented—the contest was between V.P. Singh and Sunil Shastri, so who was this mysterious third party? For journalists fixated on V.P. Singh, Kanshi Ram was an irritant; in turn, Kanshi Ram and his band of dedicated volunteers held the press in contempt.

It was after several frustrating attempts that I managed to attend a BSP rally and later spent hours chatting with the party cadre, learning why they hated being called Harijan (god's children) and why they detested the media. 'Harijan' was condescending: 'Are we bastards that we must be called god's children?' As for the media, it was biased, upper casteist and full of venom for the BSP. When I finally met Kanshi Ram, he denounced the Congress and the BJP as being *Manuwadi* or casteist: if one was *sapnath* (a snake), the other was *nagnath* (a cobra). I had never heard these phrases before and I was fascinated. Over the coming years, I would keenly watch the BSP's progress, marvelling at Mayawati's meteoric rise from unsung understudy to empress of UP.

Allahabad 1988 also provided a rare glimpse into the future world of alliances and coalition governments. Though the Janata Party, formed in 1977, was an internal coalition of five political groupings, it took a whole decade before, in 1989, that the coalition era would truly be inaugurated.

The V.P. Singh-led National Front government was an alliance within an alliance within an alliance. The Janata Dal, the National Front's main constituent, contained within it the Janata Party, the Lok Dal and a clutch of former Congressmen. The National Front, in turn, was a coalition of four parties—the Janata Dal, the Telugu Desam Party (TDP), the Dravida Munnetra Kazhagam (DMK) and the Asom Gana Parishad (AGP). Finally, the National Front was supported from the outside by the BJP and the Left parties. Thus there were at least eight groups within the government and, unsurprisingly, the arrangement was unstable and collapsed in eleven months! Yet it would prove to be the prototype on which future coalitions were based.

The seeds of the National Front coalition were sown in Allahabad. Though the main contest was between the Congress and

V.P. Singh, the latter was backed by virtually the entire opposition. A lasting image of that time is a public meeting attended by a galaxy of leaders, among them N.T. Rama Rao of the TDP, Atal Bihari Vajpayee from the BJP, the Lok Dal's Devi Lal and P. Rajeswara Rao from the Communist Party of India (CPI). As Allahabad watched, the men linked hands and raised a salute to V.P. Singh—a symbolic gesture that foreshadowed their coming together to form India's first real coalition government.

The National Front coalition would break up. Yet, in doing so, it would alter Indian politics in a way few would have thought possible at that time.

A MIRACLE CALLED INDIAN DEMOCRACY

The website of the Election Commission of India, like all governmental offerings, is excruciatingly dull; but it is a fund of information. In its archives are details of every single election contested in independent India—in all, fifteen Lok Sabha elections, 309 Assembly elections and a dozen or so in states which have since been reorganized or renamed or dissolved.

There is also an enormous amount of election trivia: size of the electorate, number of political parties, voting percentages, number and spread of polling stations and so on, besides hundreds of press releases, manuals and handbooks of instructions for polling and returning officers.

What if an absorbing narrative were to breathe life into these statistics? The facts are so remarkable that you wonder how and why India holds together, how and why democracy thrives in this unlikeliest of countries, and how and why this saga has missed being told and retold in the manner of a sacred mythological epic.

The truth is that Indian democracy is truly home-grown; compared to the West where the upper echelons feel more engaged with democracy, it works in reverse here—with the elite's dissociation from democracy (also known as the 'secession of the rich'; a new term for this group is Resident Non-Indians) contrasting sharply with the mass embrace of adult franchise.

Though elections have hardly improved the lot of the poor and the wretched, surveys conducted by several organizations, including the well-respected Centre for the Study of Developing Societies, tell us that they feel uplifted and empowered by the act of casting their vote. This must explain the underclass's sense of pride and ownership towards elections and why this segment, though lacking the education of the wealthy, is so politically plugged in. On the election beat, I have always been amazed by the amount of information to be had from the ordinary voter; amazed too that people so poor and deprived could be so positive about an event that still doesn't touch their immediate lives.

Nothing captures this paradox as does the eastern state of Bihar: abysmally poor, low on social indices, and yet full of sparkle. Travelling in the state for the 2000 Assembly election, I was struck by the eloquence of its people; they seemed wiser in many ways than those who condemned them as illiterate and backward.

In the Dalit bastis of Jehanabad, people wore tattered clothes, worked as bonded labour, suffered the indignity of not being able to exercise their franchise, but had an innate understanding of democracy and greatly valued their vote. In Pai Bigha, where eleven Dalits had been killed by the Bhumiar-led Ranvir Sena the previous year, the village *karta* (headman) spoke of his constitutional rights and explained the Sena's hostility in terms of 'feudal systems' and 'land ownership'. I recalled Laloo Prasad Yadav's words that while he was far from giving his people *swarg* (heaven), he could claim to have given them *swar* (voice). At that time I had dismissed it as Laloo-speak. Standing in Pai Bigha, I connected with the deeper meaning of the words.

Years later, during the 2009 election, I would meet Mohammad Faheem, a young Muslim boy, jobless and very obviously poor, in a backward qasba in Sambhal in western UP. Bright-eyed and earnest, Faheem backed Manmohan Singh for prime minister, because he had 'managed India's economy brilliantly'. I asked him about rising prices. 'Yes, that hurts,' he said, 'but we need to take a larger view. Sixteen banks have gone *diwaliya* (bankrupt) in the US, none here.'

My eyes misted over. So much wisdom, and we call these people ordinary?

The wonder of Indian democracy is the greater for the odds against its birth and the odds against its survival. Up until the 1950s, the Indian nation was a problematic construct. There were three separate Indias at the time of independence—the provinces directly under the British Empire, the 544 princely states under British suzerainty, and the enclaves under French and Portuguese occupation.

Many of the princes were despots with just a few acres of land. Others presided over states so large they maintained armies comparable in size and competence to the Indian Army. Loyalty to the Indian nation was an alien notion in many parts of the country at the time; enormous persuasion and imagination—for the latter read force—was required to bring them around. The 'one nation, one people' slogan of Hindutva jingoism is quite clearly of recent origin.

At the end of a gargantuan exercise, completed before the first election in 1951–52, fourteen administrative units emerged from 544 states. It was a stupendous feat. Sardar Patel, the architect of unification, rejoiced in it even as he worried about the future: 'Almost overnight we have introduced in these States the superstructure of a modern system of government. The inspiration and stimulus has come from above rather than below and unless the transplanted growth takes a healthy root in the soil, there will be a danger of collapse and chaos.'*

Patel's fears were not unfounded. If integration imposed modernity on an essentially feudal sub-structure, the existence of a multitude of castes, communities, tribes, religions and languages,

*V.P. Menon, *Integration of the Indian States*, Orient Longman, 490.

each a sub-nation in itself, added further layers to the complexity as did extreme poverty and debilitating illiteracy, not to mention the communal spectre raised by the violent partition of the country. The easiest way out of this mess would have been for the new country to have become a military dictatorship. If not that, a Hindu India would have been perfect foil to the newly-created Islamic Republic next door. Or at the least the founding fathers could have restricted voting to the educated. Yet modern India opted without hesitation for democracy with universal adult suffrage.

Had Patel been alive today, he would have been a proud man: sixty-two years after its troubled birth, India stands as a lone democracy surrounded by countries with different degrees of dictatorship. Never has an Indian government been undemocratically overthrown. The administrative baton has passed from government to government through elections held without a break except for a single aberration—the Emergency of 1975—thanks to which the general election of 1976 was delayed by a year. Yet it is a tribute to the democratic spirit of India that Indira Gandhi called the 1977 Lok Sabha election and lost it too.

FRAGMENTATION AND CONSOLIDATION

The sustainability of the Indian parliamentary system is no longer in doubt. If democracy is about devolution of power and greater representation, then Indian democracy has struck deep roots. The evidence is in the astonishing transformation of the political landscape. If India's biggest achievement post-independence was the conversion of hundreds of small enclaves, potentates and estates into compact, manageable states, six decades later the trend would seem to be in the opposite direction with soaring sub-regional ambitions causing smaller and smaller states to emerge from the bowels of the bigger states.

There are other signs that the once centralized polity is fast fragmenting: political parties have mushroomed; regional parties are not just growing in numbers, they all want a role at the Centre, which means that they must raid each other's bases even as they eat into the vote banks of the so-called national parties. UP provides graphic evidence of this cut-throat competition. In 1989, the Congress lost its upper-caste and Muslim votes to the BJP and the Samajwadi Party (SP). By 1991, it had lost its Dalit votes to the BSP. A decade later, the BJP would find its upper-caste base poached upon by the SP and the BSP.

And yet curiously there is also the reverse tendency towards consolidation—not the gargantuan consolidation of the earlier, single-party kind, but small consolidations within the overall trend of fragmentation. The examples are once again to be found in UP—in the 2009 resurgence of the Congress, and in the attempts at reaching out by previously exclusivist identity-based parties.

The Congress's revival in UP was in the order of things: for if the Congress's rivals fattened themselves on the party's vote banks, it stood to reason that the cycle of poaching would at some point benefit the Congress. The Congress won twenty-one Lok Sabha seats by snatching small shares of votes—Muslims from the SP, forward castes from the BJP and non-Jatav Dalits from the BSP.

Clearly, to be able to win in UP, a political party must try and approximate the old Congress formula of bringing three or more castes under one umbrella. In its heyday, the Congress relied on a combination of Brahmins, Muslims and Dalits. The SP grew by adding Thakurs to its Muslim–Yadav base, while the BSP captured office by standing the Congress formula on its head. Earlier, the umbrella was large enough to hold whole caste groups; in today's fragmented polity, parties must compete for fractions of the caste groups, resulting in a profusion of smaller umbrellas, each holding within it slices of two or more castes, and each held by a different party. To understand just how small the umbrella can get, consider the fact that the twenty-one seats the Congress won in UP in 2009 came from a mere 18.25 per cent of the votes polled.

What explains the opposing impulses of fragmentation and consolidation? Fragmentation is a factor of caste and regional aspiration while consolidation arises from the urge to succeed. The most breathtaking example of this is the transformation of the BSP from an abrasive, exclusivist party to one propagating inclusion. The BSP's *Brahmin jodo abhiyan* (take Brahmins along campaign) was audacious beyond imagination. This was the same party to which had been credited the slogan, '*Tilak, tarazu aur talwar, joote maro inko chaar*' (Thrash the Brahmin, kshatriya and bania). With the change in the party's strategy, the slogan too changed, to '*Hathi nahi, Ganesh hai, Brahma, Vishnu, Mahesh hai*' (It is not just the elephant [the BSP's electoral symbol], but also Ganesh, Brahma, Vishnu and Mahesh).

Who would have thought that Mayawati, who rained abuse on upper castes, calling them—among other names—Manuwadi and Aryan, would come to embrace them? That her new-age slogan would include the Hindu divine trinity? The BSP's benign re-birth might seem paradoxical when judged by its history: it was a party born in opposition to Manuwad whose core voters were historically oppressed by upper castes. Yet the party went against its grain in order to have a shot at power.

The aggression of the early BSP consolidated its core Dalit vote. The more Kanshi Ram and Mayawati targeted Manuwadis (specifically, upper-caste Hindus), the more Dalits gravitated towards them. Today, such is the identification of UP's Dalits with the BSP that close to 80 per cent vote for it. But the core vote was not enough to win the BSP power, and hence its pursuit of the same upper castes that it so loudly denounced. The strategy fetched it brilliant dividends in the 2007 state election, though in the 2009 general election, the party's vote share would dip by three percentage points, indicating a measure of disillusionment with the Mayawati government.

So, a decade into the new millennium, it is a deeply complex political India that we confront. On the one hand, the polity is fragmenting with sub-nationalism assuming micro forms: for instance, two new parties contested the 2009 general election—the

Praja Rajyam in Andhra Pradesh and the Desiya Murpoku Dravida Kazhagam in Tamil Nadu. On the other, there is evidence of some consolidation—within every state, parties are adding to their core constituencies to try and secure a vote share large enough to win power in the assemblies. At the same time there is a clear third trend: of once fiercely provincial state parties expanding into other states to raise their national profile; of them wanting to transcend the narrow, subaltern image that at one time was so important to their politics and to their sense of who they were.

For political parties seeking to enlarge their roles at the Centre, the national-party tag is a status symbol, an affirmation that they are in the big league. Mayawati and Laloo Prasad Yadav would be loath to be called regional leaders, though in actual fact their areas of influence remain UP and Bihar. Indeed, today every regional satrap, from Mayawati through Mulayam Singh Yadav, Chandrababu Naidu, Laloo Prasad Yadav, Nitish Kumar and Ram Vilas Paswan, is a shadow prime minister in his or her own perception.

Whatever the eventual outcome of these overlapping trends, one thing seems certain: India is culturally, socially, demographically and politically too diverse for it to be ruled by any single party with an extreme vision. The exclusivist *bahujan* (Dalit)-based BSP metamorphosed into an inclusivist *sarvajan* (all communities) party to achieve majority in UP. The minority-bashing BJP ruled at the Centre but only by shedding its bigotry, at least outwardly, to appease its coalition partners. Even Narendra Modi, he of the Gujarat anti-Muslim pogrom, had to don the mask of 'development' to deflect attention from his sordid past.

FROM THE 1950s TO THE MILLENNIUM

The first Lok Sabha election was held over five months between October 1951 and February 1952. In all, twenty-six states, excluding Jammu and Kashmir and the Andaman and Nicobar Islands, went to the polls which, in a resounding slap to those who doubted the wisdom of the Indian masses, saw a voter turnout of 61.2 per cent. Yet this was a small beginning.

Over the next fifty-seven years, Indian elections would become the largest such exercise in the world, reaching state-of-the-art standards in the 2004 general election with the Election Commission of India dumping the traditional ballot paper for the sophistication of the Electronic Voting Machine (EVM). In that election, forty-six foreign delegates would watch wonderstruck as Indian voters—the bulk of them poor and semi-literate, and many disabled and needing to be carried to the polling booths—used the EVM as if born to it. In the 2009 general election, the Election Commission of India would enroll 713.77 million voters, deploying a polling staff of 47 lakh to oversee an impossibly vast network of 8.34 lakh polling stations, some of them located on terrain accessible only by helicopter. When bad weather prevented landing, voters would trek to the booths, escorted by army and paramilitary personnel.

For an idea of the scale and grandeur of today's election as well as the socio-political changes it represents, compare the following sets of statistics.

The second Lok Sabha election, 1957

Size of electorate: 17.3 crore
Number of states and Union Territories: 17
Number of political parties: 15 (4 national and 11 state parties)
Total seats: 494
Number of candidates: 1,519
Number of independents: 481
Share of votes:
  National parties: 73.08 per cent
  State parties: 7.60 per cent
  Independents: 19.32 per cent
Congress performance: 371 of 494 seats for a vote share of 47.78 per cent
Cost of holding the election: Rs 5.9 crore

The fourteenth Lok Sabha election 2004

Size of electorate: 67.14 crore
Number of states and Union Territories: 35
Number of political parties: 753
(6 national parties, 45 state parties and 702 registered unrecognized parties)
Total seats: 542
Number of candidates: 5,435
Number of independents: 2,385
Share of votes:
National parties: 62.89 per cent (56 per cent excluding BSP and NCP)
State parties: 28.9 per cent (36 per cent including BSP and NCP)
Registered unrecognized parties: 3.96 per cent
Independents: 4.25 per cent
Congress performance: 145 of 543 seats for a vote share of 26.53 per cent
Cost of holding the election: Rs 1300 crore

In the fifteenth Lok Sabha election held in 2009, the number of registered unrecognized parties rose to 1000. But more incredibly, the Congress, exceeding the wildest expectations, crossed the 200-seat mark.

The statistics would hold within them three different narratives: first the remarkable journey of the Congress; second, its attempted displacement by the BJP; and, finally, the growth and significance of the regional and subaltern parties.

THREE DIFFERENT NARRATIVES: THE CONGRESS, THE BJP AND THE REGIONAL PARTIES

As the party of independence, led almost entirely by members of the Nehru–Gandhi family, the Congress enjoyed first-mover advantage for the first three decades. Through this time, the party had a two-thirds majority with a vote share between 44 and 47 per cent. Power sat lightly on Jawaharlal Nehru. He was gentle and broad-minded with a progressive, if impractical, world vision; he might have been a benign king to his adoring subjects.

Indira Gandhi evoked love and hate in equal measure, and the Congress under her became authoritarian and repressive. Yet Indira showed daring in office—bank nationalization, thumbing her nose at the United States, the Bangladesh war, etc.—thanks to which she would occupy a unique perch in history, going beyond Nehru in the popular imagination and earning the grudging admiration of peers and successors. Generations to follow would vote her India's best prime minister.

Indira concentrated power in her hands, demolished institutions, treated the constitution as if it belonged in the waste bin and heaped humiliation on her opponents. The slogan 'India is Indira, Indira is India' bespoke of an arrogance that would become the Congress's trademark for all time to come. A quarter-century after Indira's death, the Congress continues to come across as haughty and imperious, despite a steep fall in popular support and despite losing elections four times between 1989 and 2004 (1989, 1996, 1998 and 1999). As in 1977, each of these defeats was brought about by an opposition stirred to unite against the Congress because of the party's overweening sense of its own uniqueness and importance.

Indira Gandhi chopped and changed state leaders at will. A cartoon of the early 1980s had Congressmen lining up to greet Indira, only to have her point to one of them and say: 'Hey you! You are the next chief minister. What is your name?' Rajiv Gandhi, though closer to Nehru in deportment, was not above showing a subordinate his place. In 1982 when he held the post of general secretary of the All India Congress Committee (AICC), he publicly rebuked then Andhra Pradesh Congress chief minister T. Anjaiah, unaware that this would unleash a wave of Telugu pride and rebound on him in the form of the TDP led by N.T. Rama Rao.

The Congress under Rajiv Gandhi was also bitterly opposed to the Mandal Commission report, refusing to admit that the commission's recommendations had a significance that went beyond job reservation. Mandal represented unfulfilled subaltern aspirations and it unleashed what French scholar Christophe Jaffrelot was to call 'India's silent revolution'. The OBC upsurge changed the class and character of Indian politics, ending upper-caste dominance in Parliament and in the state assemblies, and leading to a spurt in the growth of regional and identity-based parties.

The Congress's conceit is explained in part by the charisma of the Nehru–Gandhi clan, held to be the nearest thing we have to royalty. But it is also explained by the party's pan-India presence and its strong vote base. In the 1999 Lok Sabha election, the party crashed to its lowest-ever tally of 114 seats. Yet, even at its worst, the Congress had a vote share of 28 per cent, a 21 percentage point slide measured from its own high of 49 per cent in 1984, but nationally the highest vote share held by any party.

The party's born-to-rule attitude was reflected in the September 1998 Panchmarhi resolution which rejected coalition building as a route to power. Panchmarhi happened in the backdrop of a momentous event—the assumption of office by a thirteen-party coalition led by Atal Bihari Vajpayee. The BJP, thirsting for power but unable to attain it on its own, had wisely reached out to allies. The lesson this taught the Congress was valuable; yet, even in the 1999 general election, the Congress chose isolation to alliance-making. In 2004, the astute Sonia Gandhi, gauging the restlessness in the party—Congresspersons hate being in opposition—embraced coalitional politics to dramatic effect. The Congress returned to power at the head of the multi-party United Progressive Alliance (UPA). The Congress had beaten the BJP at its own game. However, the party's rank and file strained against the limitations the compromise imposed on them. Unable and unwilling to accept a situation where previously subservient regional satraps dictated to them, they beseeched the 'high command' to rethink the alliances about to be finalized in UP and Bihar for the 2009 general election.

As the UPA's first term came to an end, the tensions bubbling under the surface burst into the open. With the RJD, the Lok Jan Shakti and the SP deciding to go their own separate ways (after seat-sharing talks failed), the UPA went into the 2009 election unrecognizably truncated. It was a crazy gamble, yet the Congress leadership, now fortified by the presence of the young Rahul Gandhi, was inexplicably gung-ho, especially about going it alone in the heartland. At an informal meeting with a small group of journalists, the Gandhi son spelt out the thinking behind this: alliances were useful in the short term but they demoralized the cadre and shut off growth avenues. The Congress needed to look at the long term without bothering about victory and defeat, he said. Rahul disagreed with the argument that India's diversity was best represented by a multi-party government; rather than depending on other parties to provide it, the Congress ought to accommodate the diversity within itself—by allowing fresh talent to come in through free, fair and regularly held organizational elections.

In the event, Verdict 2009 proved to be a Congress blockbuster. The 206 seats the party won in the fifteenth Lok Sabha election had been made possible by a uniformly good showing across the country, a better-than-expected landslide in Andhra Pradesh, and, most amazingly, by a bravura performance in the heartland. The Congress picked up twenty-one seats in UP, coming second behind the SP, but finishing ahead of the BSP.

Verdict 2009 was undoubtedly historic. The UPA was the first government since 1984 to have returned after completing a full term in office. More to the point, it had returned, not on the back of an emotional issue—assassination, war, etc.—but had been judged on performance. The precedent to this went all the way back to the 1971 general election which Indira Gandhi won on the platform of *garibi hatao* (remove poverty). But even this comparison would fall short given that 1971 was a mid-term election. The UPA's second mandate would stand out by other yardsticks. Election 2009 was fought against the backdrop of the world's worst slowdown since the 1930s and its impact was felt in India too. But, incredibly, the UPA government faced little anti-incumbency, because of a series of welfare measures such as the National Rural Employment Guarantee Act (NREGA), the waiver of farm loans, the Right to Information Act, etc. And although reports from elsewhere suggested that the UPA was on the whole ahead, I would see the pro-Congress mood for myself in UP where I travelled extensively through the election month. I was not convinced of this at first, but as the month wore on, I got used to people telling me that they respected Manmohan Singh, that he was the man to trust in difficult economic times. Rahul Gandhi topped the charts as a future leader while the troika of Sonia–Rahul–Manmohan Singh got high marks for decency. Yet for all the groundswell of opinion in favour of the Congress, I was not sure it would win as many seats as it eventually did because UP's distinctive recent characteristic had been the assertion of caste and identity politics.

That the Congress defied the odds to make a return in India's prized political state suggests a fatigue with the same politics that defeated it in the first place. Congress persons from UP would describe this as the end of *jaat-paat* (caste) politics. However, on current evidence, it is far from clear that we are witnessing a long-term trend of Congress revival (or of the decline of coalitions)—whether in UP or in India as a whole. The Congress won twenty-one seats on a smallish base of 18.52 per cent in UP, and country-wide it won 206 seats though polling only 28.5 per cent of total votes cast. Compare this with 2004 when the party won 145 seats for a vote share of 26.53 per cent (two percentage points less than in 2009) and 1999 when it had only114 seats though polling 28.30 per cent votes (0.02 percentage points less in 2009).

The story of the BJP—formerly the Jan Sangh—is in many ways the opposite of the Congress's. The Jan Sangh played no significant role in India's independence and carried the taint of communalism which limited its appeal to a narrow, rabble-rousing upper-caste base. Wherever possible the Jan Sangh formed small provincial alliances, but the party acquired a national profile only in 1977 when it merged into the Janata Party.

The BJP would be repeatedly shunned because of the politics of Hindutva. Nonetheless, it fought hard to end its isolation—by co-opting the lower castes (the term social engineering was first made famous not by Mayawati but by BJP ideologue K.N. Govindacharya), and keeping an eye out for future allies. The BJP recognized alliance-making as a means to power, and power it wanted at all costs—both for power itself and to deepen and widen its vote base. The BJP has been in the vanguard of most anti-Congress coalitions—from the earliest coalitions formed in the northern states to coalitions formed at the Centre in 1977, 1989, 1998 and 1999 (it headed the last two).

If the Congress was arrogant towards allies and made a fetish of its supposed superiority, with the BJP the logic worked in reverse. The BJP sought out partners who were at once attracted to and repelled by it. The BJP was the natural ally of parties that opposed the Congress. But the association meant loss of Muslim votes. By 1996 the Babri Masjid stigma had made the BJP so much the untouchable that a Janata Dal-led coalition (called the United Front) took the help of the Congress to keep the party out of power. But the Congress's vanity would rear its head again, resulting in the rupture of the United Front, most of whose constituents walked into the waiting arms of the BJP. The BJP's 1998 alliance included such die-hard anti-Hindutva parties as the TDP, the National Conference and the Trinamool Congress. The self-proclaimed 'Hindi-Hindu-Hindutva' party's 1999 alliance even managed to accommodate the atheist and anti-Hindi DMK.

Post the birth of the BJP, Indian politics has alternated between anti-Congressism and anti-BJPism. In the anti-Congressism phase allies coalesced around the Hindutva party, only to move away when Hindutva became the larger threat. In the 2004 election, the pendulum once again swung against the BJP; and though the party psyched itself into believing it was on a hat-trick, in reality it had been badly hit by the departure of allies such as the National Conference and the Lok Janshakti Party.

By 2009 the tide should have turned in the Hidutva party's favour. Yet, a full five years after the Congress had been in power, the on-again, off-again pattern of relationship between the BJP and its allies broke. In this election, a sizeable section of the regional parties, now led by a Left Front swearing vengeance against the Congress, would form a loose front against Sonia Gandhi's party. But the BJP, far from being able to capitalize on the mood shift, would continue to lose allies, the hardest blow being dealt by the Biju Janata Dal exiting on the eve of the election. The deserters, nine of them by now, all cited one reason for opting out: the BJP's anti-minority policies. The exodus combined fatally with the BJP's image—of a party irretrievably wedded to old shibboleths. Verdict 2009 set the BJP back by two decades—the party's tally of 116 seats for a vote share of 18.8 per cent was the lowest since 1989.

Like the BJP, the regional parties grew in opposition to the Congress, but where the BJP is centrist–upper casteist in orientation, the regional parties are mostly OBC or Dalit-based and advocate a virulent brand of federalism. The earliest regional parties date back to before independence, among them the Shiromani Akali Dal in Punjab and the Jammu and Kashmir-based National Conference. The trend picked up momentum after the formation of the rabidly pro-Hindu Shiv Sena in 1966 followed by the (then) separatist DMK in 1967. Today there are more regional parties than one can count: as against seven national parties listed by the Election Commission for the 2009 election, there were forty-four regional parties and 1,000 registered unrecognized parties.

The regional parties form a huge block but they have never been able to leverage this to come to power—except when propped up by a mainstream party. The reason is twofold. First, in the history of the Lok Sabha, the non-Congress, non-Jan Sangh/BJP parties have never held the majority of the seats. This happened despite the fact that the regional block commanded an impressive share of the vote. In 2009, for instance, the BJP and the Congress together polled only 47.35 per cent of the votes cast, though winning as many as 322 seats. The second factor is the lack of unity among the regional players. In UP, the BSP and the SP are adversaries. In Tamil Nadu, the DMK is implacably opposed to the AIADMK. This mutual incompatibility, not to forget the competing egos of state satraps, all but rules out the regional parties uniting to claim power—even if at some future date they win a majority of seats. The Congress's second successive win in 2009 pointed to the failure of the BJP, of course. But it was also a stinging indictment of the third front brand of opportunistic politics.

SO ALIKE, SO DIFFERENT: MAYAWATI AND NARENDRA MODI ON THE CAMPAIGN TRAIL

Which politicians from among the current crowd would qualify as the personalities of the millennium? Without any doubt Mayawati and Narendra Modi. Mayawati and Modi tie on all counts: charisma, popularity, impact and sheer grit. But they stand out for another reason: both won theoretically implausible victories, in May and December 2007 respectively.

Nevertheless, they couldn't be more dissimilar. Mayawati draws phenomenal crowds who listen wordlessly to her droning oratory, stirring themselves only to shout '*Behen Mayawati zindabad*'. Modi is a riveting demagogue and his audiences, though comparatively smaller, throb to his fiery rhetoric.

Personality differences aside, the stories of Mayawati and Modi could be the stories of two contrasting Indias at the turn of the millennium. One is desperately poor and underdeveloped, but alive to the dynamics of socio-political mobility. The other is prosperous and on the development fast track, but without the caste-churning necessary to shift power—this is part of the reason for the BJP's uninterrupted rule of Gujarat.

The public reactions to Mayawati and Modi reflect this divergence. Modi draws his voters from across Gujarat but is extremely popular among the urban better-off—the same people who find Mayawati obnoxious, crude and unacceptably self-obsessed. Those who love Modi, love his arrogance and love his unconcealed love of himself. To this class, Modi is 'Mard Modi'—macho, powerful, proud of his Hindu warrior image, and for that reason unforgiving of anyone with a different world view.

Mayawati's supporters are crowded around the bottom of the social ladder, with Dalits forming the core. To them she represents the dream that they would like to live, and it is a dream that they live through her. This class does not despise Modi as his supporters despise Mayawati. But it feels no affinity for him.

I interviewed Mayawati obsessively through the 2007 Assembly election in UP arriving at her rally in Sultanpur to a most astonishing sight. The messiah would show up hours later but thousands and thousands of women, babies tucked under their arms, were already trudging on foot to a ground that would soon fill to overflowing. Over the next five hours they would sit motionless, not taking a break, not even asking to quench their parched throats, as lesser functionaries sang paeans to Maya's upper caste–Dalit social engineering, and held out hopes of her 'early' arrival.

Mayawati's arrival broke the discipline but only momentarily. The crowds that had risen like a tide for a view of 'Behenji', just as quickly sank down, watched over by volunteers of the Bahujan Samaj Force, a stern paramilitary-like organization in charge of audience control. On stage Mayawati, in reality quite tiny, looked large, almost towering. Her speech was without humour, without the flourishes of her rival. But it was no less effective. As Maya departed, her voters rose too and filled the far corners of the meeting ground with full-throated cries of 'Jai Bhim'.

Mayawati's rallies are brisk, conducted with military precision and imbued with a sense of mission—no fussing around her, no garlanding, no flatterers sneaking up to her for favours. Modi's rallies are equally mesmerizing but because of the crackling chemistry between him and his audience. On the campaign trail in the December 2007 Gujarat election, I caught up with him in Mahua, off the Bhavnagar coast. In the audience were dozens of crazed fans, all wearing life-like Modi masks. As the real Modi bantered and provoked, the multitude of Modis in the audience clapped and cheered, revealing quite clearly that in Gujarat the Modi cult had touched bizarre heights.

In the run-up to the election, Modi (he cut me in mid-sentence when, during an interview, I asked him about Muslims) had vowed that he would not deflect from the theme of Gujarat's development. But with reports of Sonia Gandhi drawing massive crowds in Gujarat, Modi swiftly transited to Hindutva, rousing his voters to near hysteria with deliberately provocative allusions. Now it was Ram and Sita that had them charged up: Modi asking, 'Tell me, was Ram born, was Sita born?' to roars of 'Yes, yes.' In another meeting it was Sohrabuddin Sheikh, who was killed in a fake encounter in 2007, that had the crowd screaming. Modi asked them, 'What should I have done to him?' and the response was, 'Kill him, kill him.'

Modi fought this election with one hand tied behind his back, thanks to an abrasive personality that alienated much of his own party, the Sangh Parivar and his administration. Indeed, in this election, the Rashtriya Swayamsevak Sangh (RSS) and the Vishwa Hindu Parishad (VHP) fetched up on the same side as Modi's opponents. But in the end, the opposition proved unequal to his popular appeal. He connected with his voters directly—over party, parivar and government.

DEMYSTIFYING ELECTIONS

We saw earlier that the poor and the oppressed have a greater stake in democracy than the materially better off. For the disengaged, democracy is nothing if not a euphemism for frequent regime change, which in turn is shorthand for delays, instability and uncertainty, not to mention corruption and endless red tape. A multi-party alliance, with its discomfiting imagery of a bandwagon of wobbly parties, strikes terror in the elite heart.

Prima facie, the cynicism is not unfounded. Democracy as a lofty ideal is a good distance from democracy as it works on the ground in India. Indeed, like a Charles Chaplin film, Indian democracy can be accessed at two levels. In its dead serious avatar it is about the might of the vote, the devolution of power, the constitutional vision of equality and equity.

But equally significant is the tragicomic side: splits and mergers, a proliferation of parties, defection, rigging, purchase of votes. A lot of this has serious implications; but a lot is also—unintentionally—funny. Since the first general election in 1951–52 political parties have multiplied with the same ease as they have divided and subdivided; that is, over this period many new parties have emerged as the offspring of the old.

The Socialist Party split from the Congress in 1948; it spawned the Praja Socialist Party (PSP) only to rediscover its Socialist Party identity. The reborn Socialist Party then reunited with the PSP to form the Samyukta Socialist Party (SSP) from which re-emerged the PSP. Even as the Socialists made merry, came a procession of kisan parties, all variants of the latter-day Lok Dal. The Socialist and the Lok Dal factions merged into the Janata Party which transmogrified into the Janata Dal. The rump became a one-man party while the Janata Dal, in turn, splintered into countless Janata Dal, Lok Dal and Socialist factions.

How does one track a family tree such as this? Sometimes help can come from unexpected quarters. When, in November 2007, the Karnataka-based Janata Dal (Secular) was in the throes of one more rebirth, party leader M.P. Prakash came to the rescue of journalists struggling with their math. The Janata Dal had split thirteen times since its 1989 debut, he informed us, adding helpfully, 'No one need be surprised if the parivar splits for the fourteenth, fifteenth or sixteenth time.'

The Janata Dal at one time held Laloo Prasad, Nitish Kumar, Ram Vilas Paswan, Mulayam Singh Yadav, Naveen Patnaik and Deve Gowda. Today all six men run their own parties.

This is small change compared to the 702 'registered unrecognized parties' that participated in 2004 Lok Sabha elections. (The number rose to 1,000 in 2009.) Of the 702, a vast number, 530 to be precise, do not even show up on the Election Commission of India's website. Of the 172 that are listed, as many as 109 were shown as having own 0 seats for a vote share of 0.00 per cent! Did this mean these parties polled no votes in the seats they contested? No. A more likely explanation is that they did receive some votes but the numbers were too low to register on the national radar. The 530 consigned to oblivion clearly polled no votes at all.

The bulk of the unrecognized parties are self-evidently non-serious. Some are also strangely named. Where else but in this country will you find a party by the name, The Religion of Man Revolving Political Party of India (TRMRPPI for short)?

Others could have dipped into a cache of familiar prefixes and suffixes, judging by how many of them turn out to be permutations and combinations of Bharatiya, Rashtriya, Janata, Samata, Samajwadi, Lok, Jan, Bahujan, Shakti, Dal, Manch, etc. At last count, there were 122 parties with the prefix Bharatiya, thirty-eight with the prefix Akhil Bharatiya and twenty-four with the prefix All-India. And these are parties that do not even count locally.

Is this proliferation of political parties a testimony to India's diversity? At one level it is. But their existence could be to collect funds, to launder money, to access official facilities, to grab land, to cut political deals, or simply to gain respect. The better ones could be dummies used by the biggies to cut into the votes of their opponents. *Vote katwa* (vote cutting) parties are legion in UP and Bihar. Once they've performed their vote-cutting function, these parties typically leave the fray. Children of political veterans float parties to keep the house allotted to the father. Some parties cause havoc just by being present. For example, an opponent of the RJD could float a similar sounding Rashtriya Janatantrik Dal to confuse the former's voters.

There are other elements of the Indian election that are at once amusing, fascinating and disquieting. From the outside, the party system appears quite well ordered, with the ruling party and opposition rigidly defined, their ideologies sharply contrasting and the two sides perennially at war. On the ground, politicians are often one happy family, defecting easily from party to party, hopping as easily from ideology to ideology, and able to justify each move and counter-move with the same absolute conviction.

A friend and I discovered this apparently simple fact of electoral life while travelling in UP to cover the Lok Sabha election of 1989. By day, we would find the politicians in combat mode—snarling at one another, hurling charges, and full of righteous indignation about the opponent's politics, policies and ideology. By night, they would be sipping tea and exchanging gossip in convivial togetherness.

In one such *adda* (meeting) we ran into Atma Ram (name changed), a contact from an earlier election. A self-confessed goon and booth-capturer, he had started his political career as one of Sanjay Gandhi's henchmen. By 1989, however, he was a changed man, having defected to V.P. Singh's side and sworn off his more colourful past. Atma Ram, now contesting on a Janata Dal ticket, sat surrounded by his former friends from the Congress. Seeing our raised eyebrows, the group roared with laughter. Atma Ram shared delicious nuggets about booth-capturing with us. His theory was that no election can be rigged against the will of the people. As proof he cited the 1977 Lok Sabha election which Sanjay Gandhi wanted rigged. But the design was foiled because 'in the polling booths we were thrashed so badly by angry voters that many of us landed in hospital'. Atma Ram was in hysterics as he related this.

He argued that rigging could enhance a verdict but never defy the undercurrent. This was what made Indian democracy intrinsically good. True enough. The Congress failed to rig in 1977. It failed again in 1989 but not for want of trying. Despite widespread violence, V.P. Singh won. Atma Ram won too, evidently benefiting from his own wisdom.

I tested this hypothesis in Bihar, notorious for electoral malpractices. But Atma Ram was correct. Laloo Prasad won because he was popular. And he lost because he was unpopular. The evidence is in the victories he pulled off with all the controls imposed by T.N. Seshan. Besides, rigging (vastly curtailed after Seshan) was a game played by both sides. A top Bihar politician admitted this to some of us. Eyes twinkling, impish grin in place, he said: '*Hum bhi chhapte hain, woh bhi chhapte hain*' (They stamp votes and so do we).

Bihar taught me other tricks of the trade—the whys and wherefores of defection, for instance. Researching the results of the February 2005 Assembly election, I was intrigued by the sudden rise of the Ram Vilas Paswan-led Lok Jan Shakti Party (LJSP). The LJSP had come from nowhere to bag twenty-nine seats in that election. Poll pundits hailed Paswan as a worthy rival to Mayawati.

In truth, the LJSP's 'historic' rise was defection-enabled. Thirteen of the party's twenty-nine winners were defectors who had won the first or second position in the previous election. There was a story in this.

There are two options before a newly formed party without a base. Plod, expand your base and pick up a few seats. Or simply buy out the winners or runners-up from the last election, and map a rich harvest.

Defectors can be done in too. Members of Parliament from the Jharkhand Mukti Morcha (JMM) famously came to grief in 1996 because they deposited their loot in the bank. Parliament-watchers will vouch for an even more incredible hard-luck story. This was of a member of Parliament who had broken with V.P. Singh to become a minister in the 1990–91 Chandra Shekhar government. One day, the man was found sobbing his heart out in full view of

Parliament's Central Hall. Reason: of the three instalments promised to him only one had been paid. Years later (in 2008), the Lok Sabha would witness the actual spectacle of bundles of currency notes being brought in as proof of a bribery attempt.

From time to time I recall Atma Ram's assurance that Indian democracy is intrinsically good. The small wrongs cancel each other out, leaving the big picture intact.

THE MANY FACES OF THE INDIAN ELECTION

The Great Indian Election not only covers a mind-boggling canvas, there are subtexts and layers to it that need telling over several volumes and is beyond the task of this essay. Some issues are too obvious to be missed: the business of predicting elections would certainly be one them; another would be the election's dismaying paradoxes.

For the reporter sweating it out on the election beat, the exit poll or the opinion poll, with its sassy presumptuousness, is a slight like none other. No journalist worth her salt will stand for her own punditry being challenged. And yet, admittedly, these polls make for riveting viewing on television.

In the early days, the wise anchor and his earnest assistant would inspire awe with their mastery of such mystifying things as the swing factor (change in the strength of a party between two elections), the split factor (fragmentation of opposition votes) and index of opposition unity.

The Information Age has taken the gloss off these television polls. In the villages of UP and Bihar, voters will freely discuss 'egjit' polls, casually asking the visiting hack if she is an exit pollster; at the same time they show amazing sophistication in understanding that these are mock, not real, polls.

Too much polling and too many wrong calls have lowered the credibility of exit polls. Yet curiously, today, the exit poll market is many times its original size, with competing television channels dumping the old, stodgy format for the '*break ke baad*' brand of thrills and suspense. In its new sleek avatar, psephology is less statistical jugglery than entertainment in the same league as soaps and reality shows.

The many paradoxes that Indian elections routinely reveal include dynasty, parties without internal democracy and the twice sanctified Narendra Modi.

The Indian electoral arena is packed with dynasties. In its issue dated 12 April 2004, the weekly newsmagazine *India Today* estimated their number at more than a hundred. In the 2009 Lok Sabha, parent–child and uncle–nephew pairs would become the norm rather than the exception, causing much intellectual anguish: What kind of a democracy elects sons and daughter, nephews, and nieces?

India's First Family (the Nehru–Gandhis) is at once its most loved and most hated dynasty. But there is also the Scindia dynasty, the Karunanidhi dynasty, the Mulayam dynasty, the Abdullah dynasty, the Chautala dynasty, the Bansi Lal dynasty, the N.T. Rama Rao dynasty, the Laloo Prasad dynasty and so forth.

Perhaps because of a value system rooted as much in liberalism as feudalism, rural India shows none of the urban discomfort with this phenomenon. Thus 'Italian Sonia is first an Indian bahu'; Rahul (Gandhi) is of course the 'natural heir'; and 'So what if Rabri (Devi) is an unlettered housewife?'

Moreover, India's success with elections has also not translated into inner-party democracy, though parties do go through the motions of holding elections. In the Congress, the 'High Command' is the last word on every appointment, every decision. In the BJP today, L.K. Advani seems to be playing that role.

The trait gets magnified in the state satraps. All India Anna Dravida Munnetra Kazhagam (AIADMK) party persons live in fear of Jayalalithaa and compete to tattoo 'Amma's' name on their forearms and wear rings and pendants embossed with her pictures. In some southern states, party persons are also apt to immolate themselves to prove their loyalty to 'The Leader'. BSP members of Parliament will vanish at the sight of a reporter lest they should fall foul of the 'martial law commander' (their name for Mayawati).

Finally, any study of elections will have to deal with the conflicts and dilemmas that arise when the election transforms into a people's court. Jayalalithaa shrugged off the corruption charges against her with the unforgettable '*Makkale Mahesan*' (voters are god). Twice-elected Narendra Modi is another challenge to democracy. I remember the anguish of an NGO friend when the newsmagazine *Tehelka* reopened the issue of the 2002 riots just before the 2007 Gujarat Assembly election. 'Why are we making the riots an election issue? He will win again and claim a second vindication for the riots.' He won, and won resoundingly.

Are we a lesser democracy for all this? No. Our apparently fragile democracy has proved its toughness. Dynasts, dictators, fascists and unruly legislators have all to answer to the electoral test—and this test is a playing field so level, the mightiest crumble here. Remember, Indira and Sanjay Gandhi were trounced by unknowns. More important, elections have a natural way of limiting excesses. If Jayalalithaa was elected, she was also summarily thrown out.

To go back to Atma Ram's wise words—Indian democracy is innately good. There cannot be a better tribute than this to a democracy that started out tentatively, adroitly negotiated the hurdles along the way and survived as the largest political experiment in the world.

‘Om Sweet Om’

. . . .

Renuka Narayanan

Adi Shankaracharya, Chaitanya, Shirdi Sai Baba, Ramakrishna, Swami Sivananda, Swami Chinmayananda. Just a random pick of dead gurus of the last twelve centuries—the real article, miracles witnessed, great deeds of intellectual and spiritual conquest recorded.

Satya Sai Baba, Sri Sri Ravishankar, Baba Ramdev, Mata Amritanandamayi. Another random pick of today's leading gurus, who presently make India 'Om Sweet Om'.

What's the difference between the legends of yore and the media savvy mavens of today?

The bottom line seems to be: the great gurus of old wanted our souls; the god squad of today want our money in exchange for feel-good exercises, holy ash and trinkets. That seems to be the accepted view on the majority of the modern gurus and godmen peopling our religion channels and community halls, not to mention our prayer rooms and bedside tables, in modern India. Their works are wholly honourable: building schools, hospitals, shelters for orphaned girls, homes for mentally disabled children. The gurus know their public. If they want to tap India's charitable impulses for a do-good agenda, the way to Indian wallets is through their owners' spiritual insecurity. The ground is fertile because of centuries of religious conditioning, making India the card-carrying civilization of the 'Spirit'. Indians have grown up overdosing on capital letters in religious tracts (where do you think Arundhati Roy caught the bug?): the Immortal Spirit, the Self, the Absolute and, on a more familiar note, 'O Thou Supreme Bliss of Devaki!' (this last addressed to Lord Krishna in grandfatherly translations of the Foundational

Indian Epic, the Mahabharata). Almost the first formula that nice little children learn is *Mata-Pita-Guru-Deva*—Mother, Father, Guru, God. (This is cleverly twisted by Hindu modernists to say, 'Look how we honour the Feminine! Mother comes first!' Oh, pooh. Everyone learns by age five that, goddesses aside, Indian society, Hindu or otherwise, is mostly a very old Boys' Club, pretending to be hip and reconstructed in professions like journalism, medicine and banking, but not bothering anywhere else to even fake that they know how to spell e-q-u-a-l-i-t-y.)

So, on top of the heap, before human beings leave off and god begins (mostly Mr God, though the goddess is big, too, in Hindu sentiment), the person right up there in this ascending order of people you traditionally honour is: the guru. He—and, very occasionally, she—doesn't need a college degree or even a measly diploma in god-school to hold sway over the populace. Their 'inner power' or their devotees' perception of their inner power is enough to give them quite extraordinary clout over very important people. Film stars, governors of Indian states as large as France, tycoons with private planes (rumoured to party like Arab sheikhs and fill swimming pools with imported champagne and strawberry blondes), ex-princes, politicians, the high court judge and the cokehead—all bite the dust and touch these gurus' toes.

Why do all these people kowtow to the guru? Traditional respect? Possibly, which is another way of saying that we are hardwired to prostrate ourselves before funny men (or women) in orange (or white) hung about with beads and beards. As the now overworked Indianism goes, 'We are like that only'.

However, other factors may be at play, more to do with the nature of modern Indian experience than spiritual hardwiring. Consider this. In the early noughties, as the religion columnist for *The Indian Express*, I found myself on the national highway to Agra with a busload of well-heeled, perfumed people headed out from Delhi. The Confederation of Indian Industry (CII) was holding a jamboree there and, for the climax, it had invited the hottest guru of neo-nirvana, Sri Sri Ravi Shankar, head of the Art of Living foundation. 'He's the poster boy of CII,' whispered a sleek, Cambridge-educated corporate man to me, preparing to scatter rose petals in Shankar's path by way of traditional welcome.

With India's economy booming, Shankar and other New Age gurus were increasingly sought after as overworked Indians looked for new ways to cope with the pressures created by their materialistic lifestyles. 'Many people who come to us suffer from stress overload. They live pressure cooker lives. They need a way to decompress,' said one of Shankar's key followers, a programme director for the movement, which offers courses tailor-made for executives.

The telegenic Shankar zooms around the world to minister to stressed-out heads of state and their wives, to ministers and captains of industry and economy. He once spoke at the ultra-exclusive World Economic Forum in Davos, where political leaders come to pow-wow with the elite of the business world. He says his programme of short, medium and long breaths has been taught in 145 countries to at least 20 million people over the past quarter century. A student of Maharishi Mahesh Yogi, who famously taught 'transcendental meditation' to the Beatles in the late 1960s, Shankar says his goal is to make the world happier by showing people how to breathe properly. He calls breathing 'the forgotten secret of life' and says it can bring inner peace. 'For every emotion there's a corresponding breath, so when you're angry you have short fast breaths and when you're happy you take long deep breaths,' he explains, as frequently reported by the world media. 'By breathing in certain rhythms we release negative emotions.' The guru, who added the (traditionally) permissible second honorific Sri to his name to distinguish himself from the Indian sitar maestro Ravi Shankar, also says his breathing programme 'keeps you young'.

'Don't I look young?' asked the 1956-born Shankar of executives at the CII retreat, with the trademark giggle that punctuates most of his sentences. Shankar naturally looks the part of New Age guru: white robes, shoulder length black locks that he keeps tossing back, black beard. He gets by on just three hours of sleep a night, he says, snug in his headquarters outside Bangalore City, in a special hut full of love tokens from devotees, including a red velvet heart cushion with white curly letters on it saying 'I Love Guruji'.

Critics accuse him of offering nothing but 'don't worry, be happy' platitudes. Before he was granted a visa to Pakistan, embassy officials in New Delhi contacted 'neutral' (meaning not-rabidly-Hindu) writers and Indians supposedly in the know to check whether he propagated 'Hinduism'. He does not, but yoga is consistent with the Hindu philosophy of the unity of mind, body and spirit. Shankar maintains his huge following among India's upper crust with not just breathing but also the singing of devotional Hindu songs of traditional origin. When I last looked in on the Art of Living headquarters, Shankar's happy Hindu bhajan-band featured a good looking 'swami', Nikhil, who led the singing in a huge auditorium. Holding a mike, he swayed and crooned: '*Sundaraanana Bhasmabhushita*' (O Beautiful Ash-Smeared One)—to Lord Shiva.

High-profile devotees at Shankar's feet included a liquor baron, a former Miss Universe and film actress Khushboo, who has a temple dedicated to her in south India by passionate fans. 'Guru to the rich and famous'? But a former cokehead-jailbird from a village in the truly rural state of Haryana tells me how he now teaches other men in other jails to breathe and feel better. The huge central Indian state of Madhya Pradesh even contracted Shankar's Art of Living foundation to teach yogic breathing and meditation in every one of their thirty-four jails. 'We LOVE Guruji!' a posse of indignant followers appeared to be saying as they glared at me, conversing as I was with the cokehead, just asking him questions, friendly-like.

The community of Shankar's blissed-out believers is still likeable in a distant 'I'm just a spiritual tourist' or 'spirituality is my hobby' way. They don't assault you in the privacy of your home as a friend did—a mad, bad, pub-hopping, 'good girls go to heaven, bad girls go everywhere' person—who had suddenly discovered Buddhist chanting, Japanese-style. It swept away Delhi's educated class like a tsunami in the 1990s and shows no sign of retreating in the noughties. Called Sokka Gakkai, it was founded by a Japanese gentleman called Daisaku Ikeda. Its practitioners gather in groups and chant '*Namyoho Rengekyo*', the Japanese version of the Sanskrit '*Om Mani Padme Hum*' (Hail to the Jewel in the Lotus). I ran into a Japanese contingent at Hiroshima on 6 August 2002 and they came right up and asked me—quite aggressively, I thought—to 'promote' their movement in India. Back in Delhi, I saw posters of Daisaku Ikeda: his face beside those of Mahatma Gandhi and Nelson Mandela, no less. Low on modesty, strong on 'positioning', as they'd say in marketing terms?

My friend, otherwise a Peshawari Khatri fiercely dedicated to the Hindu hill goddess Vaishno Devi, described the orderly organization of groups and sub-groups in the Sokka Gakkai. She told me of their scroll, called the Gohonzon, which they focussed on while chanting and how helpful and sincere the members were, especially if someone was sick or troubled. 'If you get more people to join, then you get a trip to Japan,' she revealed, and showed me a little bead necklace carefully wrapped in a square of cherry-blossom printed silk. 'This represents the human body, see, this big bead is the head and these are the limbs,' she said, pulling at it. And then came the Sumo-squat: 'You should join us, you have God in you!' she said dramatically. Alas, instead of being nice about it, I leapt up, swatting at the snug pocket of my jeans, yelling, 'Where? Where? Out!' She did not ask me to her birthday party that year but it made me wonder at the evangelical hubris and horrible intrusiveness of Jehovah's Witnesses and the like ringing your doorbell and inquiring about the state of your soul. It's one more occupational hazard of living in the modern Indian metropolis today, where all our souls, it seems, are up for grabs in the Great Guru Bazaar. One wonders what the slick formula of the Sokka Gakkai has to do with the Buddha back in sixth century BCE. While the chanters I met in Delhi were undeniably full of good feeling, I sensed an attempt to project Daisaku Ikeda as a world leader, bucking for a Nobel Peace Prize. There was something political about this; it wasn't just about the spiritual practices of Sokka Gakkai adherents.

While religion and politics have long been intertwined in every religious tradition, something about modern forms of power encourages the coalescing of religious feeling around single, cohesive centres. This, together with the fact that Indian cultural reflexes operate powerfully and instinctively when a guru is in the mix, makes some trends in the modern Indian spiritual bazaar more comprehensible. In January 2005, a Muslim 'Babaji' from Lahore sang *shabad kirtan* (Sikh devotional music) at the India Habitat Centre, New Delhi. The Stein Auditorium was packed to the gills and there wasn't even any standing room. And yet, everyone nicely made room as people kept pouring in. The organizers appealed to the audience's charity because the Babaji, not surprisingly, found it hard to make ends meet in Muslim-majority Pakistan singing Sikh scripture. They placed a large bowl at the edge of the stage. It was remarkable how everyone quietly lined up to put money in it, like one does at the gurdwara when kirtan is being sung. The bowl soon overflowed with hundred-rupee notes and more. It was more than a regional sentiment of 'Punjabiyat' being honoured here—after all, the singer sang songs compiled by the Sikh gurus.

Here's how I understood the phenomenon: the Guru Granth Sahib is the focus of prostration and prayer in a gurdwara. It embodies the spirit of the great Sikh gurus who suffered every kind of medieval torture for the sake of religious and political identity. This attitude of reverence for gurus, especially given the awe-inspiring history of the Sikh gurus, resonates powerfully among the majority Hindu community, for reasons as political as they are religious. Hindus have scattered regional guru figures of past eminence but not a centralized, monolingual guru-based historical tradition as the Sikhs do. Centralized and charismatic figures of devotion such as gurus (dead or alive) also allow for a centralizing of political identity.

The early 1990s saw the rise of the Hindu nationalist Bharatiya Janata Party and its assortment of affiliated right-wing groups—often glossed as the Sangh Parivar. The Sangh Parivar told Hindus, in voices both earthily coarse and ethereally spiritual, that they needed to stop 'cowering', reclaim their religion with public pride and assert their religious rights over mythical temples. While Hindu temples have always been political in the Indian subcontinent, with political power often being legitimized by and even being perceived as flowing from the consecration and patronage of specific temples, everyday religious practice among the citizenry shows no evidence of having come under a centralized, absolutist yoke. One school of thought says that this flexibility in everyday practice is the reason that Hinduism remains the majority religion in India today—political haranguing of the common Hindu is not necessary for the preservation of the religion. Nevertheless, a certain 'come out of the closet' mentality and a more public flaunting of Hindu identity have resulted from the efforts of the Sangh Parivar.

For all the above reasons, gurus and godmen have never had it so good in modern India. Adherence to one's personal guru allows a modern Hindu to take part in public prayers, attend public ceremonies of worship, set up a whole culture of worship and affiliation in fact, without having to make it ugly and too obviously political. Everyone else—Muslim, Christian, Buddhist, Sikh—has a congregation and a community. They all have a place to go to. But the decentralized, everyday practice of Hinduism tends to be a lonelier, if freer, place with no massive group of brethren to give comfort in numbers. The modern Hindu follower of the guru partakes of the human and social comforts of congregation that he sees other communities enjoying.

Of course, gurus also performed important political functions before these modern times, but then, as now, they were so useful politically precisely because popular religiosity was so strongly rooted. The angry regional and Hindu politics of the Shiv Sena in Maharashtra draws its charge from popular historical narratives about the Maratha warrior hero Chhatrapati Shivaji and his guru Samarth Ramdas, whose *Dasabodh* is still learned and recited aloud in Maharashtrian Hindu families. Sri Samarth Ramdas was born in 1608 CE in Jaamb village in Marathwada on the auspicious day of Ram Navami as the second son of a pious couple, Suryaji Panth and Renuka Bai. His parents named him Narayan. His wedding was arranged in 1620. As per custom, he sat across his bride-to-be at the ceremony with a screen between them. When the priests said, '*Saavadhan!*' (Alert, O bridegroom), Narayan reportedly vanished. Later, they discovered that he had gone to Tafali village near Nasik. There he practised meditation of the Gayatri and Rama Mantras, chanting knee-deep in the waters of the holy river Godavari from early morning until noon. He begged for alms and attended spiritual discourses in his free time at various temples in Nasik and Panchavati. Ramdas also studied Sanskrit and copied in his own hand the Ramayana of Valmiki. (His manuscript of the epic is still reportedly preserved in the collection of Sri S.S. Dev of Dhubliah.) After rigorous penance of Rama Japa for twelve years, he came to be known as Samarth Ramdas (the Enabled Servant of Rama). At twenty-four, Ramdas went on a long pilgrimage to pilgrim centres like Kashi, Haridwar, Rishikesh and so on for nearly twelve years. Tradition has it that Lord Panduranga Vittal (Vishnu, as aspected at Pandharpur in Maharashtra) himself appeared to Ramdas, took him to Pandharpur and gave him *darshan* as Sri Rama. In Pandharpur, Ramdas encountered the saintly, sweet-natured Tukaram and other saints of the medieval Bhakti period. Both the saints spread the message of bhakti by travel.

While on pilgrimage, Ramdas observed and studied the social, political and economic conditions of Indians and their utter helplessness. He began a campaign for social upliftment, preaching his philosophy between Mahabaleswar and Kohlapur in Maharashtra. At Singanvadi, Ramdas met Chhatrapati Shivaji, the then ruler of

Maharashtra. Shivaji became an ardent devotee. Being a passionate follower of Sri Rama and Maruti (Hanuman), Ramdas installed shrines of Rama at Champavati. He inspired Shivaji in his fight against the particular tyranny of the Mughal Aurangzeb (d. 1707) who, unlike some other rulers of his dynasty, bequeathed a legacy of Hindu–Muslim hatred that still plagues the subcontinent.

Ramdas had many disciples, including many noblewomen. He sent them all over India to spread a fresh awareness of the Hindu religion. His disciples and ashrams in the north helped Shivaji in his political and cultural agenda. The *Dasabodh* and other literary works like the *Manache Shlok* (verses addressed to the mind), *Karunashtaka* (hymns to god) and Ramayana (describing only the conquest of Lanka by Sri Rama and the vanquishing of Ravana) remain hugely popular even today. Ramdas's organization spread south as well and he appointed Bhimaswami, his direct disciple, as the *mahant* of the Thanjavur Matt in the Tamil region.

This influential guru of Maharashtra breathed his last in 1681 at Sajjangad near Satara, a fortress given to him by Shivaji as his residence. His samadhi at Sajjangad is still a place of pilgrimage. The last instructions of Ramdas to his disciples were:

> Do not think much of your bodily wants. . . Keep the image of Sri Rama in your heart. Repeat the name of Sri Rama always. Annihilate lust, greed, anger, hatred and egoism. See Sri Rama in all creatures. Love all. Feel His presence everywhere. Live for Him alone. Serve Him in all beings. Make total and unreserved surrender unto Him. You will always live in Him alone. You will attain immortality and eternal bliss.

On Guru Purnima in July each year, crowds flock by the lakh to their spiritual teachers for *darshan* and *diksha*.

After Ramdas, the next guru of eminence was the nineteenth century Bengal-born Sri Ramakrishna Paramahamsa, whom adherents all over India still affirm as the most outstanding guru of modern India. The Ramakrishna Matt lights up the history of twentieth-century India as a genuine and sincere movement of social and cultural service. Sri Ramakrishna transcended all religious divides, having personally investigated and practised each of the major religions, to a level of 'Oneness' practised through social service. He revitalized Hinduism across east and south India while reforming it of ritual, just as his Punjabi counterpart, Swami Dayanand Saraswati, did with the 'back-to-the-Vedas' Arya Samaj movement in Punjab and parts of Rajasthan. The difference is that while Sri Ramakrishna is hailed as a guru, Swami Dayanand's muscular Hinduism took on a political tone in the Punjab, which was partitioned on Hindu–Muslim lines.

Intriguingly, another guru intensely cherished by modern Indians crosses Hindu–Muslim communal lines, melding the two in himself and in his following: Shirdi Sai Baba. Lines of devotees, which include a huge proportion of young Indians, can be seen winding around several blocks on his special day, Thursday, at temples dedicated to him. This turn-of-the-nineteenth-century guru's life and teachings were first documented in Marathi in 1910 as the *Sai Satcharitra* by his devotee Hemadpant. It has been translated into various languages since then, including English, and his devotees come flocking from regions as far apart as Gujarat and Andhra Pradesh to Shirdi in Maharashtra.

Baba's story may be said to begin when Chandbhai, the headman of a village called Dhoopkhede in Aurangabad district, went looking for his horse in a forest. Suddenly he heard a voice say, 'You look tired. Come here and rest for a while.' He looked around and saw a young fakir beckoning. The fakir smilingly asked him, by name, what he was hunting for. This surprised Chandbhai and he wondered how the fakir could possibly know his name. He hesitantly replied, 'I have lost my horse and have been hunting everywhere for it.' The fakir told him to look behind a particular clump of trees. Chandbhai was amazed to find his horse grazing peacefully there. He thanked the fakir and asked him his name in turn. The fakir said, 'Some people call me Sai Baba.' The fakir then invited Chandbhai to have a smoke with him, as was and is the sociable practice of traditional society. He got the pipe ready, but there was no fire around to light it with. The fakir casually thrust a pair of tongs into the ground and brought out a burning coal. Chandbhai was wonderstruck. 'Surely, this is no ordinary person!' he thought and invited the fakir to pay him a visit at home. When Baba went to Chandbhai's house next day, he found everybody in a happy, festive mood and the house gaily decorated. He discovered that a wedding party was setting out that very day for Chandbhai's wife's nephew's wedding.

The bride was from Shirdi and the *baraat* was going there for the ceremony. Chandbhai invited Baba to accompany the baraat, and once there they camped in a field next to the temple of the powerful local deity, Khandoba. Sai Baba stayed on at Shirdi thereafter. He lived at first under a neem tree and begged for food like mendicants do. He then wanted to live in Khandoba's temple but the priest forestalled him at the door saying nobody was allowed to actually live in a temple and he could try the mosque. So that's what Baba did. He preached at Shirdi all his life and performed numerous miracles to convince people of god's existence. He healed diseases and provided moral and material comfort to his devotees, attracting people of all faiths. Baba passed away on 15 October 1918. It is hard to find offices in modern India without at least one benign calendar portrait of Shirdi Sai Baba or a porcelain statue of him on an office desk.

In contrast, Satya Sai Baba, a going-strong-for-forty-years godman with a trademark head of frizzy hair and the mandatory orange robes, is headquartered at a lush, well-run complex called Whitefield just outside of Bangalore. Just as the Israelis made oranges grow in the desert, Satya Sai Baba greened an arid patch of earth, set up hugely successful hospitals and educational schemes. He is known to regularly produce holy ash and even a Swiss watch under duress, all with a faraway enigmatic air and a shake of an orange sleeve, to reward the deserving and well-connected: 'To her that hath shall be given.' His popularity has withstood decades of attack by the rationalists' associations and even a scandal (of pederasty) in the Indian press (which died out for lack of proof).

What is interesting in the guru–godman pattern is that they seem to be essentially either refuges in a stressful world or rebels against any overwhelming religious and political orthodoxy. The Sikh gurus and Samarth Ramdas led movements against Mughal oppression. This is usually oversimplified as being movements against Islam. But it is only when Islamic orthodox views came down heavily on civil (and therefore religious) liberties that there was a counter-movement. This happened to Jesus as well. It did not happen to the Buddha because he was a Sakya prince and a dazzling novelty, but when Buddhism became institutionalized in India, it led to turf wars for royal patronage between Hindus and Buddhists. I was told in Japan, in 2002, by the head priest of the Hachimangu Shinto shrine that Buddhism succeeded better in Japan than in its native place because the Buddhists who went there learnt from their mistakes in India. They were content to live good lives and eventually drew massive popular support through exemplary behaviour instead of evangelizing against the prevailing Shinto (ancestor worship) creed.

This thought came to haunt me in Iran where the Sufis were persecuted by orthodox Shias for political reasons (or as the Chinese government banned the Falun Gong, for example). Driving through the ancient south Persian province of Fars, I thought of its famous son, whose name spells courage in Islam. Abu-al-Mughith-al-Husayn-ibn-Mansur-al-Hallaj (858 CE–26 March 922 CE) was born in the village of Madina al-Bayda in Fars. He grew up amidst cotton fields, the son of a cotton-carder ('al-hallaj'). His grandfather was a Zoroastrian and his father a simple Muslim, while he, in classic 'little Sufi' pattern, forsook his playmates to learn the Koran by heart and study with local holy men. He married, had three sons, went on Haj and travelled up to Gujarat, Sindh and even China, teaching and writing. Many followed him with love on a second pilgrimage to Mecca, but jealous mullahs kept him out. He then settled in Abbasid Baghdad. His guru, Shaykh al-Junayd, believed that mystic teachings should be kept secret and shared only with the worthy. But al-Hallaj was so god-intoxicated that he told everybody, just as Ramanuja, founder of the Sri Vaishnava movement in India, climbed a temple spire to shout aloud the life-giving mantra '*Om Namo Narayanaya*' so that all could hear and benefit. Believing in the perfect Oneness of the One, al-Hallaj once declared, '*Ana al-Haq!*' (I am the Truth). This gave the orthodoxy their chance to brand him a *zindiq* (heretic), since *al-Haq* (*Satyam* or Truth) is one of Allah's ninety-nine names. The caliphs colluded, fearing he had stirred up anti-monarchic sentiments during his wanderings in their far provinces. Al-Hallaj had a long trial and was locked into a Baghdad jail for eleven years before being publicly tortured and crucified. Many wrote that he was serene throughout and even forgave his executioners. What al-Hallaj wrote in the *Diwan al-Hallaj* was curiously like the Hindu worldview of Advaita: Oneness with god—'I saw my Lord with the eye of my heart and said, "Who are You?" He said, "You".'

For a sample of how these grand thoughts are parlayed into modern guruspeak, we have only to consider this rather unexciting early twentieth-century piece of writing by Sri Aurobindo (*Letters on Yoga*, Volume 1, Section Four, *Reason, Science and Yoga*):

> What is this Ananda [divine bliss], after all? The mind can see in it nothing but a pleasant psychological condition—but if it were only that, it could not be the rapture which the bhaktas and the mystics find in it. When the Ananda comes into you, it is the Divine who comes into you, just as when the Peace flows into you, it is the Divine who is invading you, or when you are flooded with Light, it is the flood of the Divine himself that is around you. Of course, the Divine is something much more, many other things besides, and in them all a Presence, a Being, a Divine Person; for the Divine is Krishna, is Shiva, is the Supreme Mother. But through the Ananda you can perceive the Anandamaya Krishna, for the Ananda is the

> subtle body and being of Krishna; through the Peace you can perceive the Shantimaya Shiva; in the Light, in the delivering Knowledge, the Love, the fulfilling and uplifting Power you can meet the presence of the Divine Mother. It is this perception that makes the experiences of the bhaktas and mystics so rapturous and enables them to pass more easily through the nights of anguish and separation; when there is this soul-perception, it gives to even a little or brief Ananda a force or value it could not otherwise have, and the Ananda itself gathers by it a growing power to stay, to return, to increase.

To me, this is classic self-conscious modern obfuscation. It profits both seeker and reader to go more directly to the texts. For instance, anger management is a major area of urban concern. Instead of regurgitated soul talk like the sample above, holy texts (which the more hands-on gurus effectively quote from) are direct and upfront on such matters.

The ancient *Yoga Sutra* by Patanjali, a spiritual best-seller, of which there are several retranslations, says: 'The mind becomes tranquil and pleasant by the cultivation of friendship, compassion, satisfaction and indifference respectively, towards the happy, the unhappy, the blessing and the blight.' The Bhagavad Gita, by which Hindus take oath in court, is quite stern and contemptuous about the following eight deadly sins: 'The doer who is unbalanced, vulgar, obstinate, deceitful, malicious, indolent, despondent and procrastinating is of a raw nature.' The Aitareya Bhramana (Rig Veda) says disdainfully: 'Speech that is haughty or mad with fury is demoniac (*rakshasa vaak*).' Thiruvalluvar, pillar of ancient Tamil pride, glorious root of India's *other* classical tongue, scolds, 'Girls are supposed to be shy by nature: real shyness refrains from a mean act.' In fact, he divests himself of two more aphorisms on the subject: 'The plant betrays the soil, and speech betrays the person of birth' and 'a smiling face, a generous heart, sweet words and no scorn are said to mark the well-born'.

Fourteen centuries later, Guru Nanak Dev says, '*Mane jeetai, jag jeetu*' (Who conquers his mind-heart, conquers the world). Remains only Mahatma Gandhi to activate ahimsa into the political weapon of non-violence and declare: 'True ahimsa means complete freedom from ill-will, anger and hate, and an overflowing love for all.'

Indeed, beyond gurus, communal discord and angry politics, India never fails to enchant with her hidden harmonies. Many Muhurrams ago I attended a ladies' Muhurram majlis in Delhi dressed in my abaya. Marigolds, lights and agarbattis were set before the *alams* (banners). The majlis was extremely moving and later the Rampur shahzadi, who was there, invited me to Panja Sharif at Kashmiri Gate in the walled city. This is a general majlis that the Rampur Nawab family has endowed since before Independence. Earlier, there were barely ten Shias in attendance but now the majlis attracts a thousand people.

Leaving the car on the main road, we went through narrow gullies to a large hall packed with seated men. A large banner proclaimed, 'Live like Ali, die like Hussain' and a fiery, incredibly pink-cheeked imam was sermonizing from a high chair. We were taken right behind the imam's stage to a little screened-off, mattressed corner from where I peered through opaque black drapes at the assembly: it was like being in a remake of *Mere Mehboob* for me, the archetypal urban Hindu who's usually found in jeans and a tee. The imam thundered on about Islamic morality, rousing great shouts *of 'Naara-e-Hydari! Ya Ali! Ya Ali!'* The imam turned out to be a Gujarati called Maulana Kalb-e-Rushaid, from Mahua. 'That's where my dear friend Morari Bapu (a top guru) lives and works. I like him very much,' he said, disclosing that he had had ten years of Koranic education at the Sultanul Madrasa in Lucknow before obtaining his PhD in Islamic law at Qum in Iran. He'd been imam-e-jumma at London, Paris, Tenerife and Reunion Island and now served Delhi. We were amused to realize that we'd both lapsed into French—his was better.

Equally astonishing was my encounter with the Sikh who recited *noha*, the Muhurram narratives. About 1400 years ago, Mohyal Brahmins had fought for Hazrat Ali at Karbala and were known ever after as Hussaini Brahmins. Now I discovered Mahender Singh of Lucknow, who has recited at majlis for fifteen years, while all around him young men beat their chests to cries of 'Hussain! Hussain!'

Theatre man Aamir Raza Hussain, a majlis organizer, told me, 'Once, every Hindu home in Awadh would put up a little *tazia*. And Muhurram in India has so many Hindu links.' Take the Hindu banjara tribe in Mayawati's constituency, Akbarpur. During Muhurram, they paint their homes like they do for Diwali and wear red, the colour of celebration. 'This is one day that Imam Hussain and his mother come to our house,' they say sincerely.

Speaking of mothers, the sacred feminine has managed to assert itself with vigour on our time as befits a land that enshrines a Mother Goddess. I witnessed a truly extraordinary sight in September 2003 in a football stadium in Kochi, where thousands flocked for the fiftieth birthday celebrations of Amritanandamayi 'Amma', the 'hugging saint'. A group of Brazilians had travelled three days across the globe to be there; bands of supposedly inscrutable Japanese broke down in tears; a souvenir shop busily sold Amma dolls, right down to frilly innerwear. Among those present were Yolanda Young, daughter of murdered civil rights leader Martin Luther King Jr, and Lynda Evans, the gorgeous blonde star who played Krystle in the American teleserial *Dynasty*. It was incredible to see Amma, a tiny figure, perched onstage while thousands sang Upanishadic peace chants in sweet harmony. What—who—was this phenomenon? Reporters from the international press gaped at the crowds and muttered 'Hokey!' The *Washington Post,* the *New York Times* and Charles Haviland of the BBC were there, too. He reported:

> The followers hope to add to the 30 million hugs given out over thirty years by religious leader Mata Amritanandamayi. Ms Amritanandamayi—known to her followers as Amma—began a four-day celebration on Wednesday to mark her fiftieth birthday on Saturday. Deputy Prime Minister Lal Krishna Advani is among those

> attending in the southern state of Kerala. Organizers believe that over the coming days 500,000 people will join the celebrations. Religious leaders and businessmen from all over the world, including Hotmail founder Sabeer Bhatia, are scheduled to attend.

Yolanda King said, 'The most profound thing about her is she doesn't preach from the platform of one religion. She touches everybody. So Christians love her, Muslims love her, everybody loves her.'

Amritanandamayi, whose name means 'Mother of Absolute Bliss', was born to a poor family in a southern Indian fishing community. She refused school and then marriage, preferring to meditate. She began hugging devotees at a young age. In the 1980s Amritanandamayi founded an ashram to receive followers and dispense more hugs. In 1993 she served as president of the Centenary Parliament of World Religions in Chicago (where Sri Ramakrishna's lead follower, Swami Vivekananda, had won fame and friends with his 'Brothers and Sisters of America!' speech) and later spoke at the United Nations. In 2002 she was awarded the Gandhi–King Award for Non-Violence.

Amma has helped found schools, hospices and hospitals for the poor. Birthday plans included talks on conflict resolution, religious discussions and, of course, heaps of hugs. The inauguration of Mata Amritanandamayi Matt's future charitable projects included an all-India free legal cell comprising 1008 lawyers dedicated to serving the needy; building 100,000 free houses for the destitute throughout India; 108 free marriages for poor couples (108 is the auspicious number of beads on a prayer-bead necklace) and 25,000 devotees pledging the donation of their eyes after death. When it was my turn to be hugged, I asked her if she did not feel tired. 'Only an ayah feels tired. A mother does not,' she said firmly.

For those who cannot abide the hugger-mugger of large gatherings, a handy bliss-out before leaving for work or after the chores at home are done is available to them on thirteen spiritual channels, Hindu, Muslim and Christian. For at least three hours every afternoon, housewives can tune in to the Aastha or Sanskar channels for discourses, devotional music, Ayurvedic cures and health advice. Likewise, the Muslim channels answer questions on whether it's Islamic to invest in mutual funds and reassure ladies from Hyderabad who are haunted by a 'bad djinn'. The Christian programmes are bought from the US and are unabashedly Bible-thumping. Good News TV, a Christian spiritual lifestyle channel which has a wide reach in Tamil Nadu, claims to have programmes for children and adults with a healthy dose of spirituality. One of the top-rated shows on religious channels is the Rama Katha. It is a four-hour-long programme—even longer than a Bollywood film—but with a dedicated audience. Religious channels are the biggest development in Indian television in the last decade. Their viewership is equal to that of English news and movie channels and is higher than business news channels. While 55 per cent of their audience is over thirty-five years of age, surprisingly, the next big chunk of the audience is between fifteen and twenty-four. A proper public survey is awaited, though private channels have made their own market surveys and hug the findings close while periodically considering their own primetime shows packaging 'spirituality'.

What the ancient teachers make of this modern guru bazaar is a riddle to be answered perhaps in the hereafter. Meanwhile, as a devoted public rocks in ecstasy without the slightest trace of substance abuse, the guru's managers are scampering to the bank. Giggling.

Finger-lickin'

. . . .

Vikram Doctor

It starts in childhood. As children we are greedy and it is a hunger that will not be satisfied with the good, safe, nutritious food that our parents conscientiously feed us. We always have a sense of something more, something being denied to us, which we both want and fear: in reality children tend to be conservative eaters, and it is being forbidden that matters more than the food.

So we want it—whether it's the 'grown up' food, spicier, stronger, more expensive that our parents order in restaurants; or the subtly different dishes in our relatives' homes; or the savoury smells from neighbours' kitchens, so near yet so different; or the food in our classmates' tiffin-boxes which we'll happily swap in the lunch break, what is banal for them being deliciously different for us.

All these though are usually ultimately permissible, so they pall. What remains enticing is what we are sternly told is entirely out of bounds. Never eat street food, we are told, for fear of getting cholera, diarrhoea, enteritis, typhoid, tapeworms, trichinosis. Street food, we are told, is made from the worst ingredients (cat's meat usually, which is hard to imagine given the difficulty of catching cats in anything like the quantities required). It is greasy, over-spiced, full of MSG and unhealthy in every possible way. If we are religious, it is polluting. If we are vegetarian, it has hidden meat. If we are foreign, it is dangerously local. If we are local, it is made by unwelcome immigrants. If we are on a diet, it is the end. No wonder we find street food so alluring.

In Ambai's story 'Journey 3', a young girl, Mythili, is sent to the Mariamman temple that her mother won't visit, but still propitiates to prevent smallpox. She enlists their servant woman, giving her food for the offering, money for the jutka ride to the temple and many warnings not to take Mythili to '*that* side', meaning the stalls near the non-Brahmin temple. But '*that* side' is too enticing. They save money by taking the bus and spend it on food from '*that* side': 'hot, spicy fried peanuts smeared with chilli and turmeric; jujube fruit; ripe tamarind; parrot-nosed mangos; and sweetened balls of gram'. They eat it all, even 'piping hot chicken pillau on sewn-leaf plates, the chicken meltingly soft, with cinnamon, clove and pepper…' Upset stomachs ensue after every temple visit, but the lure of '*that* side' is always too strong, until one day Mythili's younger brother insists on coming along and gives the secret away. There are no more visits to Mariamman.

The person who longs for street food in Gita Hariharan's story 'The Remains of the Feast', is not young, but very old. The narrator's great-grandmother is ninety and dying when she is suddenly possessed by an urge for the food she could never have all her life. She inveigles the narrator into becoming her accomplice: 'I smuggled in cakes and ice cream, biscuits and samosas, made by non-Brahmin hands into a vegetarian invalid's room.' But her great-grandmother's cravings are not assuaged and she wants more—soft drinks, garlic, cakes laced with brandy and bhel-puri from the bazaar. When her family tries feeding her gruel she goes wild: '"No, no," she screamed deliriously. "Get me something from the bazaar. Raw onions. Fried bread. Chickens and goats."'

Madhur Jaffrey's mother was as adamant as most against street food, yet she knew there were times her family could not resist. She tried replicating it at home, adding the aromatic kewra (screwpine) essence that seemed to be the secret ingredient in the kebabs and other grilled meats. But at times, at birthday parties or when unexpected guests came, her husband overruled her and sent the driver to the lanes of Old Delhi for bazaar food, and all she could do was make a palliative gesture. Madhur Jaffrey recounts in her *Ultimate Curry Bible*:

> The driver would go with the car to the crowded old city, to the area around the seventeenth century mosque, Jama Masjid, and bring back dozens of breads and kebabs all wrapped in starchy white cloths sent along by my mother. How these made the food cleaner, I do not know. Even before the cloths got untied, there was that irrepressible aroma of kewra emanating from our dinner-to-be. We knew we were in for a treat.

Stories like this cast street food as a symbol of the other side of the ordered life of home and approved society. It is the life that lurks alluringly *that* side, the life denied which you grasp for at death, the life that you try to sanitize with white cloths, but still wafts irrepressibly through. It is common in Indian narratives for food to stand in for all the temptations of life simply because it is the one temptation we can admit to, hunger the one urge which it is permissible to talk about. And street food in particular appears in narratives about the competing claims of the home and the world. It is as an offering from that outside world, spicy, savoury and replete with hidden dangers to test the boundaries of home.

It happens when you go with your friends for your first forbidden street-side meal, when you bring home from the street the sort of food that you can't cook at home and when homebound wives buy food brought to them from off the street by travelling salesmen. A weekly idli seller is the catalyst for the affair in *Second Thoughts*, the rare novel in the Shobhaa Dé canon not set in the world of celebrities and glamour.

It is the story of Maya, a bored suburban housewife who falls for Nikhil, the handsome son of a neighbour: 'Every Tuesday Vishwanath brought a batch of fluffy, white idlis steamed by his wife to the building and went from flat to flat asking the housewives if they want to buy some.' Maya is buying a few when Nikhil passes outside her door and she offers him one. 'I stood there holding the sambhar container and stared fascinatedly at Nikhil's rapidly moving jaws. Three idlis disappeared down his gullet within seconds.' Maya is soon as lost as those interloping idlis!

It isn't just Indians who feel the dangerous lure of street food. Tourists might talk fearfully about 'Delhi belly', avoid ice and brush their teeth with mineral water, but there is also the belief that you can only really know India if you've grappled with street food—and the churning bowels that are the almost required consequence. A.A. Gill, the much-feared restaurant reviewer for the *Sunday Times* in the UK, wrote after a visit to Mumbai: 'Tourists tend to be particularly squeamish about eating from the gutter, but the street is no more poisonous than the big hotels: it is the most exciting place to graze.'

Yet Gill frames this endorsement with a soliloquy on shit. It is visible all around you in India, he notes: 'You're never further than a couple of yards from a turd.' He does try to make this sound enticing: 'Shit happens in India, and then they grow vegetables in it. It's a neat Hindu wheel of virtue, but the food is so fabulously good, it's worth the midnight runs.' Gill also suggests that Westerners are as responsible, having grown used to such an antiseptic society that they fail to take the elementary precautions of washing before and after meals that Indians always do. Nevertheless his message is clear: street food is wonderful, but comes with shit, both before and after.

This fetishization of street food implies an option: if one doesn't give in to its dangerous delights, one can always eat the blander but safer options of home or room service. But for many no such option exists. They have no cult of street food because for them it is just food, sustenance that happens to be in the street because there is nowhere else they can go to eat. They eat at village markets, in small towns near temples or mosques or alongside railway stations and in big cities almost anywhere. To fill their needs stalls are set up, fires started, food made and sold.

Most often this food is not what we commonly associate with 'street food'. Not the chaats, bhel-puris, golguppas, pav bhajis, kebabs and kulfis that middle-class Indians get nostalgic about when they speak of street food. These are there, of course, as special treats, but the street food that sustains those with no choice is usually simpler stuff. What you will often see is the most basic yellow dal and rice, served in massive stomach-filling portions. If it's a sandwich it won't have fancy fillings, but boiled potato and onions, enlivened by a thin layer of chutney. Boiled eggs are among the most common street food, not something to fantasize about, but good to eat, peeled, quartered and sprinkled with salt and chilli powder. Fried fish will not be expensive pomfret but cheap and tasty *bangda* (mackerel) or *tarlya* (sardine). A dessert could be ice cream with falooda noodles and swollen *sabja* seeds, or the rustic treat of *kharwas* or colostrum, the first milk from a cow or buffalo after giving birth, so rich and thick it sets to a jelly (though lacking a constant supply of calving cows in the city, kharwas sellers often set it with cornflour instead).

Every weekday near the offices of Mumbai's Nariman Point or the stock exchange at Dalal Street women stand with large stainless-steel containers from which they dish out a basic lunch of dal-roti-sabzi, fish curry–rice or puri-bhaji to hungry office goers. In the old business area of Ballard Estate, where roads are wider and parking possible, lunchtimes find a congregation of cab drivers eating dal-roti lunches from similar stainless-steel sellers. In the evening in the busy suburb of Bandra old men and women set up tables outside their small cottages and sell prawn cutlets, egg rolls and beef chops kept warm in insulated vessels. It is a taste of Bandra's vanishing East Indian past.

During Ramzan at Mumbai's Minara Masjid, in the middle of the crowds all intent on breaking the fast with rich, greasy food, you will find a matronly lady in a *rida*, the dress of Memon Muslim women, busily frying delicate little pancakes of rice flour, coconut milk and egg with sugar crystals sprinkled on top. They are called moroli and are a speciality of Memon homes. In the south Indian dominated suburb of Matunga on the pavement near a temple with a gaudily painted *gopuram* a man swirls batter in a round pan to make appams which he serves with a potato curry familiar to any Malayali.

All this is street food by virtue of where it is consumed, but it is home food too. And the irony, given how street and home food are pitted against each other, is that this is where the roots of most street food lie. One strand of street food, it's true, comes from the traditional snacks that have always been sold by hawkers at markets or outside temples. These snacks are sweet, salty, sour or all three and are usually made in advance, so the hawker can just set his basket down and start selling. Peanuts and puffed rice, kulfi and kairi (green mango) slices, chikki and chiwda, and even more complex variations involving chutneys and assembling, like bhel-puri and ragda pattice, are all examples of this snacky street food.

But there is another strand of street food that involves fresh cooking and this is often home food that has made its way onto the streets. Those who make it may be on the streets themselves, or not far from it. Making and selling food is always something that recent immigrants do, because they have to make food for themselves anyway. And in a large city like Mumbai there will usually be others from the same region ready to buy.

It works like this. A group of men from a region come to the city for work, staying together for support. They take turns to do the cooking, but after a while they pool their resources and make one man the permanent cook, or get a younger brother from the village, or perhaps one might take the leap and bring his wife. The designated cook makes food from their region for them, and sometimes if they have space this may become a full-fledged dining club, mess or *khanewal*. The word spreads among compatriots who start dropping in to eat and the khanewal becomes a canteen.

Word spreads further to curious outsiders and the canteen becomes a restaurant, modest but open for business. There are small Goan joints in Mumbai like New Martin's, Snowflake or City Kitchen which started this way, or Gujarati thali places like Friends Union Joshi Club which preserve the club aspect of the khanewal (you can still buy monthly dining tickets), or Konkani eateries like Anantashram where the setting of one small table to each chair, with no group dining allowed, recalls the functional feeding aspect of these places. That this process never stops is shown by how small African canteens have come up to cater to Nigerians and other Africans now eking out a living in Mumbai.

But a khanewal/canteen is possible if you have space, and increasingly immigrants don't. With city rents putting even upmarket restaurants out of business, many immigrants can't afford a room in which to sell food. So they start selling on the street. They face problems from crowds, heat, dust, rain and police harassment. (The last is relatively easy to take care of given a perpetually hungry police force.) Yet it works well enough for many, and, as more come to the street and start competing, new kinds of street food evolve.

The vicissitudes of urban life also mean that long-term residents can end up like these immigrants. The closure of the old urban industries like textiles in Mumbai has thrust many on the street, sometimes literally to live or at least to make a living. Such processes happen in all cities, but Mumbai is where you see it is most dynamic, since this is where the most people come and where the scale of change from old industries has been the starkest. And accordingly Mumbai is the Indian city most often associated with street food, especially abroad and under its old name. It is not an infallible rule, but if you are looking for Indian street food in another part of the world your best bet is to look for a restaurant with Bombay in its name. Bombay House, Bombay Palace, Bombay Bites, Little Bombay are all more likely to serve desk-style snacks than a Taj Mahal or Jewel of India, and popular snacks like Bombay mix (chiwda) and Bombay potatoes (dry, spicy potatoes) reinforce the connection.

This is unfair to other Indian cities which have their distinct street food styles, many of which are hardly found in Mumbai. For example, it is hard to find the fat little stuffed crisp fried paratha of Delhi's Parathewale Gali or Kolkata's mutton chops or the 'thengai-mangai-pattani-sund*aaaaaaaal!*', the dry salad of boiled peas, green mango and coconut shavings, that hawkers cry out on Chennai's beaches. Still Mumbai is where you're likely to find the most variety and also the most invention as street food sellers keep trying to stay ahead.

An early example of such innovation came after Partition when refugees were settled in camps in areas like Sion Koliwada, which takes its name from the city's Koli fishing community. Perhaps it was from these Kolis that the refugees acquired the seafood to which they applied their characteristic ajwain spiked red masala. They fried and sold it by weight with an onion kachumber, and this was discovered by the city's students always on the lookout for cheap food. They found it an ideal accompaniment to beer and were soon making weekend trips to the stalls set up by refugees near the camps.

Today the refugees have moved on, and so has their seafood, now dubbed fish or prawn Koliwada and found at all the city's seafood restaurants. A few by-weight places still exist, like the perpetually crowded stall that sits surrounded by shoe shops on Linking Road in Bandra. But the street food buzz has moved on to new innovations like the spring dosa, surely the bastard child of adjoining 'Madrasi' and 'Chinese' stalls. Someone must have stuffed a dosa with leftover Chinese stir-fry—the need to reuse leftovers always being a driver for innovation in the food business—and cut the result into fat slices, and the spring (roll) dosa was born.

Such innovations don't always work—I do not predict a great future for the egg-sambhar-uttappam that I recently saw advertised on Juhu Beach. But the ability of street food sellers to respond to new trends and tastes is truly remarkable. For example, of late, a counter movement has been building up to take on the perception of street food as unhealthy. This does not take the form of direct refutation but the far more effective way of providing healthier-seeming options. Beautifully arranged plates of cut fruit are now widely available with wedges of watermelon, cubes of papaya, slices of pineapple and dark red beetroot. A trend that I think has come from Gujarat is for dispensers of herbal and vegetable juices to set up temporary shop, often a parked van, to catch early morning and late evening walkers. A similar trend that might catch on is from Chennai. Stalls have come up across the city selling 'health soups', like tomato or the more unusual plantain-pith soup.

That health juice van shows how street food is going upmarket. Five-star hotels like the Taj have long had faintly implausible versions of some street foods on their menu. They are usually made competently enough, perhaps just with too much care in the making, whereas part of the street food style lies in its super-fast, no-time-for-niceties, slapped-together technique. Besides you're always distracted by the incongruity of not having the chaos of the street around you and paying twenty times for the experience.

Malls are now joining in with food courts which provide an approximation of street chaos in the noise from the children in the entertainment area and crowds milling around looking for a table at which to sit. The food courts have stalls that sell all the street staples and this can look like an attractive way of eating them under a roof, which is not a restaurant, and with perhaps higher hygiene standards. But one bite of the food convinces you otherwise—since it usually tastes stale and tired, having been made long before in a central kitchen, the antithesis to fresh, made-in-front-of-you street food.

Short of these extremes though there's another type of street food provider, more organized than a hawker, less formal than a sit-down restaurant, better tasting than food courts. These are the takeaway counters set up by restaurants to increase turnover and reduce overhead. Many customers don't bother to take the food home, but eat on the spot, perched against trees, sitting in their cars, sometimes making use of plastic chairs and tables that the restaurant provides quite in contravention of municipal laws. This form of street food is particularly welcome for those with fears of eating at entirely roadside operations and allows access to the wider range of food that can be made in restaurant kitchens.

For the outlets it also helps take care of a spill-over crowd who might otherwise go somewhere else. On weekends, for example, when the lines of people waiting to sample the north Karnataka specialities at Halli Mane in Bangalore can be dauntingly long, an easier option is to grab the akki rotis and ragi rotis from their counter outside. This also works for chefs who can't afford or don't want the bother of a sit-down place.

This is particularly true of Mumbai where a chef as well known as Ishtiaque Qureshi, from the family that made dum pukht famous, has opted to dispense his excellent Avadhi food from Kakori House, a small kitchen in a back lane of Bandra. It's primarily a base for home deliveries, but there are always those who can't wait and eat his meltingly soft galouti kebabs right outside in the lane. Since this is exactly how people in Lucknow would eat them at the famous Tunde Mian's, it's arguably even more authentic than the formal dum pukht experience.

Mumbai doesn't just receive street food trends like this, it exports them as well. Bhel-puri, the city's signature mix of puffed rice, thin chickpea noodles (sev), crushed hard puris, several chutneys and other tangy-sweet ingredients, is now globally available. Pav-bhaji, the gloopy mass of spicy mashed vegetables bathed in butter and eaten with soft pav buns has, perhaps mercifully, not done as well. (I'm not a fan of this over-spicy, over-greasy, over-everything dish.)

Another export, Tibb's Frankie, is a rare example of a street food deliberately created as brand. In 1967, during the Beirut stopover that was usual for long-distance air trips at that time, Amarjit Singh discovered stuffed pita bread snacks. Back home he recreated them with Indian spices and parathas, and it was a hit. He sold it through branded outlets across the city, and his family is now trying to franchise it outside Mumbai.

The real challenge though is being mounted by the one street food that any Mumbaikar will tell you is really emblematic of the city. This is vada-pav, a ball of spiced mashed potato dipped in chickpea flour, deep fried and then sandwiched in a chutney drenched pav. In Suketu Mehta's *Maximum City* one of the leaders in Chhota Rajan's gang describes Mumbai as the vada-pav eater's city: 'It is the lunch of the chawl dwellers, the cart pullers, the street urchins, the clerks, the cops and the gangsters.' Take any popular vada-pav stall like Aram opposite CST Station, M.M. Mithaiwala in Malad, Mama Kane in Dadar, the famous Khidki Vada-pav in Kalyan or really any nameless cart where the vadas are fried fresh, the bread is chewy and the chutney tangy, there are always people hanging around for the next batch of vadas to be done, and then they can barely wait for the seller to tear the pavs open before they press their money on him, demanding a vada-pav, or two, or perhaps a whole packet for the office. Aram has a McDonald's just a stone's throw away, which can only dream of such demand.

Vada-pav is not like the street food you eat as a treat, like bhel-puri, but a basic one, like those plates of stainless-steel stored dal-chawal. Yet it has acquired the esteem of the fancier street foods. Ordinary workers fill their stomachs with vada-pav (children begging at traffic lights ask for money for a vada-pav), but yuppies will also stop to have one as a guilty snack (the bread and potato combo makes it an anti-Atkins diet bomb). Office all-nighters in Mumbai are driven by vada-pav as much as pizzas, and a socialite stockbroker was known for throwing champagne and vada-pav parties at the time of the Union budget.

The story of vada-pav is worth examining to understand how street food can have dimensions that are far more than just food. For something so essential to Mumbai today, its origin is relatively recent. Pav, the chewy square bun, has long been part of the city's life, perhaps dating back to when the Portuguese, who have the same name for bread (pão), first settled on these seven islands. It could also have come later when Goan immigrants opened the first bakeries in Mumbai, followed by immigrants from Iran at the start of the last century. Only a few of these bakeries survive with their original owners, like the Carvalhos of American Express or the Zends of Yazdani, but pavs continue to be made by the north Indian immigrants who run the bakeries today.

The other part of vada-pav, the deep-fried mashed potato ball, is probably Maharashtrian. In local parlance, 'vada' refers to something deep fried and, confusingly, can mean three things: a type of thick puri made in Konkani cuisine, the deep-fried savoury doughnut from south India which is what most people outside Mumbai think of as vada, and the potato ball of vada-pav. Potatoes came to India in the nineteenth century, planted by the British in the hill areas of the north, and they spread fast, at least in urban areas. Sliced thin or mashed they were dipped in chickpea batter and deep fried as a snack.

The real inspiration with vada-pav was putting the two parts together, along with enough chutney to moisten the pav and add spice to the blandness of bread and potatoes. Ashok Vaidya, a street food seller in the central Mumbai area of Dadar, is often credited with doing this. The innovation caught on rapidly, as is not uncommon in the highly competitive street food trade. One day you hear of something new and interesting in one corner of the city, and then suddenly it's in three other places, one of which is calling itself 'the original'.

Vada-pav caught on fast for several reasons. It is convenient to eat, with the pav serving as convenient container (when the pav is torn open, one side is left intact, so if you hold it properly you don't get grease on your hand). It offers a perfect balance between moist (chutney, potato) and dry (pav), bland (potato, pav) and spicy (chutney). It requires really basic ingredients, so anyone can make it. And it is somehow uniquely filling and tasty. In *Maximum City* Mehta muses that it is 'a good mouthful, a good mouth-*feel.* My stomach is getting filled, and I feel I am eating something nourishing after a long spell of sobbing.'

The popularity of the vada-pav did not go unnoticed. The Shiv Sena was in its combative nascent years at that time and saw how such an impeccably locally-generated snack could be co-opted as a symbol (the small fact of the non-native origin of its ingredients being ignored, of course). Politicians have always been aware of how strongly street food can connect as a metaphor—perhaps because they have to eat so much of it while electioneering. Laloo Prasad Yadav is the master of this with comments like '*Jab tak samosa mein rahega aaloo / Tab tak Bihar main rahega Laloo*!'

But Laloo and samosas could not be closer than the Sena and vada-pav. Conspicuous consumption of vada-pavs became almost de rigueur at Sena meets and rallies, and the party also played a key role in expanding its production. Party leaders realized that vada-pav stalls could provide employment to the rank and file who they counted on to power their agitations. In between flexing the Sena's muscle these men were allowed to set up vada-pav stalls near Sena shakhas, where they naturally found a ready market. 'It's really the only successful employment generation scheme that the Sena has ever set up,' a Marathi political journalist tells me dryly.

During the 2008 Lok Sabha by-election in Thane, Mumbai's satellite city, vada-pav was again part of a political battle. Cashing in on the Sena's vada-pav history the party's executive president Uddhav Thackeray announced a scheme for a vada-pav sellers' union to sell a branded 'Shiv' vada-pav. The Nationalist Congress Party senior leader R.R. Patil slammed this as an insult to Shivaji, drawing a furious response from Thackeray. Not to be left out, the Republican Party of India leader Ramdas Athavale announced plans for a 'Bhim' vada named after Dr Bhimrao Ambedkar! 'Our Bhim vada is to provide employment opportunities to backward class youth,' he said, adding that he hoped it could bring all Mumbaikars together.

In that Mr Athavale was probably correct, since it is no small measure of the appeal of vada-pav that despite the Sena's attempted co-option the vada-pav remains a universal favourite. People have even found interesting ways to subvert it—for example, replacing the standard red garlic and green coriander chutneys with south Indian coconut chutney, or Gujarati sweet date chutney. Eventually this has led to entirely new snacks, like bhujia-pav, with the pav being filled with pakoras or dabeli, where it's stuffed with a mash of vegetables with sweet-spicy Kathiawadi masala and pomegranate seeds for crunchy-tangy contrast.

Today with corporatization being the new buzz word and supermarkets replacing kirana shops and bankers chasing Bollywood to invest in their films, the vada-pav is going down that route as well. JumboKing is a chain that has come up to give vada-pav the modern fast-food treatment. Started by a young MBA couple, Dheeraj and Rita Gupta, JumboKing has set up takeaway outlets across Mumbai, offering basic vada-pavs that cost just a few rupees more than the real roadside ones. They also offer options like spicy chickpea topping or explosive Indo-Chinese 'Schezuan' sauce. For a few rupees more you'll get a plastic glass of lassi and even a 'healthy' vada-pav with a brown bread bun!

Now JumboKing is going national, and according to Dheeraj Gupta the Mumbai image is part of their marketing plan. 'Mumbai has the aspirational appeal which will lend credibility to the humble vada-pav,' he says. But the company is willing to tweak the product for local tastes. In Gujarat, for example, he admits they had a tough time initially getting customers. 'This is when our market research team told us that vada-pav in Gujarat is sold with the bread buttered like in pav bhaji,' says Gupta. 'We made this simple change and our volumes jumped 250 per cent within one month!'

JumboKing is not the only company trying to brand vada-pavs. Goli Vada-Pav is another, and so is JustDesi. The latter's selling point is a larger, softer bun and the use of a George Foreman like grill to press and grill the vada-pav before serving. Quite honestly this is awful, too soft and characterless, and I'm not a great fan of JumboKing either, which tends to make the vadas too spicy, when the real heat should come through the chutneys.

But the potential does seem to exist for the vada-pav to go national or even global: I'm told you can now get it in London's Borough Market for four pounds. Anthony Bourdain, the New York chef turned author and TV star, has rhapsodized about the perfect balance between hot vada, cool pav and spicy chutneys: 'It was just perfect, the colour, texture and flavour.' Dubbing it the Bombay Burger, he told me it was a noble dish, in the best tradition of great working men's dishes from around the world.

I've dwelled in depth on the vada-pav to show how fast a street food innovation can catch on, acquiring a mythology of its own and becoming such a part of a city's culture that it can become a symbol for the city and can use the city's image to market itself on a larger stage. But it is just one example from the wide range of Indian street foods. I can't attempt to describe them all here, but I can offer a rough system to categorize them.

As with any such system this one is fairly arbitrary and can—and should—be argued with. One of the joys of street food is how it allows for discovery and passionate debate. We love to argue about which hawker has the best kebabs, which corner of the city has the best bhel-puri, which street you must always slow down on to catch the kachoris only found there. We eat, we argue, we go out to eat more and compare and argue, and the arguments are never resolved but a lot of street food gets eaten.

My system doesn't start from the food or where it comes from or what ingredients it uses. Instead it starts from the street and the footprint the food has on it. Because, as all street food sellers know, their domain is a contested one, always potentially encroached on or evicted so they must be sure of their space and how they use it. Street food sellers are marvels of efficiency, managing knives, chopping boards, skillets, stoves, storage and cleaning in just a few square feet of space.

The first type of street food in my categorization has the smallest footprint. Just a cloth spread out on the pavement, an open shopping bag or at most a pushcart is all that's needed for street foods that are not cooked but just dispensed. The cooking is either not needed or done beforehand, like the homemade biscuits, cakes and other snacks that some enterprising families make, the women cooking at home and the men going out to sell. It could be the jaw-breaking toffees, with all their different ingredients—peanuts, cashews, sesame, amaranth seeds and others—all set hard in sugar candy. It could be the kulfis that immigrants from Uttar Pradesh come to Mumbai to make and sell across the city during its sweltering summers, carrying them on their heads in cloth-wrapped earthen pots. Or it could the bananas that can always be found on street-corner carts, in curvy bunches of green, yellow and red for the ultimate safe and energizing snack. There is a dismaying tendency in supermarkets to move towards selling only the tasteless, flawlessly yellow Cavendish that dominates global markets, but in the street you will still find the great Indian varieties like elaichi, rasthali, rasa-balle and karpuravalli.

There is another kind of street food that you will never find in supermarkets. These are the foraged foods, gathered by the poor, often tribal people, from wild or wayside plants in the country and sold in the city. Some like amla, jamun, phalsa, bilimbi and bel are well known, sweet-sour staples of the carts set up near schools. Others are more offbeat like jungli jalebi, an edible tree pod that's gets its name from its pinkish spiral shape. As with most such fruits it is more astringent than sweet, with an odd taste that explains why it will never be widely popular, but there is enough evident demand for it to be sold in the city.

In Mumbai there is an old man who sits in front of the museum with an ivory coloured cylinder in front of him. It is the pith or root of a tree, from which he slices off thin flakes, faintly sweet, with a crisp texture. The old man calls it Ramkandh, which sounds like it could be the name for any kind of root that the mythological hero might have foraged during his forest exile. It is strange to find something that seems so archaic in the middle of a busy city, yet the old man is always there, sitting by the side of the road, with the root before him. There are no shops for such foods, no markets where those who gather them can sell, but the street always has space.

The second type of street food doesn't need much more space, but more effort goes into its making. These are foods that do not require cooking on the spot, but do need final assembling. This type of street food combines different ingredients—crisp and chewy, sweet and sour, flaky and moist, liquid and solid—but they can all only be combined at the last minute which is what the street food seller does.

Golguppas or pani puri are the supreme example—crisp brown spheres broken and filled to be eaten with only microseconds to spare. So are all the varieties of paan—sweet, astringent, laced with potent secret ingredients. Paan has gone upmarket and you can now buy it in flashy glass-panelled shops, but there are still street corner sellers with lines of customers and backed up cars waiting for their daily fix. Ice-golas have, mysteriously, still to make it in restaurants (with the exception of a few like Mumbai's Swati Snacks), so remain on the roadside as perhaps the most dangerously alluring street food on a hot day—slabs of ice waiting to be scraped into shards, compacted on a stick and dipped in syrup, a mixture of both welcome coolness and lurking bacteria in the melting ice.

The assembling of such street foods is a performance, and watching it is part of their consumption experience. In his novel *Beach Boy* Ardeshir Vakil elevates such a bhel-puri performance into near poetry. The narrator, Cyrus, describes the ritual of waiting for the bhel-puri man's arrival, and then the anticipation as he is sighted walking slowly with the tools of his trade, a big tin box carried on his head and an hourglass shaped cane-stand carried under his arm. Crowds of schoolchildren gather as he sets the stand down with the box on top and opens it to remove the packets of ingredients. Unhurried by these imploring crowds he sets to work:

> My eyes fix on this man's fingers. His nonchalant air as he peels another purple onion and slices it in half. He wipes the knife. No chopping board, so the whole operation has to be performed in the palm of his hand. He makes horizontal slits across the onion-half, the vertical ones tilting the flaked onions into a stainless-steel box.

A potato comes next, still mysteriously hot, which is peeled and cubed in the same freehand style. The impatience of the crowd mounts, but the man is not bothered.

> The bhaiya cuts a lime in half, he shreds some coriander leaves, he lifts up a box and slides out a sheaf of pages torn from a magazine. The paper is thick and durable but not glossy—perfect for the food it will hold. He folds one sheet over and makes a wide cone-shaped vessel.

Now all that it left is the assembling.

> He takes a fistful of mamra and drops it into the paper cone; this is followed by fingerfuls of sev, onion and potato...He gives each of the chutneys a rattling stir: a red one with chillis and garlic, a brown one with tamarind and a green one with chillis and coriander. He pours a spoonful of each of the chutneys into the paper cone and mixes all the ingredients together. The final additions come according to the customer's taste. A squeeze of lime, a few coriander leaves and a sprinkling of raw tangy mango, a last fingerful of sev...

When he finally gets his bhel-puri Cyrus feels almost disappointment: 'I had no reason then to stand around watching him prepare the dish.'

In this whole performance it is worth noting how Vakil includes the preparation of the paper cone for the bhel as a key element. Receptacles are an important part of street food and can take many forms. Paper cones are most common, with thick magazine pages for greasy food and newsprint for drier foods like nuts. Absorbent newsprint is used for greasy foods, but when it comes to plates, paper has been mostly replaced by foil, better able to contain hot, liquidy foods.

The ecologically conscious can hope to find plates and cups made of pressed and stitched leaves, but their extra cost is sadly making them rare. The same goes for the earthen cups promoted by Laloo Prasad Yadav—if you ask for them at railway stations, they are either not in stock or cost a little extra, so plastic cups persist.

Street food in general depends too much on plastic and foil these days, and this is one reason it's attacked as polluting. Both street food sellers and consumers would go a long way in redeeming themselves if they could return to recyclable receptacles.

The last street food category is the most contested because it includes all the types of street food actually cooked in the street. Cooking implies relative permanency—one can't go wandering around with a pan of boiling oil, so one must be able to claim a spot in the street for at least the time of cooking. Cooking also means fire and that means smoke, smells and possible conflagrations, which all spell problems.

This is the type of street food directly affected by the Supreme Court's unfortunate order of February 2007 banning Delhi's hawkers from cooking food for sale on the streets. According to the order, which was on an application from the Municipal Corporation of Delhi (MCD), 'cooked food items properly packed may be sold'. This allowed dispensed street food and, with some stretch, assembled street food too, but it was 'clear and categoric that cooking of any food items shall not be permitted at all'.

Reaction against the order was strong. In the *Hindustan Times*, Vir Sanghvi, then editor in chief and a noted food writer, lamented that the judges were no longer eating street food: 'They have now reached such elevated levels in their careers that they no longer dash out of the office (or the courtroom in their case) for a quick plate of channa tikka...not for them the roadside supper of freshly roasted kababs, still smelling of charcoal as you pop them in the mouth.'

Sanghvi and others, like Pushpesh Pant, a professor at JNU who has chronicled the street food of Delhi, lambasted the order not just for nannying but also for sheer lack of logic. Pant pointed out that street food cooked in front of you, often by methods like deep-frying, was the least likely to have hidden bacteria and was probably healthier than food served in fancy restaurants: 'The *khomcha-redhi-thelewala* can't keep the leftovers in a deep freezer for reuse and the *dona-pattal-kulhar* used by them are entirely biodegradable.'

Sanghvi also drew an unfavourable parallel with restaurants to counter the MCD's assertion that the food stalls were a fire hazard. Kitchen fires were a danger, he agreed, but they were more likely in restaurants: 'We've all heard of exploding gas cylinders and badly maintained cooking rangers. But an exploding chaat-wallah?' Activists pointed out that the ban would only benefit the police, who would just raise their rate of bribes from the already burdened hawkers.

This was just the latest episode in a long-running battle over street food that is being fought in the courts, in newspaper columns and also, agonizingly for the hawkers, in the streets. On the one side there is usually the municipality and urban organizations like Mumbai's Citispace that tend to represent the interests of property-owning city residents. On the other side are the hawkers and, quite often, the media which tends to take a sympathetic view of street food if only because street food has a nostalgic appeal. We may not eat it much these days, but we like remembering youthful days where we imagine we were carefree and bohemian and had iron stomachs. Sanghvi adds a socio-political dimension to this nostalgia when he writes: 'The death of the neighbourhood chaat-wallah will also mark the death of the India we grew up in. It will re-emphasize the isolationist nature of our cities as middle class enclaves in which the poor are no longer welcome.'

Rather surprisingly, given day-to-day municipal persecutions, the pro-street-food position also includes the government. The ministry of urban employment and poverty alleviation makes much of its income-generation possibilities for the poor, while the ministry of food processing has plans for establishing food streets and for upgrading the quality of street food. This sort of contradictory position is quite consistent with central government institutions like this, far removed from the demands of street food vendors and their opponents, but it does lead to odd situations where on one day you can read of hawkers being evicted and on another about plans to promote food streets built around them.

The courts have also been contradictory in its several verdicts that touch on street food issues. In cases like Olga Tellis vs Bombay Municipal Corporation (1985), Bombay Hawkers Union vs Bombay Municipal Corporation (1985), Sodan Singh vs New Delhi Municipal Council (1989) and Maharashtra Ekta Hawkers Union vs Municipal Corporation Greater Mumbai (2003) the courts have shifted between recognizing the right of hawkers to ply their trade and the need for reasonable restrictions on this right, between advocating hawking zones and warning that allowing permanency to hawkers would put them on par with established shops, between allowing the sale of fruit juices but not solid foods, allowing cooked foods and cut fruits but not the actual cooking of this food.

In all these contradictions we can see perhaps the same mixture of appeal and anxiety that governs our personal reactions to street food. The courts can see the value of street food to thousands of vendors and consumers, yet can't shake off the views of propertied elites that these people should just *go away* and do it in private. But as in all such activities, people never do, and shamefacedly or on special occasions even propertied elites will join in. Despite more than a year of the ban, and despite much harassment of hawkers, walk beside a railway station in Delhi, down a back road or behind a local market, and street food sellers continue as they always will.

They start well before dawn in Mumbai. As fishing boats come into harbour there are women frying the catch fresh on the side. Outside medical colleges motherly old ladies dispense hot plates of khichdi and poha to sleep-deprived young interns coming off the night shift. In bakeries the first trays of pav are being baked, and on kerosene stoves at street corners potatoes are being boiled to make the first vada-pavs of the day. And as the first deliveries of milk are made, the chai-wallah starts the boiling that will barely stop through the day.

As dawn breaks, the early walkers come out on the seafront promenades and the van drives up to start selling herbal health juices. Outside railway stations, commuters who have abandoned their breakfasts to catch the train can quickly fortify themselves with masala omelettes or plates of egg-bhurji, the spicy scrambled eggs that are one of the most universal, if little acknowledged, Indian street foods. The first idlis of the day come steaming out of the cooker, ready to be served with freshly ground coconut chutney and freshly made sambhar.

As the day goes on and the first commuter rush is over, the ladies with the stainless-steel boxes ride into town, sharing the trains with the dabba-wallahs who carry their competition. By noon they have set up their stalls alongside the Nepalis running 'Chinese' stalls and Biharis who can make perfect south Indian dosas. The lunch crowd lingers till almost 3 p.m. but, in the full heat of afternoon, it is the cold drinks stalls, sugar-cane juice crushers with their grinding rollers, kulfi-wallahs and sellers of plates of perfect cut-fruit who command attention.

Evening is perhaps the peak time for snack foods like vada-pav which commuters grab to sustain themselves on the long journey home, or perhaps a boiled egg, shelled on the spot and eaten in one mouthful. It is also the time for bhel-puri on the beach, or pani puri on the promenade as families take an evening walk. At kebab stalls the hot coals send sparks flying as they heat the tandoors from which the kebabs and naans will be pulled for the evening meal. Behind the Taj Hotel eager tourists line up for their 'authentic Mumbai street-food' experience at Bade Miya, while more knowledgeable Mumbaikars head for Nagpada where the meltingly soft and juicy kebas at Sarvi qualify as street food since they are grilled on the roadside, then served inside the restaurant.

And then it is past midnight and restaurants are closing and soon it will be time for the last train. Yet in patches across the city you will still find street food sellers frying the last vada-pavs, scraping bhuna-ghosht or pav-bhaji around the tawa, scrambling eggs for the bhurji that never tastes as good as when served up to drunk revellers pouring out of nightclubs or weary staff that finally manages to kick them out.

Finally even these last vendors will wind down, eating the leftovers for their own meal. Soon, nearly all the street vendors are asleep with the city, except for the all-night tea sellers on bikes with big kettles, tacitly tolerated by the police who need them most of all. In less than an hour the cycle will start again, street food sellers keeping pace with the city that sustains them and they in turn sustain.

Chak de India!

. . . .

Soumya Bhattacharya

In the decades to come, that instant on the evening of Monday, 24 September 2007, will become a conversational touchstone, a sort of Kennedy moment for most Indians. *Where* were you when Sreesanth, running back from short fine leg, caught Misbah-ul-Haq off Joginder Sharma in the final over of the World Twenty20 Championship final at the Wanderers in Johannesburg?

As I write six months after it happened, it reminds me—in kind but not of course in degree—of that *other* moment, *the* Kennedy one in Indian cricket (in Indian sport, in modern Indian popular culture. Are they all the same thing?): *Where* were you on Saturday, 25 June 1983, when India won the World Cup final against the West Indies at Lord's?

There have arguably been greater, more famous victories (and with cricket fans, arguing about these things is going down a dangerous road; we can spend months on a desert island replaying and pitting India v West Indies, Port of Spain, 1976 against India v Australia, Eden Gardens, 2001), but if I were to somehow pin down the instant when India's love affair with cricket took a turn for the passionate, overriding, nation- and nationalism-defying obsession that it has become, I'd go back to that summer's evening at Lord's, that night in India turned as vivid and brilliant as day by the fireworks that wouldn't stop and the streams of people on the streets.

Some sections of this essay appeared, in somewhat different forms, as parts of articles published in the *Hindustan Times*, the *Sydney Morning Herald*, Cricinfo.com and the *Observer* (London).

Where were *you*?

I was thirteen years old, at a restaurant in south Kolkata, listening on radio to the moment on which the match turned—Viv Richards pulling Madan Lal, mistiming it a fraction and Kapil Dev running backwards, with the sun in his eyes and his heart in his hands till he had caught the ball. I was at the restaurant for takeaway. I had given up the match for lost, and offered to go and fetch dinner. There was no other customer, only surly waiters, who seemed suddenly transformed, incredulous and delighted at the fall of the wicket. I whooped and cheered, and began to run around the deserted restaurant, arms outstretched, doing the aeroplane imitation I had perfected as a little boy. The waiters joined me.

On the evening of the final in Johannesburg in September 2007, we had all given up the match for lost, and then counted it won, and then given it up for lost again and then, never mind, stopped thinking about what would happen because the frenzied exciting succession of moments was swallowing everything else up, leaving no room for contemplation—or hope or fear or doubt.

I was in the Mumbai office of the *Hindustan Times*, the newspaper I work for. There we were, a hundred-odd people on our floor: the know-alls and the know-nothings; the ones who take pleasure in saying they don't care about the game; the ones who think it's left field to say that it's not only they who don't bother but *no one at all* bothers about cricket that much any longer (why, didn't we notice, football was becoming the new cricket?); and the ones who reference point their lives with cricket and were the real sceptics of the Twenty20 format.

No, this wasn't cricket as we adored it, this wasn't, well, cricket at all, we the Twenty20 sceptics said, but when the moment came and the men in blue took the field and play started, we simply couldn't bear to turn away. It's work, we told each other quietly, we've got a newspaper to put out, and there is no news more worth paying attention to tonight than this game.

It was the same in every office around India. Or at least the ones in which people had to stay back between 5.30 p.m. and

8.45 p.m. The rush hour that day was at half past three: the rush to get home from work, fix the drinks, open the packets of munchies, get to the sofa in front of the television. Our office was like a mini stadium—the same collective desire that makes the atmosphere crackle with electricity; the shared keenness of everybody wanting the same thing and no one daring to hope too much for it. And then—as Diwali arrived in Delhi and Durga Puja in Kolkata before they were due, amid a flurry of fireworks and reason-defying abandon—not too long after the game had begun, Joginder Sharma (inexperienced, under pressure like never before, hero or villain for life over the course of the next few balls) took the final wicket and it was all over.

Was it? Or had it all merely begun?

Over the following days, culminating in the team's homecoming and triumphant victory procession from Mumbai airport to the city's southernmost tip, talk of a New India, a Young India, a Fearless India, playing without fear of vertigo after having climbed higher than anybody could have expected, became the delirious staple of Indian public life and discourse. The urchin who had watched the game with his nose pressed against the shop window on Gariahat Road in Kolkata, the industrialist popping Dom Perignon at the Taj Mahal hotel in Mumbai, the sniffy executive who pretended she couldn't see why there should be such a fuss about cricket—they were all borne aloft and swept away on the wave of generosity and self-congratulation.

And we, the sceptics? We smiled indulgently, said this wasn't quite a *real* triumph as triumphs go (oh no, this wasn't even *comparable* to the Tests won in Adelaide in 2003 and Multan the year after), and waited for the cheerleaders of Dhoni's side to start saying—after the first falter of the same team—how this was a bunch of overpaid, talentless, arrogant young men who model for consumer durables when they ought to be out on the field sweating it out in practice.

The sceptics did, however, acknowledge something that night. We were well aware of the fact that the men who comprised the heart of this team would in time hold in their hands Indian cricket's future. They were the men who would first comprise the national one-day side with an eye on the World Cup in 2011. And, in time, would take over from the presiding legends—Sachin Tendulkar, Rahul Dravid, V.V.S. Laxman, Sourav Ganguly and Anil Kumble—the stalwarts of our most sensational, most vaunted triumphs in international cricket, in Tests, the most challenging version of the game we so adore.

The future was here, and we could do nothing but embrace it.

I am no fan of Twenty20 cricket, but I can see why people love it, why it's such a smash hit. It's short and exciting; it simplifies the game; makes it more inclusive and opens it up to a new, wider audience. No one has the time for the five-day version any longer, the world has moved on, our lives are on fast forward, and we can't afford to track a game over the better part of a week. (This last argument is as puerile as it is philistine. It's like saying, because it takes so long, we shouldn't read literature, we should consign James and Flaubert and Dostoevsky and Updike and Roth to the dustbin, and stick to only reading text messages on our mobile phones or menus at restaurants.) Twenty20 doesn't work for me because it whittles down the unique soul of cricket: its sense of narrative, of contemplation that it offers, of the stringing out of things on a long high wire of protracted drama and tension, of its sense of slowly unfolding drama over days.

But I am aware that I sound anachronistic. Twenty20 is the future of the game—or at least it will be the cornerstone of the popularity of cricket in the future. Conceptualized by the Indian cricket board (no surprises there) and backed by the International Cricket Council (ICC), the Indian Premier League (IPL)—a Twenty20 tournament of eight teams comprising players from all over the world who were bought, American football-style, at auctions by franchisees of the teams begins its much-awaited second season in April 2009. It has begun to redefine the boundaries and the very notion of the game.

Who knows, this may well be the form of cricket that my daughter, now six, will grow up to admire. Of course, it helps—and it will help—that India won the inaugural World Twenty20 Championship in 2007. (I remember how we overnight became devotees of the one-day game after winning the World Cup in 1983. It turned out that we had previously scoffed at it not so much because we were purists but because we were hopeless at it.)

The biggest thing Twenty20 has going for it is that it is a version of cricket, and in India, any version will do. In our collective consciousness and in our popular culture, there is nothing quite like cricket. There never will be. And we are always happy, almost all of us, to make room for it, any version of it, and welcome it in our midst.

~

In the opening pages of *A Season with Verona* (a riveting account of following the Italian team, Hellas Verona, through one league season), Tim Parks tells us the etymology of the word 'fan'. It comes, he writes, 'from fanatic, from the Latin *fanaticus*, which means a worshipper at a temple'. It's particularly appropriate, that origin, when it comes to talking about cricket and India, because one of the truisms we have about cricket is that it is like a religion for us. (You tend to see these silly placards at stadiums too. A misleading platitude masquerading as an original aphorism.)

Cricket like religion in India? Oh no, it isn't. Religion, as Martin Amis writes in his 2008 collection of stories and essays, *The Second Plane*, 'is a belief system with no basis in reality whatever. Religious belief is without reason and without dignity, and its record is near-universally dreadful.' Religion led to the bloodbath that accompanied the birth pangs of India or, more precisely, the birth pangs of the two nation states of India and Pakistan. At least 200,000 people died. It led to riots that convulsed Mumbai and threatened to tear apart its secular fabric for ever. It prompted the pogrom against Muslims in Gujarat—one of the worst pogroms in the history of modern India. It is behind the series of bombings that have convulsed India and killed hundreds of people over the past two years.

Religion has scarred India more deeply than anything else. Cricket is the balm that heals. That's a huge thing, but it's not the only reason why cricket is so essential, so central to our country.

As the most visible expression of national identity, or an obsession or a dream, cricket is the only thing that unites a country as diverse and as contradiction fraught as India. Cricket is the glue that binds together the less than 2 per cent of Indians who have access to the internet and who are at the forefront of and the biggest beneficiaries of the country's economic growth, social change and IT revolution and the huge percentage of the population that gets by on less than a dollar a day.

India, with its dizzying economic growth rate, inflation and meltdown notwithstanding, is expected, along with China, to alter the geopolitical map of the world by the middle of this century. But the vertiginous growth is making wider the gulf between the educated urban elite (which is driving and thriving on India's rapid transformation) and the 70 per cent of the population that still lives in the country's vast rural hinterland.

The only thing that these two sections of India's population have in common is their passion for the game. Otherwise, they could well have been living in two different worlds. If the urchin on Gariahat Road in Kolkata who watched the Twenty20 final with his nose pressed to a shop window was ever to meet the bloke popping celebratory champagne at the Taj Mahal hotel, they would only ever have one thing to talk about: cricket.

For a burgeoning, confident, aggressively consumerist metropolitan elite, cricket has fostered a strong sense of national identity. For these people, scornful of politicians and too self-absorbed to be really bothered with their shenanigans, the game has become the most triumphant mirror of the ideas of nation and patriotism. For millions of Indians (the ones who live on minimum wage, never take holidays, have no other avenue of entertainment, can afford merely a community television on which to watch the matches), exulting in the success of eleven men on a green field is as close as they will themselves ever get to success. These Indians are not proud of their city, town or village, their backgrounds or their careers; they have little to look forward to in terms of what their country might have to offer them or what they might themselves be able to give. They only have cricket.

Unsurprisingly, we have appropriated cricket for ourselves: it is *our* game. It belongs to us (and, we often think, *only* us) as much as we belong to it. Three decades ago, I—or hundreds of thousands of little boys growing up in a city in India, besotted with the game, in the throes of their heightening passion gradually transforming into a lifelong affair—considered any cricket played on the subcontinent as an approximation of the real thing. *That* happened on English cricket grounds. A seven-year-old in Delhi or Bangalore today believes that the game played on his home ground is the genuine stuff; all else is a diluted version.

The manner in which India has made cricket its very own—in terms of the money it generates, the frenzy it engenders and its intrusion into every aspect of public life, from pop culture to politics—is a signifier of India's post-colonial present and newfound poise and confidence. Like the English language, cricket was a game made popular in India by the British. And like the English language, Indians have over the years appropriated it in a very Indian way. It is not merely that cricket touches more hearts in India than in the land of its birth; the pitch and tenor of the unbridled enthusiasm India has for it is very different from what you see in, say, England or Australia or New Zealand or South Africa.

Whether we like it or not, cricket has moved from the margins to the centre of our lives and public discourse. It flows into and colours areas of our lives with which we had once believed it had little to do.

In January 2008, on the heels of Indian spinner Harbhajan Singh being charged with having abused Australian all-rounder

Andrew Symonds during the Sydney Test in January 2008 (the charge was, after an appeal by the Indian team, watered down to using offensive language that was not racist; Harbhajan's penalty turned out to be much lighter than what had been initially recommended), the *Hindustan Times* conducted a nationwide poll about the whole affair. Only 14 per cent of the respondents thought that the continuing controversy was 'just about cricket'; 86 per cent believed it had wounded national pride.

Who said it was *just* a game anyway?

Indians take cricket seriously and think of it in terms of things like national pride because, among other things, cricket is really serious business now. The English writer Tim Adams, in a discussion of the professionalization and the commodification of tennis in his book *On Being John McEnroe*, turns to the cultural historian Johann Huizinga for an explanation of how things have become so. As players have become serious businessmen, mini-industries, 'a far-reaching contamination of play and serious activity has taken place. The two spheres are getting mixed. In activities of an outwardly serious nature hides an element of play. Recognised play, on the other hand, is no longer able to maintain its true play character as a result of being taken too seriously and being technically over-organised. The indispensable qualities of detachment, artlessness and gladness are thus lost.' It is exactly the same with cricket.

The feeling has been reinforced by the shift of the financial nerve centre of the game to the subcontinent and the staggering sums of money at stake. The arrival of satellite television widened the reach of the game like never before. Giant corporations, sensing the new opportunity and the new audience that was making vastly keener and more aggressive India's original passion for cricket, moved in with their fat wallets.

From the 1990s, as satellite television began to penetrate wider swathes of Indians, cricket on the subcontinent began to exponentially increase the amount of money it generated from advertisements and television rights. Billboards of Indian companies began to be seen in tournaments played outside India. It made perfect sense for the big companies. The number of views was shooting up, and Indians, sitting in India, were watching, for instance, India v England at Headingley. By advertising there, through satellite television, you were getting as many eyeballs as you wanted of consumers in India.

By the time the World Cup in England came around in 1999, several of the main sponsors—Hero Honda, Pepsi, LG—were targetting subcontinental audiences. Along with its heart and soul, the game's money muscle had swapped homes. Now, towards the end of the first decade of the twenty-first century, India has become the key to the financial health of the game, to its very well being.

Today, India controls more than 70 per cent of cricket's global revenues. Television advertising spots of a few seconds between overs sell for thousands of dollars. After furious bidding, global media rights for international cricket in India between March 2006 and March 2010 were sold for $612 million. Last year Nike won the five-year rights to sponsor the Indian cricket team's official kit for $43 million. Many of the Australian players make most of their money from endorsement deals in India. And the $550 million that the ICC received for sponsorship and broadcast rights to the 2003 and 2007 World Cups and three Champions Trophies would not have been possible without the advertising and satellite television money from the subcontinent.

In February 2008, at a luxury hotel in south Mumbai, the auction for players to take part in the first season of the IPL in April took place. The proceedings (which married Bollywood stars, industry captains and cricketers in a glamorous, cash-rich wedding) overwhelmed the television channels and the front pages of papers. Players' services for forty-four days of Twenty20 cricket between teams that comprised Indian and international players were auctioned to the highest bidder. Each bidder was a franchisee of a team, something like a club owner in European football. Mahendra

Singh Dhoni's services were bought for $1.5 million, and several other rising Indian players like young Ishant Sharma and Rohit Sharma were assured of the sort of money they could scarcely have dreamt of twelve months ago.

The Indian board came out of all this rather well. Within days of the auction—and with the season yet to begin—the board had earned $723 million through franchisee rights (that is, the money gleaned from individuals in exchange of the rights to become franchisee of a particular team) and $5 million via title sponsorship rights. A chunk of that $723 million will be distributed to the cricket boards of countries from which players will participate in the league.

It's hardly odd that other cricket boards (and the ICC) hold the Indian board as much in awe as in fear.

We saw that most recently after l'affaire Harbhajan and the loss of the Sydney Test to Australia in January 2008. India was right to have felt robbed; there were eight crucial decisions that went against the team. But it is India's financial clout that allowed its cricket board to arm twist the ICC into sacking the controversial—and thoroughly incompetent—umpire, Steve Bucknor, for the subsequent Test at Perth.

Divorced from the context, though, the removal of Bucknor was a good thing. If players can be dropped for not playing well, why not officials who often hold the players' futures in their hands? It has happened in football, and it is high time that it did in cricket. International cricket is a highly organized business. There is no place for incompetence in corporations.

But that isn't the point here. The point is that India could do it because it holds the purse strings of international cricket. It got away with bullying the ICC earlier (in South Africa in 2001) and it will again. Money doesn't merely talk. It screams so loud that it silences any opposition.

When India asked for Bucknor's removal, the ICC boss, Malcolm Speed, gave in because it was the most expedient way to hold the tour together. (He didn't of course admit to the fact that he had yielded.) The financial and political implications of India pulling out of the tour—and its subsequent fallout—in terms of the future of the game were too enormous to gamble with, or even to contemplate. Several former cricketers have made this point, though few as strongly as former Australia captain Allan Border. 'They [India] have probably too much say in matters even though it's a global game,' Border told an Australian paper in February 2008.

A lot of us over here, though, can't get enough of India's financial muscle in the world of cricket—and the frequent flexing of it. It's a small world when it comes to cricket, but here is at least one thing in which we are dictating terms to the rest of the world. At least off the field. Here, too, as in the matter of Twenty20, I am a little anachronistic. I think that sort of thinking is too shrilly self-righteous and misguidedly jingoistic to afford any comfort or pleasure. Besides, if the wheel were to turn—it usually does—and the balance of financial power one day shifts away from India, there will be others more than willing to do to India what India is now doing to them.

And on the field? Well, at least we aren't doing too badly there either. At the time of writing (and given that this is Indian cricket where so much can change in such little time, one is always likely to be overtaken by developments sooner rather than later), India is the Number 2 Test side in the world. In 2007 it beat England in a series away from home—the first occasion it has done that since 1986. In early 2008 it returned from a magnificent, memorable tour of Australia, where—led with remarkable gumption by Kumble in the Tests and Dhoni in the one-days—it showed that it could play with bottomless reserves of grit, that while it could be cornered the team could not be written off, that it would neither be bullied nor bowed without battle.*

*In end 2008, the India–Australia series, seen as test cricket's premier conformation, saw India convincingly win the second test at Mohali.

In Australia, India lost the Test series 1–2. On the toughest tour on the planet against the best team in the modern game, most teams return whipped and whimpering, usually having lost every Test. India followed up its showing in the Tests by winning the one-day tri-series against Australia and Sri Lanka. It was the first time ever that it had done so. It decimated the world champions in the finals, beating them twice within four days. Suddenly, *anything* seemed possible.

It is always rash to speak of a reinvention and renaissance after one one-day series win—just as it is stupid to speak of desolation and hopelessness after one defeat—but there did seem to be something swirling in the air of the Australian summer. It was to do with the things we have seen in this Indian side that we have not seen before—or seen, but very rarely. A new poise, a new self-assuredness, a new courage and confidence.

Will it last? Can it? Who can tell?

Either way, there is one thing that is indisputable: cricket is the only team game which we are really any good at. Who is to blame if it is then the only team game in which we are remotely interested? For us, nothing will ever become the new cricket. If there is ever to be something like that, it will have to be some version of cricket as we know it now. A quick pop quiz: India won an international football tournament in late 2007. Who did we beat? Where was it played? Scores, anyone? Answers on a postcard please.

~

The covenant between a team and its fans is inviolable, sacrosanct. We can never bear to not follow our side when it plays. This comes with its inevitable disappointments and misery but our allegiance remains unbroken. It is not like colas or cars or credit cards or the insurance policies the players endorse. Don't like it? Flush it down the toilet. Sell it off. Exchange it for something better. Buy a new one.

When things go wrong on the pitch, some of us go on mock funeral processions. Some of us burn effigies. Both gestures are as banal as they are despicable. But none of us can stay away. (Not being able to stay away is in the nature of addiction, which always has irrationality at its heart.) If we are able to, television ratings would slip and channels wouldn't pay millions for satellite rights and companies wouldn't put their money where the nation's heart isn't. The fact that they do suggests that there are millions of us out there.

All of us think we have a stake in the Indian cricket team. We have invested our emotions, our passions, our frenzy, our whole *lives* in following our side. There is simply too much riding on those eleven men, we believe. The Indian cricket team is, for us, like a giant corporation. How its stocks rise and fall has a bearing on our lives. We can't support another team. We can't be bothered to care half as much about any other game. It's either this or nothing. And nothing is so much worse.

I have always wondered why the average Indian does not carry over such strong feelings into other walks of life. We make so much of one defeat on the cricket field that we ask for the captain to be sacked and denounce our players as wimps and threaten to attack their families. But we don't ask for our politicians to be hanged and quartered for corruption; we shrug and make do when the roads in our cities are disgraceful; when we see—especially after having returned from our trips abroad—how shameful our public transportation is.

Why is it that we don't protest? Why do we reserve our outrage only for cricket?

My guess is this: we can't allow our players to slip—it would be too much of a blow to our sense of self-worth.

~

Our obsession with the game is not merely to do with fandom, though. Never mind which social class or region they come from, many of cricket's devotees in India passionately believe that they one day will become the stars others will watch. This conviction has been strengthened by the fact that the game has opened up; it is no longer the bastion of a particular social class or region. How many cricketers does Mumbai—once the crucible of Indian cricket—have in the national team now? How many players from the middle or upper-middle class? It doesn't matter any longer.

Sourav Ganguly, India's most successful captain ever, comes from Bengal—a state without a tradition of producing any cricket player of note. Dhoni, the man in whom we are investing our hopes for the future, is the son of a railway ticket collector from Jharkhand—a young state without a tradition of producing, well, anything respectable. Irfan Pathan is the son of a muezzin in Baroda. Virender Sehwag is from dusty Najafgarh, a place not many Indians knew existed before he exploded on to international cricket. R.P. Singh's father has a modest job with Indian Telephones in Rae Bareili. Praveen Kumar, the man of the match in India's unforgettable one-day triumph against Australia in Brisbane in March 2008, is from a family of wrestlers in Meerut. They have turned cricket into the new meritocracy. And everyone is invited.

Thanks to the IPL, Dhoni earned about Rs 6 crore in a very short season of neither terribly demanding nor intense play in a form of cricket not even Twenty20's most ardent admirers will consider the premier form of the game. A Delhi University professor, in comparison, the *Times of India* calculated, will earn one-third that amount over a career spanning thirty-five years.

In New India (a new country where we have reinvented the language to turn an adjective into a proper noun), where we have learnt to slough off the old diffidence about affectation, ostentation and acquisition, this sort of money (this sort of a *career*) has its unique allure. 'Greed is good,' Gordon Gekko told us in Oliver Stone's film, *Wall Street*, in 1987. More than two decades on, the young inhabitants of New India are echoing that. Money—and its visible manifestations—is good, it is power in a way it wasn't ever before. And we need it, need more of it, and the ways in which it can be acquired hold a sort of talismanic value. (This is neither a good thing nor a bad thing. It is just how things *are*.)

In a way, of course, the evolution of the new meritocracy began with Sachin Tendulkar. Now a senior statesman of the team, Tendulkar has dominated India's collective consciousness in a way no other sportsperson (no other *person*) has. One reason for that of course is that he has dominated his sport in a way no other sportsperson has in India's history. Ramachandra Guha tells us in *A Corner of a Foreign Field* that when Tendulkar bats against Pakistan, India's television audience is greater than the population of Europe. Tendulkar has bridged something more critical than the digital divide: he has bridged the generation divide. Their admiration of him has made fathers and sons agree, for once. But that is not all there is to it.

Tendulkar arrived at precisely the right moment. Early on in his international career, India's protectionist economy opened up, giving birth to a new class of wealth creators. And in those days, Tendulkar—more boy than man, prodigiously gifted and astonishingly mature for his years—embodied all the qualities that this new class treasured: he was a world beater, a global citizen, smart, well-dressed, a self-made man. And the money he earned—huge sums, unthinkable sums—was more than any sportsperson had earned before him.

The cultural critic and author, Mike Marqusee, was one of the first to spot this in an article for *Wisden Asia Cricket*:

> The intensity of the Tendulkar cult is about much more than just cricket. Unwittingly and unwillingly, he has found himself at the epicentre of a rapidly evolving popular culture shaped by the intertwined growth of a consumerist middle class and an increasingly aggressive form of national identity. National aspirations and national frustrations are poured by millions into his every performance.

Whether by chance or by choice, Tendulkar became Indian cricket's first global brand. In this too, as in much else, he was the pathfinder. Nearly two decades after he started, he is still at it. Only the iconography has somewhat changed. It's bound to. Arguably the greatest (or at the very least, the most durable) batsman of the modern age has gone from being a thin sixteen-year-old with a golliwog mop of hair to a man with two nearly grown-up children. From the son most fathers would love to have, he is now the father most sons would love to have. The brand positioning has altered (he endorses life insurance these days) but the cachet of the brand remains the same.

Without him, there would have been no Yuvraj Singh or Dhoni or any other Indian cricketer as global brands; had he not been such a success, the allure of cricket as a life-transforming process would not have been so well defined, and the dream of that alchemy would not have been dreamt by hundreds of thousands of young men across India today.

They do dream. On the Maidan in Kolkata, in Shivaji Park in Mumbai, on the barren fields in the wastelands of Bihar, in posh cricket academies all over the country. The boy with his state-of-the-art kit in an affluent, urban family believes he can emulate his heroes—that *that* life, that fame, can be, *will* be his—with as much fervour as the boy in a dot of a village with his makeshift stumps and inadequate gear. What does it take, they ask themselves, just *what*? Talent, rigour and a lucky break. Look at Pathan. Look at Joginder. Look at Praveen, at Ishant, at R.P., at Sehwag. Look at Dhoni. If they can, why not me?

Only a select few break through to that stratosphere. Perhaps even they are aware of how slim the chances are. But that in no way dilutes the intensity of their desire. For is that not the stuff dreams are made of?

~

Television first introduced me to cricket in the summer of 1974. I was four years old at the time and living with my parents in a flat on Bolsover Street in west London. The television itself was an object of wonder for me. I had never seen one before (remember, this was still 1974, and India, when I left it for England with my parents a year previously, was a long way off from having television).

I was of course no stranger to the radio but the fact that you could merely flick a switch and bring into your home moving pictures and sound at the same time seemed magical. I would gaze enraptured at the set in our living room even when it was turned off; I would stare unblinkingly at it just after it had been switched off, watching the screen lose its glow, become a dimming speck of gradually vanishing light.

And when it was on? Well, I was in front of it for as long as I could.

One of the big things on television that summer was India's tour of England. Or at least it was for my parents. India arrived in England, after having beaten in the past three years the West Indies in the West Indies and England at home and away. London in the 1970s was not quite the multiracial, multicultural world capital that it is today, and no one could have imagined then that India would three decades later be seen as an emerging world economic powerhouse. My parents had little to show off to their English friends and colleagues as contemporary Indian achievement and glory. They—a couple in their thirties from one of the world's poorest countries, my father trying to make his way in a white collar profession like medicine in London—were hoping that the Indian cricket team would exemplify the best that India had to offer.

The series showed how misguided their hopes were.

India lost the first Test at Old Trafford by 113 runs. In the second at Lord's—which unfolded not very far from where we lived—India were so abject that it was thumped by an innings and 285 runs. Following on, it was all out for 42 in the second innings. The summer of '74 earned a new nickname: the summer of '42.

It was the first series that I ever followed, and it was good training. It was appropriate preparation for the years of torment that were to follow: of waking up at 3 a.m. and hearing us getting a pasting; of staying up the whole night and watching us getting thrashed; of skiving off work (or school or family responsibilities) to see us savaged, decimated, humiliated, murdered. I didn't know then, but a lifetime of misery lay ahead of me.

I found out, bit by bit, as I began to realize that I was in for the long haul. It happened through listening to cricket commentary on a reliable, well-travelled Grundig radio in Bankura, a small, backwater town in Bengal where I lived with my parents for a little less than two years. (The radio was a wedding present; my parents took it with them wherever they went.) There was Test Match Special on short-wave, commentary in rich, plummy accents and often incomprehensible jokes that made me create for myself a vision of what it must seem like to watch cricket at Lord's with the slope of the nursery end in front of me. (Big mistake, I later realized on first visiting Lord's as a spectator. Distance had bred enchantment as only distance can, and the radio—and my age, six—had allowed me to mythologize the experience as only six-year-olds can.) There was commentary at all odd hours of the day and night when India toured Australia or the West Indies. And there was commentary from games played in India. The reception would vary, the sound sometimes crackling and fading, but I kept my ears to the radio, sometimes giving it a good shake or slap when the sound waned. Often, it worked.

Kolkata, the closest venue for the international cricket that I heard relayed, was a couple of hundred kilometers away. But my love for cricket blossomed in Bankura precisely because I was so far way from any real action.

I became obsessed with the game through radio commentary and pictures in black-and-white magazines and heroic re-enactments of whole Tests in our backyard. (Single-handedly. Not only playing on behalf of both teams by throwing a ball against the wall and hitting it, but also keeping a running commentary and cheering resoundingly if things were going well for India. Which they usually did because the flow of the match and its outcome were in my hands.)

You didn't go out with friends in Bankura. (There was nowhere to go to.) You didn't watch television. (There was no television.) You didn't listen to music. (There was no music store to buy tapes from.) You didn't go to the cinema. (There was one cinema in the town and not once, in the two years that I spent there, did they show anything remotely resembling a film which my parents would let me go to.) You didn't read much. (The two bookstores sold school textbooks. Anything else had to be brought back from Kolkata on our occasional visits.)

As entertainment, cricket was all there was for me. What could one do but embrace it?

Soon enough, I got close to real action. I first went to Eden Gardens when the West Indies came to play in the winter of 1978. And then, I went for every international game there, for a quarter of a century. As the years rolled by, the options of how to follow cricket multiplied. It became a veritable buffet, an unfolding of a panoply of delights: television began live telecasts; satellite television arrived; the internet came with its ball-by-ball reocunting; and the glut of sports channels began their endless re-runs of famous matches and splendid innings.

Sometimes it seems hard to escape cricket in India. Even fans like me—especially the older ones, who are middle class, not far away from middle age, socially active and parents, the ones who need to strip away all the clutter, arrange their schedules so that they can make space in their lives for the cricket—aren't complaining. We can't get enough of it. Cricket reminds us of things in our pasts; it is central to the lives we lead now; and it will be crucial—and here I can speak only for myself—to the future. (More of that in a minute.)

Even now, when I watch the game broadcast from Australia, I think of the first time, over February and March 1985, I watched on television cricket played in Australia, a country I then defined solely in terms of its cricket grounds. It was the Benson and Hedges World Championship of Cricket.

Remember the bikinis? When I think now of what I remember most about first watching cricket played in Australia, it seems to be the bikinis. But that tournament itself was thrilling. India won, beating Pakistan in a day-night final. Ravi Shastri emerged as champion of champions and took the team on a ride around the MCG in the Audi that was his prize. For me, a teenager watching in the living room of our south Kolkata home, in a not-so-liberal, not-at-all liberalized India, seeing a car like the Audi—and the fact that an Indian sporting hero could now possess it—was a thrill. But the sight of all those toned female bodies and the Channel 9 cameras lingering over them in their jokey, nudge-nudge-wink-wink slow tracks was a far bigger, almost illicit thrill.

Of course, there was the magnificent Channel 9 coverage. A whole generation of Indian cricket fans growing up in the 1970s had never ever seen anything like that before. Used—and that too only just—to Doordarshan's stodgy, boring, shot-from-one-angle stuff and execrable commentary, the manner in which cricket could be brought alive on television, made spectator-friendly, participatory and exciting was a revelation. Angles, cameras, experts, debates, urgency, the *details*: how I loved it. It seemed like justification for being a fan.

I watched India's 2007–08 tour to Australia on TV at my Mumbai home. (The one before that, I had seen at grounds in Australia—an absolute carnival of celebration, of leisurely delight.) I no longer find the bikinis as much of a novelty as I used to. Also, frankly, not half as much of an attraction. And with the technical sophistication in the coverage of cricket in India now about world-class, Channel 9 doesn't seem *that* different any longer. (In any case, I don't watch Channel 9 at home but Star or ESPN.)

A lot has changed. But there is one thing that is common even now to my first experiences of watching cricket in Australia: the unrivalled pleasure of getting up in the morning to watch the game. Could anything be better, quite so unsullied an enjoyment? I go to sleep in delicious anticipation, looking forward to waking up and watching. I start the day with the game, mind uncluttered, nothing having yet happened to ruin my day or mood.

I go to bed with the remote on my bedside table. Wake up and smell the coffee? No, wake up and watch cricket. There's nothing quite like it.

I know there are millions who do the same thing, who feel the same way. Perhaps you—having come so far in this essay—do too.

As I get older it becomes ever more apparent that cricket is a window on to a parallel, perhaps a better, universe. Its disappointments do not have a bearing on my job or my family; its thrills are other-worldly. I need only to press a button on my remote, and I will be transported. I will have escaped.

On bad days, I have a fantasy in which I'm much older. I often find myself imagining the worst. (It's not quite a daydream, it's not quite a nightmare—the fear is real but it's also indulgent, even comforting.) My career is over (as the years go by it's something that becomes less and less difficult to envisage); I have arthritis or some other debilitating but not life-threatening illness which leaves me just about housebound; my daughter has left home; my parents are dead; my wife no longer finds me an amusing or interesting companion; and I no longer write or get published, so reading becomes less of a motivation and pleasure.

What will I be left with then? What will prevent me from going over the edge, becoming a slobbering old man drooling into his bowl of anodyne soup? Should such an eventuality come to pass (and with life, you just never can tell—life does have a habit of coshing you over the head), I know I will always have cricket. At the flick of a switch and the turning of a knob, with the riffle of a newspaper or the click of a mouse, I will be able to summon those familiar images, those thrills, that other world. Even when all else is gone.

When I was young, I never thought of these things—one doesn't think of growing old when one is a child. Now I fear the loneliness that age might bring. And I hug cricket to myself because one day it may be all that's left.

~

I am writing this in the early-morning quiet of my Mumbai home. My daughter has gone off to school. My wife is pottering about in these rare hours that she has to herself. These are hours I, have to myself, too, before the ebb and flow of the day begins to tug at me.

It's time to recall last night's game, relive the thrill of watching India win a close match, let the unparalleled joy of having watched India do the unprecedented—win a triseries in Australia by grinding the world champions into the dust—wash all over me again. I know there are so many others all over India who are doing the same.

So I close my eyes and see them again, our boys from the white-hot Australian summer, sprinting across the Gabba in Brisbane as though they never want time to catch up with them. Sreesanth with the tricolour and his exaggerated, faux-movie-star air; Harbhajan twirling his souvenir stump above his head, thumping his chest; Dhoni as composed in his bearing as his batting is unfettered, trying not to show how overwhelming the moment is; and Praveen Kumar, the young find, the surprise package, the man of the match, with a goofy grin that suggests he can't believe that he is the star of the sort of spectacle he used to watch on television.

The day's papers are in front of me. The *Hindustan Times* has put out a photo feature on how fans in Mumbai watched the game and how they celebrated. There is a group of young boys in Shivaji Park (where Sunil Gavaskar and Tendulkar were raised), in cricket gear, bats held triumphantly aloft, faces creased in smiles of unalloyed delight that only children can experience. There is a photograph of a set of smartly dressed young men, their drinks on the table, letting out a collective whoop of joy at a club in

Mumbai's western suburbs. And there is a photograph of a crowd packed tight on the pavement, gnawed by suspense, watching the game outside a jewellery store. The crush is so great that some of them, even after craning their necks, can probably see merely the score at the bottom of the TV screen inside. Some look like students, some like travelling salesmen, some like odd-jobs men.

My eye is riveted by a man right at the periphery of the crowd. His arms are bent, one raised, the other stretched out. Between them he supports on his shoulder what looks like a very heavy cardboard box. He must have been on his way to deliver it somewhere. Now he stands rooted to the spot, uncomfortably rooted, his eyes fixed on the television—or the little of it that he can see from where he is standing. He can't tear himself away. Work can wait, so can making a living. For that moment, in the tense moments of a critical match, it is cricket that matters. It's all he has.

The rest of life can happen between overs.

It's a typically Indian story. Cricket as participatory mass spectacle, as street theatre, as national discourse, as catharsis. Cricket as a field of dreams. It's all we as Indians have in common.

Going Against the Flow

. . . .

Indrajit Hazra

'Monster, I do smell all horse-**piss**; at which my nose is in great indignation'—*The Tempest, Act 4, Scene 1*

'No pleasure compares to this'—*Gopal Bhar, court jester in the court of Raja Krishnachandra of Nadia, on the relief of finally defecating*

Epiphanies are single-window moments of staggering lucidity that confirm a truth. The young Ramakrishna Paramahansa had his epiphany when he swooned upon seeing a flock of white birds against a sky of dark clouds and understood that we are all playthings of the Mother Goddess. Joan of Arc, struck by a shaft of sunlight—and a bipolar condition—realized one fine moment that she had a hotline to God and was chosen by Him to lead the French into battle against the English. Isaac Newton had his understanding of the universe once the apocryphal apple landed on his head.

I had my epiphanic moment one day in the early 1980s.

My father and I were visiting relations of ours in Bardhaman town, some hours away by train from Calcutta. We stepped out of the local train on to the smudgy platform. But before getting on a cycle-rickshaw, I needed to pee. Desperately.

Now I don't know whether it was the Jesuits at school finally getting to me or some other more practical reason, but I decided to do the desperately necessary act not on the next-to-me tracks or against any of the graffiti-doused walls nearby, but inside a white-tiled room on the platform that was the Bardhaman Station public lavatory.

My father showed brief puzzlement and may have asked me once whether I was sure I wouldn't prefer to take a leak on the tracks or somewhere in the bushes yonder. Public hygiene was vaguely connected in my mind with the moral science classes we used to have in school. And perhaps it was a feeling of being civilizationally superior that made me insist that I use the public toilet for the purpose it was built.

The moment is as clear in my head as triple distilled vodka in an expensive bottle. I swung open the electric blue wooden door of the station lavatory and encountered Hell.

The insides of the room were, like the outsides, made up of gleaming white tiles, signifying that the lavatory was a new construction. It was an Indian style loo with a pair of white ceramic crumple lines for the positioning of one's feet. These were almost hidden by tumultuous Van Gogh-meets-Jackson Pollock swirls of something unnameable. In this bog bath, I stood—aghast—the pressure in my bladder forgotten, my nose blinded by signifiers that signified only one thing: pissshitsofthardwetrunnysnotorgyhell.

My moment of truth had come. And the truth remains with me till this day: we are filthy people.

Now, along with that other national consolation for our collective failings that tells us that since we invented the zero we must be civilizationally smarter than other cultures, there's also the one about cleanliness and hygiene. The thesis goes something like this: as individuals, Indians are hygiene-obsessed. Apparently, in our private spaces—that is with our bodies and in our homes—cleanliness is next to godliness. The argument is that overtly or otherwise we are Brahminical in our rules and taboos about personal hygiene which thereby makes us, especially when compared to Western people (think Viking marauders; think the Black Death), gleamingly clean folks.

Well, textually, we do sound squeaky clean. The pre-defecation chant from the Vishnu Purana, for instance, tells us quite clearly that the right thing to do is to put the sacred thread around your right ear when taking a dump or a pee—facing the north during the day and south at night. And just in case you always wanted to know but didn't know whom to ask, the Puranic text also tells us that once the deed—that is No. 2 a.k.a. the Big One—is done, do wash the *linga* (genitals) once, the *guda* (anus) thrice, the left hand ten times, the right hand seven times, and both feet with water and earth (which, I guess, would be soap today) thrice. The same manual states that a person should urinate at least 10 cubits away from any source of water, 40 cubits away if there's a river or a temple nearby. And if it is defecation you have in mind, then ensure you're at least 100 and 400 cubits away from a water source and a river/temple respectively. The Koran has a similar kit for those seeking help in the personal hygiene department.

These are nice, although a tad anally retentive and quite male-centric guidelines.

So what happened at the Bardhaman station loo? So what happened everywhere around us? Why the gagging stench, the wanton droppings, the relentless torrents, the effortless easings? And why this Cartesian divide between private and public hygiene? Is there really such a Cartesian divide at all? I have visited enough bathrooms in urban middle-class India to know that this private-public division is highly exaggerated. But why then, in the Socialistic, Democratic Republic of India, is public hygiene so shit?

More than twenty years after my epiphany at the mouth of hell, why is public hygiene in this country such a pissshitsofthardwetrunnysnotorgyhell? Well, for starters, the 'sacred' manuals are as integral to our daily ablutionary lives as the Ten Commandments are to the good people of Las Vegas.

So let me take the bull by the tail. According to the *National Human Development Report 2001*, 80 per cent of Indians either defecate in the open or use unsanitary latrines and public toilets. To put this in a more lucid perspective, out of the 1.2 billion people in the world who defecate outdoors, 665 million are Indians. And that, according to numbers released by the World Health Organization and UNICEF in July 2008, is despite the fact that 'open defecation' figures in developing countries are down from 31 per cent in 1990 to 23 per cent in 2006. Some 200,000 Indians have gained access to improved sanitation between 1990 and 2006—the halcyon 'liberalization years'. That's a jump from 14 per cent to 28 per cent in the intervening sixteen years. Nevertheless, in terms of the potty index, we're yet to be Superflush India.

Sewerage facilities are available to about 35 per cent of India's urban population. As for bucolic rural India, 14 per cent have access to sanitary toilets. Thus, my dear reader sitting with this slim volume on your favourite seat with the seat down, we have a huge supply–demand problem. But really, how desperate is the demand? As the Urdu poet Chirkin rather cryptically remarked: 'The virtue that I will earn now/ will all be invested in toilets/ This time I visit your home/ I will never pee there.'

Even among people with access to flush toilets and the theoretical notion that peeing out in the open is a disagreeable thing for the surroundings that one shares with fellow carriers of bladders, public urination isn't really considered nasty business. Not really. The thought of holding on to one's bladder till one reaches the correct 'receptacle' is considered somewhat pointless, outlandish, 'foreign', even 'unmanly'. And it is interesting that women, with the same bladder functions and requirements as men, do not succumb to this male temptation. This brings me to a consideration of the matter of shame. For a man, there is no shame if he takes out his urinary utensil, stands or squats and does the needful in the presence of others who echo his shamelessness by not finding anything awry at all about human waste being deposited on the streets or against a wall. 'Holding back' until you can't 'hold back' any more is an alien concept for Indian men in general. The emergency 'gotta go when you gotta go' bar is set so low that a tickle under the belly is enough to engage in an 'emergency' relief operation. I can safely say that there is no Tycho Brahe in this country—I refer here to the Danish astronomer, who, in October 1601, after refusing to leave the dinner table to pee because of his insistence that manners must be maintained, died painfully after his bladder burst.

Forty-five years before that particular tragedy struck in Europe, here in Mughal India, an important plan was being put to work. Now, sitting-type toilets at Lothal in Harappa, some 60 kilometres away from present-day Ahmedabad, have been found to have existed around 2500 BC. But since then, as far as 'public facilities' go, India had nothing to show. So it was left to Emperor Akbar, having just taken over the reins of the Mughal Empire from his father Humayun, to commission in 1556 a public toilet in Alwar that would cater to a hundred families. The Mughals had *ghusalkhanas*—but these were private, luxurious bathrooms that doubled as massage parlours for the rich. Akbar decided that the time was ripe for public facilities.

Well, the hundred-family Alwar public toilet was made. But very soon, the people realized that the conditions were so bad, so unsanitary, that no one in their right mind—except perhaps future visitors to the Bardhaman station loo—would enter this building. Most people went back to shitting in the open (good fertilizers) or inside the usual dirty, decrepit toilet blocks.

Which is the story that is replicated to this day. Why pee in a public, nasty, smelly place whose dire conditions are magnified by being enclosed within four walls when there is an open world outside where the chances of stepping on someone else's leftovers is diminished considerably? Even a nasty, smelly place whose dire conditions are magnified by being enclosed within four walls is preferable if it is private.

And who's upsetting whom if you're taking a leak outdoors? No one bothers to 'commit no nuisance'. And at the risk of sounding glib—that's because no one minds—or, at least, minds enough. Not you and I. And not the law (which is another way of saying, 'you and I'.)

Speaking of the law, imagine my middle-class excitement when I read a news report in May 2008 that seemed to suggest that the law was at last changing tack (at least in New Delhi). Two Delhi gents by the names of Baljit Singh Sabharwal and Harjit Singh had been arrested in the evening after they were caught urinating on the premises of a Metro rail station. This, I thought, was the radical moment in India's history of hygiene. The war against 'public relief' had at last begun in earnest. But on closer inspection, I realized that there was more to it than the law cracking down on two people 'committing nuisance'. It turns out that Sabharwal and Singh might have been slightly tipsy and may have had a round of fisticuffs with the Central Industrial Security Force (CISF) personnel who caught them peeing. So, coupled with bad behaviour, it was a cumulative offence: peeing in a public spot *and* getting into a scrap.

I wonder what the story would have been if the CISF blokes had just told them to stop peeing inside the Metro station and if the two 'offenders' had quietly zipped up and gone home? I ask because the law does actually have something to say even regarding sober, non-violent public urinators. Section 308 (I)(i) of the New Delhi Municipal Council (NDMC) Act 1994 rather colourlessly states: 'No citizen shall use or permit to be used as a latrine or urinal any place not intended for the purpose.' The rules are slightly kinder for minors, with the citizen being told to 'take all reasonable means' to prevent children under 12 from 'easing' in 'a public street or a public place'. Hefty fines come as punishment.

One would have thought that armed with this piece of municipal legislation, the authorities would ensure that at least city slickers would raise the threshold of urinary release to more challenging heights. But it turns out that the NDMC folks are still trying to work out a proper deterrent. The last debate that took place on the need to get serious about Section 308 (I)(i) and have a proper workable quantum of punishment in place got stuck at the philosophical–ethical stage over whether there really were enough public lavatories in the city for pressurized citizens. Cracking down on public urinators who may not have a choice of public lavatories may just be wrong.

So has there been a construction spree in sanitary public loos since the historic arrest of Baljit and Harjit? I'm afraid not. And the answer lies in our return to what I had mentioned before: the absence of a culture of shame in publicly taking out your penis and letting an arc of warm urine out on to the streets. At least in the West, the act of public urination has been seen as a symbol of political defiance, a rebellious outpouring, an anti-social gesture. Thus, the arrest of rock stars in 1960s' London. Thus, the locking up of hippies who overturned the law by defying sanitation rules. But here, public urination is just a piddle on the street.

With such a tradition, is it even worth griping about that other common public habit in our phlegmatic nation: spitting? The notion of clearing your throat, going deep down and vacuuming the slosh up to your mouth and then hurling it as a projectile after being rolled on the tongue may actually sound more offensive to many of us than the act of public peeing. But the fact is that from the window of a bus, from the driver's seat of an auto, from the passenger's seat of an auto, from the insides of a car, from the balcony and the terrace, from the pedestrian and the person sitting down, spitting is the nation's most prevalent, yet unconscious, visible bodily function. It's a habit, not a felony.

I've seen old people in middle-class households using spittoons, metal vase-like objects that are steadily filled up with senior citizen phlegm. Sure, the respiratory tract has its own unwanted by-products. But when did it move from the indoors safety of an Awadhi-style spittoon to the outside, where the world is one giant spit bowl? Like the treacherously low threshold of the male urinary urge, why is spitting a reflex action—for both sexes—in this country?

Once again, let the law clear its throat and say what it has to about public spitting. Section 268 of the Indian Penal Code defines public nuisance in the following manner:

> A person is guilty of a public nuisance who does any act or is guilty of an illegal omission which causes any common injury, danger or annoyance to the public or to the people in general who dwell or occupy property in the vicinity, or which must necessarily cause injury, obstruction, danger or annoyance to persons who may have occasion

to use any public right. A common nuisance is not excused on the ground that it causes some convenience or advantage.

'Omission' might as well be 'emission' and it applies to spittle as much as it applies to urine. But then, is anyone injured, brought into any danger or—above all—annoyed by these errors of emission? Going by the ubiquitous nature of public spitting—and public peeing—I can't see anyone complaining. When was the last time you registered your annoyance legally about that man crypto-puking on to the road?

The West Bengal Prevention of Spitting in Public Place Act of 2003 banned public spitting. Section 7 of the Act punishes the spitter with a fine up to Rs 200. I don't know of a single booking made till date that takes recourse to this rather specific law.

And if translucent/transparent oral emissions were not bad enough, there is the additional sub-genre of hurtling paan *peek*, that torrent of red betel leaf cud that gushes out like blood from a gargoyle's mouth. Again, the flow comes from everywhere. But it is especially visible in corners of staircases in office buildings and housing societies. These spots, considered no man's land—owned by no private party and therefore ready game—are almost synonymous with paan peeks, most of them looking like stage designs from low budget slasher movies. The fact that these stains bother no one aesthetically (forget hygienically) suggests that we may be hardwired to tolerate them—the way Westerners tolerate, nay appreciate, that disgusting habit of blowing their noses loudly into a piece of cloth, as if fart sounds turned into something nice and baroque once they come from an orifice different from the usual one are to be tolerated. Is it again that whole Lucknawi *tehzeeb* thing gone outside the spittoon? Or do we blame Jagdeep as Surma Bhopali in *Sholay* for giving a new lease of life to these garish projectiles?

But being inured to arching betel juice hardly takes us off the hook when it comes to cleaning our noses in public. I have been told that pinching the phlegm out of the nose and letting the snot trampoline out is the most hygienic form of cleansing one's nasal passages. True, the honks of the Westerner blowing into the handkerchief are missing. But instead, not only are we treated to a display of what nose dribble can do when under the influence of nose muscles and gravity, but the sonic equivalents of the Western nose blow also arrive. The bathroom—private or public—once again extends out into the slimy streets of twenty-first-century India.

Public relief, in its truest sense, is about relieving oneself in public. And it is here that I can just about manage to latch on to that genuine irritant that is scratching in public. By public scratching, as you may have gathered, I don't mean tending to that itch on the elbow or feeling that stubble or even tackling that nasty rash near the armpits. I mean the visual—and hopefully innocuous—sign of 'touching oneself'. Just as people wearing a strong perfume are unable to smell it, people scratching their genitalia from outside their trousers—and, I'm afraid, saris—are probably oblivious to the fact that they may be doing what they do. Since this action can't, by any stretch of legalese, be categorized as causing harm or danger to anyone, the only recourse left to those of us who are annoyed is to show, um, annoyance. In other words, there's nothing you can do about that motley crew in front of your house scratching themselves while you have those European house guests over to dinner.

What is it about this country that makes private space tumble out into the public? Is this the dourful half of the joyous conflation of the religious with the secular and the metaphysical with the physical that is to be found in Rabelais' *Gargantua and Pantagruel* and Shakespeare's comedies? Such celebration of the body physical in its scatological excesses is one thing, but it is quite another to relish the early morning sight of rows of umbrellas under which rows of female bottoms line up, hovering above the railway tracks around Bombay's Chattrapati Shivaji Terminus.

Like poverty and beggary, the public filth from private orifices has become almost indiscernible to our senses. Unlike poverty and beggary, it is not a simple matter of class deprivation. That class does play a large role in our attitudes towards public relief and public nuisance—the two ends in this excretory give and take—is that the middle-class and above are one with the bathroom-less when it comes to tolerating the mess. Yet, on a personal level, I discovered that the public toilet does not necessarily have to be a horror zone only when I started visiting the insides of hotels. For me, the definition of a 'five-star hotel' remains one that has nice bathrooms. There have been moments when, travelling from one place to another, the urge takes over. In school, while travelling by public bus, this duration of pain and hidden humiliation would occur like clockwork—from the time the bus reached a particular boys' school till the moment it crossed a neighbouring girls' school.

Whether years of forcing myself not to be humiliated before the bus crossed the girls' school has wrecked my erotic drive is not for me to say. But, perhaps, all bodily functions are connected to each other. And it was not until I discovered the religious relief of using the closest hotel loo in times of trouble that I really managed to exorcize my ghosts.

At the risk of sounding Trotskyite, I find it staggering that hotels, with their necessarily spic-and-span lobby floor loos, are, for the most part, left unutilized, while men with heavy bladders take recourse to walls and other open-air venues. One understands that the leisure industry can't simply open up these nice places to all and sundry. But there is the other fear, vocalized to me by a friend in the food and beverage industry, about the possibility that all and sundry might turn these gleaming rooms with flush toilets and tinkling urinals into latter-day cesspools.

Such is this fear—the modern, urbanite's twist on the old caste defilement routine—that it would perhaps be the ideal catalyst to get clean public toilets constructed on a war footing. If it was India's rising middle class that spurred the creation of the Tata Nano which will bring the automobile experience to 'everyone', the time to make the clean 'hotel' toilet experience as widely available should be upon us any time now. Courtesy, perhaps, Sulabh Shauchalaya? Or ITC?

But there could be another way out in never-administratively-dull India. Take the revolutionary endeavour that the town of Musiri in Tamil Nadu embarked on in July 2008. The strategy is so easy-peasy that it makes you want to flush: pay people to use the loo. Users in this town have been offered up to Rs 6 each time they use the facilities, with the by-products of the visitations being utilized for fertilizer research. The first Ecosan Community Compost Toilet (ECCT) in Musiri is already operational and the payment to the customers-cum-providers is made, on a monthly basis, to all ECCT card-holders. According to the Society for Community Organization and Peoples Education (Scope), the number of users of the toilet has gone up by 90 per day since the introduction of the scheme, with about 200 people using the toilet every day.

There's no point talking about social engineering and other stratagems that curb public relief and make people change their shitty ways without bringing the Mahatma on board. For a lot us, the Mahatma has been about basically two things: non-violence and his fetish for hygiene. (The sex bit is more about non-sex, so…) The man was clear on one thing: '…in our approach to private and public sanitation lies our commitment to true freedom and dignity.' I can't see that being remembered by too many of our parliamentarians these days.

But Pratima Sen and Srinanda Sen in their *A New Approach to Sanitation for the Poor* (2000) do recognize Gandhi's role in trying to drive home the point about the need for public hygiene. As they put it, 'Toilets govern a lot of human issues: personal hygiene, public health, street behaviour, crime rate and above all dignity and self-esteem. Gandhi was not naïve when he harped on the centrality of sanitation in development.' In this respect, Gandhi was a strong advocate of doing away with one major obstacle—the traditional caste custom of having Dalits clean dry latrines. In his Sabarmati ashram, Gandhi did not allow toilets in the private homes on the compound. This ensured that everyone used the row of public toilets at the end of the ashram. As a rule, everyone, no matter what social status or caste, would be put on duty to clean the toilets.

I can't quite see the Sabarmati formula being replicated across India. I, for one, would prefer higher sanitary standards as well as a better trained sanitary workforce for such an enterprise to work. But I do think that the man got it right when he considered public hygiene—or, rather, the lack of it in this country—as something that needs to be worked on, and not necessarily with a long bargepole.

But public hygiene's most risible and visible syndrome-cum-disease is not a billion people peeing out in the open, but in the way we look at public space. What seems obvious to the most India-travelled firang and invisible to the most socially conscious, scraggly bearded desi is the garbage that we are content to spew out on to our streets. From the mash of coconut shells, shit, discarded food, plastic packets, used sanitary napkins, vegetable rinds, muck from somewhere horrible emerges this innate ability to consider garbage heaps as part of a bigger 'authentic' picture. How one can or might need to overlook filth on the roads is something that will remain a mystery to me. And to add fuel to the piles, these are the very zones chosen, almost in a weird call for symmetry, by the peeing and spitting public.

In the peeing, shitting, spitting, scratching swirl that we find ourselves in, public relief has the overwhelming upper hand in the war against 'nuisance'. I have done the deeds myself (confined, though, to the first two categories), so I know the monster from the position of (over?)familiarity. I have urinated in mossy public places, on a tree trunk opposite a Paris church, on roadside gutters, on to the street, into the bushes and, of course, on a wall that blunts the many flows and turns them into reverse rivulets. I have also defecated on an army helicopter that did not have any 'facilities', flinging my deposit from a small hole marked 'urinal' and thereby earning the reprimand from patriotic friends: 'You care a shit about Kashmir!'

So I know that the phenomenon of relieving oneself in public places is not a response to the unavailability of sanitary public lavatories alone. I also know that at the heart of the problem lies the fact that we just don't think that there is a problem. Pissshitsofthardwetrunnysnotorgyhell is just a string of letters thrown in for effect by semi-Jesuit-trained, Western-style potty mouths being self-righteous about Real India's Reality.

So the fact is that whichever way you want to play this thing, we are filthy people. Because of circumstances, but not entirely because of circumstances. And those half-felt signs, 'Commit No Nuisance' might as well be saying 'Do No Wrong'. In the battle between the physical and the theoretical, a sign does nothing, even if it uses the word '*prasrab*' and is therefore understood by the 'violator'.

There are two ways in which public relief can be tackled in this country. One, to have more public toilets like the good doctor Bindeswar Pathak's Sulabh Shauchalayas. And the other, which I will shortly reveal, is a tactical strategy to actually stop our men from peeing everywhere.

Some years ago, after a hefty round of drinks, my cousin and I were returning home. I won't tell you who was behind the wheel, but the urge to emerge from the car and urinate came simultaneously to both of us. Being mature by now and having grown tired of retelling misadventures involving our bodily functions, we wanted to 'hold on' till the nearest hotel—since it was too late to enter a restaurant. Unfortunately, after decades of having a low threshold and being part of a society that did not think it wrong to have a low threshold, we decided that the deed had to be done immediately.

The car was stopped, the belts were loosened as we clambered up against a footpath that faced a red wall. And the pressure was released to a blissful tinkling sound. I was only one-fourth into my de-stressing activity—I wouldn't know at what stage my cousin was in his urinating action—when we heard shouts: 'Oi, oi…' followed by the choicest of Hindustani expletives. As the quality of mercy that droppeth like gentle rain was stoppeth midway, the bewildered duo—that is us—wondered what had happened. Why suddenly this furore about two blokes peeing on a wall in a city that never batted an eyelid at such public relief activities?

Then I had an epiphany.

Let all the country's walls, corners, roadside bushes and downtown gutters be pasted with images of deities and things religious. No one will commit nuisance without facing the consequences. You see, my cousin and I had just quarter-peed on to a temple wall. The process of cleansing filthy people had quietly begun.

India Commuting

. . . .

Manjula Padmanabhan

Right until the moment that I sat down to write my piece for this collection of essays, I had expected to make a patchwork quilt of some fifty years of train journeys, from early childhood to now. Then I opened a new file on my laptop and in that instant the gently bubbling spring of memories changed into a trickle of stale anecdotes about lost tickets, colourful fellow passengers and the time I threw up all the way from Madras to Bombay courtesy my mother's mutton sandwiches. I've told these stories dozens of times and though they're reasonably entertaining when accompanied by cheese sandwiches and tepid coffee, they are not exactly marble-plaque material.

I no longer travel as much as I used to, so I realized I would need to go on an actual journey by train in order to remind myself of what it was like. But one journey would not stand in for the generality of the Indian Railway Experience. Yes, I could have made a number of trips, perhaps on each of the major lines or in a circuit through each of the metros. But I'm an extremely sedentary and lethargic person. Such a programme of activity would have left me so exhausted that I'd never have got around to writing about it.

So I decided to fashion an amusement from scratch, using myself as fall-gal and the Indian Railways as my stage. I decided to go on an actual trip from Delhi to Chennai, on the Rajdhani, but to treat it as if it were an amalgam of all my previous trips. This approach will not satisfy the reader who is looking for a 'how to' guide for navigating India's railways, nor will it be useful for the backpacker who wants to travel as cheaply as possible while sleeping on the hardest and most inhospitable seats. Some bits are made up and a couple of bits belong to stories told me by other travellers. Yet, in its own way, it is true and the people in it are real—perhaps more real, ultimately, than the version of myself that I present in this account.

I am five-foot-five, fifty-six years old and look as if I eat eight large meals a day. My close-cropped hair is going grey. I wear contact lenses which give me a permanently startled expression and my clothes are normally loose, baggy and dark in colour. Nevertheless, I knew that on a train travelling from north to south India, surrounded by sober, respectable fellow citizens many of whom would be south Indians, I would draw attention to myself just by being different from the norm for my age and social class. Either they would see my name on the ticket collector's passenger list, assume that I was a Tamilian and try to engage me in conversation, or they would suspect, from my short hair and broad gauge, that the name was a decoy of some sort and regard me with narrowed eyes for the duration of the twenty-eight-hour journey.

Naturally, then, my first priority was to create a disguise for myself. Stage magicians will tell you that the main part of a successful trick is misdirection—drawing attention away from the mechanics of the trick by doing something just outside the plane of intention. With this in mind, I did two things. The first was that I bought myself a set of clothes of the kind that I never normally wear: a salwar-kurta 'suit' made out of cheap shiny cloth, mud-brown in colour, with an all-over print of dull red flowers. On my feet I wore a pair of vomit-pink slippers, one size too small and I took care to paint my toe nails metallic sea green two weeks in advance of the journey, so that by the time I boarded the train my feet looked moth-eaten and diseased.

My second move was to shave my hair off.

My reason for taking this drastic step was simple: I didn't have the time or inclination to grow my hair out, yet a woman with short-cropped hair not only suggests that she makes regular trips to a hairdresser but also that she has the money and leisure to pay for such indulgences. By contrast, a shaven head, in India, instantly communicates a message of traditional values, self-sacrifice and, most importantly, loss. A woman will not normally remove her hair except for sober reasons—the loss of a spouse, catastrophic illness, mental derangement, louse-infestation or in quest of a favour from the gods. Whatever the cause, nobody doubts the credentials of a tonsuree. The very nakedness suggests an exposure to the elements and an absolute lack of secrets that is pitiable and for that reason, disarming.

I used an electric hair-clipper that I'd bought two years ago in London in a bid to liberate myself from the tyranny of hairdressing parlours. The first time I turned it on, it made such an unholy racket that I shaved off my eyebrows in sheer fright and never tried it again. Sure enough, this time around it was as manic as ever and sprayed hair all over my bathroom, baying like a motorized banshee. But at the end of half an hour, I'd been transformed from a fat, middle-aged woman into an androgynous gnome with a faintly repellent brown-domed head. Perfect!

For luggage I had a shoulder bag, as grey and scuffed as if it had been a football in its past life. For food I carried a packet of sandwiches and a plastic water bottle. For money, I had ten thousand rupees in cash in the form of 500 notes. I tucked these into a money-belt that I strapped to my right thigh. In a little cloth purse that I tucked into my shoulder bag, I had ten one-rupee coins and ninety rupees in small denomination notes.

I got to the station an hour early, so that I could study the reservation charts at leisure. No doubt I would have experienced a superior level of drama and tension if I had forced myself to travel by unreserved third class, but I am not enough of a masochist to exercise that option. Instead, I was in a Second A/C sleeper compartment. From the lists posted behind glass, I knew the names of the people with whom I would share my two-tier cubicle. Three passengers with the same surname were travelling together, two of them female. This most likely meant a family of two adults and a child or a couple with an unmarried sister. There were two others, both men, who shared their serial numbers with ours, in the paired bunks along the corridor. One was a Srihari and the other a Kumaran. But people who sleep in the corridor bunks are pariahs amongst the reserved-class-wallahs. Whatever their actual status outside the train, within the train they look thin and reedy, sitting with their shoulders hunched up above their ears, staring out of the windows like dogs whose masters have gone away on long leave.

Among the passenger names, I could make out three south Indians, one Bengali, two Maharashtrians, a lone Sardar and two foreigners. The rest of the names belonged to communities and states that were not recognizable to me. With two exceptions, the compartment appeared to consist entirely of men travelling on their own, with no common surnames to connect them.

The two exceptions were a family of six in the cubicle next to mine and, in the middle of the carriage, one cubicle occupied by three ladies listed only by their first names: Misses Mary, Augusta and Josephina plus one Mrs Molly George who might be an attendant to the first three or an unrelated passenger, I couldn't tell. This zone of femininity was the Rajdhani's version of the women's compartment. Though it wasn't quite as much like a travelling hen-coop as its counterparts on other trains, it nevertheless afforded its minor privacies in the form of a fitted curtain and no corridor bunks. I never travel in a women's compartment if I can help it. One, because its acronym is 'WC' which makes me feel I've booked myself into the toilet, and two, because from all accounts of train-dacoity, it is clear that social carnivores routinely begin their raids in the women's compartment. Not only are the gold-bedecked prey-species helpless as trussed chickens behind lockable doors, but other passengers can pretend that they have no idea what was going on in that hallowed space reserved for the delicate sex when asked for witness accounts later on.

I waited until there were only five minutes left to board the train. Red-tunicked porters no longer swarmed near the entrances of the carriages and non-travellers were starting to detach themselves from the relatives they had come to see off. Female passengers and children had already disappeared inside, while male passengers were stubbing out their bidis, clearing their throats and hawking for one last time over the side of the platform, as if to rid themselves of the last burdens of the capital city before stepping into the train.

I grabbed the handrail and crawled on board with the feeble mannerisms of a person too down-trodden by the vicissitudes of reality to believe that she can lay claim to anything as bold as vigorous movements. I wore a limp grey dupatta coiled like a dead python around my neck, its tail held to my mouth, as I feigned uncertainty about the exact location of my seat. I was perfectly aware that it was in the very first cubicle of the carriage's aft-entrance, but I walked past that space to peer instead at the numbers of the bunks in the neighbouring cubicle. I stood in the corridor, blinking owlishly out of round-framed glasses.

A plump woman dressed in a bright cotton sari with an elaborately woven pallu drawn over her head was seated at one of the window seats. Within two seconds of my pausing at the entrance of her cubicle, her head swung away from the window, to glare at me. Less than ten minutes had passed since she'd entered the train and yet here she was, in full possession of what had now become her ancestral berth—the seat where generations of her clan-members had been born and reared and had eventually died.

'What do you want?' she demanded. Beside her, squatting with her feet up on the seat, was an old woman so enfeebled that she looked like an inanimate collection of stick-like limbs held together by a winding sheet of thin white cloth. Her presence on the reserved seat guaranteed that she was a widowed mother or mother-in-law, but years of neglect had so reduced her that she had become, for all practical purposes, a waste-basket into which food scraps would be tossed now and then.

Opposite Mrs Plumpness, at the other window seat, was a young boy with his head buried in a cheap comic book. The fact that he did not so much as twitch as his mother spoke to me revealed that he was the adored, the pampered, the *only* son of the family. He was as scrawny as a field cricket, but his aura was that of a lion residing amongst mice.

The woman spoke Gujarati-flavoured Hindi. 'What's the matter?' she barked. 'Can't you speak?'

I said, affecting a moth-coloured voice that fluttered feebly from one soft syllable to the next, 'I…I was just…looking for my seat…'

I too spoke in Hindi, but because I was mumbling, I managed to hide the fact that I speak it inefficiently. There is a very specific reason I am uncomfortable speaking in Hindi. It has to do with Hindi's gender-specific verb endings. In English, the verbs a woman uses are indistinguishable from a man's. But in Hindi our verbs part company from the world of men, in a way that I find annoyingly and demeaningly separationist. I realize that those who grow up speaking Hindi do not experience this level of unease and find the idea quite ridiculous. Yet for me, accustomed as I am to the neutrality of English, whenever I am required to use gendered verbs, it's as if I've been forced to cover my head in a veil or bind my feet, or in some other way draw attention to a self-effacing Otherness that for many people is the very definition of femininity.

'*Seat!*' exclaimed Mrs Plumpness. 'There are no seats here—no vacant seats,' she said. 'All are taken! Where's your ticket—do you have a ticket?'

I began to pick at my shoulder bag, rooting within its flat outer pocket for the ticket that I knew was folded in half and tucked into the strap of my bra. I could feel the lady's hackles rising as I hunted. My very breath upon her threshold was a threat, an offence. Had she been a wolf, she would have been on her feet by now, lips drawn back in a snarl. As it was, I could see from the corner of my eye (as I pretended to look for my ticket), that she was rigid with attention, her entire being focussed upon me.

'One…one minute, please…' I stammered.

Just then a powerful tremor travelled up the spine of the train, causing the grey floor to jerk beneath all our feet. A sharp trill sounded outside, warning all loiterers and casual hangers-on to step down and return to the platform. The PA system then sneezed loudly, and gave out a brassy *DING*! Inside the compartment, bodies were hurtling this way and that. Voices were raised in excitement—a child had been left outside, an uncle remained inside, last-minute altercations took place between porters and passengers, and leavers and lingerers defined themselves for a final time. A hasty man pushed past me in order to enter the cubicle I was standing beside, giving me the ideal opportunity to lose my balance.

'Oh!' I said, crumpling onto the seat as the voice-over began to drone out a welcome message, first in Hindi then in English. The jostler was Mr Plumpness. Mrs Plumpness sprang to her feet, emboldened by her husband's presence. 'See!' she said, speaking in Gujarati. 'This female wretch is trying to grab a seat…'

A second whistle sounded and a more powerful tremor succeeded the first one, accompanied by a sustained squeaking shriek of metal joints and stays, rivets and bolts, leaf springs, wheels, cogs, shafts and axles—all the constituent elements that make up a train's substance being called upon to exercise their power and to do whatever was required of them in the vast linkage of small parts that made up the great mechanical whole. Then another jerk and another and another, each one gradually wearing down the inertia of each twenty-tonne carriage, each shift conspiring to exchange stillness and inaction for progress and forward momentum.

In the midst of all this controlled hubbub, I found (or pretended to find) my ticket.

'H-here it is,' I said, from my position on the seat. A girl had come up by then, a younger relative perhaps, a cousin or minor in-law. The way she trailed the man suggested that she was related to him rather than to the woman at the window. His younger sister, perhaps.

'What's the matter?' she asked, upon seeing me.

The man snatched the ticket from my fingers and began scanning it with minute attention. He was a short figure, with a roll of fat that hung loosely around his belly, a pneumatic tyre that needed pumping up. Thick black hair was plastered down tight against his skull and he had a broad face with jutting cheek bones, coupled with a weak, recessed chin. He wore rimless glasses with gilt ear-pieces, and his jaw muscles tensed regularly, as he masticated a wad of paan in his mouth. Three men pushed through the impromptu knot that had developed in the corridor on account of me, passing onward without pausing. The train was starting to pick up rhythm. Outside, the figures standing on the platform were slipping past, waving their hands, falling back, receding into memory. The journey had begun.

'This baldie is trying to grab one of our seats,' said the woman to the husband, casually heaping contempt upon me with the epithet she chose. The confidence with which she used the word suggested that she didn't expect me to understand her language. How could she know that I had Gujarati relatives, and had consequently caught the gist of what she had said? I recognized with satisfaction that she had registered my bald head and had assumed it was the result of some misfortune. Her hostility towards me seemed fuelled by her instinct to distance herself from my inauspicious presence as quickly as she could manage.

The man turned to me and said, as he returned my ticket, 'Look—your seat is the next one—see?' His syllables slopped out untidily because of the wad of paan in his mouth. Two tiny rivulets of red spittle appeared at the corners of his lipless frog-mouth as he handed the ticket back to me. 'It's just next to this one,' he said, making a flipping motion with his hand, 'on the other side of this partition.'

He turned to his wife and said, in Gujarati, 'She'll go now.'

Then he sat down on the seat opposite the one I had collapsed onto and, as he did so, he, his wife and the girl who had been lurking just behind him dropped me from their collective consciousness as completely as if I had been a soap bubble that had blinked out of existence.

It was quite astonishing.

I found that I was forced up and onto my feet, expelled into the corridor by the sheer force of their inattention.

Score one, I thought to myself. Seven to go.

~

Turning to my left as directed, I went towards my designated seat.

Two women had settled down beside each of the two windows. One was middle-aged and the other one was considerably younger, suggesting that they were, as I had expected, a mother and daughter pair. The older woman wore a green silk sari with red border and the girl wore a white blouse over jeans. The blouse was of fake eyelet-lace, by which I mean it had the white-on-white embroidery but without the distinctive tiny apertures—eyelet-lace without the eyelets. The man connected to this party was absent, but in the corridor the two pariah-bunk passengers had taken up their positions at the window seats. One was an old man whose face was the exact colour of a faded brown paper bag that has remained unattended on a windowsill for many years, even down to the speckles of tiny black fly droppings and splotches of dried rainwater. He wore a dull grey shirt and white pyjamas. At his feet lay a small cloth bag and on the overhead bunk were six identical cartons each with a picture of idli-trays displayed on one side.

Opposite him was a nervy young man who sat coiled tight as the spring in a battery compartment when the battery is in place. He looked as if he were in his early twenties, with his skin still stretched tight over the bones of his face. He wore glasses and his hair was cut short with no parting. Above his upper lip, he wore a crisply laundered moustache, while the ochre-brown skin of his cheeks was that painful shade of greenish blue that I associate with recently shaved facial growth. He wore a fresh, checked shirt and nicely pressed grey pants, and on his feet were a pair of new grey Nikes. If I knew nothing else about him, I would guess that he was a scion of the BPO empire, a new recruit whose recently acquired

American or British accent would still be twangy with pride. He would be unmarried but actively searching for a partner now that he was virile with money. He sat with his back to the wall of the carriage, facing in the direction of the cubicle but not looking at the three women within his field of vision. Staring at women was an activity no longer suitable to someone at his current station in life. Under his seat was a shiny black sling-bag with the Nike swoosh on it. One of his legs was crossed over the other and the foot that dangled in the air vibrated like a tuning fork.

According to my ticket, I had one of the two window seats in the cubicle. It was the older woman, as it happened, who was occupying my place. The seat numbers were clearly marked on the side of the compartment, so she must have known that she was not in her seat. Nevertheless, in the time-honoured manner of someone who does not intend to give up a coveted position unless forced, she did not so much as raise her head to look at me as I stood at the entrance to the cubicle. To meet the gaze of the rightful owner of a seat is to acknowledge that he or she exists, which leads to loss of seat, loss of face, loss of every warm and worthwhile thing.

Instead of challenging her, however, I sat down at the other end of the seat from her, and stared down at my feet, hunched over my sling bag. I had been practising this posture for a whole week but it was only now, surrounded by people who judged me entirely by my appearance, that my mind emptied itself of coherent thoughts and my personal horizons shrank to a few yards around me. Having created an outer shell that radiated hopelessness, my interior world now misted up and became insubstantial. While with one side of my mind I congratulated myself on having succeeded so well, with the other I worried that I might never be able to turn off this disguise.

When the man of the family appeared and took his place on the seat next to his daughter and opposite mine, he began drawing off his shoes, unbuttoning his bush shirt and making himself comfortable exactly as if he were in his own home, alone with his family. None of the three glanced at me, nor did I look up at them.

Meanwhile, the train was gliding through the city at a comfortable, loping pace. The great iron beast that tames the horizon and devours distances was merely sauntering along, gathering speed for the time when it would break free of the city's confines.

The compartment, being air-conditioned, was a closed capsule of chilly air that was punctured every few minutes by someone entering or exiting. As the cubicle I was in was right by one of the two self-sealing doors that contained the cooled air, I was keenly aware of this parade of passers-by. I registered them mainly as pairs of trouser-clad legs hurrying this way and that, because I continued to sit in my prawn-like posture, staring at my feet. To begin with, every passenger in the interior of the carriage needed to visit the bathroom, singly or in pairs, which meant that at least fifteen people passed by our cubicle in the first half hour alone, once in each direction. Then, at least half of those who had gone to the bathroom and returned to their seats needed to get up again to stand in the small vestibule just outside the air-conditioned zone and smoke. I knew they had gone to smoke because of the scent of cigarettes that wafted back into the compartment upon their return.

Whenever someone came or went, one of the two heavy blue damask curtains draped across the entrance to the cubicle was sucked out the door, enfolding that person in its suffocating embrace. After a brief battle, the person would emerge and carry on. This was hard enough for passengers, but it was especially tricky for the housekeeping staff, who sometimes had to wrestle their way past the curtain while carrying loaded trays of food, stacks of bed linen and heavy caddies of boiling tea or coffee.

The catering personnel consisted of three youths in smart black uniforms, black caps on their heads and neat white aprons across their fronts. They spent the first hour of the journey conveying loads of trays, hot-water flasks and stacks of plastic cutlery down through the corridors to other sections of the train. They were followed by the bed-linen staff, dispensing sets of blankets, sheets and miniature pillows, each as flat as a mouse pad and each within its own starched pillow slip. Then there was the lone, melancholy floor-swabber looking reproachfully in the direction of cruel passengers who had neglected to foul up the floor sufficiently to keep him in full employment.

It was only after all these people had come and gone that finally the ticket-collector, a dapper little penguin of a man, appeared with his clip-board and pen.

He turned immediately to me, with his hand held out in mute demand of my ticket, sitting down as he did so, at the edge of the seat opposite mine. He did not, in the slightest way, give any indication that he'd noticed my shaven head or, if he had, that he'd come to any conclusions based upon it. For him, I was one of forty-six passengers on the Nizamuddin-Chennai Central Rajdhani Express. So long as I had a valid ticket, it made no difference whether I was dread-locked or tattooed, covered in warts or swaddled in silk.

The moment he sat down, I realized that I had unconsciously been waiting for him. He was my deliverer and saviour. Uncurling myself, I looked up and gave him my ticket while saying, in my normal speaking voice, 'Excuse me, but could I exchange my lower berth for the upper one?'

From the corner of my eye I saw three faces swivel towards me.

I had been listening to the low murmur of their conversation for some time, and knew that they were Marathi-speakers. But they were also urban people for whom English would at the very least be familiar, if not in fact the language in which they conducted their professional lives. I did not have to actually see the expressions on their faces to know that they were looking exactly as amazed and shocked as if a stray dog on the street had suddenly straightened up, jumped onto a motorcycle and roared off into the sunset.

Score two, I thought.

Six to go.

~

When I had clambered up to my second-storey eyrie, I made a rough diagram of the berth position in the carriage, based on what I remembered from the reservation chart. The number sequence began with A, which is where I was. B was occupied by the Gujarati clan. C was the one in which the lone Sardar was quartered, along with three others whose names were not recognizable to me. D was the women's compartment, in the middle of the carriage, with only four passengers in it and no corridor bunks. E contained the two foreigners as well as two of the three south Indians I had noticed. F contained six men with no shared surnames, G contained military personnel and H was home to the Bengali, two Maharashtrians and the remaining south Indian. The Bengali was a doctor, but of course reservation lists do not distinguish between medical and academic degrees.

One of the black-clad attendants came along to ask about meal preferences. When I had reserved a vegetarian meal for dinner, I got down from the bunk and began to walk slowly down towards the engine-end of the bogey. The feudal family had already drawn its curtains around its borders, sealing itself in. The younger woman, whose original seat was in the corridor, had now been sucked behind the fortress walls for her own protection. Possibly, she would even sleep in there. A train is an alien environment, after all, for the hot-house flowers that respectable Indian women are brought up to be. To be horizontal and asleep in the corridor, vulnerable to every passing glance while hurtling across the countryside was a fate that no one would wish upon a genteel young woman. Either Mr Plumpness or the old lady would take her place in the corridor, I felt sure.

When I came abreast of compartment C, I discovered that the lone Sardar of the reservation charts had unaccountably multiplied.

Maybe he had requested an exchange of seats with friends who had been accommodated elsewhere. Whatever the case, there were now six large bearded men in that cubicle. They had stripped down to their banyans; one of them was wearing a bright blue-checked lungi and the other five were in loose white pyjamas. All six had removed their turbans and two had let down their beards. They were playing cards, laughing raucously and scratching under their armpits as I passed. The curtain that should have shrouded the entrance to their cubicle was faulty and refused to remain in place, so their revels were plain to see. They had positioned a tin trunk in the middle of their cubicle and were using it as a table. A small electronic noise-maker had been slung from one of the upper bunks, its chirping racket competing with the muzak that was piped into the cabin through the PA system.

Right next to them was compartment D, the women's compartment. Here the curtain had not only been drawn, but was buttoned up tight on the inside. It was a fitted drape, secured in place with velcro so it was not possible to see into the space even when the train was going at full clip. All the lights were blazing behind the veil and I could hear a low hum of conversation. From beneath the lower edge of the curtain, a white-socked foot encased in a sturdy black sandal extended into the corridor.

Was it an invitation? Or a plea for help?

I smiled to myself and walked on.

I went directly to the bathroom now, not pausing to look in on the cubicles that I passed along the way. There are two styles of bathrooms on the Indian Railways, Western and Indian. When I was little, I had always been told to seek out Indian-style toilets for reasons of hygiene, but I always found them terrifying. The sight of the track-bed racing by beneath the train, as glimpsed through the glory hole, unnerved me. Just the notion that the train's tight skin was porous after all, riddled with gaping, unguarded vents, was frightening, as was the sensation of air rushing up against one's bare bottom. Even now, all these years later, I cannot look down that crude, black pipe without feeling an irrational desire to keep my clothes, cellphone, handbag and all my cash clenched between my teeth before perching above the aperture, for fear that I will lose all my precious items to The Abyss. Even though I knew that the Western-style toilets were exactly the same except for the presence of the porcelain throne, and even though I could still see the blur of the track-bed speeding by underneath and even though the commode rarely had a lid, still, the mere presence of the seat between me and the void was reassuring.

On this occasion, however, the reason I was hurrying towards the Western-style toilet had nothing to do with fears or comforts. It was just the one that happened to be farthest from my designated seat and therefore less likely to be used by the passengers at my end of the cabin. Once inside the little room, I exchanged the dead python around my neck for a black chiffon dupatta which I'd brought along with me. I wrapped it around my head, tying it into a tight, neat chignon. Even though the result did not look like hair, it tamed the nakedness and made it acceptable. Then I took out another dupatta, a pale pink *ikat* this time, which cut down the grim factory-hand styling of my kurta, and arranged it around my shoulders.

Then I approached the cubicle nearest to the bathroom on the engine side of the carriage and boldly stuck my head through the curtain. 'Excuse me,' I said, as four faces turned in my direction, 'which one of you is Dr...?' In my mind I had renamed him 'Dr Bong'.

One of the men put up his hand as if he had been in a classroom. 'I am,' he said automatically, before realizing that perhaps less enthusiasm might be in order. 'Is there some problem?'

'If you're a medical doctor...' I said, my tone suggesting that I believed he must be. Privately, I had my doubts. He had responded to the question with a guilty start and his movements, as he got to his feet, were slower than I would have liked. He had a bristly moustache, a broad, domed forehead, and a mane of straight black hair that covered the back and sides of his skull efficiently. He was of medium height, stocky, bush-shirted and wearing pale grey trousers and black socks on his sandaled feet. He had large, expressive eyes, thick-rimmed with lashes and I was surprised to observe that he wore contact lenses. As a lens-wearer myself, I tend to notice such things. 'I'd like to consult you about something...'

The other three men in the cubicle were looking up with goldfish expressions, their eyes perfectly round and their mouths agape. They clearly believed that an emergency of some juicy feminine nature, for which they would have ring-side seats as companions of the doctor, might be about to unfold.

He came out into the corridor as I moved back towards the door that would take us into the vestibule of the carriage. 'I'm a journalist,' I said, when we were no longer in the air-conditioned capsule. 'I'm writing an article about medical emergencies that have taken place on board a train and I wondered if you'd be willing to talk to me about your experiences?'

I had been staring straight into his eyes as I spoke and I saw his pupils dilate as he realized he was not going to have to perform open-heart surgery on board a moving train after all. 'Ah,' he said. 'Well. I...well...that is...I...' Now he was perspiring. His eyes were darting about like fish in a tank that's been left out in the sun.

'It's all right if you don't want to,' I said, hoping to reassure him.

'...actually, I'm *not* a medical doctor,' said Dr Bong, blurting this out with a burst of energy. He relaxed, now that he'd made this confession. 'I'm not a doctor at all. But I always sign up with that title because professionals get preference on the railways. It's an informal rule—you know, politicians, military people, police and then professionals. Also, in case someone falls sick, they like to feel they've got someone they can turn to...' Then he remembered that I'd said I was a journalist. 'Of course...that is...I...uhh...'

'It's all right,' I said. 'I won't mention your name in my article. What happens if there's an actual medical emergency?'

'There's always some other doctor on board,' he said. 'Usually two or three. One time I was on board a flight and a pregnant lady began to have contractions. When they called for doctors, one of the hostesses turned to me because she'd seen my name on my boarding pass. I stood up and went along, just as one of the other doctors got there before me, a gynaecologist. But I was already standing up, so I went along anyway and watched the whole drama. They kept the plane circling till the baby was born. At the end, all the passengers cheered and many people shook my hand as if I had done something great!' He was grinning. 'What newspaper are your writing for?'

'*The New York Times*,' I lied.

'Really?!' he exclaimed, looking impressed. 'Are you on their staff or...?'

'I write a regular column,' I said. 'They pay very well. What d'you do when you're not pretending to be a doctor?'

'I work for an ad agency in Cal,' he said, but his eyes flickered sideways just before he answered. He was probably lying about that too. I saw him glance up at my head, his eyes narrowing as he noticed that I was apparently bald.

'Cancer,' I volunteered, before he could frame a question.

'Oh!' said Dr Bong, jumping back. Or maybe it was just the violent motion of the train. We were flying along now, in the way that trains have, the carriages flinging themselves from side to side, the rails rattling, the air whistling through the windows and the floor jittering up and down.

'Don't worry, it's not infectious,' I said, leaning towards the man. 'Both breasts are gone. The doctors gave me two months to live, but I survived and a year has passed. I'm still on therapy,' I touched my chiffon-covered head. 'Lost all my hair...'

'Very sad, very sad. Well...I...I think...I'll get back to my seat,' said the fake doctor. He seemed desperate to get away.

'I can show you my prosthetics, if you're interested!' I called after him. 'They're made in Taiwan, vanilla-flavoured and very natural to the touch...'

He scurried away with his head tucked between his shoulders, like a mouse running from an owl.

Score three, I thought to myself, *but only just*. Right up until the moment I said the word 'cancer', he'd been potentially interesting, a minor deviant. I like minor deviants. I might be one myself.

~

In the section next to the doctor's were four burly men in paramilitary uniforms and two smaller men in civilian clothes. All six seats had been blocked under the military quota in the reservation charts so I didn't have any names to go by. Two of the uniformed men were in the corridor and the other two were sleeping in the top bunks of the cubicle, their feet sticking out into the corridor. They had not removed their boots, I noticed.

The two smaller men were sitting on their respective bunks when I looked in on them. They too had pulled out one of their tin trunks for use as a table, but instead of a card game, they had placed their respective tea-trays on the trunk-top. The overhead light had failed in their cubicle so they would have been doomed to darkness if not for a jaunty candle in the shape of the number '1' that one of them had lit, securing it inside an enamel shaving-mug. They had drawn back the curtains of the cubicle so that the corridor's light would spill into their shadowy domain, making it easy for me to peer inside and ask my question.

'Excuse me?' I said.

Both men looked up. They were mismatched in the way of famous comedy pairs—Laurel and Hardy or Tom and Jerry—something intrinsically funny about the differences between them. The tall, broad one said, 'Yes?' while the smaller, more delicate one just nodded, with his head cocked to one side.

My immediate impression was that they were both young, perhaps in their twenties. Travelling salesmen was my first guess regarding their careers, but they might just as well have been cousins going home for a clan gathering or graduate students taking a Puja break. They were dressed decently, but without any flair. In the dim light all I could see was that they were clean-shaven, wearing long-sleeved shirts, with their luggage stowed neatly under their seats. The big one's hair rose up in a poll of black curls on top of his head while the smaller man's hair was straight and slicked back, parted on one side: a large hearty rabbit and a small nervous mongoose.

'I'm doing a survey,' I said. 'Is it all right if I ask a few questions?'

'Sure, sure,' said Rabbit, as he shifted his bulk aside very slightly, as if to make space for me, except that there was plenty of space and therefore no real need for him to shift.

'Usually, we are the ones asking the questions,' said Mongoose, unexpectedly. 'Never mind! We will give the answers this time.' He said this with a straight face, neither smiling nor frowning. There was something melancholy in his sobriety.

We were all speaking in English, though theirs was more accented than mine.

I said, 'Oh! Does that mean you're...?'

'Media consultants,' said Rabbit, turning the palm of his right hand up, as if this were a self-evident fact. Something in the way he performed this gesture made me want to giggle.

'We do market surveys,' said Mongoose, nodding morosely.

'Really!' I said, smiling too brightly. There are certain circumstances which cause me to laugh uncontrollably. I produce a loud, chuckling rattle—sub-machine-gun with a touch of hyena—that is difficult to turn off once it gets started. I grow breathless, my sides ache and my eyes stream with tears. The fits usually occur when there is an obvious trigger, such as a comedy film or the company of friends, but sometimes, as on this occasion, the hysteria rises inside me like a volcano of soap bubbles for no clear reason at all. An image flashed before my eyes, of me with my shaven head and green-painted toe-nails falling off my seat howling with laughter, as the two media consultants looked on, puzzled and a little pained. I clamped my hand across my mouth, hoping they wouldn't notice.

'How about you?' asked Mongoose. 'You are in survey business also?'

Further images were flashing in my head: scenes from Peter Sellers's movies, of Herbert Lom's face starting to twitch as crazed cackles leak out of him. I feared something similar was about to happen to me. I began massaging my cheeks as if I was in pain.

'Uhh,' I stammered, 'not really, no. I'm...I'm a journalist...'

'You should let *her* ask the questions,' said Rabbit to Mongoose, in a reproachful tone.

The smaller man turned towards me, his eyes trusting and morose. 'Please, ma'am, you go ahead and ask. We will tell you anything.'

I was very grateful for the relative darkness of their cubicle. Sucking in a deep breath, so that the giggles were pushed back down into my stomach, I said, 'I'm doing a series of articles about reincarnation. Maybe the two of you have some interesting stories to tell me?'

There was a brief silence. Rabbit cleared his throat and shifted slightly in his seat. Looking straight ahead as if reciting a passage he had memorized, he said, 'Well...speaking for myself alone, I can say I take six eggs once a day.'

'*Eggs*?' I asked, unsure of what I'd heard.

'Hard boiled,' he said, thinking that I'd wanted clarification.

Mongoose was shaking his head from side to side. 'He refuses to listen. I have told him so many times, but still he eats them. He says it is a question of faith.'

'Just a moment,' I said. 'Why are we talking about food?'

'You asked about it, so I am telling,' said Rabbit, turning his palm over once more.

'It is true,' said Mongoose. 'We have been travelling together on field trips for three years. He takes six eggs every night before dinner...'

'I'm sorry but...what do eggs have to do with reincarnation?' I had gone to a stage beyond laughter now. There was a floating sensation in my head, as if my giggles had transferred themselves to my sinuses without pausing to be released along the way.

'You can read it in the papers every day,' sighed Rabbit, raising his eyes to the ceiling with a long-suffering expression. 'Some people are dying, some people are getting attacks. Excess of eggs leads to catharsis of the hearteries, leading to incarnation. But I am still eating my six eggs a day because...because...it is my *belief*!' He closed his eyes.

'No one can help him,' whispered Mongoose, 'no one.' He seemed on the verge of tears.

I got to my feet, knowing that I would explode if I remained in their company a second longer.

'Thank you!' I managed, before I fled. 'You've been very informative!'

Score Them, I thought to myself. They seemed not to have noticed my appearance at all! Five to go.

Dinner service had begun in the carriage and I returned to my cubicle, going straight up to my berth. I had reverted to my former appearance but it took me a while to bring the laughter under control. It didn't help that I could feel the gaze of my cubicle-mates flickering in my direction every few seconds as if they expected me to sprout wings or at the very least revert to my earlier prawn-like condition. Their curiosity was like an ultrasonic vibration that they were sending out in pulses, willing me to come down to their level so that they could quell the disturbance that my presence had produced in their midst and tame me with questions. If any one of them had stood up and addressed me directly, I would have been forced to answer them. But I was sure they'd never overcome their reserve enough to make the first move, and I was right.

I ate my sandwiches, drank my water and went to sleep without exchanging a word with them.

~

The train reached Nagpur half an hour behind schedule the next morning, after the breakfast service. I ate my omelette, bread and coffee up in my eyrie, no doubt causing intense disappointment below. It would be acceptable if home-cooked food was scarfed down furtively because, after all, many Indians routinely segregate their eating arrangements within their own homes, men eating separate from the women, women having exclusive dominion over the kitchen, some areas of the home being out of bounds to menstruating women and so on. But food from railway kitchens is eaten de rigueur in full view of other passengers and pleasantries must be exchanged between strangers who would otherwise never share any part of their lives with one another. I believe the reason for this conviviality is not broad-spectrum friendliness, as is often believed, but a method of neutralizing the unhealthy vibrations that result from sharing space with people belonging to the 'wrong' castes or hierarchies in the course of a journey.

By remaining out of reach, I had effectively blocked the natural channels by which potentially malign energies are contained and anaesthetized. Initially, I must have appeared to be so wretched as to be beneath attention. But after I had revealed that I was an English speaker, it must have become necessary to assimilate me and to understand, at the very least, what type of threat I posed to decent society by being shaven-headed—whether I was merely eccentric, or a widow, or, worst yet, a widow belonging to one of the Troublesome Minorities. By remaining stubbornly out of reach I had robbed them of the opportunity to know what type of negative influences they had to guard themselves against.

Nagpur was journey's end for them, so the family was forced to leave the cabin with a sense of unfinished business. Just as they were about to leave, I saw Mrs Red Border shooting desperate glances in my direction. At the very last moment, I relented and looked down towards her. Instantly, she threw her head up, aimed an angular smile in my direction and said, 'Good morning!' in the same tone of voice that would normally be used for saying 'Goodbye!'

I flexed my mouth upwards, without really smiling. *May the Confusion be with you,* I beamed telepathically in her direction. *May you always wonder who and what I was. May your stern and rule-bound existence be infected, forever, by the Contagion of Doubt.*

~

The train emptied out at Nagpur. The two corridor passengers connected to my cubicle had got down in Bhopal, the night before. The contents of the women's compartment were revealed to have been nuns—three neat women dressed in black shifts and white wimples, with a plump woman in a blue nylon sari following in their wake, a fond relative by the looks of it. The Sardars went too, brooding and moody now, as if a single giant headache throbbed in all six of their turbaned heads. Their beards were neat, their turbans tight and their checked shirts long-sleeved, yet they looked diminished compared to the previous evening, all the joy drained out of them.

Only a scattering of newcomers climbed back on the train and by 7.30 we were on our way once more. My cubicle now contained only one other person, a thin, dark, catlike man. He wore spectacles, a white shirt and black pants. His first act upon claiming his berth, the lower one diagonal to mine, was to remove his belt, coil it up and stow it in the wall-pocket. His luggage consisted of a shiny black soft-sided carry-all and a small flat briefcase. The moment the train began to move, he took the briefcase over to the two corridor seats which were still extended in the 'bed' position, removed his shoes and folded his legs up in a lotus pose. Then he drew the curtain just enough so that his head and shoulders were hidden from view, opened the briefcase and began to feed, all his movements quick and precise. He was exactly like a cat applying itself to its food bowl with complete concentration. I couldn't see what he was eating and I didn't attempt to, since it was clear that he valued his privacy. When he was done, he closed his briefcase, drew back the curtain and returned to his seat in the cubicle. Opening a newspaper, he began to read it.

I decided he must be a police officer of some sort, an inspector perhaps—too small-made and self-contained to be army, too self-assured to be a mere pen-pusher, too modestly dressed to be a bureaucrat. He didn't glance in my direction even once, but in the way that he disappeared behind his curtain, it was clear that he was conscious of my presence. It was an odd thing. His lack of interest was discreet rather than insulting. I could not assign a score to him or to myself—the ideal situation. A fellow-traveller should be willing to acknowledge the presence of others, whoever they are and whatever they look like, in a calm, uncomplicated way. Neither party should be in a position to register a victory over the other, in the sense of taking something from them that they didn't intend to give away, such as their peace of mind or their equanimity.

I went prowling through the cabin once more. The egg-eating media consultants had gone and so had the military personnel. No one had taken their place. The women's compartment now contained a young mother, two small children and an elderly female who looked like an animated prune, with dark purple skin and a desiccated manner. They had left the drapes drawn back, so that as I passed I could hear the older woman's nagging voice, pick-pick-picking at the younger woman, who looked down meekly, smoothing down the little girl's hair. The other child was still a baby and had been placed belly-down on a pillow beside her on the seat.

In the place of the Sardars were four new people, all men. They appeared to be unrelated strangers in the way that they were setting up separate domains for themselves, two in the cubicle, two in the corridor. One of them was tall, with curling salt-and-pepper hair, blue jeans and a cotton shirt that looked as if it might conceal a designer label somewhere upon itself. He wore stylish reading glasses and had an Orhan Pamuk novel in his hands. He might have been the CEO of an ad agency and seemed faintly out of place on the train. But then again, maybe not. There is a certain logic by which potential air-passengers choose to travel by train because it confers a pleasing *We, The People* coolness upon them.

The foreigners were still in place, now sitting at the window seats and reading books. Beside them were two others who may or may not have been there from the start. I had not paid enough attention to them the previous day to be able to tell. The fake doctor was still on board but neither of us acknowledged the other, he perhaps because he genuinely didn't recognize me without the black chiffon dupatta wrapped around my head. The feudal family in the cubicle neighbouring mine had got down at Nagpur and three young boys with IT written all over them had taken their place. They had festooned themselves with wires and audio-devices, with at least three laptops in plain view and a table fashioned out of two brand-name desk-top computers still in their original cartons blocking up the space between the two lower-berth seats.

The corridor berths were all but empty.

The compartment which had contained six unrelated names was now occupied by just one passenger. One robust-looking older man, wearing a white-on-white kurta-pyjama and reading the newspaper, occupied the whole of the cubicle with an air of having captured the castle. He had items of luggage on each of the other bunks and three pairs of shoes took up the floor between the two lower bunks. By his side, in the wall-pocket, a transistor radio chirped a cricket commentary. On the tiny bed-side shelf between the two windows, there was an old-fashioned wind-up alarm clock and several of the railway's diminutive flasks, as if he had set up a relay of hot beverages to drink.

I walked up and down the corridor once, twice, unsure of what to do with myself. It was not yet nine o'clock in the morning. I had already called my home in Delhi to confirm that all was well, and had also called ahead to my mother and sister in Chennai, to confirm that they were alive and healthy too. I had books to read and Sudokus to solve. But I had set out eight missions for myself and had only completed four so far.

Sure, I could go and talk to the foreigners—but I felt bored just thinking about it. Most foreign tourists are so inured to being riddled with questions that they probably feel insulted if no one pesters them for jobs or sexual favours within the first half-hour of their being on a train. The local pair looked as if they had been in India long enough to have become professional answerers. I could generate the likely conversation we would have without needing to actually speak to them:

Where are you from?

'Germany/France/Italy/Holland/Israel…'

What do you do?

'Taking our "gap" year before university and travelling around the world.'

And?

'We love/hate India and wish we could stay here forever/leave at once.'

What are you reading?

'Orhan Pamuk.'

How can I get a visa to your country?

'Go away, please.'

Score to me, but in a tired, routine way—nothing I could take personal credit for.

The young mother was already too harassed. The elderly gentleman was too comfortable. The IT boys were too hooked up to be coherent. Talking to them would be the equivalent of leaving messages on a stranger's answering machine.

The countryside was streaking by outside, an anonymous blur of village huts, mounds of dried cow-dung, shoals of little village children trooping off to school, buffaloes wallowing in a filthy pond, green fields, palm trees, crows, cinema posters, trucks backed up at level crossings, a lone bullock-cart plodding along.

Yes, I could go and talk to the curly haired CEO. In fact, he would be my natural target, a person belonging to the same social class as me, though he didn't know it, since I was currently in disguise. But I could tie my chiffon dupatta around my head and wear the *ikat* dupatta and explain what I was up to.

'My plan was to speak to at least one person in each of the eight cubicles in this carriage,' I could say to him, 'while disguised as a lower-middle-class woman who has shaved her head and is therefore likely to be taken for a widow.'

If he asked me why on earth I wanted to do something like that, I could say, 'Because I am tired of being predictable, remaining within my social class, being easily identified as such and having only one dimension. As a traveller, I want to explore not only other places, but other states of being too—to be someone else and especially to be someone that others don't like to engage with. It's so unpleasant to be openly disliked that maybe it's necessary to know what it feels like now and then. As an education—or an inoculation. For who can say when one might not, after all, become that thing that other people despise? Isn't it best to be prepared, so that when the time comes we have some prior experience to protect ourselves against the unkindness and lack of consideration we will face?'

And maybe the CEO would recoil from this admittedly somewhat deranged agenda. Maybe he would tell me that it was manipulative and anti-social to set out deliberately to mislead others. To which I would say, 'You are perfectly right to react this way and I cannot justify my behaviour except to say that it's what I wanted to do, and now I've done it and am feeling like a big-game hunter romping home with a bag full of trophies...'

But I didn't speak to him and this conversation didn't take place.

Many people spend the entire transit between the terminii of their lives being someone *else*. The *else* is defined by everyone around them, people who hem them in and create a context for them, without attempting to understand who each individual really is or could be, if he or she were given a fair chance; rigid, rule-bound, judgmental people who treat another person's reservation ticket as if it didn't count, as if it didn't exist.

Yet every single traveller has a true and valid reservation ticket, just one and in just one direction. This is true even for those who believe in reincarnation. Because look: each specific life is unique and unrepeatable. Personally, I do not believe in immortal souls but even if such things do exist and even if they do return to this physical dimension that we call reality, flying back and forth between the worlds as predictably as Arctic terns flying between the Poles, there is still no question of any one person returning to the same life, to the same time frame, to the same parents and to the same friends.

So the journey is all, the journey is everything.

I spent the remainder of my train ride suspended between my destinations, enjoying the sensation of being anonymous, like a balloon without a string. I didn't speak to anyone else and no one spoke to me either. As a woman travelling on my own, none of the men around me would have felt it was safe to speak to me—I might take offence at their unwanted attention and/or became inappropriately familiar with them.

The train was running a full hour late by the time it pulled into Chennai Central, at 10 p.m. The only other thing I had in my little shoulder-bag was a set of my normal clothes and I changed into them when we reached the Basin Bridge Junction. I wore the black chiffon dupatta wrapped around my head and I could see at once, in the mirror of the bathroom, that I had returned to my usual self. My mother was going to be furious at me for making a public spectacle of myself by shaving my hair off, but I had planned to tell her that I had done it as a dare.

The catering staff came by to accept tips fifteen minutes before arrival, followed by the bed-linen boy and the floor-swabber. He was looking much happier now, at journey's end, since there was so much debris to attend to: cigarette butts and orange peels, biscuit wrappers and empty cellophane sachets from the single-use plastic cutlery handed out at each mealtime, crushed styrofoam cups and a pair of grey socks.

The great iron beast slowed down as it passed through suburban commuter rail stations, speeding up and slowing again each time, until finally the end was in sight and it began decelerating for one last time.

Braking…braking…braking…and…

Stopped.

The station was flooded with the unnatural golden sunlight of sodium vapour lamps, boisterous with activity, despite the late hour. As I queued briefly behind other passengers waiting to get off, smiles and small pleasantries were exchanged:

'—a whole hour late!'

'—family will be worried!'

'—never happens on the Rajdhani!'

'—where are you putting up?'

I was no longer an unfamiliar, disturbing object wedged awkwardly into the shared universe of other lives. I had returned to my safe, familiar self, as a middle-aged upper-middle-class woman traveller, perhaps travelling home to my family, perhaps visiting friends on holiday, perhaps on work, perhaps on transfer.

Then we spilled out onto the platform, like hundreds of vari-coloured glass beads, bounding away to the infinity of our otherness. I called my mother and sister on my cell phone to say that I had arrived, caught a call-taxi from the stand just outside the station and, in twenty minutes, I had reached home.

The Spiritual Army and Navy Store

. . . .

Pratik Kanjilal

Every Delhi party features this long, awful Sargasso Sea moment when the drinks have been cleared away, dinner is yet to be served and the small talk falters. People slump in sofas looking trapped, desperate for someone to play Boy Scout and break the embarrassing silence. In one such awful moment, I did the Boy Scout honours. I turned to a greenhorn attaché at the US embassy and for want of anything better asked him the traditional stupid question: 'So, how do you find India?'

'It's just as I expected—very superstitious,' he said brightly. He'd seen a monkey god, snake gods, retired bureaucrats worshipping sacred trees in city neighbourhoods, kids at the stoplights every Saturday demanding ransom on behalf of Saturn, and watched news of witchcraft, black tantra, *jadu-tona* and human sacrifice on the telly. We are so totally immersed in a culture of superstition that we don't even notice until a firang points it out.

But weeks earlier I had been in firang country trying to find my way out of Atlanta in order to drive to Alabama. After hours of being lost, I found the Interstate exit and floored the gas pedal. And there, nestling in the grass by the concrete, was a sign. It looked like a regular road sign, but this was a Sign from Above. In huge capital letters it spelt out one word: REPENT. Repent, rash mortal, because you're going to hit the Interstate, which might take you straight to the Pearly Gates and the guy with the big ledger will have unpleasant questions for you. To my un-Christian eye, it looked remarkably like superstition. John Berendt's non-fiction account *Midnight in the Garden of Good and Evil*, set in nearby Savannah, features a voodoo woman who flings grave dust at her client's enemies and no one finds it odd. It sounds crazy but

Georgia, the home state of CNN, UPS, Delta Air and Coca-Cola Corp., is a mighty superstitious place.

As you see, one person's faith is another person's superstition. Your God could be my juju. And what I regard as anciently sanctioned liturgy may be evidence of primitive fetishism to you. The idea of superstition is culturally relativistic and the phenomenon shares a lot of ground with organized religion, which some regard as nothing more than superstition organized and vouched for by wily priests. In the Orientalist discourse of the last three centuries, elements of Indian faith and ritual have been routinely misreported as superstition. So that attaché was clearly wrong. India looks excessively superstitious only when seen through Western eyes—or Westernized eyes, which is much the same thing.

Taking the argument further, India is a madly multicultural society and each of its constituent cultures may look superstitious when seen through the eyes of another. And within each of those cultures, social and economic status can make a huge difference to what is deemed superstitious behaviour (see Possession, p. 403). When a Dalit Union minister was pulled up for participating in shamanistic rites, he angrily inquired how his beliefs were worse than those of upper-caste people who flock to the wellness guru Sri Sri Ravi Shankar and his Art of Living.

And, finally, how do you tell belief from superstition in a country where the silicon age lives cheek by jowl with the late Stone Age? Who is more superstitious—the day trader who will not buy stock over the Internet on Tuesdays because it spells certain ruin or the tribal who believes that sickness is caused by witchcraft and that he must save his society by killing the witch, an action which he does not regard as murder (see Witchcraft, p. 392)?

The decentralized nature of Hinduism, the majority religion in India, makes it fairly unique among world faiths. It has no mother church like St. Peter's, no central shrine like the Kaaba, no messiah like the Buddha and no central document like the Granth Sahib. In fact, no one is in charge and everyday, ritualistic Hinduism can be regarded as a collection of cults. The Hindu pantheon grows from the ground up, freely absorbing folk traditions from beyond the pale in the form of new cults. If they are well received, they spread widely and become part of the ritual calendar. At the same time, central beliefs and myths may fall into disfavour and linger on in marginal communities in forms which the mainstream disparages as superstitious. By usage, superstitions assume the status of approved religion and vice versa (see GHATOTKACHA TEMPLE, p. 399, KARNI MATA, p. 402).

Indian culture and faith are eternally evolving, absorptive, eclectic, lateral. As Mark Twain noted (in *Following the Equator*) on a visit to Varanasi in 1896, 'There is a chance for everything in [this] admirably stocked and wonderfully systemized Spiritual and Temporal Army and Navy Store.' Which is why the Western notion of superstition, which is defined as faith unsanctioned by a church, is of little diagnostic value here. Actually, it hasn't worked too well in Europe either, where it was invented. Coined in early Rome, 'superstition' is among the sneakiest, dodgiest words in the lexicon of ideas. It seems to derive from *super*, Latin for 'above', and *stitio*, which is a close cousin of the Sanskrit *sthiti*, signifying location or standing. So the word literally means 'standing over'. This may signify a power over and above the physical world, but there is really no satisfactory explanation for this curious phrase.

Vague terms are shape-shifting weapons, particularly handy for vilifying the Other. The Roman historian Tacitus declared that Christianity, which was just getting into second gear in his time, was a clutch of the most benighted superstitions. With the zeal of the new convert, the Holy Roman Emperor Constantine retaliated later by denouncing the paganism that preceded Christianity as superstition. As the Christian faith consolidated itself in Europe, the term acquired a generally accepted default meaning—belief that is pre-Christian or un-Christian, and therefore to be deprecated as unreal, illogical and unenlightened.

In living memory, differences over what constitutes superstition have been strictly Christians versus the Rest of the World fixtures, and the Christians were winning the series. But let's step further back to the era of European exploration, when the Rest of the World—including India—swam into Europe's ken. When Vasco da Gama reached Calicut in search of 'Christians and spices', the Zamorin's men took him to what is believed to be the temple of Mariamman, the goddess of choice for relief from smallpox and other terminal misfortunes. And, convinced that they were among the Christians they had come to seek, the Portuguese knelt and paid homage to the idol of the mother goddess, which they took to be the Virgin Mary. They also paid their respects to the personages depicted in frescoes on the temple walls, venerating them as Christian saints, though they did seem rather fierce and sported devilishly long teeth.

By the time the Europeans had progressed from trading posts to colonies, the scales had fallen from their eyes. They were sure that they had not found Christians but the Other. In the popular Western imagination, India became home to superstitious races worthy of Christian derision. The stereotype, born of a European narrative of history, lingers on though perceptions are changing. The notion of karma, once disparaged as fatalism, mutated into a hippie chic catchword and is now New Age slang. And in 2008, Barack Obama sought a presidential nomination with a little image of the monkey god Hanuman in his pocket. It is surmised that he had picked it up in South-East Asia, where he spent part of his childhood. If a future president of the US is comfortable with that, maybe we're not so superstitious after all. Maybe we've just been misrepresented by people who had limited experience of the East and found it mysterious, inscrutable and generally scary.

On the other hand, this little flyer arrived in my newspaper this morning. It's printed in Hindi and English on something like toilet paper. It's from one Guru Raj Bharti, Uncrowned Emperor of Matters Spiritual and the Seven Deadly Arts. If I call the Emperor on the mobile number he has thoughtfully provided, he will rid me of angst arising from setbacks in business or a failed career in cinema or modelling, domestic uproars, divorce proceedings, bigamy, rivalry, bad loans, barrenness, masturbation, love marriage or bloodstains appearing mysteriously on the walls of my home. In return, all he wants from me is a pack of joss sticks and two limes. And twenty minutes of my time. And my wallet, naturally.

In retrospect, I agree with the greenhorn American I had met. He might be CIA or something, but he was telling it like it is. Guru Raj Bharti exists, whether we regard him through Orientalist glasses or in the clear light of day, and we clearly live in a God-awfully superstitious country. The pages that follow will reveal just how flamboyantly, colourfully superstitious we can get.

STARCRAFT

'The only function of economic forecasting is to make astrology look respectable,' John Kenneth Galbraith once lamented. Perhaps that explains why the art has always enjoyed enormous credibility in India, where there are very few certainties in the rational domain. Here, astrology has been a fact of everyday life for at least one and a half millennia and its popularity seems to have increased with time. Once dependent on the patronage of royal courts and prominent merchants, astrologers have been embraced by the middle class, which has been growing in numbers and means over the last two centuries and particularly rapidly in recent times. Meanwhile, they are still patronized by the political establishment and, despite the example set by the rationalistic Jawaharlal Nehru, India has had prime ministers and chief ministers who would not move a muscle without a soothsayer saying so. Few political leaders will go to the polls or make an alliance without consulting the omens. When Prime Minister Manmohan Singh successfully fought off a no-confidence motion in Parliament in July 2008, he wryly advised his opponent L.K. Advani of the BJP to change his astrologer to better his political fortunes.

Among the common people, no action of any importance is contemplated without due diligence done by the astrologer. Even rationalists who have dispensed with everyday articles of faith may still consult an astrologer before a life-altering event, such as marriage. In earlier times, the soothsayer's hold on the imagination was complete, as this news item from the *Tribune* of Lahore dated 24 June 1882 will show:

> It is reported from Bombay that a Bania named Trikamdas, an inhabitant of Ahmedabad, was informed by a Brahman that his death would take place on a certain day in the month of Vaisakh. Thereupon the Bania repaired to the holy shrine of Palitana to perform his funeral rites. But not dying on due date, he returned to Ahmedabad and interviewed the Brahman, who said that he had made a mistake in the calculation, and that Trikamdas would die in the month of Sravan. The devotee has thereupon gone back to Palitana to die.

Europeans who dealt with Indian kings as agents, advisers, diplomats, mercenaries or plain visitors frequently wrote of their exasperation with royalty's dependence on astrologers. They would not clinch a deal or go to war at the decisive moment if the omens were not right. They took astrological advice even for routine domestic matters like the annual move from summer to winter quarters—often just a move from one wing of a building to another. The pioneering photographer Louis Rousselet, in India to document royalty, had to wait for days to go on a tiger hunt with the Gaekwad of Baroda in 1875, because the astrologers found the stars unpropitious. The Frenchman, whose classic frames now sell for princely sums, found the Gaekwad extremely superstitious but was happy to see that in the end even royalty was exasperated and defied the astrologers.

In medieval times, *rajpurohits*, the court priests who doubled as astrologers, were often as close to the king as generals or ministers—or even closer, because they dealt in personal affairs. In Rajputana, their havelis were built right outside the inner city walls. In Jaisalmer, the priest's home was actually inside the fort complex. And in Udaipur, the magnificent Purohit's Haveli was built on the highest ground in the city, the only exception to the injunction that no one could build as high as the king.

Now that royalty has gracefully abdicated to commerce, astrologers have sought out new, middle-class constituencies through the media, particularly television. Most of India's three-hundred-odd television channels, including those focussed on news and current affairs, feature astrological content. Some channels exclusively run astrology and related programming 24x7 and newspapers and magazines have always carried horoscopes. In their defence, viewers who run their lives by media astrology say that they are just getting their mental wellness fix and that their habit is no worse than the American obsession with the therapist. In 2001 the government even sanctioned university courses in Indian astrology at the urging of Murli Manohar Joshi, who was Union minister for human resource development in the BJP-led National Democratic Alliance government. Fortunately, it turned out that young people are rather hard-headed and strongly preferred a certificate in Java over one in *jyotisha* and these courses did not really catch on.

In India, astrology is par for the course but sometimes it does offend public sensibilities, like in the 2007 wedding of Aishwariya Rai and Abhishek Bachchan, in which the most successful actress in Bollywood married into popular Hindi cinema's first family. Naturally, every media astrologer and his aunt wrote up the couple's horoscopes and it became public knowledge that Aishwariya Rai was *manglik*. The *manglik dosha* ('flaw of Mars') is a condition affecting people who have Mars in the 1st, 4th, 7th, 8th or 12th house of the lunar natal chart. A manglik can safely marry only another manglik, whereupon they cancel out each other's flaws. Bachchan is not manglik and if he went ahead with this marriage he would apparently come to a sticky end after an unnaturally short lifetime made hellish by marital discord, bad luck and poor health. The approved method for dealing with a woman with the Martian flaw (which is dangerous only in women) is to marry her to an inanimate object, on which Mars presumably vents his baneful influence, before the real marriage. The luckless groom is usually a banana or pipal tree in this ritual wedding ceremony called the *kumbh vivaha*. The real husband, whom the woman marries later, is thus saved.

Rai was apparently married to a banana tree (see TREE MARRIAGE, p. 408), though the Bachchan family denied this. However, in the year in which the couple married, the family did exhibit a bout of extraordinary religiosity and left no place of pilgrimage unvisited and no deity unpropitiated. It was said that they were taking out extra insurance cover against the Martian flaw.

The Abhishek-Aishwariya affair drew adverse public attention because all the parties involved, including Abhishek's parents, are role models for Indians. They were called superstitious and sexist but what they did—or rather, what they denied doing—is no more than what many Indian families would have done irrespective of their status. And if they were modern and progressive, they would have denied it just as vehemently.

In a similar incident back in 2003 Karnamoni Hansda, a nine-year-old Santhal girl in a village near Kolkata, was found to have a tooth embedded in her palate, which is considered a bad omen in her community. As an antidote, her family married her to a stray dog of the neighbourhood in a ceremony attended by a hundred wedding guests who were wined and dined as custom demands. The girl's opinion was canvassed and she expressed no objection to marrying the dog, whom she knew and liked. Her community clarified that the girl would be free to marry a regular human later. Intriguingly, the dog's name was Bachchan.

Some stories about soothsaying suggest that it was never taken in deadly earnest. For instance, childless women are reported to have enjoyed a special rapport with astrologers in the past. This occasioned much sexual innuendo because, owing to the nature of their problem, they consulted soothsayers secretly, after dark. They were mercilessly ribbed if they happened to lose any jewellery, the assumption being that they had used it to pay an astrologer for services rendered. But if the consultation was successful, the ribbing turned nasty because, though they had given the family a child, they had clearly bartered it for not only the lost ornament but also lost virtue.

Recently, life science experiments aboard the space shuttle have come to the support of astrology. It has been demonstrated that variations in gravity—planetary influence by another name—affect living tissues. Spiders spin their webs differently, the heartbeats of goldfish change, immune systems become weaker and gene expression is altered. The salmonella organism, shot into space, returned to earth three years later in a spectacularly virulent form. And it turns out that it may be impossible to get pregnant in space—space-born children may be, well, inconceivable. So there could be something to claims of planetary influence, though it may have nothing to do with astrology.

However, a recent study proposes to make that link. In 2001 the BJP-led government had launched courses in Hindu astrology which Murli Manohar Joshi had termed jyotirvigyan—astrological science—under the University Grants Commission. He claimed that sixteen Indian universities were already offering courses in subjects much like astrology and he was only formalizing an existing trend. The move was strongly resisted by rationalists, partly on principle and partly because the minister was committing fresh funding to astrology while starving established disciplines, but to no avail. Ironically, Joshi was a professor of physics before turning to politics.

In September 2008 the Lal Bahadur Shastri Sanskrit Vidyapeeth's department of medical astrology announced initial findings of a UGC-funded project. They had matched the case histories of more than 1000 hospital patients with their horoscopes and claimed to have found a correlation in 75 per cent of cases between the incidence of disease and astrological predictions. There is nothing wrong with conducting such studies—they actually clear the air and advance the debate from the level of claims and counterclaims to that of factual evidence. However, it goes without saying that findings should be subjected to rigorous peer review by the scientific community before they are accepted.

Astronomy and astrology evolved in various cultures in prehistoric times when the human race graduated from the hunter-gatherer mode to less interesting ways of making a living. It probably originated as a single discipline, a purely practical science helping to accurately plan the planting and reaping of the agriculturist and the annual migrations of pastoral life. In fact, our activities are still ruled by the heavens. We consider ourselves modern because we plan our lives by the clock and the calendar, forgetting that these are in turn based on the movement of the stars.

Presumably, astrology broke away from the common discipline when the study of the heavens assumed a body of religious and symbolic meaning. But in India the two were perhaps never clearly set apart. The mathematician and astronomer Varahamihira (sixth century AD), one of the 'nine jewels' of the court of Emperor Vikramaditya—India's King Arthur—is best known for his encyclopaedic *Panchasiddhantika*, which contains the essence of five earlier astronomical treatises which are now lost. However, he is almost as well known for the *Brihat Jataka*, a core text of Indian astrology, or jyotisha. A millennium before Tycho Brahe, who organized the data behind European astronomy and laid the foundation for Kepler's work, Varahamihira worked on standardizing accurate star charts and produced path-breaking solutions in trigonometry. But outside of academia, he is remembered only as the father of Indian astrology. His son Prithuyayas added to his canon with the *Hora Saara*. As the title suggests, it is about horoscopy.

The names of the texts summarized in the *Panchasiddhantika* arouse some suspicion that Indian astrology may not be entirely Indian. Great swathes of Greek, Roman and Mesopotamian thought may have all but smothered the local brand. The texts

Varahamihira summarized include the *Paulisa Siddhanta*, the work of the Roman star-watcher Paul of Alexandria (fl. 378 AD), and the *Romaka Siddhanta*, which enumerated other traditions current in the Roman Empire. Varahamihira's book also provided complete tables based on Ptolemy and in his *Brihat Samhita* he urged the reader to respect the Greeks, though they were *mlechhas* (ritually impure aliens), because they were champion scientists. Evidence of Mesopotamian influence is seen in jyotisha's adoption of the sidereal zodiac, which was a Sumerian innovation, rather than the tropical zodiac used in Western astrology. Similarly, the twelve-sign zodiac we use was dreamed up in Babylon. And traces of Persian astrology are also suspected to be lurking in there. The only indisputably Indian element is the system of lunar houses and the schema of the heavenly bodies: the sun and the moon, the five planets from Mercury to Saturn, and the two 'shadow planets' Rahu and Ketu, which are really the lunar nodes (the eclipse-rich points where the moon's orbit crosses the apparent path of the sun through the skies).

The native authenticity of Indian astronomy can neither be established nor disproved because Alexander the Great, the young man in a hurry of the old world, muddled the historical record. In the fourth century BC, Alexander's armies swept through half of Asia like a runaway kitchen blender, whirling Greek, Persian, Middle Eastern, Mesopotamian and Indian culture into the great salad bowl from which the Hellenistic age would rise after his passing. Not until the exploits of Genghis Khan (which brought us, entirely by the way, the Mughal Empire) would Asia see such a violent churning of culture and society. The Indian predictive arts were shaken and stirred by this maelstrom and may not have remained authentically Indian. A system could be basically Indian with a strong Mesopotamian *tadka*, as in the case of sidereal astrology, or it could be a chutnified version of a Greek method, as in the case of numerology.

Today, Indian astrologers remain as open to change as they were in Alexander's day. Early adopters of IT, they were advertising 'computer astrology', which takes the drudgery out of astrological computations, as soon as cheap, grey-market PCs arrived in the early 1990s. Astrology programs were among the first software packages written in India. Today, from the digital city of Hyderabad there are reports of astrologers camping outside hospital maternity wards with laptops and printers ready to spit out an infant's natal chart the moment its head pops out into the world. More infamously, gynaecologists are harassed by parents to prescribe a caesarean section, though a normal delivery may be entirely possible. A caesarean allows parents to exactly time the birth for an auspicious moment prescribed by their astrologers.

Computer-savvy astrologers hit the superhighway soon after the Internet was available in India. They were getting business from the diaspora on email at a time when most executives did not know how to switch on a computer. Of course, Indian fortune telling has always been an export-oriented industry. It was first taken westward more than a millennium ago by the gypsies, where it lingers on as fairground entertainment.

Today, Indian astrology is a major export industry. Apart from providing web services, astrologers are body-shopped to countries with a large diaspora population. In the UK, people of Indian origin have a decent share of the £40 million soothsaying and spiritual wellness industry, competing aggressively with the beads-and-baubles New Agers of the Stonehenge–Glastonbury circuit.

Europe already had regulations controlling this sector and in 2008 Indian soothsayers have come up against a non-tariff trade barrier in the UK. Along with their British peers, they are now required to state that their services are 'for entertainment only' and not 'experimentally proven'. If a *gunin* or tantrik fails to make these declarations in their shingles, advertisements and printed matter, including cash receipts, they can be prosecuted just like any service provider for predictions that go wrong.

It's not much fun being a soothsayer if you have to declare yourself to be an entertainer up front, but things could be worse. In Moscow in July 2008 Grigory Grabovoy was brought to court in a steel cage and sentenced to eleven years of hard labour after taking money from people to raise their loved ones from the dead. In 2004, for instance, he had approached the mothers of the 186 children who were killed in a disastrous military operation to liberate them after Chechen fighters took them hostage in their school.

There is indeed something ghoulish about the manner in which Grabovoy preyed on recently bereaved people who were particularly vulnerable to his pitch. But he is only an extreme example of the method used by almost all practitioners of the various arts of fortune telling who regard it as just another business rather than a calling akin to religion.

Now, prognostication alone does not make for a sound business plan. It's not very remunerative to tell someone they're headed for big trouble. There's much more money in it if you can also tell them how to avoid it. So after he tells your fortune and predicts a sticky time six weeks hence, your astrologer may produce a numerological solution involving changing your name, address or telephone number. And he may suggest that you wear a gemstone next to your skin which will set the influence of the stars at nought and favourably redraw your fate line. This stone may be precious or semi-precious, but either way the sticker shock will stun like a phaser.

Which brings us to the financially rewarding world of numerology and gemology. The former is probably not of Indian provenance and almost certainly owes to the Greeks. Pythagoras of Samos, the very man whose method of calculating the hypotenuse of a right-angled triangle is the bane of every schoolchild, pioneered a whole system of philosophy which sought the music of the spheres in number sequences. Number theory and the formal study of sound owe much to his work. So does numerology.

Gemology, on the other hand, is very definitely Indian, though it was briefly in vogue in another form in medieval Europe where compendiums of gemstones known as lapidaries were published. But it was a passing phase and the only stone which remained popular in Europe was the bezoar, a hairball or calculus found in the stomach of ruminants, some other animals and even humans, which was regarded as an antidote to poison. The belief is not entirely baseless. Some hairballs can in fact precipitate arsenic, a popular poison in ancient times. But even the bezoar is not of European provenance. The name is a corruption of the Persian *pad-zehr* (protection from poison) or *be-zehr* (poison-free), clearly indicating its Asian origin.

STONES AND NUMBERS

In May 2008 Bharti Telecom, which owns the Airtel mobile phone network, proposed to make an audacious takeover bid for the South African mobile network MTN. The projected $50 billion deal would have made it the sixth biggest mobile telco in the world, with 130 million subscribers in more than twenty countries. It would have eclipsed all previous overseas mergers and acquisitions of an increasingly aggressive India Inc. Deals of this size are often initiated on important public dates so that the PR blitz can piggyback on routine media coverage of the day and add to the perceived cachet of the event. World Telecom Day, 17 May, would have been a natural choice, but the market punters brushed it aside in favour of 23 May. Only because Bharti CEO Sunil Mittal's birthday is on the 23rd (of October, though) and the number sequence 23 apparently features in his driving licence number, his mobile phone number and credit card numbers. Analysts frankly admitted that Indian businessmen are superstitious and, when they make big gambles, sentiment often rules over market logic. As it happened, Bharti's bid was delayed beyond the 23rd. The deal fell through and Anil Ambani's Reliance Infocomm stepped into the breach with a bid of its own.

Numerology has been around as a prognosticative art for a long time, but it developed into a corrective therapy only in the twenty-first century. Strange, but true. The notoriously superstitious Bollywood crowd went for numerological rehab and, since they're the role models for half the subcontinent, everyone followed in their wake.

Unlike the arcane art of astrology, numerology is quite amenable to DIY. The principle is very simple: add up the numerals in your date of birth until you arrive at a single numeral. Opinion is divided on what works better, just the date of month or the whole date, including the year. Either way, once you have a single numeral, you can take it to any fortune teller and set him to work.

There isn't much you can play with here because your date of birth is set in stone—or a government certificate, at least. But your name is free range. Each letter has a numerical value according to its place in the alphabet sequence. Add them up as before and you're cooking. What, you got a six and wanted a seven? No problem, just add an 'a' somewhere in your name. Wanted nine? Fiddle the letters some more and you should get there. And thus acne-ridden hard-luck girl Manisha is erased forever and the incredibly fortunate and attractive Minissha is born. Arun the loser must die so that Aroon the god in human shape can live.

On similar principles, the movie *Krish*, which was destined to be a hit anyway because of a gigantic international marketing and distribution campaign, was rechristened *Krrish* just to make sure. And *Singh is Kinng* was given an extra 'n' on the advice of cult numerologist Jhumani, who had earlier reset the name of the epic *Jodha-Akbar* to *Jodhaa-Akbar*. He also set the release date of *Singh...*, 08.08.08, because eight is the producer's lucky number and 2008 offers a hat-trick. He left it at that but the Chinese inaugurated the Beijing Olympics on the same day, on the eighth second of the eighth minute of the eighth hour of the evening—that's 08.08.08.08.08.08. They're clearly more obsessional than us. Incidentally, even foreign brands are not exempt from numerological renaming. The Indian version of *Big Brother*, hosted by Shilpa Shetty who won the UK show after a race row, is called *Bigg Boss*.

The most successful soap operas on Indian television, made by Balaji Telefilms, have names which start with the letter K—*Kyunki Saas Bhi Kabhi Bahu Thi*, for instance. The trend apparently started when astrologer and tarot reader Sunita Menon identified K as the lucky letter for Ekta Kapoor, who runs Balaji Telefilms. Maybe she did get it right. The 'K serials'—which soon became KK serials as Kapoor took out double insurance cover against bad luck—are brain-deadening, unwatchable, and yet are the most successful Indian soaps ever.

As you see, our new obsession with numbers extends well beyond the self. Mobile phone dealers allow people to pick their own numbers to accommodate their numerological needs. Car salesmen time their deals so that they are able to pick up a favourable licence plate number for their clients. Practising Muslims prize the sequence 786, the numerical representation of the first line of every surah but one of the Quran—'Bismillah' for short. But faith in this number is not restricted to Islam. Amitabh Bachchan, a practising Hindu, wore 786 on his sleeve in two films in which he played a porter—*Deewar* and *Coolie*. The former became one of the biggest hits of all time and while shooting for the latter, Bachchan suffered a potentially fatal injury but recovered completely. Curiously, triskaidekaphobia, the global dread of the number 13, which causes hotels, office buildings and apartment blocks to skip rooms (and sometimes whole floors) of that number, and airplanes to skip the thirteenth row, only affects the urban upper classes in India.

Like numerology, gem therapy is an ancillary industry of astrology. It claims to work by using stones associated with the nine heavenly bodies—the sun, the moon, the planets Mercury to Saturn, and the lunar nodes Rahu and Ketu. Practitioners may be *anukul-vadi*, believing that a gem acts exactly like its associated planet, or *pratikul-vadi*, and support the opposite principle. Either way, they prescribe stones that the client is supposed to wear in contact with the skin, set in rings, lockets or amulets. Like doctors, they frequently change their prescription as therapy progresses. Old stones are removed from the client's person and fresh varieties added to the bouquet. Only the criminally rich would be able to bear the cost of treatment were it not for a buyback system in vogue among gemologists. It keeps clients from going bankrupt. More importantly, it discourages them from seeking second opinions from competitors, who will not buy back gems prescribed by the first gemologist. They will, rather, scoff at them as flawed or fake.

Gem therapy finds its textual basis in passages in the Puranas, but the correlations between gemstones and heavenly bodies are laid down in Varahamihira's *Brihat Jataka*:

> The ruby stands for the sun, the pearl for the moon, emerald for Mercury, the diamond for Venus, red coral for Mars, yellow sapphire for Jupiter, blue sapphire for Saturn, hessonite for Rahu and cat's eye for Ketu.

Together, they make up the navratna or nine jewels, a term which has been in use from the Golden Age of the Gupta Empire (320–500 AD), when it was used to describe the nine leading talents of the Gupta court. This could be the era in which gem therapy originated.

Gemologists are obsessed with the 'purity' of stones. In order to be effective, says the *Garuda Purana*, a gem must be lustrous and should not have a granular appearance or visible cracks or fissures in its body. The wearer of a flawed stone is guaranteed to come to a sticky end.

In recent years, gem dealers have started selling guaranteed pure stones internationally via television and over the Internet. On television, they have been hawked by once-leading film stars like Jackie Shroff. Stars are a natural choice because, like other high-risk operators such as stock market investors and entrepreneurs, movie people are seriously into gemology. For reasons which are not obvious, it is also wildly popular in eastern India, where people can have their fingers totally encrusted with rings.

Other forms of fortune telling are also in vogue in India. There is palmistry or cheiromancy, imported from Europe and improved upon (the wrinkles of the forehead are often read, for instance). Phrenology (reading the skull) and physiognomy are not unknown, but again are imports. Local flavours include bulls which are led from door to door and are trained to answer questions about the future with an affirmative nod or a negative shake of the horns. Geckos are prognosticatively potent: if one falls on your head, you will marry royalty. If one clucks just after you speak, what you've said is definitely true. Birds, the most prolific omen-bearers of the ancient world, still do service in the form of tame parrots who pick out a client's horoscope with their beaks like a tarot reader picks cards from a deck. Crows are also watched for signs. Their flight patterns, eating preferences and the cadence of their cawing apparently have prognosticative value. They are particularly useful in determining whether a funeral sacrifice has been successful by observing how they eat the ritual offerings left out for them. Curiously, the crystal ball, the stock in trade of the European fairground gypsy, is unknown in India, the country of origin of all gypsies the world over.

VASTU

Vastu is the ancient Indian system of planning and architecture which seeks to bring man-made structures into harmony with the environment and thereby secure a wholesome lifestyle for inhabitants. Indubitably ancient, references to this art are found in the Puranas and compilations of ancient lore assembled in Gupta times and later, apart from the central treatise, the *Vishwakarma Vastushastra*. Given that urbanization was a late development in Aryan civilization, which was originally a pastoral culture, vastu may be pre-Aryan (bearing in mind, of course, that the provenance and trajectory—and indeed the very existence—of 'Aryan' culture is deeply contested). It's entertaining to speculate if it may have been used by the Indus Valley civilization (3000–1500 BC), a culture so obsessed with orderly town planning that its English discoverers put it down for a soulless bureaucracy.

The principles of vastu have always been observed by rural folk, and in the cities the fortunes of the art are now in the ascendant thanks to the real estate boom fuelled by India's growing prosperity. For instance, here's an advertisement for a vastu-compliant home which went on sale recently:

> The house is positioned exactly according to the four directions. The entrance is East Facing. Light comes in to the centre of the house from all four directions. There is a pond with a waterfall to the northeast of the house. The property is protected to the South. Great care was taken to ensure a flat building pad within the vastu fence. The first floor bedrooms ensure a solid *vata* pacifying night's sleep, while still providing awesome views. The pop-out porch off the master bedroom makes for an exquisite sleep area with the moonlight flooding the space with soma from the moment the moon rises in the east until it sets in the west. The rising sun illuminates the front door year around as it slowly moves from the south to the north and back. On the day of the equinox, it is directly in front of your front door.

Sounds like a fancy bungalow in Lonavala or Pachmarhi? But the concluding lines of the advertisement point to another continent altogether:

> It is an astronomer's delight with the night-time planets readily visible from the instant they rise until they set. A computer program accompanying the home sale enables you to follow the night sky 365 days a year.

A real estate deal with software thrown in free could happen only in America. In fact, this advertisement is for a clifftop home in North Carolina, one of the many vastu-compliant homes that dot the landscape of Europe and North America.

In America, Maharishi Mahesh Yogi's Global Reconstruction Programme for Permanent World Peace has been energetically promoting 'Vedic' architecture and vastu. John Hagelin, Harvard postgrad, former grand unification theorist and superstring-wallah and now the late Maharishi's minister for science and technology, has urged George Bush to close down the south entrances of the White House, whose incorrect positioning is apparently responsible for the chaos that Dubya's reign has let loose on the world. No. 10 Downing Street also has an entrance similarly placed, which explains why Tony Blair was such a disaster for British Labour. And the entrances of our own Parliament are a bit out of kilter too, which is why our legislators are able to entertain the nation with their antics on Lok Sabha TV. Clearly, the British got it wrong wherever they went. They should have consulted the Indians. We know better. We've always known better.

These days vastu extends well beyond the home. The rural police near Nagpur have recently been caught running a controversial experiment using vastu to cancel out 'bad energies' on dangerous stretches of highway in order to reduce the number of road accidents. They allowed a pyramid power promoter to build vastu pyramids lining the road. The number of accidents did indeed go down, but the police suspect it had more to do with the installation of speed guns than pyramid power.

Originally, vastu was probably just a sensible way to lay out a building. A house oriented according to vastu principles typically enjoys a lot of light and fresh air. In a hot, humid country that means dwellers will have better general health. The art does not stop at planning a house but also prescribes its landscaping—again, on common-sense principles. Papaya trees, for instance, are to be planted near the kitchen, where they will thrive on runoff water and wastes thrown out.

Kautilya's *Arthashastra*, the world's first book on political economy and governance, includes common-sense layouts for royal camps and stables for cavalry and elephant which are very reminiscent of vastu. The book also has plans for the ideal capital city and state, laid out to simultaneously secure the objectives of military and political security and public health. Cardinal directions are not specified, but the meticulously detailed, four-square arrangements of royal quarters, camps, stables and other institutions of the state are also very reminiscent of vastu plans.

But in our times, vastu is ruled by the most inscrutable laws. For instance, loads cannot be placed in the centre of the drawing room—no, that icon you snitched from the Konark temple can't be your talking point. Bedrooms must be furnished so that people sleep with their heads to the south. However, children must sleep with their heads to the east or west, and must cram for their exams facing east. Staircases are the worst. The number of steps must be chosen so that on division by three, two is the remainder. This is a modulo operation, a procedure which entered Western math in 1801 and finds use in computer logic. What does it have to do with building staircases? Go figure.

Nothing is known of vastu's relation to the similar art of feng shui, but in the early Buddhist period China looked to India for religious and cultural guidance, much as medieval England looked to France to be instructed in fashion, a tradition that the modern world still follows by oohing and aahing over gaudy Hermès scarves. It is not unreasonable to speculate that vastu may have crossed the Gobi Desert with Chinese monks on their way home from India and fathered feng shui. So an Indian school of practical architecture and planning may have travelled to Shanghai and Nanking to spawn cute frogs and lucky bamboos while at home it slowly degenerated into an obscure art which tells you which wall to hang your Husain canvas on, according to the direction in which the horses are galloping. And now, thanks to globalization which has brought us the cheap and cheerful China Bazaar, feng shui has come full circle to compete with vastu on its own turf, and is perhaps winning.

WITCHCRAFT

In December 2003 J.S. Bhatti, superintendent of police of Bijapur, Karnataka, was arrested on the charge of having his wife Vimla murdered by four witch doctors. He suspected that she had been bewitching him in order to make him impotent. Apparently, Bhatti admitted that he had sent the witch doctors to her, but only to neutralize her witchcraft. Things went out of hand and they strangled her to death, presumably in their efforts to throttle the demon within her.

This case was particularly shocking because the perpetrator was a senior policeman, serving in a district where the literacy rate is above the national average. If he believed his wife to be aberrant in any way, he had access to psychiatric help. But he hails from Bastar district, part of the tribal belt spanning the backward areas of Bengal, Bihar, Orissa, Jharkhand and Chhattisgarh, where black magic and witchcraft are still aspects of everyday life. Nature clearly won over nurture. Of course, it is not unknown for city dwellers to seek out tantriks who advertise their skills in the newspapers cheek by jowl with escort services, Russian masseuses and institutions holding out the promise of a college degree even if you've flunked school. But it is the exception rather than the rule.

Tribal communities are the main repositories of witchcraft, a remnant of the pre-Aryan animist faith of this region. The controversial archaeologist D.D. Kosambi, who analysed myth and folklore in his work, has plausibly speculated that India originally had a matriarchal society which was overrun by a warlike patriarchal culture (in fact, few tribal societies are patriarchal). Assuming this to be correct, it would have been politically prudent for the latter to demonize the religious leaders of the culture they had displaced as witches. And yet, the memory of their former social and political importance would linger on. Perhaps that is why people hate witchcraft and also consult witches to deal with adversity in business or love, unfaithfulness, childlessness, enmity, hauntings, sexual dysfunction, or simply to counter witchcraft previously done on them. Tantriks have combined witchcraft with the darker side of Hinduism to offer special, stomach-turning services. None of this makes news, except when it results in murder.

G.C. Dyson, who served as an administrator in Punjab in the early years of the twentieth century, wrote of a childless woman who went to a holy man for fear her husband would take a second wife. She was told that if she wanted to bear a son, she should kill a girl aged less than ten, cut out her liver, fry it and eat it. She did so, could not conceal the corpse well enough and was caught.

In 2006 there was an action replay in a house in Noida, a Delhi suburb, where children were sexually abused and killed. The Nithari serial killings are being investigated by the Central Bureau of Investigation. One of the accused has apparently confessed to cutting out the livers of the children and eating them fried to increase his sexual prowess. It's exactly as the holy man had prescribed in the case reported by Dyson a hundred years ago.

Today, thanks to increasing access to modern medicine and organized religion, the position of the witch doctor in society is slipping. But the accusation of witchcraft is widely put to political use to punish women who transgress social norms or resist the advances of powerful men, or simply to rob them of their property. Typically, victims are powerless women. Women of locally important families are almost never targeted, except by their own relations, who may have an eye on their property.

Faith in witchcraft remains a reality in the tribal belt where people—usually women—identified as witches are routinely tortured, mutilated and killed, sometimes with the collusion or acquiescence of their own families. It is estimated that at least five 'witches' are attacked and tortured every month in Jharkhand alone. Some of them do not survive the ordeal. In 2008 a 'witch' in a Bihar village was tied to a tree and beaten with the police standing by and the television cameras rolling. It shocked the nation, though the woman survived largely unhurt. Far worse routinely happens out of sight of the authorities and the media. Jharkhand now has a law making the accusation of witchcraft a criminal offence, the first of its kind.

Incidentally, there is a crucial distinction between Western and Indian ideas of witchcraft. The Western witch (or Christian witch, until the recent revival of Wicca) is regarded as party to a pact with the devil, while Indian witchcraft is neutral to notions of good and evil. If someone has bewitched you, it is not at all sinful to bewitch them back.

JADU—TONA

Witchcraft is related to jadu-tona, South Asia's own take on voodoo, which shares some common ground with the better-known African and South American versions. The tools of the black magician's trade include the classic dolls pierced through with pins; the autochthonous *tona,* a charmed object, often a container of excrement or urine left in the path of the victim; and magical spells intended to make the victim waste away, bleed to death, lose their souls or go insane. Not just people, even animals, homes, institutions and auspicious events such as weddings or celebrations can be cursed. Naturally, counter-spells are available for every spell. Just good business strategy.

Black magic is no longer very popular in most parts of India, but it remains a craze in some areas of Pakistan and is found to some extent in the Indian states bordering that country. But the black magician's pharmacopoeia remains sought after everywhere for cures to sexual problems. In the old quarter of almost every Indian city, you will find billboards and shingles of quacks selling philtres and tablets for dysfunction. Even small pharmaceutical companies are in the business. Their herbal concoctions or *totkas* can be bought over the counter at chemist's shops and are even advertised in newspapers, though this practice has always been frowned upon. The American historian Katherine Mayo commented on these philtres in *Mother India*, a book which raised tempers almost as high as *The Satanic Verses* when it was published in 1927, and is still regarded as a classic Orientalist text:

> A sidelight will be found by a glance down the advertisement space of Indian-owned newspapers. Magical drugs and mechanical contrivances, whether 'for princes and rich men only', or the humbler and not less familiar '32 Pillars of Strength to prop up your decaying body for One Rupee only', crowd the columns and support the facts.

Mayo records that between 29 December 1922 and 4 December 1925, in the undivided Punjab, fifteen Indian language newspapers were prosecuted for publishing such advertisements. Seven were Hindu publications, seven Mohammedan and one Sikh. Just like in the present, faith in totkas afflicted people across all religious boundaries.

SUNDRY WONDERS

Miracles and other instances of the unexpected, inexplicable and plain bizarre litter the Indian faithscape, occasioning no more than a raised eyebrow even in the unbeliever. And there are about a million superstitions that really have nothing to do with belief. The world over, people believe that it's bad luck if a black cat crosses your path. In India, a cat of any colour will do. If it crosses the path of your car, you must brake to a halt immediately and switch the engine off for a moment before it's safe to carry on. You must do this even if your car happens to be in the middle of a highway.

When you set out from home, you must never reverse your car out of the garage, but inch forward a bit before you engage the back gear. You'll never get anywhere if you start a journey going backwards. And when you get out on the road, it is auspicious to see an elephant ambling along in the direction you're going, for that is the emblem of Ganesha, god of ventures, and he will speed you on your way. Truckers, rough and ready people who can't be bothered to wait for elephants to happen by, speed up their rigs by tying an old sandal to the fender for its sympathetic magic.

Most importantly, when you pick up your car keys and step out the door, pray that no one says, 'Hang on a bit', or asks, 'Where are you going?' For then it's best to go back indoors, step back out the door and start all over again. And if you're a good householder, the door will naturally have a lime and a few chillies hung on a string from the lintel to keep spooks at bay. Ironically, these are the very condiments which are served to every guest in a feast.

The origin of these superstitions is not always obvious but others are more amenable to rational analysis, such as the ones relating to darkness. Women are advised not to leave their hair open after dark and must not cut their nails, use scissors or sew at night. And they must never sweep the floor after sunset for fear of sweeping away Lakshmi, the goddess of wealth. And no one, but no one, should utter the word 'snake' in the dark.

These prohibitions make perfectly good sense in a home without electric lighting. Women who leave their hair open after dark may have trouble getting it all together again in a poorly lit room, if you bear in mind that women frequently had hair down to their knees. If they used sharp instruments in the half-dark, they could cut themselves. If they swept the floor, they could permanently lose valuables they may have dropped. And snakes are simply too dangerous to be called up in the dark.

But most superstitions are vestigial proscriptions and prescriptions from so long ago that their basis is no longer obvious. And given the cultural diversity of India, they number in the millions. Here's a small sampler, culled from past and present, to give you an idea of the variety and peculiarity of human belief in the subcontinent.

Blood and Water

In June 2008, during an anniversary celebration at St. Michael's Church in Mahim, Mumbai, the faithful noticed that a painting of Jesus had begun to bleed. The rivulets of blood authentically followed the folds in the Redeemer's drapery while he smiled benignly upon the congregation. The painting was under glass and would have been difficult to tamper with. The church was mobbed by devotees. People of all denominations queued up for hours to see the miracle and photograph it with their cellphone cameras. The police had to be called in to maintain order and local youths took over traffic control on the roads.

Almost a year before that, in August 2007, a child wading at the mouth of the nearby Mahim Creek, a famously dirty rivulet emptying into the Arabian Sea, sipped a handful of the sea water and found it sweet. In the days that followed, hundreds of thousands of people converged on the creek to drink the miraculous water. People of all persuasions arrived from all over the state of Maharashtra and took the water away in bottles. They included Hindu ascetics, though the miracle was attributed to the Muslim saint Baba Makdoom Shah, whose shrine is nearby. The municipal corporation repeatedly warned against the health hazards of drinking the water of the creek, which is not potable. No one paid any heed and they were apparently none the worse for it.

About the same time, the Virgin wept in a Kochi church and the likeness of the Shirdi Sai Baba emerged from patches of damp on a monsoon-wet wall in Surat, reminding people of the time it had appeared at night in storm clouds over Kashmir, dramatically lit by a flash of lightning.

Two other miracles coincided with the Mahim Creek wonder. In Agra, a fast observed by a girl brought on rain and in Bareilly, on 20 August, a Durga image drank some milk which was offered to it. The news from Bareilly spread rapidly and that night people stayed up in cities and towns across north India trying to get their local deities to drink milk. It is said that many succeeded.

Milk Mania

Bareilly was a late rerun of the biggest miracle in contemporary India, when the entire Hindu pantheon simultaneously developed a voracious taste for milk. Sometime before dawn on 21 September 1995, a priest in a south Delhi temple made a ritual offering of milk to an idol of Ganesha and was amazed to see the elephant-headed god suck it up with his trunk. Awed, he told someone about it. In minutes, the story was moving faster than Internet urban legends. In an hour, it had assumed proportions that a viral marketer would die for.

By breakfast time, the milk story was the fastest-travelling meme in living memory. Hordes of people were taking milk to the local temple to try their luck. In cities and towns all over the country, traffic snarls built up that would last well into the night. By lunchtime, the story had spread to Indian communities in the Middle East, the UK, the US and Canada. British supermarkets in areas preferred by Indians reported spurts in milk sales. In Delhi, the epicentre of the faithquake, sales shot up by 30 per cent.

It wasn't just temples that were mobbed. Ganesha icons are collectibles even among the ungodly and people raided the homes of friends who harboured Ganeshas in order to feed them milk. Soon, even the god's parents, Shiva and Parvati, were putting it away at a fantastic rate and the taste for milk then spread to the rest of the very sizeable Hindu pantheon.

Humourless savants from the government's department of science and technology visited temples, replicated the miracle and concluded that it owed to capillarity—the surface tension of the milk was forcing it into the minute cracks and fissures on the surface of the stone idols, making it seem as if they were drinking it. Capillarity is a phenomenon known to every high school science student, but it cut absolutely no ice with the faithful. As we saw, the 'miracle' was enthusiastically welcomed back when it ran again twelve years later in Bareilly.

Capillarity explained the 'how' of the milk miracle. But it's also useful to ask: why? Who benefitted from this mass hysteria among Hindus worldwide? Probably, someone who wanted to test how fast a whisper campaign could travel through the faith and to what extent it could urge people to action. It's a speculative thought, but sobering. In the years after the milk miracle, administrations have been taken aback by the speed with which Hindu mobs organized in a series of sectarian riots. It was almost as if the organizers had done a dummy run. Maybe they had—in Delhi in 1995.

Monster Love

Manali could be the only place on earth where a she-monster and her son are reverentially worshipped. We're talking about a genuine, certified monster, with her genealogy established by holy scripture. Hidimba was the sister of the demon ruler of the Kullu region in the lower Himalayas who was killed by the Mahabharata hero Bhima. He married her and they had a son named Ghatotkacha before he moved on with his brothers. She brought up the child, installed him as king and then moved to a forest by Manali to meditate in the hope of being elevated beyond her monstrous status. Her prayers did not go unanswered. Hidimba Devi is now the presiding goddess of the region and, until the abolition of the monarchy, no king of Kullu could be crowned without her blessings.

Her temple, a simple wooden pagoda, was built in 1553 at the spot where she meditated and is the venue of an annual fair, the most important of the area, to which all the lesser deities of the region are brought in procession. The shrine has no idol. There is just a gigantic rock face on which, when the firelight strikes it right, you can see the imprint of a human foot, a waterfall, a nameless being or just about anything. Nearby is her son's shrine, which is just a tall tree. At its foot, the faithful leave tin models of whatever they wish for—little villas, cars, trucks, television sets. And nailed to the tree are scores of human outlines cut out of tin sheets, their arms and legs splayed out like stick figures.

In the Bhima–Hidimba story, a folk historian might see a parable of the conquest of the aboriginal population of the mountains—demonized as monsters—by Aryans. An Aryan leader could have made a matrimonial alliance to cement his community's hold on the region and left behind his son to rule in his stead. In fact, aboriginal 'wild people' called Razees were known in the hills until fairly recent times. The British soldier Donald Macintyre wrote of seeing a hunter-gatherer couple clad in leaves in 1866. They spoke no known language and when they were given some money they tried to eat it. These aborigines had been driven into the forest by the Ranas and Gurkhas of Nepal, and finally exterminated.

And the tin figurines nailed to the tree? Interestingly, early Christians often referred to the Holy Cross as a tree. Christ was said to have been 'nailed to the tree', just like the figurines. Not sure what the implications are for the intriguing monster shrine at Manali, but human sacrifice in ancient times is not beyond belief.

Khamb Baba

In 1877 Sir Alexander Cunningham, founder of the Archaeological Survey of India, noted an ancient pillar standing on the banks of the Bes river in Madhya Pradesh. Known as Khamb Baba, it was venerated by the local fisherfolk who, to this day, daub it with vermilion, tie threads around it, burn incense sticks at its base and occasionally hold ceremonies on its plinth in the course of which one of their number becomes possessed. He then proceeds to exorcize any devils which may be infesting the congregation. The devils are then tied to Khamb Baba or nailed to the column and thus rendered harmless.

Some years after Cunningham's survey, another archaeologist scraped off the vermilion and discovered an inscription recording the conversion to Vaishnavism of Heliodorus, ambassador from the Greek ruler of Taxila to the Sunga empire, circa 113 BC. Chauvinists take it as evidence of the irresistible power of Hinduism before which no benighted foreigner can stand, but all it means is that the first Hare Krishna in the world was a Greek diplomat.

The Heliodorus Column, as Khamb Baba is properly known, is set in Vidisha, one of the oldest kingdoms in India, which dates back to the Mahabharata era. In his youth, about a century before Heliodorus, Emperor Ashoka served as viceroy here, lived in nearby Ujjain and married Maharani Devi, the daughter of a Vidisha banker. A Buddhist, she is said to have left him after the carnage of Kalinga, and this rejection may have had something to do with his famous conversion. Close by is Sanchi, the Buddhist complex from where Ashoka and Maharani Devi's children, Mahendra and Sanghamitra, set out to proselytize Sri Lanka, bearing a branch of the tree of enlightenment. Their project was part of the biggest missionary enterprise in ancient times that reached out to lands from China to Rome. And against this magnificent sweep of history, the column that a Greek diplomat set up here to announce his conversion to the local faith is now the prison of sundry devils exorcized by a fisherman in a frenzy.

Goddesses: Human and Fictional

Santoshi Ma, or 'Mother of Satisfaction', came out of nowhere in the 1960s when her story began to circulate in a DIY pamphlet. It told a *vrata-katha*, a morally instructive tale read out at fasts held by Hindu women. It remained an obscure cult until 1974, when a Bollywood movie based on the story and made on a tiny budget with little-known actors became a box-office hit on par with multi-star blockbusters like *Deewar* and *Sholay*. Within months Santoshi Ma's cult, which prescribed fasts—and, curiously, the avoidance of limes and bananas—had swept north India like a tidal wave.

Though Santoshi Ma's scriptural credentials are sketchy at best, viewers treated the movie as if it were scripture itself. Cinema halls where it was screened became impromptu shrines. Viewers arrived freshly bathed and left their footwear at the door, as they would in a real temple. And when the goddess appeared, the screen was showered with offerings of flowers and money, just like in a temple.

The cult remained wildly popular for decades and is still practised, though the following has decreased.

There are similar reports concerning Babu Devkinandan Khatri's *Chandrakanta*, a wild yarn rife with romance and intrigue set in a fictional fortress modelled on Chunar fort near Varanasi. Published at the end of the nineteenth century, it is regarded as the first novel in Hindi and is widely quoted in learned literary discourse. In the popular domain, it is still avidly read in the Hindi belt. A television serial adaptation by Neerja Guleri in the mid-1990s got a mixed reception because it played fast and loose with the text, but a movie is in the pipeline starring Amitabh and Abhishek Bachchan. Now get this: over the years, there have been reports from Uttar Pradesh of Chandrakanta, the heroine of the novel, being worshipped in villages as a goddess. Fiction has become faith—faith with absolutely no reference to religious authority, and therefore a kind of superstition.

But even that pales into insignificance compared to what's happening in Tamil Nadu, which has temples dedicated to living screen goddesses. A fan is building a temple for Namitha, the reigning Tamil sex siren, with her idol duly installed. Khushboo already has a temple in Tiruchirapalli, though the actress was born Muslim and got into trouble with conservatives in 2005 for saying that men should not expect their wives or girlfriends to be virgins.

Rajasthan's Rat Temple

Deshnoke is a little Rajasthani town in the middle of nowhere—which is a rather accurate description of the Thar desert—but hundreds of thousands of people come here every year from all over north India to visit its only attraction, the temple of Karni Mata. The Mata was a local woman of god who had foretold the success of the young Rao Bika, who came to the wilderness to start his own kingdom after a tiff with his father, Rao Jodha, founder of Jodhpur. Karni Mata's influence grew dramatically when, with a bit of help from her, Rao Bika founded the powerful kingdom of Bikaner.

Karni Mata took a curiously indulgent view of rats and today Deshnoke is one big rat sanctuary, with their holes pock-marking the sand dunes miles out of town. The rats, called *kabas* to distinguish them from common or garden rats, run in hordes in the temple, where they are lavishly fêted. They are believed to be the reincarnated spirits of the Mata's flock. Apparently, she cut a deal with Yama, the god of death, allowing them to be reborn only as temple rats, rather than any old thing, until they could take human shape again. The temple is run by Karni Mata's descendants, who show visitors around while they patiently wait to be reborn as rats. Stepping on a rat is mighty bad luck, because you will have to donate a golden rat to the temple. Seeing an albino rat, on the other hand, indicates that you will be lucky.

Possession

John Campbell Oman's *Cults, Customs and Superstitions of India*, which was a best-seller a hundred years ago, lists an epidemic of possession cases among his domestic staff. His chowkidar takes ill after beating off some creditors and has to plead with them to take off the 'curse' they put on him. They are initially taken aback but rise to the occasion and perform a little exorcism ceremony in return for which they are paid in full. A servant woman gets haemorrhages because of the black magic of a former lover who had cut up a lemon and squeezed it over the mouth of a wishing well, praying that her blood would leak out like the lemon's juice. A servant takes ill after pulling down some branches from a babool tree growing over the dilapidated grave of a Syed (a certified descendant of the Prophet). The departed Syed's temper has to be cooled with a libation of water from the servant's wife's hand, but a complete cure is secured only when a dose of quinine is administered to the servant. And finally, the coachman gets the falling sickness because his runaway wife has paid someone to sic a demon on him. He pays someone to boomerang the demon back on her.

Oman also refers to a common belief that the spirits of first wives are out to possess their successors and settle their hash. Second and third wives therefore wear a *thuppa*, a little silver likeness of a woman worn on a locket. At every meal, they offer some food to the thuppa before they eat themselves. And when they put on new clothes or ornaments, they ritually offer them to the likeness first.

In the twenty-first century, belief in possession remains fairly widespread. In June 2006, the Muslims of Bhalej village in Gujarat banned Mumbai singer Himesh Reshammiya's hit number '*Jhalak dikhla ja*' because it was encouraging a spook to possess people. Apparently the problem was caused by the words '*aaja, aaja*' ('come, come') in the lyric, which the spook took to be a come-hither. The village elders declared it illegal not to switch off a radio when this song was on air.

Meanwhile, Hindu women in the village were being possessed because of the Gujarati hit '*Sanedo sanedo*'. Women who sang it at a particular time of day were hag-ridden by the spirit of a woman who had died of cancer and had not been ritually mourned by her family. The local exorcists did brisk business while these songs, one dangerous to Muslims and the other to Hindus, remained hits.

The most widely publicized case of possession—divine possession, at that—in recent times was that of Devendra Kumar Panda, inspector general of police in Lucknow in 2005. He had been increasingly affected, since 1991, by the legend of the love of Radha and Krishna. In 2005 he filed for early retirement, doffed his uniform, donned female attire, lipstick, a nose-ring and an ornament on the forehead, declared himself to be the second Radha and took to singing bhajans and dancing in his office at the police station. Meanwhile, his wife filed for divorce. The media picked up his story and he swiftly became a cringe-making embarrassment for the Uttar Pradesh police.

Panda found it impossible to live in his official residence after serious differences with his wife. His wife's point of view is understandable. Apart from the cross-dressing and singing and dancing, Panda had erased his name from the nameplate of his official residence. It simply said: Doosri Radha (the Second Radha).

But only Panda's upper-class peers were embarrassed about his doings. Forced to leave home, he went to Puri to see his celestial love (like Krishna, Lord Jagannath is an incarnation of Vishnu). He was received by locals led by the secretary of the taxi drivers' union, who immediately prostrated themselves before him and venerated him as the goddess. Meanwhile, again to the embarrassment of the police, a cross-dressing constable in Lucknow declared himself to be the Third Radha and danced in the streets in drag. Clearly, there are two nations in India, only one of which finds divine possession ridiculous.

Serpent Love

In *Thirty-five Years in India,* Dr Honigberger, court physician to Maharaja Ranjit Singh, described *mar-ishq* (translated as 'serpent love') as a strange disease which he believed to be unique to the Punjab between the Indus and the Sutlej. Patients were 'troubled with fainting and dizziness, nausea, want of appetite, disinclination to work, and heaviness in the limbs'. At the height of the symptoms, they were approached by snakes and bitten. The venom did them a power of good and the victims looked upon snakes much as you and I regard our family physicians.

Dr Honigberger met several patients in Lahore and was assured that the Punjab teemed with mar-ishq cases. He examined a washerman who was aged sixty and looked eighty. Venomous snakes had sought him out for thirty years. He had initially allowed himself to be bitten once a year, and then increased the dose to once a month. Latterly, the serpents had taken to following him into the water in which he washed clothes. Dr Honigberger added that his perspiration reeked like serpents.

Mar-ishq may have been peculiar to the Punjab but the veneration of snakes is a nationwide phenomenon. The word *nag* (cobra) is a constituent of many common first names and surnames. The snake is in fact an ancient totem. The Mahabharata begins with a snake sacrifice and snake idols are often found in temples, apart from millions of votive shrines under pipal trees at crossroads and village squares. So the idea of being saved or 'treated' by a snake may not seem unusual to the religious.

Or perhaps this serpent love had nothing to do with religion at all, but was just an urban legend cooked up to diddle a firangi doctor. Or maybe the 'patients' were just snake-bite addicts—it is now widely believed that the country is teeming with venom junkies. But of course you will never meet one, so that's probably yet another urban legend like mar-ishq.

In recent times, a case of snake love got international coverage. In 2006 Bimbala Das of Orissa was cured of a lingering disease after she fed a cobra some milk. She immediately fell in love with the reptile and was married to it in a proper religious ceremony attended by over 2000 wedding guests. She also joined the Vaishnava sect which had solemnized this human–reptile marriage. However, a busybody foreign journalist smelled a rat because the reptilian groom was not present at the ceremony. There was only a gold replica in his place. The story died down amid aspersions that the snake was a figment of the imagination and the wedding was stage-managed to get mileage for the Vaishnava sect.

In July 2008 another case of snake love came to light in Solan district of Himachal Pradesh. Satya Devi claimed that snakes had sought her out and bitten her seventy times since 1980. Neighbours used to rush her to hospital earlier, but soon they became rather blasé about it. So did the patient herself. The last time she was bitten, she popped a painkiller and carried on with her life.

Military Spook

The Indo-China border in Sikkim, the scene of desperate fighting during the conflict of 1962, is patrolled by a ghost soldier. A substantial spook, the spirit of 'Baba' Harbhajan Singh holds an army commission—honorary captain on extension, because he is past the age of retirement. Uniforms are issued to him and he has his own bed in the barracks. He goes home to Punjab on leave—his picture is escorted there and back by orderlies by train and military truck. His salary is sent home to his family. He is venerated by locals and soldiers who serve in this area near the Nathu La pass, one of the most forbidding military outposts in the world, who believe that he will warn them of the next conflict, which has been imminent for over four decades. Curiously, it is reported that Chinese soldiers believe the very same thing, and set aside an empty chair for him at border talks when commanders from both sides meet.

Harbhajan Singh led a mule train during the Indo-China conflict. According to one legend, he materialized out of nowhere in the midst of an Indian Army detachment which had been ambushed behind enemy lines and led them to safety. After the soldiers returned to base, they learned that their saviour had fallen into a glacier and died three days before the ambush.

An upstanding, religious man in his lifetime, Captain Baba's stature has grown steadily after his death. His shrine in the army base has become so popular with locals and tourists, apart from soldiers, that it had to be shifted to a more accessible location on the highway to Nathu La, which carries heavy traffic now that the pass has been reopened to trade.

In 2007 the army was embarrassed when a distant relation of the Baba filed a lawsuit accusing them of promoting superstition. There is a proposal to hand over the shrine to civilian authorities, because there is now no way to stop the Baba's legend from growing. His shrine is already a popular pilgrimage and in July 2008 the Union Bank of India opened the highest ATM in the world nearby. Cash donations are bound to increase, and with it the Baba's standing can only grow.

Tree Marriage

Every year, the Hindu marriage season is kicked off in the autumnal lunar month of Kartika by the *tulsi vivaha*, a five-day ceremony in which Krishna is married to the tulsi (holy basil) plant. Interestingly, the plant is also known as Vrindadevi, or 'goddess of the group'. D.D. Kosambi read the ceremony as the memory of a matriarchal system superseded by patriarchy, recalled by ritual marriage. In his *Myth and Reality*, Kosambi says:

> Certainly, the *gokula* in which Krishna was brought up would be patriarchal, as a cattle-herders' commune. But the Vrindavana in which he played his pranks was sacred to a mother-goddess of a group (*vrinda*) symbolised by the *tulsi* plant. Krishna had to marry that goddess [to take over from her] and is still married to her every year.

In an account of his journey from Madhya Pradesh to Simla in 1835, W.H. Sleeman, General Superintendent for the Suppression of Thuggee, recounted several instances of tree marriage. An Indian friend in Jabbalpur had planted a mango orchard but according to custom could not taste the fruit before he had married one of the trees to a tamarind in the same grove. There was no tamarind, so a jasmine was substituted and the wedding celebrated with all pomp and ceremony—after the owners had sold all their jewellery and got themselves waist-deep in debt, because at least 150 Brahmins had to be fed. They did all that just to be able to eat their own mangoes.

Rainwater harvesting was a popular charitable enterprise in olden times, but it was fraught with a similar tree marriage problem. No one who built a tank could take a sip of the water before he had had the tank ceremonially married to a banana tree, grown on the bank specifically for that purpose.

It's as if trees were considered to be almost human. Which some of them may be, like the famous walking mango tree of Sanjan, Gujarat, which has been ambling along at the unhurried rate of a yard per year. The tree does this by stretching out a limb, touching the earth, taking root there and forming a new trunk. Meanwhile, the old trunk withers away. This is technically mere monopedalism, but the tree is clearly trying to get somewhere, the only one of its kind to attempt such a project. Meanwhile, its bark is being touted as a specific for common ailments like stomach aches, and the tree could be flayed alive by believers before it gets to its destination.

Baby Shower

In 2007 authorities in Bijapur district, Karnataka, cracked down on a bizarre local practice: People drop their babies from the tops of temples. Childless couples apparently make a vow at the temple to drop their babies if they ever have children. They are caught before they hit the ground in a carpet held up like a trapeze net, but several civil society groups have demanded that the practice be ended.

Sounds like a harmless if slightly cuckoo practice, right? But back in 1844, Sleeman reported the much darker original form, at a fair held in the Mahadeo Hills, where 'young men offer themselves as a sacrifice to fulfil the vows of their mothers'. Childless women pledged their firstborn to Mahadev or Shiva, the god of destruction, if they got a son. The pact was kept a secret until the boys thus born attained puberty, when their mothers told them about it and asked them to fulfil the vow. Sleeman reports that they immediately donned saffron robes, assumed the ascetic life and visited all the shrines of Mahadev all over India, finishing the circuit at the fair, where they flung themselves off from a height of 400 or 500 feet and were dashed to pieces on the rocks below.

In India, our rationalists fight on desperately, against all odds. In the 1960s and 1970s, the movement was energized by the trenchant writings of the Sri Lankan godman-slayer Abraham Kovoor, who wrote equally scathingly against superstition and organized religion. He became the nemesis of Sathya Sai Baba, the most popular godman of the time, who produced holy ash from nowhere and distributed it among his devotees. Kovoor threatened to replicate the miracle at Sai Baba's sermon, before the congregation, but the Baba managed to keep him at arm's length. In 1963, he announced a prize of Rs 1 lakh, a huge sum at the time, to any godman who could work a miracle under controlled conditions. The prize money is still unclaimed.

Today, there are rationalist bodies in almost every state, organized under the Federation of Indian Rationalist Organisations. The Delhi Science Forum and Sanal Edamaruku's Indian Rationalist Association have been fighting the good fight very visibly, and the Andhashraddha Nirmulan Samiti of Maharashtra has been campaigning for a law banning superstitious practices, but it's a losing battle. Maybe it's because rationalists are typically earnest, humourless, well-meaning do-gooders, and the competition is vastly more entertaining.

Indian superstition is so hopelessly intertwined with religion that it allows a reasonable person to take only two positions. You cannot rationally oppose superstition and support religion. You can dismiss both out of hand, like Kovoor did. An ethically problematic position, for while you protect people from charlatanry, you also deny them the comfort of faith. Far too many people in our country have only faith to help them make sense of a painfully senseless world.

The alternative is to suspend judgement, thereby avoiding the sin of scientific fundamentalism plus future embarrassment—because a lot of superstitions have a political or social basis which has been forgotten over time, and sometimes a researcher digs deep enough to find it. Equally, some have an unsettling habit of revealing a hitherto unsuspected scientific basis. Medical superstitions, for instance: the pesticidal and antibacterial properties of neem, long claimed by traditionalists, were derided, but now neem is widely used as a pesticide. Claims about garlic, turmeric, tulsi and a hundred other herbs, once regarded as folk superstitions, are being similarly revalued and they are being brought back to the pharmacopoeia. They have proved to be more credible than the wellness advice from medical doctors which floods newspapers, magazines and websites, and which changes as rapidly as the prescriptions of a management guru.

Personally, so long as there is oversight to ensure that no one gets cheated or hurt, I'm not unhappy with the entertaining medley of tantriks, snake-lovers, soothsaying bulls and colourful charlatans who people our world of superstition. They are so much more interesting than the Western alternative—conspiracy theorists, Area 51 nuts, alien abductees, scientologists, intelligent design-wallahs, little green men and the therapists who promise to make them all go away if you will only cross their palm with silver.

One of these days, I'm going to call up Guru Raj Bharti, the magus who inserted a flyer in my morning paper. You remember him, I trust—the Uncrowned Emperor of Matters Spiritual and the Seven Deadly Arts. Memorable man, unforgettable designation. I don't have any problems with my modelling career or love marriage that I need him to look into, but I shall visit him anyway bearing two limes and a pack of joss sticks as prescribed. Just for the entertainment, of course. Yeah, just the entertainment. Honestly.

FURTHER READING

Hakluytus Posthumus or *Purchas his Pilgrimes*, Samuel Purchas, printed for H. Fetherstone, London, 1625.

Rambles and Recollections of an Indian Official, William Henry Sleeman, J. Hatchard & Son, London, 1844.

The Mysteries of All Nations, James Grant, Reid and Son, Leith, UK, 1880.

Cults, Customs and Superstitions of India, John Campbell Oman, T. Fisher Unwin, London, 1908.

Secret Societies and Subversive Movements, Nesta H. Webster, Boswell Printing & Publishing Co. London, 1924. (*Caveat*: This is a politically compromised author, but great fun for conspiracy buffs. Read with fingers tightly crossed.)

Mother India, Katherine Mayo, Harcourt, Brace & Co., New York, 1927. (*Caveat*: Though reportage-based, this is a classic Orientalist text, an imperial propaganda pamphlet. Mahatma Gandhi denounced this book as 'the report of a drain inspector' and it was burned in the streets in India. It also drew irate responses from English and American readers and institutions. However, some of the reportage, though shocking, is factually correct.)

The Masks of God, Joseph Campbell, Viking, New York, 1959.

Myth and Reality: Studies in the Formation of Indian Culture, Damodar Dharmanand Kosambi, Popular Prakashan, Bombay, 1962.

The Culture and Civilisation of Ancient India in Historical Outline, Damodar Dharmanand Kosambi, Routledge and Kegan Paul, London, 1965.

Traveller's India, H.K. Kaul (ed.), Oxford India Paperbacks, 1979.

Arthashastra, Kautilya, L.N. Rangarajan (ed. and trans.), Penguin India, New Delhi, 1992.

The Religious Culture of India, Friedhelm Hardy, Cambridge University Press, 1995 (South Asian edition).

Following the Equator, Mark Twain (1897), in *The Oxford Mark Twain*, Oxford University Press, 1996.

Modern History Sourcebook: Vasco da Gama, Peter Halsall, Fordham University, New York, 1998.

Essays on Christianity, Paganism and Superstition, Thomas De Quincey, in *The Works of Thomas De Quincey* (21 vols), Pickering and Chatto, London, 2000.

Inglish Remixed

. . . .

Punita Singh

'But I never called you a monkey,' protested India's spin bowler Harbhajan Singh as Andrew Symonds strode off the field in a huff. 'I know what I heard,' said the irate Aussie and complained to the referee. Harbhajan was docked for bad behaviour and the ensuing controversy went into a tailspin, using up several tons of newsprint and hours and days of prime airtime as the national dailies and radio and television channels featured the story.

We might be guilty of aping the West in many ways, but why Harbhajan would call Symonds a monkey when such a choice of choice English epithets is available is baffling. It seems what he might have said was '*Mainu ki*?', a Punjabi phrase which roughly translates as 'What do I care?'—the verbal equivalent of a shrug to express he didn't really give a damn about an earlier exchange on the cricket pitch. Some conjecture he muttered '*Ma ki...*' in Hindi, alluding to an incestuous act with the mother, but either way, 'monkey' is apparently not what was said.

A musician friend who lives in Delhi likes to recount an incident where the reverse happened: an English word heard as a Hindi insult almost got him arrested. He was driving home after a concert with his guitar and banjo in the backseat of his car. The cops stopped him at a checkpoint and wanted to know what was in the cases in the back. The guitar, they understood, but the moment he said 'banjo', they got aggressive and threatened to lock him up for the night. Not for carrying a strange, tuneless instrument, but for abusing them. Again a case of phonetic accident: to them 'banjo' sounded suspiciously similar to another incestuous insult, this time involving sisters.

The sounds of one language can have quite a different meaning when heard in the context of another. Given the similar vocal apparatus all humans are endowed with, it's only natural that we'd end up with common sounds across languages. Phrases like '*mainu ki*' or '*ma ki*' could well be misheard as 'monkey', just as the word '*banana*' which means 'to make' in Hindi, might be misperceived as the fruit in English. Such cross-lingual phonetic overlaps could drive you bananas if heard out of context, but could have you peeling with laughter when exploited for their punning potential in a bilingual environment where the alternate meanings are evident.

The advertisements for Amul butter have acquired cult status in India for precisely this sort of linguistic creativity. The creators of the ads have been particularly adept at weaving their wordplay around topics of current interest from the world of politics, culture, sports and more. Going through their archives, one almost gets a chronological account of events, with what was big in the news at that time captured in 'utterly butterly delicious' one-liners.

> 'Ravan'ously hungry? Eat Amul'—this during the Dussehra festival season when effigies of Lord Ram's opponent Ravan are burnt.
>
> 'Amul's a Pawar-ful bond' referring to Sharad Pawar's election as chief minister of Maharashtra in the late 1980s.
>
> 'Hurroy for Arundhati! Amul Cooker Prize'—when Arundhati Roy won the Booker Prize for *The God of Small Things*.
>
> 'The three "muska'tiers"'— punning on the Urdu '*muska*', meaning butter, to announce the availability of Amul in three convenient new sizes.
>
> 'Steve Wah! Aus you like it'—playing on the last name of Aussie cricketer Steve Waugh to applaud him with '*wah*', the Urdu equivalent of 'wow', on winning the World Cup.

The Amul campaign broke new ground not just with its witty use of double entendre, but for brazenly using what linguists call 'code mixing'. Juxtaposing words from English and Hindi and other regional languages within and across sentences was a departure from the post-colonial snobbish hangover of using 'proper' English. Legions of advertisements that followed used such mixing freely to appeal to younger generations of Indians comfortable in expressing themselves in this new mixed vernacular.

Pepsi's '*Yeh dil mange* more' and '*Yehi hai* right choice, baby' and the Coke advertisements stating 'Life *ho to aisi*' and '*Thanda piyo,* enjoy *karo*' made life seem exciting and bubbly. And what better to accompany all that cola than a Domino's pizza? The 'Hungry *kya*?' campaign brought pizza to Indian homes within thirty minutes or less (even if the first syllable is pronounced to rhyme with 'fizz' by most Indians, instead of the more standard 'peet-za'). After binging on carbs and carbonation, if there's still room left in the tummy for 'something *meetha*', reach for a bar of Cadbury's as superstar Amitabh Bachchan does in the chocolate commercial.

Advertising on television and on the radio has been particularly effective in using an admixture of English and Hindi or other regional languages to reach a broader consumer base, with such advertisements recyclable on multiple language channels. With visual and auditory reinforcement of the message, more potential buyers are likely to 'get' the content of the cross-lingual advertisement, which would be tough to convey via the print medium, given its inherent limitations in capturing the phonetic features of a language.

While many sounds are common in English, Hindi and other Indian languages, there are some that aren't. It's difficult enough to try to map the twenty-six letters of the English alphabet to the forty-four plus sounds used in spoken English itself, let alone to the fifty to sixty sounds of another language like Hindi that includes nasalized vowels and consonants like 'bh', 'dh' and 'gh'—sometimes difficult for non-native speakers to articulate. Variations in transliteration also creep in because there is no standardized way to denote sounds like the consonants 'th' in *thanda*/*thhanda* (cold) or the 'dh' in *dhakan*/*dhhakan* (lid). The tongue-flapping sound in the middle of *barha/bada* (big) has no prescribed transcription symbol in English, nor do the affricates 'chh' at the beginning of *chota/chhota* (small) or the 'jh' in *jhanda/jhhanda* (flag).

The mismatch between sound and spelling can lead to confusion about pronunciation and obscure meaning. Nasalized and elongated vowels pose a real problem when transcribed in Roman script. The word '*mange*' could well be read as the English word meaning 'a contagious skin disease' or the French word meaning 'to eat', instead of the Hindi word pronounced 'maan-gey' which means 'asks for' in the Pepsi ad '*Yeh dil mange* more' ('The heart asks for more').

As a child, I remember thinking an Indian movie called *Jungle Mein Mangal* ('Fun in the jungle') was a foreign film because the words resembled German words I'd seen, albeit a bit mangled. The Hindi word meaning 'I' is particularly hard to get right in Roman script. Typically transcribed as '*main*' but pronounced as a nasal 'may', it could be read as the English word rhyming with rain, meaning 'primary' or 'principal'. The word '*chalenge*' meaning 'will go' in Hindi could be misread as 'challenge' in English.

Just as many sounds of Indian languages have no equivalent in English, some sounds of English have no equivalent in Indian languages. The short vowel in the middle of the words 'bed' and 'led', for example, has no counterpart in Hindi. Transcription of these words in the Devnagari script leads to Hindi users pronouncing them as '*bade*' and '*laid*' or '*bad*' and '*lad*'. As there is no letter in the Hindi alphabet to denote the shorter vowel sound, it's somewhat arbitrarily mapped to the nearest vowel in Hindi. Depending on which mapping a person is used to, you might hear somebody say '*I hurt my hade so I must raste in bade. I will come to work on Sunday instade*', or listen in on IT guys talking in India, and you may well hear things like '*We cannot axass the wab right now because the natwork is down.*'

The sounds corresponding to 'p', 't' and 'k' are also sometimes mis-mapped in Indian languages. Western speakers of English typically aspirate these consonants, popping them with an extra whiff of air when they occur at the beginning of words. In Hindi and Punjabi both aspirated and unaspirated versions of these sounds are used and can make a difference in the meaning of a word. Adding the blast of air to 'ph' makes '*phal*' (fruit) different from '*pal*' (moment), '*thokna*' (to hammer) different from '*tokna*' (to nag) and '*khan*' (a mine) different from '*kaan*' (ear). This phonemic difference does not exist in English. With a choice of two symbols to map each of these consonants to, pronunciation differences emerge depending on how words such as 'pig', 'time' and 'cot' are transcribed in Hindi or Punjabi. If mapped to 'ph', 'th' and 'kh', we get a more or less standard Western pronunciation. If mapped to the unaspirated 'p', 't' and 'k', we end up with a softer pronunciation more similar to 'b', 'd' and 'g', with most Westerners hearing our utterances of these words as 'big', 'dime' and 'got'.

As a graduate student in America, my phonetics professor would lightheartedly make fun of this feature of my Punjabi Indian accent: 'You need to have more aspiration,' he would pun, jabbing me with a ten-cent coin each time I asked for the time. Another Indian student from Kerala was not spared ridicule either. She had a habit of adding a 'w' before words that began with the vowel 'o', as in '*wokay*' for 'okay' and '*woh*' for 'oh'. She also had a tendency to delete the 'y' from words that began with it, as in '*ellow*' for 'yellow' and '*ess*' for 'yes', but to insert it at the start of 'em', 'en' and 'ess' when referring to the letters of the alphabet 'm', 'n' and 's'. A yemmay student in audiology, in her Malayali-accented English, 'that is so simple' sounded like '*thad is zo zimble*'. The 's' becoming a 'z' and the 'p' a 'b' are instances of what's called 'voicing' in phonetics, a feature that distinguishes 't' from 'd', 'k' from 'g', 'f' from 'v', 'sh' from 'zh' and 'ch' from 'j' as well. Her tendency to use the voiced consonants rather than their unvoiced counterparts was mimicked by other students who found her accent zimbly zindilading.

The 'z' sound doesn't come so easily to other Indians, though, as it seems to to Malayalis. Many Indians pronounce 'zoo' and 'zero' as '*joo*' and '*jeero*', as there is no symbol for the 'z' sound in most Indian language scripts. With many Persian words like '*zor*' (force), '*zindagi*' (life), '*zaroorat*' (need), '*zaroori*' (important), '*zaika*' (flavour) having gained acceptance in Hindi, however, a symbol now exists to accommodate the 'z' sound within the Hindi alphabet. In places where there hasn't been such a Persian influence, Indian English speakers continue to be confujed and yooj the 'j' for the 'z'.

The 'zh' sound in the middle of the words 'leisure', 'measure' and 'pleasure' is difficult for most Indian speakers to articulate too, as it has no equivalent in most regional languages. In attempting to form a 'zh', some speakers end up producing a 'z', leading to '*layzur*', '*mayzur*' and '*playzur*'. Others map it to 'j', saying '*layjur*', '*mayjur*', '*playjur*'. Still others map it to 'y', leading to the classic Punjabi and Hindi mispronunciation: '*layyar*', '*mayyar*', and '*playyar*'.

Like the 'z' sound, the fricative 'f' has also been imported into Indian languages from Persian and accommodated in host alphabets like Hindi by putting a dot under the symbol for 'ph'. Many Indian speakers continue to trip on this consonant, though, calling a 'fool' a '*phool*', a 'flower' a '*phlower*', a 'forest' a '*phorest*', and a 'full stop' a '*phul stop*'. Sometimes a curious reversal happens with Hindi speakers using the 'f' sound to pronounce Hindi words like '*phool*' (a flower) as 'fool' or '*pheeka*' (bland) as 'feeka'.

'V' and 'w' are sounds many Indian speakers have trouble. Instead of 'biting our Vs and kissing our Ws' as the mnemonic goes, Hindi speakers of English seem to swap one for the other, much like the 'r' and 'l' in oriental 'Engrish'. Given that there is only one letter in the Hindi alphabet that's used for both these English phonemes, it's not surprising that vi vould be confused about vich sound goes vere. After all, India is a wast country vith warious wernaculars and vi are wery likely to vind up vith wariations ven vi woice our thoughts in a Vestern tongue like English. Vi should be walorized for the wim and wigour vith vich vi do so, though.

We do indeed have varied ways of dealing with 'v' and 'w' in India. Kashmiri speakers of English tend to insert a gliding vowel diphthong like 'ew' at the ends of words that have a final 'iv' sound. So 'negative', 'positive', 'affirmative', 'native' and 'give' become '*negatew*', '*positew*', '*affirmatew*', '*natew*' and '*gew*'. Keralites do something similar and Tamilians seem to drop the 'v' altogether, as in '*fa-ee*' for 'five'. In languages like Bengali, that have neither a 'v' nor a 'w', any sound vaguely resembling them gets approximated to a bilabial 'b' or 'bh' as happens in some dialects of Spanish as well. Bhen bhisiting Kolkata, you may hear intellectuals bhocipherously debating the 'bhy', 'bhat', 'bhere' of life or strident marchers in the streets chanting something like, 'Phirst and phoremost, bhi bhant economic phreedom phor our people'.

While in Bengal, you may also hear shome shpeakers use 'sh' in English words that have the 's' sound. A carryover from Bengali, this is the reverse of what happens in neighbouring Bihar where 's' often replaces the 'sh' in English, and even in Hindi words. The 's'–'sh' confusion can usually be resolved by listeners if the substitution is in the middle of a word, as in '*educaysun*', '*naysun*', '*dictaysun*' or '*hoshpital*', '*reshtaurant*', '*penshil*', or if there is no alternate word in English that could be misperceived instead, as in '*sout*' (shout), '*sall*' (shall), '*siver*' (shiver), or '*shimple*' (simple), '*shtate*' (state), '*shilly*' (silly). Some word pairs in English such as see/she, sore/sure, same/shame, son/shun, however, could be misconstrued if the reverse sound is used, sometimes to hilarious effect, as in somebody chivalrously offering their sheet for someone to shit on.

In Bengal and the North East, the vowels 'i' and 'ee' are also sometimes transposed, as in 'The bridge over the Howrah breeze' (The breeze over the Howrah bridge). The proverb about 'Reaping what you sow' can have you in stitches if heard as 'Ripping what you sew'. And if you're in a tearing hurry to visit the beautiful bitches in Puri, Orissa, be sure to pack some suntan lotion, rather than dog biscuits. Then you can lie back in a deck chair and rest in piss.

Besides the pronunciation of particular phonemes, the overall intonation and stress patterns we Indians impose on our spoken English also give it a characteristic lilt and syllabicity. Actors playing Indian characters in Western movies or television shows typically exaggerate the 'sing-song' feature of most varieties of Indian English, as Peter Sellers did in the movie *The Party* and Hank Azaria does for the voice of Apu Nahasapeemapetilon, the Indian convenience-store manager on the long-running American cartoon show *The Simpsons*.

A promotional campaign by the convenience-store chain 7-11 caused a political furor in the US recently when they decided to dress up many of their outlets as the Kwik-E-Mart featured on *The Simpsons*. Besides dispensing squishees, crustyOs, pink donuts and other disgusting delicacies, 7-11 hired Indians, or actors posing as Indians, to run the stores and speak to customers in an Apu-like sing-song manner. The campaign could have been construed as a celebration of the Indian accent or the success Indian Americans have had as convenience-store managers in the US, if it hadn't been such a blatant parody of the stereotype. With Apu's character on the show not just altering his speech intonation, but also the expiry dates and prices of his wares, the campaign had undertones of racism that had protestors out on the streets, demanding 7-11 and *The Simpsons* atone for the slur.

In addition to swinging the pitch up and down within sentences, we Indians are creative in moving syllable boundaries around within words and accenting them differently from most Western speakers. Words such as 'develop', 'psychology', 'biology', 'conservative', 'executive', 'message' and 'encourage', often become '*dev-lup*', '*psycho-lawdgy*', '*bio-lawdgy*', '*con-ser-vative*', '*exe-cute-ive*', '*mess-age*' and '*encur-age*', in contrast with 'duh-vel-up', 'psychol-uh-gy', 'biol-uh-gy', 'conserv-uh-tive', 'exec-uh-tive', 'mess-ij' and 'encur-ij'. It's also quite common for Indians to add stress iambically to the second syllable in words like 'comment', 'object' and 'project', rather than according more equal stress to each syllable: a pronunciation difference that can make a verb out of a noun, as in 'They can project ahead with the project, provided they do not subject the subject to being treated as an object or we will object.'

Adding extra syllables to words is a common phenomenon in many of the Indian versions of English. While speakers in the south tend to strongly explode the final consonants in monosyllabic words like 'stop', 'next' and 'think', as in '*stop-uh*', '*next-uh*' and '*think-uh*', north Indians stretch words out by adding an 'uh' for emphasis, as in 'Come-uh. Take a break-uh'. Punjabis, in particular, are often caricaturized for their tendency to add an 'uh', as in the popular MTV song by Abhinav Dhar: 'My name is Manjee-tuh. Won't you come to my sangee-tuh. My girlfriend is Lovelee-nuh. Bhatinda beauty quee-nuh'. Punjabi speakers of English also tend to break diphthongs in words like 'high', 'sky' and 'try' into two vowels as in '*ha-ee*', '*ska-ee*' and '*tra-ee*' and in words like 'hour', 'flour' and 'towel' into two segments like '*aa-vur*', '*flaa-vur*' and '*taw-vel*'.

Negotiating the pronunciation of words that have a lot of consonant clusters and blends like 'bl', 'br', 'cl', 'cr', 'dr', 'fl', 'fr', 'gl', 'gr', 'lk', 'lm', 'pl', 'pr', 'sl', 'sp', 'squ', 'tr', etc., can be quite arduous for Indian speakers of English. Words with such sound combinations very often buh-reak and sup-linter into parts, adding extra syllables to words like 'clear' (*kill-year*), 'cream' (*ki-reem*), 'drama' (*duh-rama*), 'film' (*fill-um*), 'frock' (*fuh-rock*), 'glow' (*guh-low*), 'milk' (*mil-ik*), 'print' (*puh-rint*), 'slow' (*suh-low*), 'square' (*suh-quare*) and 'trip' (*tuh rip*). In the Hindi heartland, words that begin with 'sk', 'sm', 'sn', 'sp' and 'st' also acquire an extra syllable sometimes, with an 'i' added at the start while the speaker builds up sufficient air pressure for coarticulation, as in '*iss-kool*' (school), '*iss-mell*' (smell), '*iss-no*' (snow), '*iss-poon*' (spoon) and '*iss-tation*' (station).

Words that are stacked with consonants, like 'rhythm' and 'hymn' can be a challenge as well. While 'rhythm' retains its rhythm when spoken in two syllables, 'hymn' acquires a whole new connotation when broken into two syllables instead of pronounced as the usual 'him'. I once heard an Indian bhajan singer introduce himself, quite inconceivably, as a 'hymen singer'.

If you can add syllables to words, surely you can also subtract them. While Punjabis tend to add the 'uh' at the end to elongate words, they are equally able to contract them by deleting syllables, as in '*krakter*' for 'character', '*inteljent*' for 'intelligent', '*sepration*' for 'separation', '*dipty*' for 'deputy', '*famly*' for 'family', '*slekt*' for 'select' and '*krekt*' for 'correct'. And if you can break a diphthong into vowels, you can also transpose and combine vowels to make diphthongs, as in '*voilence*' (violence) and '*voilins*' (violins). The vagaries of English spelling add to classic errors in pronunciation by non-native speakers. Why should 'bowl' be pronounced like 'hole' and not like 'fowl' or 'howl'? This sort of vowel movement is common in Indian English, making bowels out of bowls and loins out of lions.

All of these peculiarities of Indian Englishes differentiate them from each other and from other Englishes of the world. Yes, English is now a noun that can be pluralized. At some point towards the end of the last millennium, enough varieties of English had sprouted around the globe for linguists to consider them as forming a language family. So we have the native varieties of English used as a first language in places like Great Britain, the United States, Canada, Australia, New Zealand and South Africa. Users of English as a second language or as an institutionalized language form an even larger category, and are generally from places such as India, Pakistan, Bangladesh, Singapore, Nigeria, Zimbabwe and the West Indies, that have had historic contact with English-speaking colonizers. Another category of 'emerging Englishes' comprises new Englishes like Chinese and Japanese English that are evolving as the need to communicate globally spurs the development of the language within countries where English has not traditionally had a stronghold.

Like 'Inglish' or 'Indlish', terms sometimes used to refer generically to Indian English, varieties such as Chinglish, Japlish,

Singlish and Spanglish, are often talked about as well. What makes them different from each other is not just their phonology, with pronunciation and intonation differences giving them a discernible sound, but differences along other linguistic dimensions such as syntax, semantics and pragmatics as well.

The syntactic or grammatical dimension governs the form and order in which words are strung together in sentences and can be quite different from standard English in these variants. Semantics determines how particular meanings are attributed to words and phrases in the lexicon and how new words are created to express meaning. Newer varieties of English are replete with such neologisms as words are adopted or adapted from local languages to suit the situation. The pragmatic dimension, which goes beyond what is explicitly stated and refers to language usage within a cultural and societal context also brings in differences in these Englishes, giving them their own distinctive identities.

In the field of linguistics, it is common knowledge that the first language of a speaker will have some influence on the process of acquisition and usage of another language. Errors in pronunciation, grammar and use of non-standard words or expressions in the second language are often based on a carryover of features or conventions from the first language. So Germanic speakers of English might mix up their 'w', 'v' and 'f' sounds and stick verbs at the end of sentences, like the bank teller I met in Austria who told me: 'Venn you your passport have, denn you your money can change'.

Given the enormous number of common Latinate words in French and English, French speakers might mistakenly use '*faux amis*' (false friends) to express themselves in English, using words that appear similar in the two languages but actually differ in meaning. When a French musician friend told me 'Zere are many pieces in my 'ouse so we can 'ave repetition zere', I was mystified for a while, till I realized she meant 'There are many rooms in my house, so we can have a rehearsal there.' The word 'piece' meaning 'room' in French and 'repetition' meaning 'rehearsal' had been dropped into the English sentence because they seemed like English words to her. Indians might be forgiven for making similar assumptions in using words like 'chalk' and 'gulley' while giving directions: 'Take the second *gali* on your left after crossing the *chowk*' sounds like a sentence with only English words.

In languages like German, French and Hindi, nouns have different genders and are used with different forms of possessive pronouns. A transfer into English can result in errors like 'her sister' even if the person whose sister is being referred to is male, or 'his brother', even if the brother's sibling is female. Unlike in English, where the possessive pronoun matches the gender of the possessor (his sister, his brother), the possessive in these languages matches the possessee's gender, rather than the possessor's, as in '*seiner Schwester*', '*seinem Bruder*', '*sa soeur*', '*son frere*', '*uski behen*' and '*uska bhai*'. Statements like 'He has gone out with her sister' make you wonder whose sister he's really gone out with: his own or someone else's?

In multilingual India, with people having different first languages, one would expect all sorts of variants of English then, with Punjabi, Malayali, Bengali and Marathi speakers sounding quite different from each other when speaking in English. And this is true to quite an extent, of course, with all the phonetic osmosis and idiosyncratic use of expressions borrowed or translated into English from assorted native languages leading to variants like Hinglish, Bonglish, Punjlish, Tamlish, Malayalish, etc.

In north India, Hinglish and Punjlish are liberally punctuated with '*yaar*' or just '*ya*', meaning 'friend', and '*achha*' meaning 'okay'. In south India, '*ma*' and '*da*' get added as fillers and tags when speaking to women or men in Tamlish and '*seri*' used in place of 'okay'. In Bonglish, '*ki re*' may get added to express disbelief, disdain or indignation, as in '*Ki re*, you are too sensitive', while '*ayi oh*' in Tamlish and '*oy*' in Punjlish might serve the same purpose.

In English, one might be casting pearls before swine when interacting with someone too ignorant to appreciate something.

In the Hinglish equivalent, one would shrug that a monkey can't appreciate the taste of ginger, while in Marathlish it would be a donkey that wouldn't know the taste of jaggery. In Tamlish, the sacred smell of camphor would go unappreciated by the proverbial donkey and in Kanaddlish, the donkey wouldn't appreciate the fragrance of musk.

All of these borrowings and interjections add local context and colour to the regional varieties of English in India. Despite such sub-cultural and dialectical differences, though, it is truly remarkable how a pan-Indian variety of English seems to have emerged across the country, with a widely shared vocabulary and commonalities in grammatical construction and deconstruction. When we diverge from 'standard' English in India, we tend to do so in similar ways for the most part, whether we're from the north or south or east or west.

An example of common usage in this pan-Indian Inglish is the omission of the articles 'the' and 'a' when they're required in a sentence, and their insertion when they're not! All over the India people are dropping article or adding to the nouns that don't need them. In few cases this can change meaning and imply opposite of what speaker actually intended to say.

If one hears 'There are few issues we need to discuss', one might conclude that there's really nothing much to discuss, whereas the speaker of Indian English might, in fact, mean that there are some issues that should be discussed. Dropping the 'a' before 'few' can alter the sense of the sentence completely. Adding an unnecessary 'the' can also lead to ambiguity: 'We have launched a satellite into the space' makes one wonder which space is being referred to. Some particular area demarcated as 'the space' or the more general 'space' that's out there, way beyond the stratosphere.

Another pan-Indian grammar glitch is the use of 'would' for 'will', as in 'The concert would take place at 7 p.m. tomorrow'. Using 'would' would in standard usage imply some sort of conditionality, but in Indian English it is used as the future tense of 'will', irrespective of the fact that 'will' already indicates the future. For someone not used to Indian English, it could be unclear whether the concert will indeed take place tomorrow, or if it would take place, provided some conditions are met, perhaps dependent on the availability of the venue or the artistes. Hearing an MC say 'The next presentation would be made by Sunil', could also make you wonder if Sunil is present to present it, or couldn't make it. The phrasing of the sentence leaves an unsaid 'but…' dangling at the end, as if to state 'The next presentation would have been made by Sunil, but unfortunately, he could not make it here today.'

Mixing up tenses and not conjugating verbs to match subjects is a common syntactical sin committed by us in Indian English. The past tense of 'He doesn't have the money to buy the ticket' is commonly heard as 'He didn't had the money to buy the ticket.' Since 'had' is the past tense of 'have', many Indians use it, regardless of the fact that the auxiliary verb 'to do' has already been conjugated in the past as 'did' and so would simply require the infinitive form 'have' with it, not 'had'. We end up with a doubled past tense that sounds odd and incorrect. Perhaps we like to emphasize that what's past is past and there's no need to get so tense about it.

Doubling comparatives and using redundant expressions like 'lot many' is also something a lot many Indians do. If something is less than less, we make it 'very less' and if something is better than better, we make it 'more better'. The meaning is more or less clear, but the phrases can sound jarring to the unaccustomed ear.

Prepositions occupy a special position in Indian English too. These little linking words on which sentences pivot can be a bit off in our usage, leading subjects astray, causing teachers to object. We go to work on car and get stuck up in traffic. We discuss about our projects, search Net to find out some information and pay attention on detail. We return to home from office and enter from the backside. We sit in sofa, listen music and take rest. We look forward for our holidays and are interested to go in a new place.

Some Indian speakers of English trip up on verb conjugation because the 's' ending in the third person singular seems like it should go with plural subjects, as in 'they likes watching movies', instead of 'they like watching movies'. Since plural nouns are typically made by adding an 's' to a singular noun, the rule gets overgeneralized and misapplied to verb conjugation. So we end up with 'he like' and 'she like' for the singular subject and 'they likes', 'we likes' for plural subjects.

Another error in pluralization, or rather the lack of it, is observed in the expression 'One of my friend visited me yesterday.' Hopefully, one has many friends and one of them visited yesterday. As one of many is being referred to, the noun 'friend' should be pluralalized, but all across India one hears 'One of my colleague', 'One of my relative', 'One of my neighbour' or 'One of my batchmate'. It is one of the common usage in our Inglish.

In standard English, turning a statement into a question usually entails a change in word order. So 'She is not going to school today' can be rephrased as a question by rearranging the words to say 'Is she not going to school today?' In Indian English, we resort to intonation to form a question by simply raising the pitch at the end of a statement, rather than by changing the sequence of words. 'She is not going to school today' spoken with an upward inflection of pitch becomes the interrogative form. While a rising pitch pattern is used in other Englishes to form questions too, it is typically accompanied by a change in word order that Indian English doesn't always bother with.

Possibly the most unifying usage in pan-Indian Inglish grammar is the overwhelming tendency to use the progressive tense for stative verbs that state what state we're in or were in or will be in. 'I am having two brothers and a sister' does not mean that my siblings are taking birth right now as triplets, but rather that 'I have two brothers and a sister'. For some reason, we Indians prefer the present continuous tense when the simple present stating this fact would do just fine. 'I was not realizing what he was meaning that time' is meaning 'At that time, I did not realize what he meant' and 'Finally, I am going to be relaxing on my holiday' would be meaning that 'I finally get to take a break'.

In the British comedy show *Mind Your Language*, the three South Asian students Ranjit and Jamila from India and Ali from Pakistan all sound alike. Besides the 'jolly good', 'thousand apologies', 'oh dearie me' and other archaic expressions punctuating their speech, a common characteristic of their language is the use of the progressive tense: 'Why you are wanting to be changing our teacher, Ms Courtney? We are liking Mr Brown'.

Other British comedy shows like *Goodness Gracious Me* and *The Kumars at Number 42* have also featured Indian English usage, with some of the expressions used by characters in the shows becoming common parlance in the speech of young Brits. The question tag 'innit' is one such term.

A contraction of the common English question tag 'isn't it', what makes 'innit' Indian is not the phrase itself, but the way it's used at the end of all sorts of statements, even those with which the verb 'is' would not fit grammatically. Indian English is replete with such usage:

> The movie was very educational, isn't it? (instead of 'wasn't it?')
>
> He is going to demonstrate a new technique, isn't it? (instead of 'isn't he?')
>
> They are going back to Bangalore today, isn't it? (instead of 'aren't they?')
>
> We will be reimbursed for working overtime, isn't it? (instead of 'won't we?')

Possibly a carryover from the Hindi tag '*hai na*?' and similar equivalents in other Indian languages, this type of indiscriminate use of 'isn't it' is typical in India. Sometimes the Hindi phrase itself is inserted into Indian English, instead of 'isn't it', as in 'We have a meeting tomorrow, *hai na*?' and the '*hai na*' is usually further reduced to just '*na*', the way 'isn't it' has been reduced to 'innit' in South Asian British slang.

Like the '*na*' in Hinglish, 'eh' in Canadian English or the 'lah' in Singaporean English, 'innit' has become more of a tag now, than a question tag per se, with the hip-hopping duo in *Goodness Gracious Me* attaching it with no compunction to statements that wouldn't normally work with a question tag: 'People got problems they wanna chat about, innit?' and 'You calm down, innit.'

Another expression used by these Bhangramuffins that's become cool around modern multicultural Britain today is 'kiss my *chuddies*'! Literally 'kiss my underpants', the word '*chuddies*' made its way into the hallowed halls of Windsor Castle recently when Prince Charles, of all unlikely people, used it in a speech honouring the contribution of the Asian community to linguistic and other aspects of life in Britain. With entries in the Collins and Oxford English dictionaries, '*chuddies*' have come out of the closet, or rather the drawers, and are enjoying their airing in the sun, however brief that might be.

In another of the *Goodness Gracious Me* skits, two competitive mothers trying to outdo each other with regard to the stellar qualities possessed by their sons, introduced '*danda*' (stick) as slang for penis: 'Your son may well be a neurosurgeon with his own private jet, but how big is his *danda, hahn*?' Other less cocky words introduced by the British Asian characters in these shows are '*pind*' (village), '*pindu*' (country bumpkin), '*lafanga*' (loafer/rogue) and '*besti*' (shame/dishonour): 'It'll be *besti* in my *pind*, man, if I marry a girl my parents don't approve of.'

The import of Indian words into English is certainly no new phenomenon. With a history of language contact spanning several centuries now, all sorts of words from South Asian languages have crept into English. Some, like avatar, bazaar, brahmin, bungalow, cashmere, chutney, chakkar, cummerbund, curry, divan, guru, jodhpurs, karma, khaki, mantra, mogul, nirvana, pariah, pundit, pukka, pyjamas, sahib, sherbet, thug, veranda and yoga, are transparently subcontinental. Other words like bandana, bandicoot, bangle, Blighty, candy, caravan, catamaran, cheroot, chintz, cot, cushy, dinghy, dungaree, ginger, godown, juggernaut, kedgeree, mulligatawny, punch, shampoo and toddy have camouflaged their origins to such an extent with their anglicized spelling and pronunciation that many Indians aren't even aware of their indigenous antecedents.

'Shampoo—an Indian word? That's hogwash!' exclaimed a sceptical friend when I mentioned it as a word of Indian descent. Well you could use it to wash hogs, but most of us use it to wash our hair. The word's origins can be traced back to '*champna*', as in kneading the scalp or massaging the head with some sort of lotion or oil. The extrapolation of the verb to the noun '*champu*', to refer to the substance itself and its use for washing hair, and mapping of the 'ch' to the 'sh' sound as in many imported English words like 'charade' and 'chic' gives us shampoo.

In an attempt to gather Indian words and phrases used colloquially in the days of the British Raj, Colonel Henry Yule and Doctor Arthur Burnell compiled their famous compendium *Hobson-Jobson* in 1886. A century later, Nigel Hankin took on a similar task, offering a new collation of Indianisms in English in his *Hanklyn-Janklin*. The name 'Hobson-Jobson' is apparently an onomatopoeic mis-transcription of the cries 'ya Hassan, ya Hussain' heard by British soldiers during Muharram. *Hanklyn-Janklin* is so named as a 'resonant tribute' to *Hobson-Jobson*. Its echo words are also in keeping with the Indian tendency to re-duplicate words into phrases like '*chai-shai*', '*pani-wani*', '*book-shook*', '*kursi-wursi*', etc., where the second word is nonsensical but expands the scope of the first.

Both these books are treasure troves of words and expressions used in Indian English, but each is bound to its time and context. In *Hobson-Jobson*, for example, the primary meaning for the word '*bursautee*' derived from the Hindi '*barsaat*', meaning 'the rains', is given as 'a disease to which horses are liable in the rains, pustular eruptions breaking out on the head and fore parts of the body'. A second meaning is 'a waterproof cloak, or the like'. In *Hanklyn-Janklyn,* there's no reference to the horse disease in the entry for '*barsaati*', but 'raincoat' is mentioned. In addition, a new meaning is offered: 'A rain shelter; usually on the upper terrace or roof of a building', which could be used as extra residential accommodation. In the century that passed between the publishing of the two books, the emphasis seems to have switched from horses to houses. Saddled with a shortage of reasonable accommodation in urban areas, many people rent barsaatis, while interaction of the common populace with horses is not so paramount.

Words can lose or gain importance over time and fall into disuse or acquire new shades of meaning. Borrowing from other languages or coining neologisms can replenish the active lexicon of a language. Keeping apace with new words-*shurds* being used in Indian English these days, we would need new editions of *Hobson-Jobson* and *Hanklyn-Janklin* by the hour almost.

Words and phrases that would have to be added in latter-day editions include '*bindaas*', 'funda', 'fundoo', '*jugaad*', 'timepass', 'item girl' and such. 'Bindaas' meaning carefree, and 'jugaad' referring to an innovative quick-fix are Indian words, but 'funda' and 'fundoo' are fundamentally English. Derived from 'fundamental', 'funda' basically refers to the basic essentials that one needs to have clear to get on in life. A 'fundoo' person is someone cool who's all sorted out, with all the right fundas, but 'fundoo' can also be used negatively to refer to a fundamentalist. 'Timepass', similar to its inverse 'pastime', refers to a frivolous activity engaged in to pass the time. 'Item girl' is the sexy new incarnation of the cabaret-dancing 'vamp' of Indian films of the 1970s. A *hazaar* other words and phrases like these have been a part of the urban patois for years now, though they still raise highbrows' eyebrows.

While the more English Indians might be disdainful of usage of such street vernacular, the ultimate reference for all things lexical, the *Oxford English Dictionary* (OED) routinely scours the Englishes of the world in search of new words that ought to be included in its volumes. Words like '*adda*', '*badmash*', '*bhang*', '*bindaas*', '*chotu*', '*gora*', '*desi*', '*jungli*', '*masala*', '*shabash*', '*tamasha*' and '*yaar*' have made their way into the OED and other Western dictionaries along with a host of others like '*bandh*', '*chamcha*', '*dharna*' and '*neta*' that are part of the common parlance in Indian English.

A recently published book by Baljinder Mahal called *The Queen's Hinglish: How to Speak Pukka* lists even more Indianisms, acknowledging the spread of their usage in the UK, even amongst non-Asian Britons. The Internet is another resource for philologists interested in word gathering. The speed of communication and ease of uploading help in maintaining online glossaries that can be updated on an ongoing basis, as in the 'desi english' listing provided by V. Subhash at http://www.vsubhash.com/desienglish.asp.

Specific settings often breed specific vocabularies, as on college campuses, in the workplace, or in the media. In Delhi University, one hears words like 'arbit' (for arbitrary), 'enthu' (for enthusiastic), 'vagueo' (for somebody noncommittal or nondescript), 'too good' (for something excellent), 'taking *pangas*' (inviting trouble) and all manner of acronyms. JLT, meaning 'just like that' seems to be a translation of the '*ainvey*' or '*aisey hi*' in Punjabi and Hindi. OHT for 'overhead transmission' is what happens in some classes when what the professor is saying completely eludes comprehension. POA is 'plan of action', as in 'What's the POA for Friday night, man? Where's the party happenin'?' CT for 'cheap thrill' is what a 'roadside Romeo' might get from 'eve teasing'. And the ubiquitous KLPD, meaning 'a real letdown' or an anticlimax, is derived from Hindi words that would be hard to translate, but roughly mean 'to be turned on, only to eventually be denied the goods'.

In Indian offices, words such as 'peon', '*chaprasi*' and '*challan*' continue to be used today, even though they seem dated in the modern MNC/BPO setting. While in the office, you should be 'in your seat' in your 'kaybin' doing the 'needful' to increase revenue in 'lakhs' and 'crores', except when you need to take a PL or CL for personal time off. If you need to go 'out of station' to work 'on tour', as it's called, 'intimate' your clients, try to 'prepone' your appointments, and 'revert' to whomsoever called when you return. When giving your email address to someone, be sure to say 'at the rate of' for the @ sign. It seems just 'at' is not sufficient to convey what that little symbol means.

The penchant for using acronyms is even more prominent in the Indian media. Newspapers are filled with them. To a reader not acquainted with the Indian police, it may not be evident what FIR, PCR, SHO, SP, DCP mean, yet newspapers often don't decrypt them. In some cases, an acronym becomes a word unto itself, as has happened with radar, laser and scuba, and we get words like 'Sail' (for the Steel Authority of India Ltd) and 'vat' (for Value Added Tax), which are imported into languages like Hindi, as is, without translation of the individual letters forming the acronym. Indigenous new verb forms like 'air-dashed', '*lathi*-charged', '*gherao*ed' routinely appear in the dailies. A 'history sheeter' is a bad character or 'miscreant': someone with a criminal record who's been 'chargesheeted' too many times, perhaps. Portmanteau words made by combining other words are also popular in the press. For the longest time, I did not know what a 'distcom' was, till someone graciously deciphered it as 'distribution company'. With electricity distribution now decentralized, a spate of new distcoms have taken charge as power players on the horizon.

Mobile phones and the web have also contributed to the vocabulary of Indian youngsters. You don't ask people for their phone numbers any more. Rather, you ask them to give you a 'missed call' so you can store their number in your digital phonebook. SMS is another useful acronym for 'short message service' that works both as a noun and a verb, as 'texting' does in the UK and other places. Another way of getting in touch would be to 'ping' or 'poke' on the Internet. You could even 'Orkut' or 'Facebook' each other and become part of a larger online community. Chatroom expressions like LOL for 'laugh out loud' and 'sup' for 'what's up?'

have become words in their own right. Even the diminutive OK has been reduced to just K.

Another whole genre of verbs popular with multilingual speakers in India has emerged by mixing verb roots or stems of one language with those from another language. Hindi speakers routinely use phrasal verbs like wait *karna*, try *karna*, accent *maarna*, phone *karna*, drive *karna*, vote *karna*, line *lagana*, service *karana*, repair *karana*, etc. Bilingual speakers using a primarily English structure come up with hybridized verb forms like '*sunao*ed', '*maaro*ed', '*palo*ed', '*manao*ing' and '*theek karo*fy'.

Another type of crossover from regional languages into English gives us modifiers like 'only', 'itself', 'just' and 'also'. The translation of the Hindi '*Woh aisa hi hai*', becomes 'He is like that only'. The '*hi*' in '*Hum aaj hi Dilli laut rahey hain*' becomes 'itself' as in 'We are returning to Delhi today itself'. The '*bhi*' in '*Woh kisi ki bhi nahi sunta*' can become 'only' or 'also' as in 'He doesn't listen to anyone also/only'.

With all of this linguistic manoeuvering, the semantic dimension of Indian English is blazing bright. If we can't find words to express what we need to express, we concoct them or morph Indian words to fit into an English base structure. It is part of 'the alchemy of English' that linguist Braj Kachru talks about in his book *The Alchemy of English: The Spread, Functions and Models of Non-native Englishes.*

While Indian English serves us remarkably well in communicating in our own milieu, communicating with speakers of other Englishes can be challenging at times. Besides the differences in phonology, syntax and semantics, some expressions may be lost because of a lack of familiarity with the pragmatic dimension of language which takes into account social, cultural and historical aspects of the interlocutors' backgrounds.

A show called *The Papdits* made for American television never really took off because of such a mismatch, perhaps, despite being co-written by the writer of the irreverent, controversial and very successful movie *Borat*. Featuring an Indian family travelling across the US interacting with real Americans (non-actors), the show showcased Indianisms and linguistic and cultural differences as in an episode in which the wife has a Tupperware party and tells the gathered American ladies: 'Today we will be selling a brand new product called a food storage container. These containers are having a magical see-through quality. They are made from a special type of glass called plastic. These are all very useful for keeping food for surprise visitor or in time of famine.'

In a country where visitors always call before coming over and there's never a famine, the social context of Ms Papdit's spiel may indeed be lost on Americans. Besides the rather pappy name of the show, it seems its tongue-in-cheek humour and self-deprecatory jokes about the Indian community didn't click with either the Americans, who perhaps didn't get them, or with Indian-Americans who are so under pressure to assimilate that cringe-inducing reminders of their linguistic and socio-cultural gaffes are not funny to them.

Getting used to another dialect of English does take some acclimatization. As a student in the US in the 1980s, I recall being shocked when asked to pay fifty dollars for a cup of coffee. How could that be? It was just a lousy cup of perk, not even a mochacino or a fancy latte. As it turned out, it wasn't for fifty dollars, but rather $1.50. The Indian way of saying the currency name first and then the amount is the reverse of how the Americans say it. They would read $5000 out loud as 5000 dollars, not dollar 5000. So the 'dollar fifty' the waitress had announced was 'a dollar fifty', as in one dollar and fifty cents, not $50. Phew! That was a relief, given the few dollars I had in my pocket.

Other situations where Indian and American English came a-clashing was in the driving exam I had to take to get a US licence. The examiner asked me to turn on the turn signal. I had no clue what that was. I looked like a blinking idiot until it clicked that it was the indicator that was indicated. In the written exam, a question about parallel parking on the pavement got me perplexed as I couldn't understand why I would need to park on the pavement and not by it, on the side of the road. It turns out the Americans refer to the main road as the pavement and what we call the pavement or the footpath is the curb or the sidewalk.

If ever stuck on the pavement in the US with a punctured tyre, curb your desire to look for the stepney in the dicky and get the spare tire out of the trunk instead. While we would open the bonnet to check on a dying battery, Americans would look under the hood. If you need alternative transport, use your cell phone to call a cab, rather than using your mobile to call a taxi. Forget about getting a lift on a lorry. Try hitching a ride on a truck instead. And don't unnecessarily 'horn please' or it'll be 'ok bye-bye tata' for you.

Differences in varieties of English will continue to trip us up occasionally, no doubt, but with the Internet, satellite television and movies and music travelling across the world faster than light, we are becoming more aware of the differences and are able to comprehend them. The flattened, globalized world and the culture of outsourcing and virtual collaborations has colleagues working together across time zones and dialectical divides and English is the medium of communication.

The Call Centre phenomenon may be decried and derided, but it has provided not just customer service agents to serve consumers across the world, but also acquainted English language users with the sound and flavour of other dialects. English is the language on which people in India have pinned their aspirations and Indians are learning to use it, any which way. With India becoming a major player in the global economy, a day may well come when, as spoofed by Melvin Durai on his website http://www.melvindurai.com/indianenglish.htm, we will be calling customer service agents in the US and UK and they will speak to us in the Indian accents they've been trained to emulate so that we feel more comfortable conversing with them!

Indian English is proliferating at an accelerated rate these days. With Indian movies and popular music propagating code mixing, English words are becoming familiar even in rural areas where people may not have access to formal education or English-speaking people. Movie titles like '*Bheja* Fry', '*Ek Chhoti Si* Love Story', '*Jab* We Met', '*Jhankaar* Beats', '*Kya* Cool *Hain Hum*', 'Love You *Hamesha*', '*Pyar Ke* Side Effects' and '*Zindaggi* Rocks' have become routine. The language the characters speak in the films also oscillates between their vernacular and English.

Songs with lyrics alternating between English and Hindi, Punjabi or other Indian languages have hijacked the airwaves. 'Where's the party tonight', 'Let the music play', 'It's the time to disco', 'We are same same but different', 'Pretty woman, *dekho na*', 'Rock and roll, *soniye*', 'That's the way, *mahi ve*', 'Pappu can't dance *saala*' and a whole host of other such tracks feature on every party playlist. Transcending class and cultural differences, Indian pop has 'all the cool boys' and 'all the hot girls' singing '*Om shanti om*', even in far-flung places across the country and the globe where the beat appeals despite some of the words being unintelligible or misheard as 'Home, shanty, home'.

Shows on Indian TV invariably end up using some form of code mixing as well. As in a popular cookery show in which the chef gave instructions like this:

> '*Ab aap* mushrooms *ko* chop *kar ke* olive oil *mein* gently sauté *kijiye. Phir thora sa* salt to taste *aur thorey se* herbs sprinkle *kijiye*—jaisey oregano, thyme, *vagehra, aur aapki* dish *taiyar hai*!'
>
> (Now chop the mushrooms and gently sauté them in olive oil. Then add some salt to taste, sprinkle some herbs like oregano, thyme, etc., and your dish is ready!)

With fourteen English words and twenty Hindi, if you didn't already understand the other language, you would with more exposure to such shows.

The direction of code mixing has become quite blurred in the type of mixed vernacular being used these days. Whether Indian words are borrowed and inserted into an English grammatical base or the other way around is hard to discern sometimes, as speakers can switch between languages mid-sentence. A Hinglish conversation I heard recently on the playing field went like this:

> 'What are you doing *yaar*? *Yeh to bilkul* fair *baat nahi hai*, man. You only said we would play by the rules, *na*? *Phir* play by the rules *hi karo. Is tarah ki* adjustment *wudjustment* will not do, ok? Come on, *shuru se* start *kartey hain*.'

Besides the cross-lingual words being inserted throughout, the first and third sentences have an English base. The second and fourth sentences have a Hindi base and the last two sentences are totally mixed. Translated into regular English, we would get:

> 'What are you doing, buddy? This is not fair at all, man. You're the one who said we would play by the rules, didn't you? Then let's just play by the rules. This sort of adjustment will not do, ok? Come on, let's begin at the beginning.'

Sometimes we end up in funny circular situations where an English word is appropriated into an Indian sentence, which is then translated back into English with comical results. For example, the word 'tension' is used a lot in Mumbai Hindi in sentences like 'tension *nahi lene ka*' meaning 'don't be tense'. The reverse translation into English becomes 'don't take tension'! The Hindi verb '*lena*' which means 'to take' ends up in other quaint combinations like 'He is taking rest right now' to mean 'He is resting right now' from the Hindi construction '*Woh abhi* rest *le rahe hain*'.

'Do you know how to swim?' becomes '*Aap ko* swim *karna aata hai*?' which gets translated back to English as 'Do you know how to do swimming?' with the auxiliary verb 'to do' added to imply the Hindi '*karna*' and the primary verb 'to swim' made into the gerund 'swimming'. 'He is travelling a lot these days' becomes '*Aaj kal woh bahut* travel *kar rahe hain*' in Hindi, which gets reverse translated to English as 'He is doing a lot of travelling these days'. Similar construction leads to phrases like 'doing painting', 'doing knitting' in Indian English. The doing can get extended to usage like 'doing my graduation' from Delhi University. And when you're done doing, you 'pass out', rather than graduate.

Other verbs and gerunds emerge in combinations like 'She is knowing playing piano' for '*Usko* piano *bajana aata hai*' which means 'She knows how to play the piano', or even 'I am knowing English speaking' for '*Mujhe* English *bolni aati hai*' to state 'I know how to speak English'!

Far from being apologetic about using incorrect grammar or non-standard pronunciation, Indians are using English unabashedly today. The advertisements on television almost celebrate such usage and misusage, with advertisements such as the one for Orbit chewing gum vouching for its whitening effect on 'teeths', which results in the bovine star of the ad receiving 'too much *rishtey*' from all the bulls in the vicinity. And the Mintrox commercial offers soothing, cool mints to offset stress because 'life eej hard'.

The Englishes of the world might be spreading in directions that make them more and more different from each other, yet the core remains the same. In his book *English as a Global Language*, linguist David Crystal acknowledges that English is splitting into local versions that may become mutually incomprehensible, but predicts that a standard dialect called World Standard Spoken English or WSSE will emerge as well, with enough convergence between the variants to allow coherent communication between speakers. More and more people will be multidialectical speakers, conversant with multiple varieties of English. He acknowledges the special place India has in the English-speaking world today, 'outranking the combined totals of speakers in the USA and UK'. With an estimate of over 200 million users of English as a second language, a number that is sure to be revised upwards periodically, it is crystal clear that Indian English has to be contended with as a major member of the family of Englishes.

We may not have received the proper 'Received Pronunciation' and our grammatical errors may have inured with habit over the years to become standard usage. Our quaint expressions and twists and turns of phrase might make native English speakers wince, but as long as we are able to get our message across, they are a valid form of communication. What will eventually be convincing is the invincibility of Indian English. It is here to stay. Hear to say.

A lot can get lost in translation. But a lot could be found. And profound. Like the other day, while warming up for a concert, a guest choir conductor from France told us to inspire and expire. In French, 'inspire' and 'expire' mean to inhale and exhale. The instruction may have been a bit disconcerting, but it was a good reminder for living in general. 'Inspire and expire' would be a breathtakingly inspiring motto to live by indeed, and 'inspired and expired' a great epitaph for a life well lived.

Talking Bollywood

. . . .

Jerry Pinto

THE SEDUCTION

My first time was marked only by boredom. A whole stable of Pintos went to see a Hindi film at Citylight cinema in Mahim, the patch of Mumbai where I grew up. Citylight was not a grand or even a good theatre, but it had the advantage of being right across the road from my home. (This meant that we could always pop back for a snack, for insect repellent, for a quick visit to a familiar and clean loo.) Since I knew no Hindi in those days, I lost the plot after the first five minutes. After I had asked various Pintos 'How much more?' about five hundred times, I announced that I wanted to go to the toilet. My mother was chosen to escort me home.

Outside, some urchins wanted to know if we were going to use our tickets to get in again.

'The film's half over,' my mother said.

'It doesn't matter,' said one of the boys. 'They're all the same.'

'Then why do you want to see this one?'

'*Majjaa*,' he said simply. (A translation of this would demand too much of the English language. Let us just say that any equivalent would have to be a composite of 'fun' and 'pleasure', and have a hint of the bazaar as well.)

My mother handed over our tickets to the boys and we went home.

Between that first debacle and my full-fledged love affair with Hindi cinema, there is a blank. Here and there I see a flash: Rajesh

Khanna collecting his blood in a wine glass and offering it to Hema Malini as an aperitif. Rajesh Khanna again, weeping as he drags the carcass of an elephant to its cremation. Dharmendra singing us the meaning of life from the back seat of a bus, to music produced by teacup and saucer, Bata shoes and Asrani's lips. Sharmila Tagore, in a bikini, water skiing with a smug look on her face that tells us she knows exactly how many taboos she's breaking.

I'm not sure where or how I watched these films, or snatches of them; perhaps these are images I saw only on hoardings and posters, or perhaps I'm telescoping memories. I was banned from the cinema except where it was deemed a good film for children, like *The Sound of Music*, *The Ten Commandments* or, oddly enough, *Mackenna's Gold*. I thought it was something to do with being Roman Catholic that all the films which were considered 'good' were English, but when I checked with friends of different religious persuasions, I found that their parents voted with their wallets for Hollywood too. Perhaps it had to do with being middle class and with English being the language of aspiration.

I didn't mind the ban, least of all the stricture against Hindi cinema, till I was in my early teens. And then—I can't figure out how—I was greedily grasping whatever came to hand, anything I could see, whenever I could see it. Suddenly I was part of a festival of emotions that swept unchecked across the great Gangetic plain, down towards the Vindhyas and over that puny barrier into the west of India. Suddenly I was part of the multitudes who are now buying 3.7 billion tickets all over the country, thus participating in one of the most important film industries in the world, and one that gives employment to 6 million people.

It is also said to be the biggest film industry on the planet.

This, of course, has been hotly contested. The argument in favour of Bollywood is that it turns out the largest number of films anywhere—nearly a thousand a year. But then, Hollywood is much bigger in terms of revenue, around twenty-five times as large as all our cinemas put together: an average Hollywood film will have 5000 prints made; a top-line Hindi film will have 500 to 700. By this yardstick, the Hindi film industry isn't even as large in turnover as the Telugu, whose revenues are said to be five times higher. But then, how exactly do we want to see it? That in Hollywood they gross more than we do, or that we make more films than they do? That we sell more tickets, or that their tickets are several times more expensive, since the vast majority are sold in dollars? Is that what it's about?

It shouldn't matter if Bollywood were an art form. But in its own self-description, in the one it has craved for decades and won only recently, Bollywood is an industry, so it *does* matter but only up to a point. For Bollywood is also an art form, a form of popular culture—perhaps the one that has the best claim to being a pan-Indian popular culture—and then it does not matter at all whether it is as big as Hollywood or does as much business or less. Because art and culture is about hearts and minds.

Not too long ago, a friend called me in a mild panic. 'I have to replace sixteen bottles by five o'clock,' she said. It was nearly noon. 'Any blood group. Can you come?' I could. I went. I donated blood; I ate my biscuits, drank my coffee and went home. My friend called the next day. '*Main is khoon ki har ek boond ki keemat chukaaoongi, Jerry*,' she said, consciously ironic as she riffed on the hyperbole of a popular Hindi-film line, promising to repay the price of every drop of my blood.

I understood. Some thanks are so deep that they can only be ironic. And when we need irony, we reach for Bollywood.

Why just irony? When we need any emotion, we reach for Bollywood. It is a parallel language, which lies just under our tongues. It's there when you need it, an entire system of shared references that needs no explanation. It has no snob value; you're not quoting Shakespeare or an apposite Latin or Sanskrit maxim here. You're just jumping into the village pond and anyone can do that. When we need a phrase to express ourselves, whether it is the superficial slights of an ordinary day or our deepest hurts, we reach for Bollywood. If a friend abandons us, we sing '*Dost dost na raha*' from Raj Kapoor's *Sangam* (1964). Every generation recognizes self-destructing love as the Devdas story—the various film versions, not the original book. A diva is an Umrao Jaan, a dreadful boss is a Gabbar Singh, a tragedy queen is a Meena Kumari.

Bollywood is not just a film industry. It is the custom-made synecdoche for India: the all-singing, all-dancing technicolor spectacle whose primary audience is a nation struggling with poverty, ignorance, corruption and intolerance. It is our national metaphor, operating on the principle that everything will turn out all right in the end, if we can only stay the distance. It is the backdrop that fills out the empty corners of our lives, maintaining a pleasant stranglehold on our imaginations. It determines—or at the very least modifies—who we see ourselves as and who we refuse to be; how we think-talk-dream-speak-love-fight. It is a place to which we can go, an illusion to which we succumb but which we can mock.

Bollywood is ours in the making and it is ours in the consumption. Popular art forms everywhere come from the space between gut and heart. In India, this relationship seems to be even more visceral. Folk performers will often repeat a line again and again for the benefit of their audiences, milking the last tears or the last laughs from it; they will move on only when they sense that the crowd has had enough. Even classical musicians feel their way through a performance, encouraged by the audience's 'wah wahs' or hastened on by pointed silences. We participate actively in our viewing of cinema too. Spontaneous applause breaks out after a well-delivered line. Small-change showers still patter and tinkle during dance sequences.

I remember watching Manmohan Desai's *Naseeb* (1981) in a Mumbai cinema. In one of the fight sequences, the lead players, Amitabh Bachchan and Hema Malini, have the villain and his moll on the run. '*Bhaag bhosdeeké* (Run, you cunt),' the man next to me shouted, his body rippling with delight as the villains retreated in bad order. In smaller towns, audiences are more direct in their demands. They let the projectionist know when they want to see a certain reel again. He always obliges. The audience for Hindi cinema determines not just how many weeks a film will play for but also *how* it will play each time.

Speaking for myself, I think my transformation from bored outsider to compulsive consumer had something to do with Bollywood being forbidden fruit. By the 1970s, the middle class had come a long way from the time when it was uncomfortable with cinema and dismissed it as low class. But in the unspoken hierarchy of pastimes, books still outweighed the movies. Although it was admitted that there could be bad books (pornography, for instance) and good Indian films (the films of Satyajit Ray, for example), the default position was: books are serious and safe; films are frivolous and threatening. Thus, films were rationed out in small doses so that no unhealthy addiction might begin. Some hope.

At Victoria High School (VHS) in Mahim, it helped that there were opportunities all around us. The mother lode was the triple whammy of big cinema houses near by: Baadal, Bijlee and Barkha. There were also, within walking distance of school, Shri cinema, Rivoli Picture House, Paradise cinema and the aforementioned Citylight. The truly adventurous among us went two bus stops south to Dadar where V. Shantaram's Plaza offered Hindi and Marathi films; or two bus stops north to Bandra where there were Bandra Talkies and New Talkies.

This meant that whenever a VHS boy felt a desire to bunk, he had ten films to choose from. Of course, this figure was more theoretical than actual. At least two of the pleasure palaces (Citylight and Paradise) were already showing reruns and one of them (Rivoli) was showing south Indian movies of the racier kind. (Or at least the posters made them seem racy. Often a single scene could be turned into an advertisement for the pornographic potential of a film: 'Chalo lover, get under cover,' a lady said on one of the posters.)

I remember queuing for hours to see *Mr Natwarlal* (1979). It had Amitabh Bachchan and Rekha and the songs on the *praayojit kaaryakram*, which played between 10.30 and 11 p.m. on Vividh Bharati, just before the legendary request programme *Bela Ki Phool*, had made it sound like a corker of a film. My sister and I stood in line for six hours and finally, finally, we had tickets for the first day, first show.

In those days, it was a big thing: first day, first show. It carried a cachet. It was an achievement, even if it was only a function of your perseverance in the face of black marketers who would have been waiting in line before dawn, sleeping in position. The ephemeral nature of cinema was underlined for us by its unavailability. If you missed the first run of a film, there wasn't much chance of catching it again, especially if it flopped. You might catch a hit in your hometown, where the prints would arrive much later; or at morning shows in good theatres; or even at the fleabags and second rung cinema halls. But if a film with your favourite star flopped, it was unlikely that you would ever find it again. All that changed with the arrival of video cassette players and recorders.

I saw my first VCR at work at an Indian Machine Tools exhibition in Vikhroli, a northern suburb of Mumbai. It was playing Shakti Samanta's *Barsaat Ki Ek Raat* (1981), and I remember the sheer excitement of thinking, 'Gosh, you can *own* a film now.'

Of course, few people owned films. They borrowed them from the video circulating libraries that sprang up everywhere; or they went to special shanties, which would show pirated films or even blue films. '*TV video bahut hua, sab ke sar mein dard hua*,' sang Amitabh Bachchan in *Jaadugar* (1989) in an attempt to convince people not to hand over their money to the pirates. But no one cared. We were liberated from that intense study of newspaper listings. We could finally choose our own films and we could see them when we wanted to, as long as the video circulating library had them on offer. Many families who could not afford a video player or recorder would hire one for twenty-four hours and watch a whole pile of movies back to back. The VCR brought the

Hindi film into the home. It shredded the pretence that Daadi-ma didn't want to watch Hindi films. Though one of the films was a picture chosen with her in mind, the old lady would often also stay awake for a good romance, and she didn't object to some blood and bullets.

Now, even that smorgasbord of cinema seems like a time of deprivation. At the time of writing, one can buy a video compact disc for Rs 29, thanks to Moser Baer's innovative reinventing of the selling of films, a move that may well revolutionize the market in the way Gulshan Kumar reinvented the marketing of film music with T-Series. Today, where pirated films were being sold, official versions are being hocked; three hours of laughter and tears and violence and music for less than the price of a cappuccino in most urban coffee shops. Television channels offer films at any given moment of the day or night and though we are now paying for direct to home transmission, the cost is still almost negligible to most middle-class homes. I now have as many films as I want to watch. If I want to anticipate my pleasures, I have channels that will play me round-the-clock promos. Whenever a big commercial film is about to release, the news channels jockey for position, like debutantes trying to catch the eye of prince charming, and promise the moon and their souls for exclusives with the stars.

~

THE SONG

If Bollywood rules our lives in the subcontinent, the Hindi film song must take much of the credit.

Surfing channels some days ago, I stopped at an incongruous scene. The channel logo said it was a Malayalam channel. The young contestant on a song competition was singing '*Tere bina zindagi se koi shikwa to nahin*' from Gulzar's *Aandhi* (1975). Neither the compere of the show nor anyone in the audience commented on this or looked surprised. Other young talents of Kerala stepped up and sang Hindi film songs with varying degrees of skill and emotion. The compere continued to nod appreciatively in the manner of the rasika and the audience swayed to the familiar tunes that have travelled relentlessly southwards. Not everyone in that studio would have understood all the words being sung, but they related to the emotion coded into the music.

The songs begin the process of familiarisation, the cinema follows after that—and suddenly, before you know it, the recalcitrant south has begun to speak Hindi. This should be an object lesson to all those who wish to legislate language on to the world. What the diktats of Delhi could not do, the seductions of Mumbai—a city that itself has small claim on Hindi or any of its variants—have achieved.

I remember the outrage I felt the first time a young Brit said, 'That's the cinema where everyone sings, innit?' Now this reductive definition no longer bothers me. Yes, Hindi films have lots of songs. They aren't just the songs of films; they constitute a parallel popular culture. They have independent lives, as British scholar Anna Morcom has pointed out. Those who hum them do not need the words, they do not need those words to mean anything, the lyrics are secondary to the emotional content of the songs and that is indicated by the melody. Once that has been received, a song may begin the next phase in its life cycle, where it may be divorced from context, where it may float free of the stars and the film itself, where it acquires a life of its own which will determine whether it becomes a classic, is remixed or simply forgotten. The songs that enter into the long-playing records of public memory find their way into antakshari, the game all Bollywoodians play, and which is the true test of both mass and enduring appeal.

Antakshari is an act of claiming mastery not just over a song or a tune but over the entire song book. It is a celebration of a shared heritage, a club to which anyone can belong except those who have not cared to listen. It is a challenge in which each group competes to display how deep their knowledge of the genre is; thus specialist antaksharis can be played with composers, singers, decades, or even a combination of the above. But most antaksharis are raucous public events, loud and funny. They are a common cultural context and the whole structure is open and flexible enough to allow the hospitable and curious Indian to extend a hand to anyone in earshot. If you know and love these songs, come and join in, antakshari says, let's make some familiar and joyful noise. Come play, because there are 30,000 songs and counting but very few begin with the 'tha' of '*Thande thande paan se*' (*Pati, Patni aur Woh*, 1978) which is what makes it all so much fun.

These songs have become the white noise of our lives. As the writer Amitava Kumar puts it: 'What is India? (Although I suspect this is very much a Hindi-speaking, middle-class Bihari's point of view.) India is ten million Tata Leyland trucks on the highways playing on their radios Lata singing, '*Tum na jaane kis jahan mein kho gaye/ Hum bhari duniya mein tanhaa ho gaye*' (You have vanished into some distant world and left me alone amidst the crowds).'

~

THE COMMERCE

'No one has offered a cogent explanation for why the Hindi film industry settled in Bombay,' Rachel Dwyer, indefatigable chronicler of Bollywood, once remarked. Writing about his actor brother Balraj Sahni in *Mere Bhai Balraj*, the legendary Hindi novelist Bhisham Sahni notes that there is no Hindi film industry in any of the states that actually speak the language. Historically, language was not an important part of silent cinema. Titles could be changed at will and written in as many languages as were needed or economically viable. But even when sound arrived in 1931, the two major languages of the Bombay Presidency were Gujarati and Marathi. The only possible explanation for the Hindi film industry choosing Bombay over any other place must be that the speculative money was in this city.

But there's a conundrum here. Businessmen are supposed to look at the profile of an industry, its history of profit making, its quality control mechanisms, its back-up systems and who-knows-what. It is true that the more adventurous or flamboyant among them are also supposed to be gamblers, but probability is said to favour the prepared mind. No one who has studied the business of Hindi film-making would ever think of putting his own money into Bollywood. Besides, speculators and chronic risk-takers, too, would retreat after repeated failure: after all, a large majority of commercial Hindi films flop at the box office year after year.

So how does the industry keep going? The easy answer to that is glamour. As a tutor of mathematics, I once taught the two hard-won sons of a dealer in zinc. Mr Jinkmandi had once invested in a film. That much was obvious from the number of stickers, pens, compass boxes and other material that was lying around the house, all of which bore the film's name. Mr Jinkmandi told me that he had lost his money on the film. He had decided he would never invest in another film. But his wife, he said, had been happy. For six delirious months, Mrs Jinkmandi had consorted with the stars. She had had her photograph taken with them. The director had invited her to the set. He had even suggested a walk-on part but Mr Jinkmandi had put his foot down. Her memories of those days when Jackie Shroff inclined a courtly ear or Govinda set her aquiver with his smile were worth the couple of crores that Mr Jinkmandi had put down.

At one time, in the palmy days of the studios, Mr Jinkmandi would not have got a look in; back then, the nascent industry did seem to be able to draw in committed and relatively clean financiers. But as the studios collapsed and the stars took over, the producers found themselves at the mercy of the whims and fancies—and often the greed—of their lead actors. As the reach of the cinema grew, so did the magnitude of the egos of the stars until finally they had managed to drive away almost all the 'good' money.

Simultaneously, the government treated Hindi cinema miserably. Taxes were high; raw stock was controlled; income tax raids were frequent. The attitude of the government towards the film industry—an old-fashioned brahmanical one, filled with a Platonic contempt for play actors and play acting—was also partly responsible for the money that rushed in to fill the vacuum. Suddenly, Bollywood was in bed with the underworld, perhaps the only section of society who had enough money and low accountability.

But the industry found that underworld dons were not just looking for a way to launder their money. They wanted a piece of the pie. They wanted a say in the casting. They wanted stars to visit them in Dubai and sing for them and dance for their birthday parties. They wanted to dictate who made what pictures, with whom and how. Middle-class fears of Bollywood were finally coming true, but not quite as one would have expected. Movie making in Mumbai had indeed turned out to be a dirty business: but it wasn't the sex, it wasn't the casting couch, it wasn't even the harm to the public aesthetic; it was the money that was dirty.

The daylight murder of Gulshan Kumar snapped Bollywood out of the underworld dream and slowly the industry has begun the painful process of reform. For a while, in the late 1990s, one heard of nothing but the corporatization of Bollywood. Films were being insured; companies were going public and even attracting foreign capital.

But the banks are now in Bollywood. This means they are investing your money in a game where the winners are a tiny percentage of the total. You might not want that to happen if you were to visit a film set. You might be forgiven for thinking the industry is in a state of terminal decline. The studios seem derelict, given over to pigeons in the rafters and goats on the plains. Everyone is either scurrying around in a terrible panic or standing around without purpose, their eyes blank, locking on to you for one moment of intense scanning until they dismiss you as someone who does not have any influence. The faintest whiff of this, a relationship across many degrees—being the friend of a cousin of an assistant director to a director whose last success happened a decade ago can be counted as enough—brings them to life. Nothing else does.

Inside, a small patch of a cavernous studio is illuminated and within it there is as much glitter, as much stimulation and as many beautiful people as the budget can stand. But the light boys and spot boys have no insurance; the extras get greasy lunches from fly-spotted vessels; the costumes come from a trunk; the toilets are backed up since the stars 'go' in their trailers and the wiring is a swarm of black-red-yellow snakes. Nothing is on time. No coherent direction emerges but over everything hangs a durable self-satisfaction, the stainless steel egos of those who know that they are part of the industry that attracts the maximum attention. After all, however secondary the role they play, this is the dream sequence for every Indian. The only thing that competes is playing cricket for India and now finally, in the era of convergence, these two dreams are coming together. The Great Gatsbys of India's mega-wealthy are now investing in the mania for cricket. The result is Shahrukh plus Sachin, Zinta plus Dhoni, and we can only imagine what that equation adds up to.

It is a damp, unhealthy place for money, this Bollywood. It defies reason and logic by surviving its worst excesses. Its observers have rung its death knell at regular intervals but no one goes to ask for whom the bell tolls. It does not go on by any alchemical magic or artistic excellence. It goes on by attracting capital.

Now that's magic.

~

THE FORMULA

One of the standard accusations against Bollywood till recently (and many still make it) was that it made films according to a formula.

I have never understood what this means.

There's a boy and there's a girl. There's also the girl's father who has disappeared, a mother who weeps a lot and a friend who cracks silly jokes. Despite father, mother and friend, the boy and the girl meet, frolic in public gardens and soon fall in love. Then society or one or more parent gets in the way and they are parted. They sing a sad song. Thereafter, someone or something or some animal reunites them.

Is that the formula?

There's a happy young man who lives in a happy small house with his brave widowed mother and his mischievous younger sister in a well-stuffed pink salwar-kameez. Then one day, he refuses to play nefarious ball with some villains. They blind his mother, rape his sister, poison the pet cockatoo and go home to a good dinner. The boy returns and drops all the gifts he has bought for his family with his first pay packet. He starts to cry, rages at god, cremates everyone, and turns into a criminal to avenge himself. Only a pretty young journalist who follows his career understands that he is not out there to acquire power or wealth, that he has a heart of gold. And she is indeed right: when he has killed all the villains, the young man turns himself in to the local police inspector who is his estranged younger brother.

That one? Was that the formula?

There are a mother and a father and two little boys. They fall foul of a natural calamity or a religious festival or a villain or a combination of all or some of the above. The children are separated from their parents and the parents too are separated. A childless police officer and his near-hysterical wife adopt the elder boy. A petty thief and a petty pickpocket and a petty bootlegger who may or may not be the same person adopt the younger boy. The elder boy becomes a police officer; the younger a petty criminal. The boys are reunited after the petty criminal has fallen in love with a rich girl and the police officer has met and been pursued by a gypsy. The young men join hands, metaphorically and literally, to beat up the villains.

That's the formula?

There's a young woman with a large carefree family for whom she slogs all day, quietly coughing blood into her hankie all night, while her boss thinks of her comely body and the young teacher across the road thinks of her as a goddess.

That one?

There's a middle-aged woman trying to look, for reasons unclear, like the young-daughter-gone-missing of a certain family. She finds a villain in the middle of this happy family she has adopted as her own. She gets on a horse, gets into a disguise, races to a makeshift stage to dance and sing her intentions and then whips the villain into a river.

That one?

In the depths of the forest, a ruined haveli with a door barred with chains and a wall-eyed caretaker who greets and spooks a young couple whose car has broken down on a full-moon night...

That one?

A young man...a gun...a girl...a gang...a politician...another gang...betrayal...a fast car...great gobs of blood.

That one?

It is obvious that no one actually knows what they mean when they say that X is a 'formula film'. The phrase suggests that there are no genres in Hindi film, one of those old accusations made by white men or coconuts (men who are brown outside and white inside) watching an alien art form and trying to squish it into categories they had created for their own dear cinema back home. They ignore, or, more likely, don't understand the ways in which Hindi cinema often consciously segmented the market.

Guru Dutt made *Chaudhvin ka Chand* (1960) to recover from the commercial disaster of *Kaagaz Ke Phool* (1959) because until then every 'Muslim social', as Islamicate films were called, had been a hit. When you went for a Rajshri Pictures film, you knew you would get two-hankie weepies with lots of young people singing beautiful songs and doing good and honourable things. When you went for an Amitabh Bachchan movie, you knew fists would fly.

So there is no one formula. And if there are patterns, that is to be expected. All forms of storytelling have their paths through the forest of human experience. And as they beat their way through the undergrowth, they craft a certain way of telling stories.

If that's the formula, sure, we have many.

~

THE HERO AND EVERYBODY ELSE

Bollywood operates with, as most popular mainstream cinemas do, a patriarchal worldview. It asks us to align ourselves with the interests of the hero. When he was a lover, we wept with him. When he was a city slicker, we followed the rake's progress. When he was a fighter, our bodies tautened in anticipation of the blows about to fall. This had repercussions for how the story was written, how the star system evolved and who got paid how much. It also meant that the hero bore the burden of the failure of the film.

The hero's dominance leaves very little space for other men. This was particularly the case before multiplexes and the metrosexual man changed some of the rules of the game. Till then, the hero's friends were almost always the comics: they wore clothes that revealed their stunted intellectual and emotional growth and they often seemed sex-starved to the point of caricature. All this pointed up the alpha male's superb lack of concern for the blandishments of the sexually available women around him. These were—and, overwhelmingly, still are—the vamps and the bad girls, whom he would always spurn in favour of his virginal heroine who would be waiting for him around the next corner.

The hero's father was a shadowy figure. He was either dead or had abandoned the family or was in jail. This left our hero free to worship the central deity, his mother, Maa, the goddess who welcomed offerings of blood. The Oedipal relationship between these two often left very little space for the heroines.

Most women in most Bollywood films were denied agency, and for all the modern gloss of the twenty-first century multiplex film, the virtues demanded of any respectable female lead are still the same: surrender, respect for the family and sexual innocence except when she is sharing the frame with the hero. Women do not do; they are done to. In the earliest phases of cinema, when their presence was a novelty, some of these women did become stars. Sulochana, a silent star of the 1930s, it is said, earned more than the governor of Bombay. But by the time we arrive at the talkies, the men have taken over. Once in every while a woman might surface as did Nadia ('Hunterwali') Wadia in the Fearless Nadia films, but even she was an exception. A whip and a pair of leather boots had alchemic power but it was ephemeral. Today, female stars still get paid less than male stars.

By the 1950s, men were defining cinema. When we speak of the golden age of Indian cinema, the defining names are male—whether they are directors: Raj Kapoor, Mehboob Khan, B.R. Chopra; actors: Kapoor again, Dilip Kumar, Dev Anand; music directors: Naushad, S.D. Burman, Madan Mohan; writers: Khwaja Ahmed Abbas, Sachin Bhowmick, Wajahat Mirza; lyricists: Shakeel Badayuni, Sahir Ludhianvi, Majrooh Sultanpuri; and so on. This should come as no surprise. Like most other industries in India, Bollywood was midwifed by men. Their morality was what influenced the development of Bollywood. It could be argued that this was basically a Hindu morality, the new, post-Partition Hindu morality that gave precedence to the Bhagvad Gita and to the idea of dharma as central to human life. But no faith can be translated into morality without it changing and being changed. If you add the needs of dramaturgy, some radical changes can be expected.

Consider *Mother India* (1957), which seems to have been ovarian in the formulation of the cinematic notion of Indian womanhood. When Radha (Nargis) is brought to her knees by poverty, widowhood (grass or otherwise is never made clear), flood and the hunger of her sons, she goes to the moneylender Sukhilala (Kanhaiyalal). She knows that she must repay him with the sexual favours that he has been suggesting will make him an easier creditor. We, as the audience, sympathize with this. Here, after all, is a woman on the verge of a breakdown. Was she to give and sell her body, who could blame her? In the hierarchy of interests, we have all been taught, the nation comes first, the group next, the family thereafter and the self, last. To sacrifice the self for the good of the family —its sons being its tenuous hold on posterity—should surely be allowed. And yet, at the last moment Radha refuses and begins the process of becoming a symbol.

This is where she performs the first of the two acts that will define her as Mother India. The second comes at the end of the film where she kills her own son in the defence of another woman who is about to be abducted and lose her foothold in society. This raises her otherwise unimaginable act to the status of disinterested benevolence; its value is enhanced since it is made at the cost of personal sacrifice.

Thirty years later— and some might argue that this was occasioned by the rise of Rekha who brought to her undeniable histrionic talent the baggage of her well-documented real-life tragedies—the courtesan began to cut a dash as a figure of romance. Of course, it is the oldest profession in the world, and members of the tribe had showed up on screen fairly regularly. Waheeda Rehman played Hirabai in *Teesri Kasam* (1966) and Meena Kumari played Nargis/Sahibjaan in *Pakeezah* (1972). But if we skip forward to films like *Bhavna* (1984; with Shabana Azmi as the eponymous lead) and *Aastha: In the Prison of Spring* (1997; with Rekha in the lead role of Maansi), we see how different the idea of sex-work is now. A woman may not just surrender to the importuning moneylender; she may turn sex worker in the interest of her family. Indeed, even the distance between Bhavna, driven by poverty to sell her body, and Maansi, who wants to be able to afford nice things for her daughter, is immense. Bhavna is seen as the victim of an unequal social system; Maansi is the victim of her own desires. But in both films we are expected to sympathize with the woman.

Each decade throws up its own notions of the abstractions that make up a moral code. Justice, for instance, took a hell of a beating with the rise of the Angry Young Man, Amitabh Bachchan, in the 1970s. Through the 1950s and 1960s, the court scene that came at the end of the film was foretold by a quick shot of the national slogan 'Satyameva Jayate' (Truth shall prevail) or by a shot of the goddess of justice wearing a bandage over her eyes and carrying a pair of weighing scales. And almost inevitably, truth did prevail, justice as a last-minute witness or a startling revelation saved the innocent and punished the guilty. Bachchan rewrote that scene forever. Now, justice would be served out on the streets and the courts would be reduced to a supporting role. Justice was often mocked, as in *Andha Kanoon* (1983) where in the climactic sequence Jan Nisar Akhtar Khan (Amitabh Bachchan) chases Ram Gupta (Amrish Puri) into the courtroom and kills him there. Then he challenges the courts to arrest him because he has already served a term for murdering the man who lies dead on the floor. Double jeopardy applies and the courts stand by helpless.

In this moment, we see the change in the definition of the hero. Until then, he was Saratchandra's Devdas, a man who cannot take on his father and so turns his rage against himself and loses. It is interesting to note that the only superstar who did not play Devdas, the self-destructive lover/loser, was Amitabh Bachchan. All the other three—Kundan Lal Saigal, Dilip Kumar and Shahrukh

Khan—have and all three films have been hits. But then Amitabh was the only actor to play Oedipus and destroy his father in *Trishul* (1975). And from Vijay, the powerful reformer of society, the vigilante who could take on the universe to keep it safe for his mother, we have now travelled to the age of Rahul. Rahul is Everyman with a manicure and a designer wardrobe. He has no agenda except to win the young woman on the train to Europe with him. His world is now intensely personal and the other Indias rarely impinge on him.

The heroine was almost always the positive pole in the moral universe of the popular Hindi film. But over the years she has begun to change too. In the 1950s, she was the woman in white, literally and figuratively. By the time B.R. Chopra released *Insaaf ka Tarazu* in 1980, she too had been reshaped by the zeitgeist. The film is best remembered for two sadistic rape sequences in which Ramesh Gupta (Raj Babbar) first rapes Bharati Saxena (Zeenat Aman), the woman who rejects his love because she is already in love with another man, and then her sister Neeta Saxena (Padmini Kolhapure). Finally, it is Bharati who takes up arms and kills her rapist, another reflection of Mother India. The climax of the film has her making a speech in court, which causes the judge (Iftikhar) to rise and renounce his robes since he is unworthy of his position.

Zeenat Aman herself is often referred to as a catalyst in the changing equation between Bollywood and its heroines. She and Parveen Babi were the new westernized heroines who wore miniskirts and swimsuits; they talked about free sex and often danced in their films without the time-honoured excuses of 'performing for charity', 'upholding our great traditions of dance' or just plain being in love with the right man and wanting to frolic a bit. But these women were still putative virgins and definitely good girls. Sheela (Zeenat Aman) may have just run out of the sea in a bikini in *Qurbani* (1980), she may be a cabaret artiste but when she discovers that Rajesh (Feroze Khan) has been stealing, she throws his ill-gotten gains into the fire. In *Purab aur Paschim* (1970), Preeti (Saira Banu) was shown drunk and staggering, clutching a cigarette and wearing a miniskirt but the love of the good Indian Bharat (Manoj Kumar) brings her home from the degenerate west where she has acquired her bad habits.

Through the 1970s, the westernized heroines were presented as *chanchal* or mischievous, perhaps a little misled, but they could always be brought back to sari-clad virtue. Whatever her dress code before love struck, a sari would always follow one of Kamadeva's flower-adorned arrows. But a few small cracks have begun to appear. In *Hum Tum* (2004), Rhea (Rani Mukherjee) sleeps with Karan (Saif Ali Khan) before they are married. Of course, this has happened before, as far back as *Aradhana* (1969) but the 'morning after' is always awash in female tears. Not so here. Rhea gets up and wonders whether Karan has realized his feelings and how special their night together was. When it is apparent that he has not, she stomps off in a huff, without a single tear. But perhaps the most telling film was *Murder* (2004). Simran (Mallika Sherawat) marries Sudhir (Ashmit Patel) when her sister dies leaving an infant to be cared for. In the line of familial duty, Simran has sacrificed her love for Sunny (Emraan Hashmi) until a cloudburst brings him back into her life and they have a frankly sexual affair. At the end, however, Simran does not pay by dying or being abandoned. The script forgives her. So does the audience. The film was one of the biggest hits of the year, which is remarkable even allowing for the number of times Sherawat and Hashmi locked lips and took their clothes off.

Until this moment, we did not want the 'bad' girl to get her man and settle down. Bachchan and Babi share the first on-screen post-coital cigarette in *Deewaar* but both die. Sahibjaan did get Salim (Raj Kumar) in *Pakeezah* but Meena Kumari had to die off-screen for the film to succeed: before her death, the film had been declared a flop. In every film in which Helen the 'cabaret dancer' found love, she also found death waiting for her.

Middle-class morality is now championed by television soaps, where overdressed women take on the world for joint family honour and jewels. But that's another story.

~

AB TERA KYA HOGA, BOLLYWOOD?

Of course, our cinema hasn't entirely re-invented itself, and perhaps *we* are to blame. As co-perpetrators of Bollywood, we can't make up our minds whether we want to be modern or we want to hark back to a rosy-tinted past. In a parallel development, there have been a whole string of retrogressive hits. This streak began with young Sooraj Barjatya's *Hum Aapke Hain Koun. . .!* (1994), in which young love is all set to sacrifice itself at the altar of duty until a Pomeranian called Tuffy plays *deus ex machina*. The next film of this kind was Aditya Chopra's *Dilwale Dulhaniya Le Jayenge* (1995), where a young man (Shahrukh Khan) courts his father-in-law and refuses to run away with his beloved when their marriage is forbidden. Then there was *Mohabbattein* (2000), also by Aditya Chopra, where a young man (Shahrukh Khan again) courts the man who drove his beloved to suicide. It fattened on the old-fashioned storytelling of B.R. Chopra's *Baghban* (2003) in which a father who has invested all his wealth in his sons finds that only his adopted son has any room for him in his old age. All these films were monster hits, which means that we saw something in them.

These films are probably our way of seeking return to a prelapsarian past. We have sought individuality by breaking with the family occupation. We have sought privacy by selling the family house and buying independent flats. But we all look back to the old homestead and now that the pressure is off and the pain of the slights and pricks is in the past, we hanker for the undivided family with all its self-sufficiency ('We had an entire cricket team at home') and its ability to account for everyone ('I never had to worry about where the children were'). These films act, it might seem, as the old moral science textbooks did. They clearly differentiate good behaviour from bad. The villains are inside the gate—the scheming uncle, the sharp-tongued aunt—and for those who have not found their way out of the family home for whatever reason, this rings a deep resonant bell.

But even as such films, once called 'family viewing' and at one time one of the great plots that drove Bollywood, become rarer, it also becomes clear that love—and not love of the socially disruptive kind—is now the prime mover. It was not always so. In the 1970s and 1980s, one of the clichés of dialogue, which a male star would say to another male star, was, '*Tumne ek dost ka dil toda, ek ladki ke liye*?' ('You've broken a friend's heart for a girl?') Into that line you could read a wealth of homosocial meanings, or simply the greater respect awarded to friendship over romantic love. Or perhaps the latest in a series of masculine wounds. The north Indian boy is wrenched from his mother and from the warm cosiness of female company. Then he is surrounded, cocooned, looked after and mauled by a bunch of men. Love breaks through this cocoon and *brahmacharya*, the phase of innocence and celibacy, is over. The young man must now take on the responsibilities of the householder; he must enter *grihasthashrama*. So that famous line may also have been the lament of those left behind in the march towards biological and social order. But whatever it was, it has died. Now the assumption is that your friends will help you woo your ladylove and once you have won her, they will fade gracefully into the background, accepting their exclusion.

Other lines have faded too. Practically nobody forbids a marriage with, '*Yeh shaadi nahin ho sakti*'. No one pleads with the moneylender for mercy with, '*Zamindar saaheb, mujhe thodi-si mohlat deejiye*'. The hero no longer comes home to declare that he has come first class first in his BA. The *dishoom-dishoom* of the fight scene has given way to the bark of submachine guns. Films no longer have to be sixteen reels. Comedians no longer have to be grotesques. To some, this is the beginning of the end of Bollywood-as-we-knew-it and the beginning of a Bollywood that is marketed for an international audience of NRIs or the high-end multiplex audience at home who live in London and New York in their heads. To others, it is the natural dialectic of every art form, especially art forms that begin to be consumed in new spaces and by new audiences.

At the same time, we can't seem to get enough of Bollywood. It's an extraordinary feeling. We are all free to love Hindi cinema as much as we want, now that we have all discovered that kitsch is cool. From being an illicit passion, Bollywood has become the new intellectual accoutrement, the hot new academic subject. Scholars of medieval art are writing stolidly about popular culture. The film *Om Shanti Om* (2007) could not have been made twenty years ago. It could only have been made in a moment in which we're all in love with the excesses of catsuits aglitter with sequins and big hair on the women. It's as if we've learnt to love only what we're about to lose.

Think of a folk dance leaving the village and arriving on the proscenium stage of an auditorium. Some steps will fall by the wayside. Others will be applauded and, therefore, repeated. A nightlong performance may be edited down to twenty minutes. The pace may be stepped up or slowed down. That's when a critic comes along and declares that the folk dance is no longer 'authentic'. That might be what's happening to Bollywood. If it's a new product out there, it's because there's a new generation of film directors taking over and they're bringing their own sensibility to the films they make. It is sometimes called *hatke* cinema and sometimes multiplex cinema and sometimes whaddaphuck cinema. But as long as it keeps offering majjaa, we'll be back for more.

NOTE

Through the course of this essay, I have used the term Bollywood, though I am aware that many in the film industry have a serious problem with it. But we cannot take pride in the way our cinema has taken its place among the cult cinemas of the world and reject the name that made it famous. We cannot pride ourselves in being India's pan-national pop culture and refuse a name popularly bestowed upon us: Google 'Bollywood' and you get 53,000,000 hits; perform the same Internet search with 'Hindi commercial cinema out of Bombay' and you get 26,000. Popular discourse will go with the name that is easier to say. Bollywood is easier to say. We make it easier to say each time we say it and we say it often enough.

Besides, those who object to it seem to feel that it might indicate that the cinema they make is derivative, a shadow version of what is turned out in Los Angeles. This argument would hold so much more water if the men who keep bleating it would actually boycott all films that are based on Hollywood originals; if they would refuse to lend their talents to such dubious and laughable enterprises; if they would spend some time thinking up new stories or spend some of their money actually making or supporting original films.

If all the above is not explanation enough, let me just say that I call Hindi cinema Bollywood with an insider's right to a name that may seem pejorative to others. I do not believe there is a Bollywood that can be composed only of those who perpetrate the cinema. Every art form includes, if only by implication, its consumers. We make it popular culture by consuming it and by naming it. And we named it Bollywood.

Chai-pani

. . . .

Ira Pande

Chai-pani, literally, tea and water, is a universally accepted Indian euphemism for a certain sum of money which always has to be kept aside for 'incidental and unaccounted expenses' in the course of dealing with officialdom. This can range from the simple sum that actually buys a cup of tea to a huge kick-back for a defence deal paid to a senior official: the difference is only one of degree. This is also perhaps why no one has actually spoken of eliminating it or even trying to tackle this problem. From time to time, outraged noises are made by well-meaning citizens and thundering editorials appear about it in national newspapers, but seriously, when so many of our elected representatives have been caught with their hands in the till and then rewarded with cabinet posts, it is a moot point whether we want this old chestnut roasted.

To understand the symbiotic relationship between the bureaucracy and chai-pani, I decided to go to the root. As ever, the best sources are our classical texts, for there is virtually nothing that our shastras have not tackled. The *Arthashastra* of Chanakya is one of the earliest treatises on statecraft anywhere in the world. Chanakya, a wily Brahmin, was to the Maurya dynasty in fourth-century BC India what Machiavelli was to the de Medicis of Renaissance Italy. It is said of Chanakya, that '...he protected the Mauryas as the eyelids do an eye.'

The *Arthashastra* discusses virtually every aspect of state life and protocol. On embezzlement alone, Chanakya has listed forty different types of graft. 'There are about forty ways of embezzlement,' he begins and then proceeds to list them as:

what is realized earlier is entered later on;
what is realized later is entered earlier;
what ought to be realized is not realized;
what is hard to realize is shown as realized;
what is collected is shown as not collected;
what has not been collected is shown as collected;
what is collected in part is entered as collected in full;
what is collected in full is entered as collected in part;
what is collected is of one sort, while what is entered is of another sort;
what is realized from one source is shown as realized from another;
what is payable is not paid;
what is not payable is paid;
not paid in time;
paid untimely;
small gifts made large gifts;
large gifts made small gifts;
what is gifted is of one sort while what is entered is of another;
the real donee [recipient] is one, while the person entered (in the register) as donee is another;
what has been taken into (the treasury) is removed while what has not been credited to it is shown as credited;
raw materials that are not paid for are entered, while those that are paid for are not entered;
an aggregate is scattered in pieces;
scattered items are converted into an aggregate;
commodities of greater value are bartered for those of small value;
what is of smaller value is bartered for one of greater value;
price of commodities enhanced;
price of commodities lowered;
number of nights increased;
number of nights decreased;
the year not in harmony with its months;
the month not in harmony with its days;
inconsistency in the transactions carried on with personal supervision (*samágamavisháṇah*);

> misrepresentation of the source of income;
> inconsistency in giving to charities;
> incongruity in representing the work turned out;
> inconsistency in dealing with fixed items;
> misrepresentation of test marks or the standard of fineness
> (of gold and silver);
> misrepresentation of prices of commodities;
> making use of false weight and measures;
> deception in counting articles;
> and making use of false cubic measures such as *bhájan*
> These are the several ways of embezzlement.

Chanakya, the old fox, then goes on to observe:

> Just as it is impossible not to taste the honey or the poison that finds itself at the tip of the tongue, so it is impossible for a government servant not to eat up, at least a bit of, the king's revenue. Just as fish moving under water cannot possibly be found out either as drinking or not drinking water, so government servants employed in government work cannot be found out (while) taking money (for themselves).

And finally, I came across this gem:

> It is possible to mark the movements of birds flying high up in the sky; but not so is it possible to ascertain the movement of government servants of hidden purpose.

HOMO HIERARCHICUS

Just as tea needs hot water, the institution of chai-pani is based on the symbiotic relationship between the politician and the bureaucrat. One without the other is a little like having tea without the leaves. Perhaps it all started with the mai-baap syndrome: a relic of the old feudal order where you came bearing gifts from your land if you sought a favour from your ruler. Whatever its genesis, it is now considered almost mandatory to offer some kind of gratification (even if a bouquet of flowers) to the person who can help you with your plea for help. From the peon who guards the entrance to offices to the PA who grants an appointment, the great chain of the bureaucracy extends like a leviathan across the corridors of power. It is best, therefore, to understand the various players that constitute this complex web.

For centuries, and long before this country was cast into the iron frame of the Imperial Civil Service, caste and gotra determined the hierarchies of power. Rulers consulted their court astrologers over horoscopes of suitable candidates to appoint as ministers and advisers. If the person had an ascendant Jupiter and a shining Sun in his horoscope, belonged to a known line of Brahmins and was proficient in Sanskrit, he was appointed to the court.

Naturally, therefore, these became the best templates for casting the new hierarchies of state power once the neo-Brahmins of the Imperial and the Indian Civil Service (ICS) were created. With slight modifications, these ancient norms have stood the test of time. Thus, if you replace the old horoscope with a good educational background, being a Brahmin with a facility for passing competitive exams and a knowledge of Sanskrit with an understanding of officialese, then you have the perfect candidate for the civil service. So, to a large extent, the ancient categories still stand as markers of fault lines across regions and administrative styles.

Let us now study a few prominent ones.

THE PENINSULAR BUREAUCRAT

This is the first kind—the Mysore Brahmin, along with his Dravidian cousins from Tamil Nadu (the famous Tambram) and Kerala (that may gradually harden into the Malayalee or Mallu axis of power)—and this is the category that stands at the pinnacle of the grand Pyramid of Power. Born and brought up in the Presidency towns of colonial southern India, the Peninsular Bureaucrat (henceforth PB) has a long and impressive lineage. The *adi purush* of this genre was an unknown Mysore Brahmin, who wore a gold braided turban on his head and always had files clamped under his armpit. To him and his ilk, we owe the land revenue records kept in scores of archives all over the country, till today an invaluable source of information and data. In a neat, slanting hand, there are precise margin notes wherein he has noted, in rupees, annas and pice, the amount of 'moneys' spent from the state treasury under various 'heads'.

The PB is also the earliest example of officialese (a form of coded language, almost as holy as Sanskrit, which in some sense it replaced) and the one who introduced Latin jurisprudence—terms such as inter alia, a priori, et al.—into the lexicon of state administration. I understand that textile historians have discovered that the earliest examples of red tape were found in the ruins of an old Mylapore *tharawad* when it was pulled down recently to make way for a new builder's block of flats. I believe traces of it were found buried under the holy tulsi plant in the courtyard.

The PB usually has long, unpronounceable names: this is because he respectfully includes all his ancestors, his village elders and his favourite gods into several prefixes (such as the initials K.V.S.K. or P.D.M.S.) before adding the Rao, Subramanium or Nair (depending on whether he is from Mysore, Tamil Nadu or Kerala) to his own (very often the littlest one), something as sweet and pronounceable as Kutty. So when someone called L.M.N.V. Rao arrives, one can tell that he comes from a village which begins with an 'L', his father was someone whose name began with an 'M' and his grandfather's name began with an 'N'. His own name begins with a 'V'. These clever mnemonic devices were adopted centuries before punch cards were dreamed up. Imagine! All that is missing in this litany is his village pin code and personal phone number but then he has had to think of forms to be filled and the spaces designated there. As the creator of several (if not all) such forms, the PB thus stops just short of those markers but he is still trying to figure out a way of doing it.

Never, therefore, underestimate the huge data bank that he carries behind that mark of Vishnu on his forehead. His disdain for short, snappy notes or for decisions that do not have back-up reasons running into pages and pages of flagged appendices stems from his firm belief that 'Yanything that is quickly done, is not praaperly done at all!'

His other great quality is his anonymity. Not for him the flashy North Indian life: no sir! He eats simple home-cooked food (idli-sambhar, dosa-sambhar or rice-sambhar) and is a vegetarian who likes vegetables which are grown only in his 'native parts' (this means his home state). His home is similarly austere and ungarnished, with basic furniture one-ly. His mornings begin with fresh *kapi*, which he drinks as he devours the newspapers and finishes a crossword or two. Then, a bath, a long puja, a wholesome breakfast and he hurries to his white Ambassador with the red light, muttering like Alice's white rabbit: 'I am late, I am late.' He is the first one in and the last one out from his office and takes no notice of the time when he prepares budgets, policy papers and drafts.

This is the person on whom the huge edifice of the government rests. He is the man whom ministers consult on matters of official propriety, state protocol, precedents and facts. He sits in on important and secret cabinet meetings, taking down meticulous notes, which he will possibly type up himself in the interest of state secrecy. He is also the person who stands respectfully behind the minister as important agreements are signed between nations. Never mind that you will never recall his face, it is his bandgala that you will never forget. Buttoned up to his neck, there is no greater symbol of discretion and rectitude anywhere in the Government of India.

THE KOI-HAI BUREAUCRAT

This one is the dark twin of the PB. In form and feature, face and limb, he is as unlike the faceless, anonymous PB as, say, Diana was from Camilla.

Born with the proverbial silver spoon in his mouth (later replaced with a pipe), this one is a born charmer. Fond of his whisky-soda and his golf, he has been educated at the best public schools of the country and has been through an undergraduate course in St Stephen's and then gone on to his father's old college in Oxford or Cambridge. This part of his life is an important part of his past for it gives him an aristocratic bearing that never goes, even in the darkest boondock posting he has to suffer in his early years. The local prince or feudal lord in the subdivision where he starts his career is often an old school or college mate. They call each other 'Bertie' or 'Pongo' or some Wodehousian name that recalls their prank-filled days at the old alma mater. Mater reminds me that his mother tongue is the Queen's English, which he speaks so suavely that he could be mistaken for an Englishman during a power cut. But then, power never gets cut when he is around. His horoscope probably had seven suns blazing in the house that denotes career.

His privileged educational background, to say nothing of the ICS ancestors behind him, gives him other advantages as well. Other bureaucrats look on with envy as he cracks jokes which begin with a hearty, 'Remember, old boy?' peppering the conversation at cabinet meetings, because the minister is another old Wodehousian mate. Koi-hai is witty, confident and sails in late to meetings without guilt. His office hours are tailored to take in power lunches, golf afternoons and bridge evenings. As he climbs the ladder, effortlessly it seems to the toiling masses, he gets enviable postings in the country's best public sector undertakings or plum foreign assignments in UN agencies. Koi-hai lives through life without once going to a Mother Dairy booth or the CGHS dispensary. This is why he has no idea of how inflation works on middle class incomes and often is the unfortunate coiner of slogans such as 'India Shining' and 'Pip-pip hurray'.

He is most comfortable with the ancien régime, disgusted with the dhoti-knicker walas (as he refers to non-koi-hais of both left- and right-wing persuasions) and distinctly uncomfortable with the rural types. However, once classed the baba log, only the most foolish among them still carry their prejudices very far. They have learnt, often the hard way, that globalized India did not just bring others into touch with the world formerly available exclusively to them, it also democratized the power base so broadly that it is now a battlefield where only the tough survive.

THE UP KAYASTH BIRADARI

Sometimes, history plays a part in human evolution. And sometimes, human evolution plays a role in creating history.

A good example of this symbiotic relationship between man and history is the kayasth civil servant, who comes mostly from Uttar Pradesh (UP), Bihar or Delhi. The kayasth was once the imperial scribe in the Mughal court, and chosen for several important reasons. Deracinated and unburdened by all the taboos that governed, say, the Brahmin courtier, the kayasth melded in him the Islamic and Hindu traditions of social etiquette so perfectly that to date no one can say where he fits in the Indian caste system. He is not immediately classifiable into any of the four classic varnas of Brahmin, Kshatriya, Vaishya or Shudra. In truth, he is a bit of all: learned in the classical languages, such as Sanskrit and Persian, he is able to straddle several planes of existence. For decades his suave manners and communication skills have won the hearts of those who do business with the Government of India. The kayasth can quote Urdu shairi, Sanskrit aphorisms and come up with the mot juste that can break the ice when horns are locked and ministries battle over budget allotments.

Up until the 1950s, the kayasth civil servant came from the Allahabad University matrix, when the Muir Hostel was regarded the nursery of the ICS. Long lines of Mathurs, Bahadurs, Narains and Dayals can be traced in the civil lists of those days. Then, post the 1960s, the power centre shifted to St Stephen's College in New

Delhi. However, what did not change was the special relationship the canny kayasth civil servant had forged with the power structure. Whitehall's Sir Humphrey Appleby, the civil servant in the long-running BBC series *Yes Minister*, that 'unflappable symbol of a machine that has no gears, only brakes', is a sort of Anglo-Saxon version of this model. The kayasth civil servant also possesses an enviable chameleon-like quality in that he can merge into the power structure so seamlessly that successive governments use the same advisers and policy planners.

Wily, quick-witted and a wordsmith par excellence, the kayasth is seldom at a loss for words or clever exit lines. Discretion and an uncanny ability to weave a power axis around him the moment he enters the upper echelons of power, the kayasth is about as difficult to prise away from the ship of state as the proverbial limpet from a sailing ship. Long after he has crossed the age of retirement, he continues to head commissions of enquiry or wield power as a governor of a state. His wife is generally a woman of substantial means (with a handsome dowry, if not handsome looks) and comes from a long lineage of civil servants herself. Thus, between them, the kayasth couple is related to virtually every other important kayasth couple. This is perhaps why, until a few years ago, every other cabinet secretary and home secretary was a kayasth.

THE SAFARI BABU

It is difficult to say when the safari suit and the civil service were married to each other but gradually the safari suit became the most popular uniform of the Government of India, known in its peculiarly Indian and official avatar as Bharat Sarkar. Just as the Gandhi topi and the dhoti were gradually dropped from the politician's wardrobe, white drill trousers teamed with the khadi bush shirt (bought at the annual Gandhi Jayanti sales from the local Khadi Gramodyog) were discarded sometime in the 1970s by the new and forward-moving bureaucrat.

With it came certain changes in the manner and pace of the sarkar. The amiable, paan-chewing, old-fashioned babu who had handled files at a leisurely pace, sipping hot, sweet chai supplied by the supplicant (hence the ubiquitous chai-pani quota mandatory for clearing files at lower levels) was gradually obliterated from public spaces. The new safari babu preferred to be treated with more style. A drink session with male friends (called a *sayshun* in matey terms, accompanied by much wink, wink and nudge, nudge) was now the best way to keep the movement of files smooth and wrinkle-free. In any case, it became firmly established by the early 1970s that nothing in the *gormint* moved without some grease. This could be something as innocuous as providing a car to drop the babu's missus to the market, or as substantial as footing the bill for the babu's daughter's wedding feast.

Matters reached such an alarming stage that Rajiv Gandhi once noted that of every rupee spent on the poor by the Government of India, barely fifteen paise trickled down. The rest got lost in the process of handling the funds. Along with the famed rope trick, the mystery of disappearing welfare funds is now a quintessentially Indian accomplishment. Files are lost in transit, relevant papers are untraceable, and all the CBI's men and all their sleuths cannot find the brain behind this heist. This is also why the same old trick is played on the Indian voter by the clever bureaucrat and politician. There are some holy cows that no finance department will ever question: schemes that relate to public welfare, anti-poverty measures, women and child (ouch!), minority matters, Dalit and unemployed youth . . . the combinations and permutations of this Bermuda Triangle are constantly invented by government servants at the time of budget plans so that money can be procured quickly before it lapses. How it is spent is another man's problem (or delight, as it may turn out).

Soon after he donned the safari suit, the Indian babu realized the benefits of hunting big game. Poverty is an industry that must be milked for all it is worth. Sometimes one wonders what will happen to ministries named Women and Child Development, Minority Welfare, NRI Welfare, Programme Implementation, etc. when India breaks free of the poverty circuit. Flood relief funds, disaster management cash, unemployment benefits—where will we ever find enough grassy meadows to put the army of unemployable men and women out to grass when that happens?

BUNGALOW BILL

This is a particularly rare breed of civil servant, for—unlike those who wish to race to Delhi and the corridors of power in North and South Block—this one never serves outside the provinces. This, in most cases, is not because his heart bleeds for the proverbially oppressed common man or *aam admi* or even the noble savage, but because life is so cushy in the outfields of power that he will happily live and retire as commissioner of a division. Bungalow Bill prefers to live in a style reminiscent of late Victorian or early-Edwardian Raj-style grandeur, so he joins the service primarily to enjoy the fruits of the service. These are first and foremost: a huge, sprawling house (called a bungalow), set in acres of land (called a compound), free electricity and water, free car and free phone, to say nothing of free rations as well.

There is a frightening quality of a time warp about life as a district collector or a commissioner. The nearest approximation is now to be seen in films about the Raj or television serials such as *The Jewel in the Crown*. Naturally, this lifestyle can be highly addictive. No wonder then that Bungalow Bill never wants to move out of the cushioned life of a late-nineteenth-century nabob. Where, he argues, will he ever replicate the grandeur of his little fiefdom?

Often the residence of a diwan in an erstwhile princely state was declared the official residence of the divisional commissioner when the merger of the princely states and the Indian Union took place. This is why the furniture and carpets alone in these bungalows are worth a king's ransom. Even though several valuable pieces have been 'accidentally' packed up with past officers' baggage when they were transferred, these old heritage buildings are awesome by any definition. A hilarious, but true, story told to me by an erstwhile commissioner's wife must be shared at this point. Their official bungalow, she told me, was so large that vast sections of it had never even been seen by her. Suddenly, it was found that the town was being raided by a cat burglar each night and no one could find out where he hid by day. One day, as she and her husband were having lunch on their lawn, they noticed smoke coming out of a window in a remote part of the house. Fearing a short circuit had triggered off a fire, everyone rushed to investigate. There, cooking his khichri on a stove sat the elusive cat burglar. He had figured that the commissioner's residence was the safest place to hide in and, when no one had caught him in weeks, he became a little reckless and started to cook his meals there as well.

Despite the generous support provided by the district agricultural officer and his team, it is virtually impossible to look after the huge acreage that goes with these residences. This is why enterprising officers cultivate wheat and cash crops, such as potatoes and onions. A large orchard full of fruit trees, such as mangoes and lemons, supply Bungalow Bill's family with enough produce to feed a small army. Add to this the cows and buffaloes, chicken and poultry pens, and you have a scenario where Bungalow Bill is like a squire of a small principality.

In addition to the fruits of the land, Bungalow Bill is served by scores of khidmatgars, paid for by the state. These range from sundry drivers to cooks, dhobis, sweepers and gardeners to personal valets (called khalasis), telephone peons and file-bearers. When Bungalow Bill leaves for office or goes to court to hear civil suits, the retinue that accompanies him would shame a visiting head of state. His cavalcade is preceded by a police escort car that races ahead of his white Ambassador and moves people out of the way. People salaam and bow respectfully as he sweeps past them and when he thinks it is time for a nap the court clerk announces the court suspended!

The official bungalow is perhaps the single most important perk of office in the civil service, for along with it comes the life-support system provided by the state. Not surprisingly, many of the old bungalows are haunted. I'll wager that the resident ghost is an old commissioner who misses this pastoral life even up in heaven.

THE ABOMINABLE NO-MAN

This is one of the most frightening types of bureaucrats, mostly because he can be found embedded at every important level of government. Trained to stall and intimidate by relentless questioning, he has perfected to a fine art the nasty business of saying no. Although his heyday was in the age of the licence raj, yet even today in the brave new world of globalized India, he can spell terror as he scans documents and proposals through his bifocals before he allows entry to an MNC or passes a payment the government owes you.

Each ministry has a Financial Adviser (FA) and in nine cases out of ten this is the Abominable No-Man. His brain works faster than any calculator and he can tell by just looking where the figures have been inflated slyly for stashing away profits, where sums have gone askew and where the government is being short-changed. No minister will ever disregard the discreet cough from the FA at the negotiating table. And when the pre-budget meetings are on, papers are presented after a silent prayer to the Almighty that the FA will overlook a certain addendum at the bottom of Annexure 3(i) in Item 4(x).

Often, this is also the species that has the smug I-know-it-all look. He knows, you see, that the buck stops with him quite literally. So sure is he that no one can get past him that he swans around with an air of impossible smarminess. His contempt for the world outside his door is palpable and his delight in pointing out the fine print that gives him the power of veto in any decision relating to his ministry has been known to raise blood pressures in the stoutest hearts.

In nine cases out of ten, the Abominable No-Man has been a Keen Type Probationer (KTP) during his training years. The KTP in the lexicon of the IAS training programme is the equivalent of the teacher's pet in school and thus cordially disliked by his peers for the same reasons. The KTP's assignments are always done on time; he is awarded the President's Medal at the end of the training period for his excellent reports and attendance. Yet, somewhere along the way to the top, he loses it. His attention is ever paid to the goal, seldom to the means. Thus, his official targets are scrupulously met, even if they are the cause of ruin and rack to countless sufferers. He is the heartless officer who will hold back pensions from being released because certain documents are not in order. His commitment is to the Consolidated Fund of India and in the pursuit of the last penny owed to the state he often loses the human touch or even the ability to smile. As he grows closer to the top, his lips thin and his brow is furrowed with deep frown lines.

After he retires, he finds he has no friends left. Call it the eternal curse of Midas but as one wise old bureaucrat once said: 'The people you meet on the way up are also the people you meet on the way down.'

THE SECURITY BRIGADE

It is difficult to say when the Government of India was taken over by the security specialists but they are here to stay. They lean dangerously from white Ambassador decoy cars as they speed down the city, sirens hooting and lights flashing madly to escort their charges hither and thither. As the years flash into decades, the security brigade is becoming like the Texan cowboy: so trigger-happy that often they shoot before they shoot a question at an imagined intruder.

One of the first rules of the power game is that once you have won the closeness you seek don't ever concede the turf to anyone else. The top guys here are those that guard the First Family. They create a cordon sanitaire so tight that no one can get within sniffing distance of the baba and the baby. Slightly less intimidating are the security personnel that surround the prime minister. Perhaps this is so because no one has so far ever threatened to kill him. They are mostly reduced to opening doors and barking down orders to traffic personnel to clean the streets of traffic for hours before he travels out of the prime minister's residence. Sadly, this proximity to power also makes them denizens of an illusionary world. Some of them actually begin to behave like the politicians they protect and if taken off VIP duty, fall prey to a terrible depression. The normal world, where people cannot be shooed off the road, or a situation where they have to queue up like everyone else, reduces them to rages of such magnitude that they can resort to violence.

'*Hum kaun hain, jaante ho?* Do you know who I am?': this simple sentence is as well-known in their circles as that line from the 1970s' blockbuster film, *Sholay*, where Gabbar Singh asks, '*Ise bata de hum kaun hain.* Tell him who I am.' Okay, so I made up that dialogue but you get my point, don't you?

The security brigade is also a firm believer in the conspiracy theory. India is under constant threat according to them: from the Pakistanis, the Bangladeshis, the Maoists, the Taliban . . . the list is endless. Every shrub and leaf is inspected; every pedestrian moved away so far that the rulers of the land never see the people they rule. Like Colombian drug lords, they live behind walled fortresses and move in cars with tinted windows. Markets and shopping areas are cleared of people, wedding guests made to stand in humiliating queues until the photo-op with the High and Mighty has been performed with the security personnel as the audience. The mahurat of weddings, even timings for funerals, are sometimes altered to suit the Great. *'Aa gaye, aa gaye . . .'* goes a ripple and necks are craned to see those who rule us. Alas, all one can see is the Black Cat Commando, Kalashnikov at the ready, prepared to shoot anyone with suspicious bearing.

However, in the provinces, security personnel undergo an interesting mutation. The Black Cats become Tame Pussycats, as they escort the boss's children to and from school, or accompany his rogue son on night prowls through the city's hotspots. The lean, mean guard becomes the amiable Mishraji or Yadavji, or sometimes just 'Shadowji'. He is an extension of the family that rules and makes full use of this heaven-sent proximity to power to get his children admitted to the best schools, his wife to get bargains from the market, his no-good brother and brother-in-law to get gas agencies, petrol pumps or at least a plot of land from the discretionary quota of the netaji.

THE KNOW-IT-ALL

One of the most hateful species of bureaucrat, he is also the worst kind to get stuck with on journeys and parties. A poor listener—let us just say that his receiver is always off and his transmitter forever on—in a loud voice he will tell whoever is willing to lend him an ear how he has saved the country from the brink of disaster on countless occasions. This is also the person who discovers his spine after he retires and becomes a furious writer of letters to the editor and can be seen at seminars and public lectures, hand eternally raised. Very often, the question he asks has little to do with the matter being discussed but everything to do with his famous opening line, 'When I was in the ministry of...'

If one were to believe every claim he makes, one would imagine that the ship of state sank after he left it. But often the truth is that he was a spineless toady who never took a decision. He discovers his lost vertebrae after he retires and when invited to speak at seminars in that famous Dead Poets' Society, the India

International Centre, he will hold his audience spellbound with the long litany of achievements that he spearheaded. He can be spotted after retirement sitting in the reading room of some public library (because he is too miserly to buy more than one newspaper now), hoping that someone in power will spot him and perhaps offer him an assignment.

The Know-It-All will lobby shamelessly for a post-retirement sinecure and continue to haunt the corridors of power until he actually gets one. The sad truth is that having milked the system for years to extract every privilege that is allowed under the rule book (and some that he slyly coaxed), he cannot survive a life bereft of the life-support system of a PA (who can handle all his personal paperwork as well), a sarkari bungalow, telephone, and a car and driver. Such bores can go on shamelessly for years, serving on commissions of enquiry that never submit their reports on time. And if they do, they are seldom worth the money that was spent on them.

Sadly, their tribe seems to increase by the year. Sometimes one is led to believe that there are almost as many civil servants serving the government after they retire as there are legitimate ones. Perhaps this makes a strong case for extending the age limit for retirement to sixty five (or until death, perhaps). After all, why should just the hustlers be rewarded?

LADY OFFICERS

It is not just enough that their gender difference demands a separate category for these officers. It is that their role and place in the civil service must be understood at various levels.

The colonial Imperial Civil Service did not have any lady officers. It was very much a male preserve and the travails of a district life, the loneliness of life in the remote outposts of the Empire, to say nothing of the gruelling calendar of tours on dusty village roads—all these were considered beyond the physical and mental limits of women.

Independence changed all that: with universal suffrage came the freedom for Indian women to choose any profession. This included the civil service. A distant great-aunt, who passed away recently at the age of ninety-something, was the first woman officer of the IAS. Aunty Esha, as she was called, was a Christian lady who married a great-uncle, privately called Uncle Tom by the family. His actual Brahmin name was Girish Chandra Joshi but after he married Aunty Esha he was discreetly cast to the outer boundaries of the orthodox Kumaoni community. Naturally, as deference to his exalted status (his wife was a member of the Provincial Civil Service of the United Provinces) he was given the respect due to a prince consort. After the merger of states took place, Aunty Esha became the first woman IAS officer in independent India.

Memories of her visits to Almora help me reconstruct what it must have been like to be an officer and a lady. She always sat with the men, talked to them as if she was one of their own gender and was looked upon by the Kumaoni women as an androgynous being: half man–half woman. In short, they never knew quite how to deal with her: she was a woman but she did a man's job and belonged to a world beyond the women's quarters.

To some extent, this confusion has remained a part of the mindset of the men who run the Government of India. Thus, while women have been given equal opportunity in terms of jobs, a subtle form of discrimination is practised against them when it comes to the distribution of power. In the states, until the late 1960s, women were seldom given independent district charge. To date, there are certain 'soft' ministries that are informally reserved for women. In all the years since independence, there has been just one woman cabinet secretary and one woman foreign secretary. The ministries of defence, finance, revenue, economic affairs or home are informally reserved for 'men only'. Ironically, in a country where women in politics have a standing and acceptance that even the UK and USA are not prepared to concede, our women civil servants are treated rather unfairly.

What is more, this debate has a distinctly male–female perspective. Thus, while most women civil servants feel that the service is blatantly sexist and patriarchal, the men make unkind remarks about those women who try to compete with them in the corridors of power. While some brave women have taken the service head on and fought court cases and media battles against unfair treatment, others simply give up the fight and float along on the sidelines until it is time to knit socks for their grandchildren.

Sadly, in the lower rungs, at the level of stenographers and clerks, women seem to fulfil most of the clichés about their tribe. From filing nails to playing Madame Defarge behind their desks, women officers are harsher, more unforgiving and impossible to rouse to efficient dispatch of work. Many suffer from a sort of bipolar disorder of being a woman in a man's world and that does them no good.

Until a few years ago, it was believed that women were incorruptible and more honest; this is no longer true. For when women fall prey to greed, they can outdo most men in this department. In Uttar Pradesh, when the IAS Officers' Association held a poll on the most corrupt bureaucrat, the winner (shamefully) was a woman.

THE GREAT TRAIN OF BEING

Think of the civil service as a long (or gravy) train: in front is the engine (the cabinet secretary) leading the long line of attendant carriages and chugging along a set path. One false move and the whole train goes off the tracks.

Behind the engine is a series of compartments. The first among these are the executive class or the luxury first-class coaches: these are the various secretaries to the Government of India. The compartments are fitted with ultra-comfortable seats and the service here is first-rate. Gloved waiters glide up and down and regularly ply the passengers with drinks and snacks and meals. These are the top-most men and women in the government: the home secretary, the defence secretary, the foreign secretary and so on. Yet, here too there are secretaries and secretaries. Although they are all entitled to the same top-class service, some are more equal than others.

The next category of compartments is a chain of air-conditioned chair car coaches. Over the years, these have become a little grubby and the service is no longer what it once was. The waiters pull out the cutlery from their pockets when they serve the meals and the toilets are to be used only when holding on to one's bodily waste is impossible. However, the air-conditioning is good and the chairs not too bad. This is where the Class I officers of the government would find themselves. Once again, proximity to the minister decides the level of service available. The simple thumb rule is: the closer you are to the source of power, the more comfortable your ride through the rough and tumble of the journey of life. The others live in hope: India's abiding faith in the great wheel of life has equipped all of us with a sense of optimism that stems from the knowledge that, one day, those at the bottom will rise to the top. All it takes sometimes is a simple general election; the rest is done by the great karmic law of the government that ordains that the kingdom of heaven is open to those who are empanelled. Others have to undergo the purgatory of a review before the sun shines again in their house of work.

Finally, there is the ordinary compartment: here, a person is lucky to get place at all. It is also the most crowded part of the train and everything operates under tremendous pressure. Everything is in short supply: from the seats to the water in the loo, and the food and bedding at night. The passengers of these compartments may complain and grumble, but it is mostly good-natured whining. Deep down, they all know how fortunate they are to find a place at all on the train that one day will reach the El Dorado of a full pension, a hefty gratuity and medical insurance till death. In India, there is no better mode of transport.

This is how the country has chugged along for millennia—on a train that is fuelled neither by coal, nor diesel nor electricity. It runs on chai-pani and as long as there is a giver, the takers will miraculously arrive. It is like the kettle bubbling eternally on the hob ready to provide succour and energy. Occasionally, there are setbacks but which railway system in the world has not faced problems from time to time? The important fact to keep in mind is that men may come and men may go but the train chugs along forever. A raid here and a graft case there may offload a few from it, but ultimately someone, somewhere devises another way to bring it back on track. The train toots delightedly and everyone lives happily ever after.

Republic of Enaristan

. . . .

Sanjay Suri

How will an Indian in India ever understand the importance of being called that word in London? That word which is never as rude to sisters as those who don't use it seem to think; those who do are only spontaneously respecting the traditions set by our forefathers and shared by so many others that we share a world with. The word that's like a punctuation mark that marks also the tone of the language before and after; the word of only apparent abuse that more often announces endearment; the word that captures a world, at least the world of the north Indian male. The word that brings down barriers and opens hearts.

I do here report my exhilaration when Mr Sidhu said it to me, but don't really expect everyone to understand my feelings on hearing it. Or the fact that Mr Sidhu and I really became friends only after that. Up until that time we had only shared some transplanted similarities of separately landed Indians; then on we became connected, rediscovered ourselves as members of a bonded community in a place where it could have been so easy not to.

It was an unforgettably blissful moment. We'd gone out shopping in Hounslow for dinner that Mrs Sidhu was going to put together for us. I was struggling with something as simple as opening a plastic bag. 'Can't do even this,' Mr Sidhu said, and that mild exasperation provoked the magic moment. Sometimes the banal, if not the ridiculous, can produce the sublime. In any case, we have all experienced those times when the expression of little irritations throw people apart and, less frequently, pull them together.

Time and place had of course to be in place for the rest to become possible. We were both categorized NRIs because our separate postmen knew our addresses by heart by now. What we shared through what others saw as our mutual NRI-ness lay less in our adoption of both India and England than, in their separate ways, their formal but uneasy adoption of us. Or, the unacceptance. Indians dislike us for leaving, maybe for getting to be the ones who left. The British, mostly, accept us the way some BJP moderates accept Muslims on the grounds that they can't after all be thrown into the sea. In India you call this kind of acceptance secularism, in Britain multiculturalism. Neither arises from the heart. It's like turning Gandhian because you've run out of ammunition.

This state is quite commonly spoken of as a spanning of two worlds, or even a shunning by them. But it is really not about either or both, but a third. Our occupation, and the perception of others, creates something other than either, just as looking through differently coloured slides creates a new colour. Rather than a bit of both, the NRI really has citizenship of a third state, and it's a little surprising why this has not so far been duly recognized as Enaristan. It is our common citizenship of this third space, state really, that made it so deeply significant for Mr Sidhu to call me, yes, that.

A word from one land spoken on the land of the other can take on quite different meanings, or at least become meaningful in different ways. Like this magical connector of a word. But in London it had progressed from connection to mark a fusion of land, location and experience; it became *bhenchod* plus. That defining word of the Indian male unfettered by shyness or sahibdom had been spoken in London. In travelling, that word too, like us, had become Enari. On the well-established scientific and sociological principle that the whole is usually greater than the sum of its parts, this word too, in travelling from one world to find voice in another, developed into something more than a linking word between individuals; in travelling like us it became the language of our third world because it informed itself that in moving from one soil to another it too had changed to take on a new meaning beyond inorganic juxtaposition. Anyone who isn't squeamish about these things will not quarrel with a suggestion that in India use of the word is traditional. In India those traditions are safe (as we hear all around us). In foreign lands you have to work at them because you need to connect with others who are also reworking these traditions into their lives. It is a deliberate means of rediscovering fellow humanity in a newly-installed world.

In saying it, Mr Sidhu had reached out. Because he said it deliberately, and not by way of reflex release of cultural baggage; that might have been the case had he spoken it spontaneously on, say, dropping some of the shopping accidentally. Mr Sidhu said it like he was almost imploring appreciation over its use, in the full confidence that I'd take it as distance-cutter, not abuse. The word was delivered self-consciously—like a verbal hug that carries the depth of a cultural bond.

The essential NRI never ever gives up saying the word—or something else of which it is the metaphorical equivalent, though somehow there isn't quite another bridging word as this one. And he must say it a little self-consciously, to emphasize linguistic rootedness that triumphed over physical transportation. Spoken in Enaristan, the word carries the magic of 'open sesame' to rediscover a newly transformed treasure.

Regular countries don't know these things. It's only the accompanied but immeasurable baggage migrants carry that can build new worlds within countries with old building blocks that take on a new shape through the transportation. Mr Sidhu and I could theoretically have left that word behind, and England is of course too ignorant to know it. But the NRI is forever trapped between the business of shedding selectively and preserving carefully. There's no preservation like self-preservation, and no self-preservation that does not include a connection with accepting others—because that is then the same thing as solitary confinement. At least as much as the hard currency he left for, the NRI seeks the currency of human connection and acceptance. Society gives us a few magic words sometimes that are a short-cut to acceptance.

Between Mr Sidhu and me, one word, one moment, transported us from circumstantial similarity to cultural commonness. That magic moment worked for me and Mr Sidhu; no doubt, other words, other ways have worked for others. But essentially, it's quite the same thing. The NRI is not just some being out to make money; he is essentially a being in a new habitat searching hard, even desperately, for connections and commonality.

I shall for long carry the regret that I failed immediately to honour Mr Sidhu as he had honoured me. I did make up for this lapse later, but only well past the magic moment. I can only say in my defence that I was overwhelmed at the time.

FOUNDER, NOT FLOUNDER

We sometimes forget, when we re-launch into our abuse of the NRI, how much more it takes to earn that title than simply to land in another country and return only as visitor. That bare circumstance can make someone an NRI for government purposes; for purpose of life, NRI means so much more, just as we are so much more than our CVs. In fact our own understanding of that somewhat scorned word the acronym has congealed into is a lot richer than the official one. It is informed by status, and then enriched by image.

We have seen for ourselves that every NRI goes through a rediscovery, even a re-assembly. That annual NRI arrival wearing something, anything, not Indian; those early photographs of Satti uncle standing before a long car; or of Billo below pigeons so well-behaved that they dropped on her not a thing; that calling of 'and' 'ayund'...the files at North Block and South Block fail completely to address the difference between the official NRI and the essential NRI.

The difference is important because every paper NRI is not a real NRI. To be a real NRI you have to do NRI-like things. A few don't; they strain to metamorphose into Western beings and therefore fail to qualify. These are nowhere people—they are not Indian, not British or Canadian or whatever, and certainly not NRIs. If an NRI is so much more than an Indian only separated from the rest by passport, paperwork and location, what then makes an NRI? The citizenship test for Enaristan included here covers several essentials, but that cannot fully access the inner spirit of the NRI. Some things just drive the NRI. Anyone can be a father, the NRI needs to be Founding Father.

Like those who appeared, made their appearance rather, at the Variety Programme of Indian Dances held by Hindu Council, Brent (Brent meaning Indian Wembley). When did an Indian in India last go to a variety show? Those delightfully unsophisticated events went out of people's lives a couple of generations ago, last honoured, that anyone can remember, only in a 1960s' film. Indian England still has them, and only because of our founding fathers.

'Halo Boab', a founding father announced from stage. He appeared to have suddenly metamorphosed from the event programme where it said 'Welcome of Guests'. It was cool to say hello to Bob whatever from stage, it was so very confident not to let stage and mike stand in the way of easy informality. And it was confident, too, to speak neither word the way the usual English do. Much more than saying hello to Bob, he was saying something about the NRI. The NRI is overawed by white attention, but never allows such awe to induce him into any compromise of the self. In fact he must not know how to. He must be aware of others but only in a way that never extends to how they might be aware of him.

One more founding father was announced; they need to be introduced in order to remind everyone just how much they have done, even though everyone naturally knows all that already. But you get these association elections, and before a voting sort of audience, it's good to let people know, again. 'Two lovely ladies will enter you tonight,' he announced. He paused with a sense that he might have to do that bit again. 'Two lovely ladies will entertain you tonight,' he continued, unmindful of what he had at first said. He, too, was saying less about the ladies and the show than about himself. The NRI always continues regardless. He must never see himself as some English would see him, or as some Indians think the English might see him. The NRI takes the position of cultural other unmindfully unembarrassed. The NRI must produce children who are embarrassed for his sake, but he must never be for his own. The children must hope that their parents will remain unwitnessed by white people; thankfully they are rarely around, and if they are, be forgiven by this culture of correctness that smothers judgement of any other.

The founding father is easy to spot even when he's not on stage, and at this event were many who were not. But they all wore the founding father badge—that ribbon frilled into flower shape above two shiny legs. There's something about Indians and ribbons that round into flowers. No one else ever seems to wear them. To Indians they are the mark of someone who is not just anyone. Everyone may not read the name and position recorded on the pink chart paper within the circling ribbon, but everyone will see the flower itself. A nameplate on your uniform at Heathrow can only make a complaint against you easier. Here, it's the mark of leadership. And, someone had to wear a suit over sneakers; we do need to be supportive of the NRI for placing himself, quite voluntarily, in that courageous position.

The NRI works on weekdays and leads on weekends. The usual English wears suits on weekdays, the NRI on weekends. These he must wear to a meeting of some association or other—the Brent Indian Association, the Baavis Gam Patidar (Patel) Samaj, the Lohanna Community of North London...any will do. It's a quite global convention for leaders to wear suits. Or for aspiring leaders. Because others must come with some ambition of joining the executive committee and then rising to presidency.

NRI is essentially a political post. At its heart, politics is an engagement with action that is driven by more than individual concern and personal wealth. It implies concern about the plight of fellow humans, fed by a sincerity that you are the one who can sort them out. If, then, fame and position come to you, that is the just fallout of your exceptional abilities and all the work you have put in. Like all presidents everywhere, the NRI president is driven by the nobility of a readiness to accept the greatest possible responsibility that the realities of the world around you will permit.

The difference between the NRI president and those of the United Nations sort is not as great as may first appear. Plenty of countries have a population of only a few thousand. The International Punjabi Society has immensely wider reach. Some Patidar samajs have membership bigger than the adult franchise of some countries, a fallout of the fact that god blessed Indians with so many of us.

We all live the difference between the world and our world, and ours is of course all that matters. Our sense of others is not the total living body count on earth, it's the number of others that are significant for us. An Indian association provides world enough to the NRI. Think of the number of times an NRI president, or even an NRI near-president, which is just about everyone, can get to speak on mike from the stage to a hall packed with people, like the better-known presidents do.

The essential difference lies in the flexibility that an NRI president brings to the job. A regular president cannot lose an election and go set up another lot of people to elect him; an NRI president can. It's like assuming presidency first and getting in the country afterwards. The NRI doesn't just understand that people can sometimes make the wrong choice—he acts on it, he chooses the people who then can make the right choice: him.

Every NRI is either a president, ex-president or near-president. The best among them are all three at the same time. You were president of another association before you left because of differences arising from the unfortunate choice of a wrong candidate in the elections to set up the association of which you are now president, while you consider, what you are told, is the option of heading another, because when you're as good as you, the word spreads.

The founding father does not like to found, then to find that he is about to be replaced by another founding father. He then founds another Indian association to father. Not a breakaway group—that is only what ignorant others say. He always founds the real group, and the real people are always with him. At some stage in life, every founding father finds himself saying mine is bigger than yours. But his faith in human judgement is weak because through his life he has seen too many others prepared to elect someone else, the wrong kind of people. It's always very trying to encounter obviously lesser people who imagine they are better than you know you are. Too often he has seen people who failed to appreciate the sacrifices he made through leading them. And yet he offers them another chance.

Maybe it was the experience of Partition that put into his mind partition as a constant possibility to ensure self-rule. So if you have an International Punjabi Society, you must also have a World Punjabi Organization; if you have a Khukhrain Biradari, you must then have another; if you have a Punjabi Society of the British Isles, you must have a British Sikh Organization. The Wanzas, Gujarat's tailors, have between them a fair directory of Wanza associations, and nothing will stitch them together again. The Patels had an association in south London and that necessarily had to be followed by a federation in north London. NRIs bond together only when they run out of a partitionable population. About the only thing founding fathers agree on after fighting and going their different ways is on the need to speak of unity.

There are of course NRIs who do not rise to presidency. They get restrained by realism. Or, as the founding fathers would say, they just weren't cut out for leadership. But have no doubt that the vast number of NRIs at some time or other take position in some association or other. And among the exceptions to those, mere membership isn't mere. On this scale every vote really does count, and Kingmaker has always been a powerful position. It can, after all, sometimes be more important to be pursued by presidents than to be president yourself. To then let drop a remark over dinner how several presidential candidates have been after you, and that you're thinking about it. The proper NRI is always, in some way or other, engaged in a civil war.

You don't get that a lot among the newer lot, which is why they can never be real NRIs; these are just upstartish relocators. Their refusal to engage in institutional quarrelling disqualifies them from real NRIhood. This unnatural abstinence of theirs leads to confrontation with a cruel truth: that the NRI, the real NRI, is a species headed for extinction. Not the new arrivals not his children, certainly not his grandchildren, will either replace or even remotely replicate his capacity to do things, undo them, and then redo them his way. Only when we have lost the subject of our contempt will we be sorry for our uncharitable thoughts about the NRI. We will want more of the old to say the same things about, but it will be too late, too late.

There's a difference between a migrant and a relocator, even if relocation lasts long enough eventually to congeal into migration. Because, unlike the NRI, the relocator of today is neither a builder nor a destroyer, or ideally both. He's in it for himself, the individual on the move with family in tow, and staying that way. He is the globalized raider, who makes his own money, minds his own business. You can't do that, the second that is, and be NRI. The NRI who minds his own business is paper NRI, not proper NRI. These new individualists betray society and history. The NRI does it for himself, but through a connection with others, through leading, or through leading others into leadership because no NRI is so unimportant that he will be just a follower. But these new chaps are proud of their disconnection, at shameful ease with being in it for themselves. The NRI created space, the new arrivals only fill vacancies.

SHINING GHETTO

That the proper NRI lives in a ghetto is a distinction that would be considered dubious only by Indian snobs. There's a case here for the critical Indian to turn some judgemental inclinations back on the self, if only for a moment. Something doesn't sound right with the questions that can get thrown at the poor rich NRI.

'What? You go and live in the West, and still stuck to your old ways, are you? Don't mingle with people from the host country? You go and live in a ghetto, with only Indians around you? What's the point of going to live abroad?' Or, 'What, just because you live abroad you have forgotten your own people, your own culture? Trying to be too much like the gora. You go and live with gora neighbours but they don't accept you, actually they don't say it but they want you out. Can't blame them, the way you go and spread filth in their country.'

The problem is in our perception. We damn a Patel for being himself, and then also for being no other. In damning the NRI either way, we might be saying more about ourselves than about him. It doesn't matter what we say so long as we're really saying the NRI can't do anything right. Or, we split the NRI into the thinking ones who live outside ghettos and the Southall types, the Wembley types. The few who've got it right, and the many who are doing it all wrong. The ones we abuse one way, the other, the other. Our own middle-class baggage—the middle class has always been the muddle class.

The NRI has frustrated the city Indian for generations. The city Indian has the sophistication, but the NRI the London address. We all dislike what we see as undeserved wealth, and the NRI presents himself as a ready species deserving of it. There will always be others who have more money, but the NRI's more is a little more exasperating. Crude fellows, England (and they call it Englaand) is so wasted on them, and to think that the British, the real British, might judge city Indians from what they see of NRIs. And the

Indian Indian's sophistication plays out unwitnessed. It's cruel to the progressive Indian that the land of Keats and Shakespeare should also be the land of Southall and the factories that the Southall Indians went to work in. That these uneducatable things should live amidst style, and that ours is betrayed by loadshedding and beggars outside the car window. We feel so unjustifiably leapfrogged over. How much better that NRI access, that address, would have been granted to us.

And never then would the Indian Indian have moved into one of these ghettos. These are for people we call all sorts of things—backward, illiterate, vague, even disgusting. But why? Living in an alleged ghetto, as most NRIs do, is sensible, natural and wonderful.

Living in a ghetto is only another extension of marrying the likes of your own; everyone does. You can globalize money but not people; cultures are not quite as convertible as currency. That word 'ghetto' is after all only an unkind translation of 'tradition'. A village that transplants itself into another's country becomes a ghetto. The principal problem with it is the perceived impertinence of setting up an Indian village in hard currency where the electricity and water don't go. The Indian village we romanticize, the transplanted one we revile.

In peculiar, even desperate ways, the NRI needs a village to live in, or the village principle to live around. Define a ghetto, say, as a neighbourhood you share in a foreign land with cultural kin. It's a club with free life membership. Nothing much wrong with that, except that it doesn't sound terribly successful. A pity that an Indian who succeeds must then show it by moving out of the ghetto, so that success has to be un-Indian in some way. You can't work for J.P. Morgan in the City of London and then go home to Southall.

But the not-so-successful stay on in ghettos, looking to other successes. Like the preservation of a daughter's virginity and promoting the chance that it will be lost only in an approved bed and at the appropriate time. This need does not just concern the NRI, it drives him. A ghetto carries administrative translation as catchment area; that means children go to the same school where others keep an eye on you, and with a far fewer number of those of the foreign kind around, it brings that much less risk of a daughter going off with a bloke of the wrong kind. University later brings no such protection, but ghetto school can give virginity a better chance up to age eighteen, and in England that's going quite far in life that way. Patel lads are not sexless, but maybe this way you can at least limit the scandal from the damage done.

It doesn't always work, of course. 'We have made money here, but we have lost our children,' a Sikh founding father announced, bravely, at a meeting on the promotion of the Punjabi language. The groans of agreement around the room were entirely spontaneous.

That is the greatest NRI concern—not the dual nationality that the speeches are about (or the one-and-a-half nationality now on offer; an Indian settled abroad can be also an 'Overseas Citizen of India', not also an Indian citizen). The concern is that the daughter growing up in England will run away with a black guy or a Pakistani. This, as parents see it, is a risk anywhere, dreaded from the day a daughter is born. But the risk is greatly multiplied for the NRI. The proper NRI will have a hard time showing off a black grandson back in Ludhiana. When whites discriminate, it's racism; when we do, we are only preserving honour and tradition. The corresponding is of course as much a fear among Indian Muslim families, but there are far fewer of these. And Muslims are in any case a great deal more, as they see it, protective of their women. They don't just move into ghettos, they build forts within them.

A ghetto keeps daughters with their own, and keeps them under closer watch than they might be elsewhere. Go to school with a bunch of girls like you, come back with them. Then on, parents are around. But spirit has a way of beating effort. Experience and averages are against that narrow space set out for the daughter. That at twenty-three she should marry a well-placed Hindu or Sikh of the fellow kind whose twenty-eighth birthday is next week, didn't you know. Pity that no one thought of stopping the Mirpuris from Pakistan from migrating as well. You can watch cricket with the enemy, but you can't sleep with him.

But the physical holding together is only one line of defence. It reinforces the second, the ghetto in the mind, or a holding on to traditional values; the two are so often the same thing. The public channel for traditional values is, what else, religion. Square mile for square mile, religious matters crowd ghettos almost certainly more than just about anywhere else on earth. These build forts in the mind, or at least that's the idea. And it helps to telescope religion into caste and club, and peopling the religious calendar to the full. It's the best bet to protect both mind and circumstance. Within these circles, otherwise conservative parents carefully allow the young to meet because they know how much worse it can get. These meetings, such peopling of places and of the calendar are really possible only in a ghetto.

It must be fortifying to be chaperoned to a cultural event on Sunday dressed up all Indian, at some time under a paper crown, and do a Krishna dance on stage where everyone applauds afterwards, never mind the quality of the dancing. These are not entertainment shows, after all; they are exercises in collective self-protection. And you are taught that the garba dance circle around the figure of Amba Ma signifies creation, preservation and destruction (in some way). And that we always begin with prayers to Ganesha, the giver. This won't necessarily plant the straight and narrow thought. What it does is to fill time with a doing of something that is so much better than what else might be done in that time. That is not a connection announced from stage at those hundreds of community events that fill every weekend, but it is the prime reason they're there at all.

An Indian woman I met boasted to me she will never drive a BMW. And then she explained. She would never go out with a man who is black, Muslim or white. Racist out and out to the correct observer, to an NRI founding father, a piece of music he's spent all his life composing. That so much NRI energy goes into making money is obvious—it brought him far, to brave that title in the first place. But even for an NRI, it's not enough just to make money. That done, he must perpetuate those similar to him. Because while money is being made, children get born, and when money is getting added up or multiplied (depending on whether you have a steady job or successful business), the children grow up to be sexually aware and then marriage-ready.

That's the day you prepare for, or protect against, depending on whether it's going right or wrong, meaning whether the offspring, daughter more than son, marries off the approved shortlist or outside. And this cannot be an individual effort since the offspring must marry within the approved circle. And so every community event is a step eventually to encourage sponsored mating.

And, finally, to do this all in a fun sort of way; it wouldn't work if it was all grim and nakedly purpose driven. It works because when you set up your own little world, you can shine in it. And who doesn't like that. The founding father can make his speeches here because where else would anyone listen. And the kids can show off their Bollywood dancing, because where else would anyone watch.

And you need a world to wear your lehenga-choli to, even if you don't go as far as the sari, and when you do, it has too much shine over something synthetic. It's all what they wear in Bollywood, and what on earth can be more glamorous than that. Bollywood brings the shine, the ghetto the confines to shine within. Every youngster is a star, because it's been so arranged. A hundred families can produce enough children to crowd a stage through a whole evening show. Then the mums and dads and relatives in tow turn up to watch; that occupies the chairs in a fair-sized hall. Together, it's a stage show to full house, with prizes afterwards to preserve and exhibit.

And all the while when no one's dancing or watching, there's the NRI gossip. And that needs the same people to come to the same place often enough. It takes, in short, a club, or a ghetto that doubles as one. The English have lost it, in the cities anyhow. It's been destroyed by the fashion of anonymity and the killing culture of political correctness. The British have become American about this: a crowd is no longer a grouping of people turning towards one another, but disconnected people sharing finite space denying the existence of the other. Connected to one another you become a crowd; connected continuously, you can become a community.

The glue of a community is gossip. The ghetto makes sure that neither you, nor your neighbour, is at much risk of minding his own business. Gossip is, at its best, only a way of being mindful of the presence of others, of engaging with them. In its most practical form, Indianness is expressed as busy-bodiness. You can't really be a busybody except around other Indians.

Never mind an argument, one way or the other, it just feels like a lot of ease. Otherwise, you wear the western dress to an asexual office; most likely you got there to meet some brown quota. You learn to explain you ways to the politely curious, if they get that far at all. It's a world of how you function, but of silence over who you are; questions get asked superficially, answered anxiously. Communication becomes explanation, and explanation a recurring appeal for an allowance of otherness.

We need to live in a ghetto because we need to live in the eyes of connected others as who we are, and not as the bearers of a certain skin colour.

ENTRY TO ENARISTAN

Following is the citizenship test for Enaristan in Britain. Candidates must concur with at least 81 of the following 101 to qualify:

1. No NRI calls himself NRI. He thinks only Indians call him that, like he thinks they think it's not a very nice

thing, but like he knows it's only because they couldn't get to be where he is.

2. When an Indian speaks wrong, it's ignorance; when an NRI speaks wrong, it's style.
3. The NRI looks better. If not, then it compensates for looks that you're NRI.
4. For an NRI every new arriving Indian is a 'freshy'. No NRI believes he was once a freshy, because he came before the word.
5. An NRI believes he has greater right to dance than an Indian. And, to dance badly and still be smarter than the Indian who dances better.
6. If the NRI can say something ordinary quick enough, it's wit.
7. An early mark of NRI speech is to say 'mourning' for 'morning', and 'having said that', 'at the end of the day', you cannot but be NRI. In India, he passes easily the 50 per cent daily quota of beginning his sentences with 'Over there...'
8. The NRI millionaire knows that making money must go with making speeches.
9. The NRI seeks titles, knighthood and lordship only because he wants the world to know his worth as well as he does.
10. The NRI knows that the caste system really means respecting dad, and his dad.
11. When Mrs NRI doesn't smile, it's okay; when Mrs India does not, she's grumpy.
12. The NRI pities the Indian who knows more about England than he does because where other people have knowledge, he has an address.
13. The NRI is a dying species but also a disappointed

species. Because in India the NRI only shone when India did not shine as much.

14. The NRI speaks of Western infrastructure like he built it.
15. The NRI never wastes land on a garden because he likes spring to be cost effective. He keeps a garden only when he has enough to show that he can also keep a gardener.
16. The NRI career must begin in a Japanese car and end in a Mercedes. Given the many successful careers visible on the roads, the exceptional among the Mercedes class may be allowed a Jaguar.
17. Road bumps in India shake up NRI insides more than they do of Indians or foreigners.
18. An NRI always tells you never to convert currency into rupees, and always does.
19. An NRI lives two lives—one from birth, the other from the stamp of permanent stay. The first life was only preparation for the second.
20. An NRI loves India so long as he can buy a return ticket from it.
21. Once an NRI, you must oppose immigration because, of course, you cannot have a little island swamped by migrants. His own arrival was an asset; that of others would be a burden to the state. He cheers the Indian team against England, but does not want more Indians to join him in such applause.
22. The NRI is a twin of the IAS officer; each believes there are two kinds of Indians—the ones who got to be like him, and the rest who tried.
23. Indians get into debts, the NRI buys repayable financing products.

24. The real status of NRI depends on something or other in India not working. If it did, he would be reduced to just a differently located Indian.
25. The NRI wife loves to take old clothes to India; it's the zero capital way of assuming conscience. This way she is not just seen to be rich, but rich in a giving sort of way, and without wasting money either.
26. An NRI loves to encounter discomfort in India in the presence of Indians; that way they know he lives better.
27. What an NRI loves about a massage in India is to figure how much more it would cost back where he lives.
28. An NRI does a bad job hiding the thought that the new cars in India take the shine off his own. He knows a foreign car is more foreign in India than in England.
29. An NRI believes Indians in India have less money but more fun, but never admits that in India.
30. The NRI is richer than India's rich. The NRI always adds a silent 'but' before wealth in rupees.
31. An NRI speaks of great sex abroad without having it. He speaks of a greater familiarity with white women than he has ever known.
32. The NRI is secretly proud that Indian children cannot produce his children's accent.
33. The NRI will remain forever disappointed over logistical difficulties in realizing the desire of multitudes of Indians to marry him.
34. An NRI is secretly proud of his children's dislike of flies.
35. The NRI loves Indians to ask him how they can get to England as more than visitors, or at least how their children can.

36. The NRI is always conscious of India's loss because he doesn't return.
37. The NRI does not like this new trend of Indians taking French holidays and Mediterranean cruises. He believes it's smarter to say he didn't than for an Indian to say he did.
38. The NRI speaks of poor Indians primarily to put rich Indians in their place. Or even against middle-class Indians who he thinks are rising higher above the middle than is good for them.
39. Occupants of Downing Street have always been good neighbours.
40. Since becoming NRI, he speaks much of the dignity of labour, because he has to.
41. The NRI is forever on stage. The higher the Indian population, the bigger his audience.
42. The opening of McDonald's in India, he knows, will be used as Indian revenge against him.
43. A good income for the NRI is justice; a good income in India is inflationary.
44. He loves to be spotted as the NRI in India, and loves to say that Indians can so spot him.
45. When the NRI chooses not to stay in a hotel in India, he is not saving money, only gracing his hosts.
46. The NRI holds every Indian responsible for bad driving.
47. The NRI these days feels reassured that Indians with less money are not therefore virginal, because what then did he lose.
48. The NRI speaks all his life of returning to India, and never does.
49. He does acknowledge sometimes that the real British

are those who ruled over his dad; the British of today are only another kind of European.

50. When the time is right, the NRI will say, gently, that funerals abroad are so much more progressive. Out there, then too, you only press a button.
51. The NRI knows you must leave India to maintain a sense of true India that Indians in India are losing.
52. The NRI is at worrying ease with all things spiritual.
53. To get pampered in India is only a privilege he offers to those doing the pampering.
54. The NRI loves Indian leaders to call him India's true ambassador, and is betrayed that more privileges don't go with such an important post.
55. When an NRI draws high interest from money kept in India, he is saviour, not investor. He remains a little surprised, but always pleased, that the money he makes for himself is seen as a favour done to India.
56. When he is not buying government bonds, the NRI speaks of investment in India as donation, and then neither invests nor donates.
57. The NRI's least favourite sentence is, 'Now you get that in India too…'
58. Now that they too wear Pampers, Indian babies are not truly Indian any more. You cannot hold a truly Indian baby without a Russian roulette sense of when it might pee on you.
59. Because Indians need visas for most countries, the NRI is naturally more trustworthy.
60. NRI women have a greater right to orgasm.
61. What to the Indian is caste, is to the NRI history.
62. The NRI knows that an Indian in India can't, really,

because someone will hear. And quiet, it's not the same thing.

63. The NRI woman is always aware of hidden advantages. The Indian woman can just as well have her legs waxed, but is so much less likely to be wearing Marks and Spencer around them.
64. When the Indian woman wears near invisible knee-highs, Mrs NRI is forgiving that the other tries.
65. When Mrs NRI uses gadgets, it's convenience; when Mrs India does, it's to show success.
66. Only the early migrants could become NRIs. Later migrants can only be upstarts.
67. The NRI finds it more natural to be written about than to read.
68. The NRI can never dress badly, only boldly.
69. The NRI woman dreams of a man who lives like an Indian and thinks like a Brit.
70. The NRI man dreams of an Indian woman who lives like an Indian and does not think like a Brit.
71. The NRI cannot distinguish between migration and making it.
72. The NRI always says India is great, but after a but.
73. The NRI is an Indian nationalist; he is prepared to be rude about India but not for others to be.
74. Every NRI is an informal consultant to the Government of India. That the government does not make good use of this is its loss.
75. The NRI does not mind so much that dual nationality will not let him contest an election, but cannot understand why that should deny him at least a Rajya Sabha seat in the winter.

76. The NRI is convinced that Indian bacteria love him very much more than they love resident Indians.
77. The NRI does not need to be badly received at an airport in India in order to complain about it.
78. The NRI is forever surprised that India's heat and dust do not show on the face of its Bollywood stars.
79. The NRI always sees less of England than the visiting Indian.
80. The visiting Brit always sees more of India than the NRI does.
81. An NRI learns to use the same language for 27 degrees in London as the Indian for 45 degrees in Ludhiana.
82. An NRI is never on time except when he is seeing someone white. If it's a white woman, he's early.
83. The NRI is clever; the Indian in India devious.
84. Mrs NRI finds it slightly annoying when Mrs India knows the names of the best cosmetic brands and, worse, uses them.
85. The NRI does the better balance with one foot in the twenty-first century and the other in a 5000-year-old civilization.
86. An NRI woman in a skirt is being Western. An Indian woman in a skirt is trying to be too Western.
87. What in an NRI kid is confidence, is in an Indian kid disrespectful.
88. For an NRI daughter to have a boyfriend is natural. For an Indian's daughter, it is immoral.
89. The young NRI has progressed further because his name is whitely edited down to the nearest syllable.
90. The NRI is sure that the English system is better than the people it produces.
91. To the NRI male, an Indian woman's legs are more leg than a white woman's legs.

92. The NRI believes he does not need to be as polite about Somali arrivals as the English needed to be about his.
93. The NRI is always surprised when a white woman won't.
94. The NRI likes Indians to come and see how he lives, but not stay with him.
95. The NRI never picks up the British habit of not staring.
96. Now that the cook-cleaner has arrived in NRI homes, the NRI woman wants to know what the Indian woman with the servant will have to say about the advantage of not having to do everything on your own.
97. Indians go to Bollywood, Bollywood comes to the NRI.
98. The NRI who takes her visiting cousin shopping is showing her the light.
99. The NRI loves Indians who make special arrangements for him partly because these make him more comfortable, and partly because these reassure him that the Indian understands the world.
100. When she leaves India, the NRI woman never quite knows how many women will copy her afterwards.
101. The NRI man ends his visit feeling sorry for everyone he leaves behind, but a little fearful that the next time he comes and goes they might want a little less to be in his foreign shoes.

Notes on Contributors

SAMRAT

Samrat is an engineer turned journalist who now works as deputy editor of the *Hindustan Times*, Delhi. In the course of research for his essay, he was forced to subject himself to much torture, including a thorough examination of his private parts at the hands of a hakim in old Bangalore.

SOUMYA BHATTACHARYA

Soumya Bhattacharya's first book, *You Must Like Cricket? Memoirs of an Indian Cricket Fan*, was published to critical acclaim across the world in 2006. His literary criticism and essays have appeared in the *New York Times*; the *Sydney Morning Herald* and the *Age* (Melbourne) in Australia; the *Guardian*, the *Observer* and the *Independent* in London; and *Sports Illustrated* in South Africa. He is an editor with the *Hindustan Times*. He lives with his wife and daughter in Mumbai.

GEETA DOCTOR

Geeta Doctor is a writer and critic. She writes on literature and the arts. What she loves most is food, laughter and the company of strangers whom she meets on her travels. She presides over a four-generation family of strong women. Among them is her ninety-year-old mother, Padma Padmanabhan.

VIKRAM DOCTOR

Vikram Doctor is a journalist based in Mumbai. He writes on food and other issues.

NAMITA GOKHALE

Namita Gokhale is the author of *Paro: Dreams of Passion*; *Gods, Graves, and Grandmother*; *A Himalayan Love Story*; *The Book of Shadows* and *Shakuntala*.

She has also written a book for children, *The Puffin Mahabharata*. Namita Gokhale lives in New Delhi.

SEEMA GOSWAMI

Seema Goswami is a columnist and author. Her weekly column, 'Spectator', in *Brunch*, the Sunday magazine of *Hindustan Times*, deals with society and lifestyle. She is the author of *Woman on Top*, a book about women in the workplace. She was previously the founding editor of *Graphiti*, *The Telegraph*'s Sunday magazine.

INDRAJIT HAZRA

Indrajit Hazra is the author of the novels *The Burnt Forehead of Max Saul* and *The Garden of Earthly Delights*, both of which have also been published in French. He is a journalist with the *Hindustan Times*, where he also writes the popular weekly column Red Herring.

PRATIK KANJILAL

Publisher of *The Little Magazine*, Pratik Kanjilal is also a translator and a columnist. His honours include the Sahitya Akademi Translation Prize in 2005 for Nirmal Verma's last novel, *The Last Wilderness* (*Antim Aranya*).

BACHI KARKARIA (RSG)

ARVIND KRISHNA MEHROTRA

Arvind Krishna Mehrotra was born in Lahore in 1947. He is the author of four books of poems, the most recent of which is *The Transfiguring Places* (1998). His edited books include *The Oxford India Anthology of Twelve Modern Indian Poets* (1992), *An Illustrated History of Indian Literature in English* (2003) and *The Last Bungalow: Writings on Allahabad* (2007).

RENUKA NARAYANAN

Renuka Narayanan is editor, religion & culture, *Hindustan Times*. She is the author of *Faith: Filling the God-sized Hole* and edited *The Book of Prayer*.

SRIVIDYA NATARAJAN

Srividya Natarajan, born in Chennai, now lives in Canada and teaches English at King's University College, University of Western Ontario. She is the author of *No Onions, No Garlic* (Penguin, 2006).

MANJULA PADMANABHAN

Manjula Padmanabhan (b. 1953), is a writer and artist. Her books include *Hot Death, Cold Soup*, *Kleptomania*, *Getting There* and *Escape*. 'Harvest', her fifth play, won the 1997 Onassis Award for Theatre. Her comic strip 'Double Talk', featuring the character called Suki appeared weekly in the *Sunday Observer* (Bombay, 1982–86) and daily in the *Pioneer* (New Delhi, 1991–97). Manjula has illustrated twenty-four books for children including her two novels for children, *Mouse Attack* and *Mouse Invaders.*

IRA PANDE

Ira Pande worked as a university teacher for fifteen years, and then as an editor at *Seminar*, *Biblio*, Dorling Kindersley and Roli Books. She is the author of *Diddi: My Mother's Voice* and has translated into English Manohar Shyam Joshi's *T'Ta Professor.*

DEVDUTT PATTANAIK

Dr Devdutt Pattanaik (www.devdutt.com) writes, illustrates and lectures extensively on the relevance of mythology in modern times. He is the author of *Myth = Mithya: A Handbook of Hindu Mythology*, *The Pregnant King* and *The Book of Ram.*

JERRY PINTO

Jerry Pinto is a poet and journalist based in Mumbai. His published works include *Helen: The Life and Times of an H-Bomb* (2006) which won the Best Book on Cinema Award at the 54th National Film Awards, *Surviving Women* (2000) and a collection of poetry, *Asylum* (2004). He has also co-edited *Bombay, Meri Jaan: Writings on Mumbai* with Naresh Fernandes and *Confronting Love: Poems* with Arundhathi Subramaniam.

ANAND K. SAHAY

Anand K. Sahay is coordinating editor of *Asian Age*, a leading Indian daily. He has mostly written stories for a living. For a long time now, he has got by by writing political columns and editorials. Widely travelled, Anand like history and has lived in London and Kabul.

PUNITA SINGH

Fascinated by the sounds of language and music from an early age, Punita Singh went on to study musical acoustics, linguistics and communication science, earning a doctorate from Washington University in St Louis, USA in 1990. Following a research and teaching stint at McGill University in Montreal, Canada, Punita returned to India in the late 1990s and has since been working with words professionally in the publishing business.

VIDYA SUBRAHMANIAM

Vidya Subrahmaniam is based in Delhi and is currently deputy editor with *The Hindu* newspaper. Before this she worked in the *Times of India*, the *Statesman* and the *Indian Express*. Starting in 1984, the year of Indira Gandhi's brutal assassination, she has tracked elections extensively, capturing in her writings the colour and splendour of the world's biggest experiment in democracy, as well as the huge socio-political transformations ushered in through the ballot.

SANJAY SURI

Sanjay Suri has been a London-based journalist since 1990. Born in Jalandhar, he has an MA in English literature from Delhi University and an MSc. in social and organizational psychology from the London School of Economics and Political Science. He is the author of *Brideless in Wembley* (Penguin, 2006).

A Short Dictionary of [Other] Things Indian

. . . .

Jerry Pinto

THE WAY WE LIKE TO SEE OURSELVES

This is indeed India! The land of dreams and romances, of fabulous wealth and fabulous poverty, of splendour and rags, of palaces and hovels, of famine and pestilence, of genii and giants and Alladdin lamps, of tigers and elephants, the cobra and the jungle, the country of a hundred nations and a hundred tongues, of a thousand religions and two million gods, cradle of the human race, birthplace of human speech, mother of history, grandmother of legend, great-grandmother of tradition, whose yesterdays bear date with the mouldering antiquities of the rest of the nations—the one sole country under the sun which is endowed with an imperishable interest for alien prince and alien peasant, for lettered and ignorant, wise and fool, rich and poor, bond and free, the one land that *all* men desire to see, and having seen once, by even a glimpse, would not give that glimpse for the shows of all the rest of the globe combined.—*Mark Twain*

THE WAY WE DON'T LIKE TO SEE OURSELVES

The Indians believe that there is no country but theirs, no nation like theirs, no king like theirs, no religion like theirs, no science like theirs...—*Alberuni*

AGARBATTI

Incense sticks. The number you light is often an indicator of how pious you are.

In Mumbai *tapori* slang, a thin young man.

AHIMSA

Mahatma Gandhi's greatest gift to the nation, which he borrowed from the Buddha, who expounded it in the Mahayana Sutras. Ahimsa does not just mean non-violence in the sense of not hurting any living being; Gandhi offered a much more complex bouquet of meanings including avoiding 'the subtle violence involved in injuring the feelings of other people'.

Like most gifts that are useful but not entertaining, Gandhi's gift is neglected.

AIR INDIA MAHARAJA

The moustachio-ed mascot of the national carrier Air India, now much neglected. The only maharaja who ever did a day of honest work.

AKHARAS

The sand pit where Indian-style wrestling is taught by aged men sitting on charpais to well-oiled young men in langots. Apart from a strenuous exercise regime, celibacy and the preserving of vital bodily fluids is strictly enforced.

Ancient religious sects comprising fearsome sadhus. They regularly go to war at the Kumbh Mela over which group should bathe in the holy waters first.

ALL-INDIA RADIO

'This is All-India Radio, giving you the news,' the lady would say. Pip, pip, pip...and all of middle India would begin frantically twiddling the knobs on their radiograms looking for Voice of America or the BBC World Service or anything that would at least pretend to have a world view and some independence.

But through rural India, through Malayalam-speaking and Tamil-speaking and Oriya-speaking and Gujarat-speaking and Assamese-speaking India, the men would gather around the set and listen to the voice from the sky (*akashvani*). Many still do.

In a largely illiterate country, All-India Radio's hand in the formation of the state has been ignored, largely because none of the historians ever had to depend on a radio set, and certainly not on AIR, for news from beyond the horizon.

AMAR CHITRA KATHAS

The only comic books—since they told the stories of the gods, saints and historical and semi-historical figures of India in standard English—that were allowed to Indian children of Generation W (the generation that came before Gen X).

Ersatz grandparents to Generation Y, especially. those who live in non-Indian nations.

AMBASSADOR CAR

For decades the Ambassador was the lowest common denominator of transport in India, uniting middle-class families, governmental bureaucrats, taxi drivers and yoga teachers. (The yoga teachers had to get the kinks out of your spine.) It was also the car on whose head sat the red lamp of authority. Its solidity, its dependability, its spaciousness and its high chassis mean that it is still the choice of the hard-working taxi drivers of most cities in India—except, oddly, Mumbai where there are Fiat taxis.

AMUL

The best butter in the world. Is all.

ANTAKSHARI

Put ten Indians on a bus or a train or in any other space where it is proposed they spend some time together and the idea of playing a round of *antakshari* (in which two teams compete to sing film songs whose lyrics start with the last letter of the previous song) will quickly be suggested. And before those who don't know enough Hindi film songs can protest, someone will be dividing up teams and someone else will be claiming that they know every song that starts with the infuriating Hindi alphabet 'thha'.

ARYANS

Allegedly, a bunch of nomads who came from the plains north of India, seeking fresh pastures for their beasts. Their arrival is called the Aryan Invasion. No one knows when this happened and some historians are not even sure it happened at all. But everyone wants to be an Aryan and every community knows that they are the real Aryans. (See also Dravidians.)

BABU ENGLISH

Kindly note that we, as a nation, were taught English in order to expedite the workings of one numbers British Empire. Thus while we would like to meet someone who still ends a letter with 'I remain, sir, your humble servant', there are many who will admit to having received your letter of the 23rd inst..

BACK-ANSWERING

To the logically minded, there is no such thing as 'back-answering' because when you simply answer, you do speak back to the person who spoke to you. To the middle-class parents and teachers of India, there is no crime worse than back-answering which includes but is not limited to:

- explaining your actions;
- pointing out some illogicality on the part of the said parents or teachers;

- pointing out something downright wrong that the said parents or teachers have said;
- not saying a word but indicating by one's demeanour that one might be doing all or any of the above.

BEEDIS

At one point, the Indian taxpayers' list was dominated by a single family that made beedis (the humble leaf-wrapped cigarettes). This demonstrates as much the ability of Indians to tolerate offensive odours as it tells you about the power of sheer volumes in the Indian market.

BENGALI TOURIST

Wherever you go in India, the Bengali tourist will be with you. Armed with the travel special of *Sandesh* magazine, he will have planned his trip, shaken out his monkey cap and sweater and muffler, inquired into the possibility of getting Bengali food where he is going, stocked up on liquid antacids and bought his tickets well in advance. Nothing will shake his resolve to see everything but nothing will slow him down very much either. The gods must be seen, the temple must be visited, a tiger must be spotted and, if possible, he should be able to come right down to the jetty where the boat rides begin before deciding that it is not worth the effort. The morning's work done, everyone in the family or group (the Bengali tourist is not a solitary traveller) will return to the hotel and foregather in one room to play cards, loll about and gossip, just as if they were at home.

BHAJIYAS/PAKORAS

Any likely vegetable, sliced, diced or otherwise mauled, dipped into a batter of *besan* (chickpea flour) and fried.

This is the problem with definitions, of course. They may tell you what a bhajiya is, but not what a bhajiya does. Bhajiyas are comfort food for the Indian masses. They bring back a time when someone in the kitchen, someone with a wispy identity, someone in a white sari perhaps, or a pair of old khaki shorts, would clean the vegetables, peel them, cut them, mix the besan with water and spices, heat the oil, mix the vegetables in the flour and deep fry the lot. These would come out piping hot, served with tea.

Today, one simply orders them from the local sweet shop because there is an acute shortage of domestic labour and when you kick all the widows out of the joint family, you end up with no one who will make your bhajiyas.

BHARATANATYAM

At one point in time, the only girls who studied Bharatanatyam were those born into the families of devadasis or temple dancers in south India who were dreadfully stigmatized by the British, who turned the word into a synonym for prostitute. The middle classes, ever willing to be colonized, took this stigma to heart and refused to let their daughters learn the dance form.

At another point in time, only south Indian middle-class girls learnt Bharatanatyam as much as Bengali girls learnt Rabindrasangeet and Goan girls learnt the piano. It was cultural training and it was supposed to make good wives out of little women.

At the time of going to print, every other middle-class girl is learning Bharatanatyam because Bollywood is hot, and a career in Hindi films is the big prize. What worked for Hema Malini can work for little Avantikalokita.

BLACK MARKET

Where everything could be bought and sold. When you could not get it where you should get it, you got it on the black market. Very often, you could not get it where you should have got it because there was a black market. Scarcity and a corrupt socialist system combined to produce a complex system of capitalist pricing. Everything had a black market in India—from milk powder to film tickets.

BLACK MONEY

Undeclared money. The money that doesn't show up on our income tax returns. The money that's handed over, under the table, and which ends up under the bed. The

Indira Gandhi Institute of Development Research estimates that India's black economy is around 18 to 21 per cent of the gross domestic product.

BUM WASHING

Without euphemisms then. We shit. Then we pour water between our buttocks from a *lota* held in the right hand and with the left hand we swish it back and forth until all that was unclean has been removed. Unless we go abroad; then we come back and start using toilet paper. Before liberalization and globalization, toilet paper was not a common phenomenon.

At one point in time, some relatives arrived in Mumbai and so I set out to stock up some of this bizarre stuff. After all, it is the kind of thing that necessitates the invention of the word, fartleberry. (No, really. The *Wordsworth Dictionary of Obscenity & Taboo* defines this as 'excrement adhering to hair around the anus'.)

At the local grocery store, I stopped and asked whether they had any toilet paper.

Of course, he did. Only he had a question.

'Sweet or salted?' he asked.

B.U.M.S.

Bachelor of Unani Medicine and Surgery. This is not a joke. Unani medicine, an ancient and revered system of healing, is obviously in need of a spin doctor.

CAMPA COLA

After the Janata government of 1977 had the *cojones* to chuck Coca-Cola out of the country, the middle classes felt the need for a disgusting dark brown drink made of chemicals and sugar that would make them burp loudly and gloriously.

CHILLIES

For a gustatory Juan-come-lately which did not reach India until the Portuguese brought it here, the chilli is now identified with Indian food. All over England, masculinity is judged by how hot you can take your curry. And the heat comes from the Bombay cherry, as the chilli was once known.

CHOR POCKET

When an Indian man on holiday wants to make a purchase, he arches his body, inhales deeply and inserts his right hand into the waistband of his trousers. There, snug against the yielding sludge of his belly, is a small pocket that has been stitched into his trousers by his tailor. It is the 'chor pocket' with which the Indian man keeps his money safe from thieves.

This is a foolproof method since most Indian men have Great Indian Paunches. This means that the roll of the belly hides the waistband of the trousers completely, making the thief's job even more difficult. The notes come out a little sodden but

Indian currency notes live longer and harder than most other currency notes and so few people notice the intense saturation with human sweat.

COACHING CLASSES

The preferred form of education in India. These are to be used in conjunction with *Competition Success Review* to get past the entrance exams to prestigious institutions like IIT, which actually start to worry when too many students get in.

COCONUT OIL

In north India, what you put on your hair as a combination of hair gel and hair food. In south India, what you fry your food in.

COUSIN BROTHER

Any cousin of the male order. The unfamiliar man you were seen with by your friends is always your cousin brother.

COUSIN SISTER

Any cousin of the female order. The girl you were seen with whom you describe to your friends as your girlfriend when she is actually a cousin.

CYCLE RICKSHAWS

The rickshaw began as a two-wheeler, powered by a man who drew it, running between the shafts. See *Do Bhiga Zamin* (Bimal Roy, 1953) for a graphic description of the life of this anonymous man. To make life easier, a cycle was attached to the vehicle. These days, you can find cycle rickshaws wherever there is extreme poverty or extreme wealth. Thus you can be cycled around the interior of a small town in India or around the squares of Amsterdam or Holland. The former will cost you a little money and may tax your conscience; the latter will tax only your wallet. For when a white man does what a black man is supposed to be doing, it's called irony. And that has a high price tag.

DHABA

Highway pit stops where heart-stop food is sold to truck drivers and the Indian middle class who want to pretend that they aspire to be truck drivers.

DIAMONDS

There was a time when there was only one source of diamonds in the world, and guess where that was? No wonder Indians have a deep relationship with the diamond.

Cynics will point to the fact that diamonds are portable, untraceable and easy to conceal when you're in a hurry to get away from the mob. And the memory of the Partition of India is not so old that there aren't some Indians who trust diamonds of one carat and above more than anything else.

DOORDARSHAN

If you are of a certain age, even a glimpse of the yin-and-yang logo of Doordarshan makes you want to hum (Tee-tee-tum-tee-tum…ta-da-da-da-da…) the station identification. For many of us, television meant the glories of the vanished socialist state. The first line that Doordarshan beamed into one's household was often an enlivening discussion on the benefits of copper sulphate on the kharif crop. But it was television and it gave birth to Prannoy Roy and it brought Luku Sanyal into our living rooms and there was the Republic Day parade and the Sunday movie and Chhaayageet and Chitrahaar and Young World and Sports Round-Up where they often showed ice-skating and the goal scored by Turkey against Egypt. Those were thrilling times but you had to be there.

DOWRY

No one gives dowry in our country. No one accepts it. If you ask anyone, they will say, 'In ours, we don't ask and we don't take.' The implication is that *other* communities take and give dowry and thus demean their womenfolk. Of course, it might seem odd that dowry deaths seem to happen in almost every Indian community—there were 6787 cases in 2005. Where there's a greedy family, an available son, some extra petrol and a complaisant police officer, a woman may be set on fire, the son may be set free and some other woman lured into the marriage trap.

DRAVIDIANS

In the view of the world in which the Aryans come down from the north for pasturage and lebensraum, the original residents of India are called Dravidians.

EATING WITH FINGERS

We eat with our fingers. Some of us eat with our hands too. Some of us even use the inner wrist and there have been reports of questing tongues scooping runaway drops of daal and curd and rice from near the elbow.

We eat with our fingers. This seems primitive but watch someone who has never eaten with their fingers try it and you will see that it requires as much skill to manipulate a fork and a spoon and a knife as it does to try and catch a pea in a floating bowl of *rassa* (gravy) with a piece of puri.

We eat with our fingers. We say the food tastes better that way. This is moot, but think about this: no one who ever eats with his fingers will ever burn his mouth.

ENGLISH

The language of aspiration for the masses. Having achieved a certain fluency in it, the language in which to announce that everyone else should be educated in his or her mother tongue. Along with our neutral accents and geographical position, the cause of the backend boom in India. The first gift of the British Raj. See also *Babu English*.

ENTRANCE EXAMS

Entrance exams to professional colleges are the Cerberuses of the elite institutions. The top management colleges will only accept the top 15 per cent. Everyone else must try and get an MBA from whichever organization they can, and once you're not in one of the top 10 institutes, it doesn't matter where you are. Naturally, the examinations have no practical value at all. No one has ever shown that the ability to crack calculus equations at high speed has anything to do with the running of big companies but there has to be a way of keeping some people out, so why not something as arbitrary as the ability to tell how many pairs of integers will satisfy an equation involving *m* and *n*?

EVE-TEASING

The young male adults of the species huddle in groups, where they hope they will be able to spot young available females.

On spotting a likely one, they make rude sounds, offer suggestions that make them repellent to the female in question, and generally behave as if it is their desire to cause as much offence as possible in the short time available. This is called eve-teasing and may explain why arranged marriages are popular in order to keep the species alive.

FEMALE INFANTICIDE

There are now 933 women to every 1000 men in India. (The UNFPA site reports that the latest figures are 896 girls born for every 1000 boys.) This means, when you scale up to the one billion people who are in India, we have around 44 million missing women.

They weren't abducted by aliens. They were either aborted when they were foetuses or they were allowed to die when they were born by a little 'benign' neglect or they were outright murdered by feeding them with something toxic.

The standard explanation trotted out was: the girl child is a burden. She has to be provided with a dowry. The poor of India see her as a luxury they cannot afford and so the girls go missing. In this way, the whole girl child problem is relocated as the problem of India's poor. It isn't our problem, not the middle-class's problem at all.

But that does not explain why affluent states like Punjab have such dismal figures. Fatehgarh Sahib, for instance, has 754 girls for every 1000 boys.

GAJRA

In the beginning, this strand of jasmine flowers served to ornament the hair of the Indian woman, perhaps to conceal the smell of congealing oil. Next, the same strand, somewhat abbreviated, was tied around the wrists of men visiting the houses of dancing girls—often located in areas without too much sanitation. Today, the gajra is beginning the slow fadeout with the sari and other niceties of women's attire. Look for the plastic versions, all made in China.

GANDHIJI

The father of the nation of India. Like most fathers, he is probably alternately terrified by and fascinated with what he has wrought.

The Rs 500 note upon which the father of the nation's face appears. As in: 'Give me a Gandhi.'

A new Bollywood property.

GANGA

By common consent, the Ganga is the holiest river in India even if it is said to be mentioned only twice in the Rig Veda.

GHAR JAMAI

A son-in-law who comes to stay at his father-in-law's house. This is also to be interpreted as a sign of lack of masculinity since he is unable to provide a house for his wife.

GHEE

The elixir of life, an offering to Agni, the libation of choice in the Vedas, if derived from the milk of the cow.

A cooking agent if derived from the milk of the buffalo.

The enemy, according to the makers of hydrogenated cooking oils, who often talk of how ghee will give you a heart attack. They do not blush.

GOA

The smallest state of the union.

Konkan Kashi or the Banaras of the South.

Rome of the Orient.

Where we go to holiday.

Where we want to buy a house.

Where the Israelis holiday.

Where the Russian Mafiosi dreams of a home.

GOBAR

Dry cow dung which is used as a fuel. Cow dung itself has many uses. It is diluted and used to wash the floors in rural India because of its insect-repellent properties. It is also used as manure. It also produces methane on decomposition, which means it can be used to produce gobar gas.

GREEN REVOLUTION

This is how you end up a nation that does not have to import food. You spray every inch of available land with pesticides and insecticides. Then you infuse the soil with fertilizers. When almost everything natural has been killed, you plant some strains of seeds you have developed in a laboratory.

It works. This might be because no one in a democracy ever died of famine; famines are man-made disasters thought up by dictators and colonial overlords and aided by war. But this should not get in the way of the celebrations.

Today, the groundwater of Punjab comes up foaming with chemicals. That's the green revolution today. You look at the state of nature and you turn a little green.

HAIR OIL

Many communities announce their collective identity to the world with the brand of hair oil they use. This is never to be used in moderation, not even by those who have no hair to irrigate.

HAWAII CHAPPAL

No one knows why these rubber slippers, known as flip-flops in the rest of the Anglophone world, are called Hawaii chappals in India. Some suggest that they let your feet breathe through their simple design—a blue V-strap that holds your feet to a flat surface of white rubber layered on a thicker layer of blue rubber. Others suggest that they look like something you might wear on the beach at Waikiki. Yeah, right.

HIJRAS

The third sex, some of whom are born with indeterminate sex organs and some of whom are castrated to become devotees of Yellamma, all of whom are demonized and marginalized.

Thus, a way of suggesting a man is impotent and effeminate or both.

A new kind of Bollywood villain.

HILL STATIONS

The British invented the hill station, a summer resort located at some considerable altitude, so that they could get away from the heat of the plains in summer; recover from insanity, tuberculosis and other diseases they contracted while colonizing the subcontinent; have sex with the wife of a higher-ranking officer. Of these reasons, only one remains to visit hill stations but she need not be a higher-ranking officer's wife.

HOLDALLS

A friend called and asked if I had a holdall. I wondered aloud if anyone we knew had one. There was a time when every family had a capacious khaki or olive-green one with leather straps. The friend called a few hours later to say he had tracked one down and was going to view it. Could I come along, I asked. I went, expecting a rush of nostalgia.

Instead, I found something that looked like a sports bag on steroids.

'This is not a holdall,' I said and I was startled to hear a trace of outrage in my voice.

'It is,' he said. 'It holds everything. So it's a holdall.'

In that sense, a gunny sack could also be a holdall. In the subcontinent, a holdall consists of a long rectangular strip of canvas folded over into flaps at either end. These flaps took the smalls, the socks and unmentionables, the sundry bits of cloth that mothers felt the need to pack, the stuffed toys. In between were laid all the longer clothes, the trousers, the shawls and the overcoats if it was a hill station trip. In the train, the holdall would be unwrapped and laid out on the berth so that it became a natural mattress with the fattened flaps serving as pillows. Thus a holdall held all and their disappearance from the Indian travel scene may well be the subject of a doctorate in the trivialized future.

HORN OK PLEASE

The cryptic sign to be found on the back of Indian trucks. No one has figured it out perhaps because no one has asked a truck driver.

HOROSCOPE

The piece of paper by which the nation of India and most of its people run their lives.

HUM DO, HAMAARE DO

The slogan of the Family Planning Association of India that everyone knows and everyone ignores.

INDIAN INSTITUTE OF TECHNOLOGY (IIT)

This is our way of keeping America running. Indians pay their taxes. These taxes go into the making of elite institutions like IIT here, IIT there, IIT somewhere else where nothing else happens. Then after hundreds of engineers have been turned out, most of them go to America and work for Bill Gates and make him richer. Bill Gates, in return, funds research at IIT so that the results can make him even richer without having to worry about visa problems. No wonder Jeff Bezos of Amazon called IIT 'a world treasure'. He would. Any American would.

PS: Once in a while an IIT graduate returns to India. He will then walk one foot above the ground in his own estimation for the rest of his life.

JAGGERY

Unrefined or raw sugar, which has been used as a sweetener in India for a long, long time. (Well, not as long ago as the Rig Veda, which mentions sugarcane but not jaggery. We have to get to the Sutra literature to find the first mention of *gur*.) By a happy combination of our new love for things unrefined and the sanctity of Ayurveda, jaggery is now the new panacea. As with all panaceas, there is no evidence for this but why let that stop you?

JAI JAWAAN, JAI KISAAN

Lal Bahadur Shastri's slogan, coined in the 1960s, exalting the foot soldier and the farmer, has joined the ranks of words that can be said without offence. No one who hails the soldier is suggesting that any action be taken against those who ordered coffins for $2500 each. No one who hails the farmer is suggesting we do something other than hand out more fertilizer subsidies so that we can poison the groundwater.

JAIMALA

An All-India Radio programme on which officers and other members of the armed forces in the far-flung reaches of the subcontinent would write in their requests. Jaimala was of course just a radio request programme, but it was also more than that. It allowed the middle-class to feel patriotic while never leaving their homes. It afforded the elder members of the family an opportunity to listen to some old songs since the jawans and the naiks and the lance corporals always asked for songs that were at least five years older, since that was what they had heard the last time they went home. And every time they played *Ai mere shah-e chaman*, the nation wept a few easy sentimental tears with its lance corporals.

KAMA SUTRA

Vatsyayana's self-help manual is the book that every Indian knows about but few have read. Everyone assumes that it is full of impossible positions requiring everyone involved to be adept at yoga and so jaded as to need a woman to spin on her haunches while impaled, but for the most part, it goes on about how a man should know how to make lemonade, what kind of wife is best, and whether a hare and an elephant can ever find happiness.

The book we quote to prove that our nation wasn't so straight-laced until the British came along and messed up our minds with their Victorian morality. Of course, this suggests that the Kama Sutra was a widely known text and written for the masses, which it was not. And it suggests that Queen Victoria ruled England for 250 years, which she did not.

KANT—LANGOT

The Hindi word for necktie. No, it really is.

KHADI

Gandhiji called khadi 'the sun of the solar system of the village solar system'. No one else calls khadi anything, though from time to time ladies who lunch will wax eloquent about our indigenous traditions of spinning and weaving.

LADIES TAILOR

What every pubescent young man wants to grow up to be.

Why?

Taking measurements for blouses, my dear, taking measurements for blouses.

LIFEBUOY

Otherwise known as *laal saabun* or the red soap, Lifebuoy has had the kind of street cred in India that brand managers would die for. But then it has a considerable headstart, having been launched in India in 1895. It is the only soap to have ever crossed 100,000 tonnes of sales in a single year. It is not a very good soap, though there are regular attempts at upgrading it and re-perfuming it and re-positioning it. But when it still has a chunk of the market, who cares? Last heard from, sales are rising due to the Swasthya Chetna project by which the brand association between the soap and health (see jingle) is made even stronger since this is an attempt to defeat diarrhoeal diseases by encouraging hand washing with soap in rural India. Altogether now:

> *Tandoorusti ki raksha karta hai Lifebuoy*
> *Lifebuoy hai jahaan, tandoorusti hai wahaan*

LOTA

The receptacle in which the water is brought to the fundament after the fundament has been fouled by Number Two. To be seen carrying it is a source of comedy in folk forms and in popular culture, since it means that one does not have access to indoor sanitation. (Poverty is always funny.)

MANGOES

An Indian fruit that grows in Harrods of London.

MONEY ORDERS

In 2006–07, India sent 77567.06 million rupees by money order. In 2006–07, multinational banks in India still needed days to transfer funds electronically from one bank account to another.

The money order will be with us for quite a while.

MONKEY CAPS

Indian men are known internationally for their bad hair. Indian men are known at home for making their bad hair look worse by wearing monkey caps when it gets cold. While this keeps one extremity warm, it prevents the wearer from ever looking hot.

MONSOONS

India is an agrarian country. It is also the kind of country where the rich and the privileged have always had a stranglehold on whatever natural resources there are. Which means that the majority of Indian farmers have spent much of their lives scanning the skies for the elusive rains.

This has translated into great music, poetry, and into a middle-class fantasia in which the rains have been specially laid on to make the world a green and fresh place for them.

MOUSTACHES

In other countries, men wear moustaches or they do not, basing most of their decisions on aesthetics or fashion. In India, men wear moustaches because a 'mooch' tells the world what you are, how far up or down in the caste hierarchy, etc. Thus moustaches have their own legends and lore. The Pathans claimed that they could mortgage a single hair of their moustaches as Pran offers to do in *Zanjeer*. The BBC reports that police in Madhya Pradesh state are being paid to grow moustaches because it commands them more respect. For further details, please see Mulk Raj Anand's *A Pair of Moustachios*.

NAADA

The string with which Indians keep their pyjamas up. This is an efficient way of fighting the battle of the bulge without resorting to new wardrobes or to new belts.

Since the naada hangs in front of the man's crotch, if left untucked, in folk theatre, and other forms that revel in euphemism, a reference to the penis.

NATIVE PLACE

The middle classes of other nations become tourists and visit other countries. The middle class of India, with the honourable exception of the Bengalis, go home to what they call their 'native place' whenever they can find the time and the train (or air) tickets. On any given day, a thousand leave applications are being filed with the same words on them, words that challenge bosses to deny such applications. Going to native place, they say, and they even mean it.

NETA

In Hindi, literally leader. In common parlance, a political leader, and thus someone believed to be venal, power hungry, corrupt and willing to ruin the country's future for his or her political present.

NO

This does not exist. (See also *Yes*).

The only time 'No' is used is when you are denying something that has happened and cannot be denied. Example:

Villain: *Humne tere bete ka qatl kiya hai* (We have murdered your son).

Mother: *Nahin*! (No!)

NOSE RINGS

Now that everyone and her brother has a pierced nose, the nose ring may not excite as much attention as it once did. But it is still an erotic sign with us, since it is supposed to be the first item of clothing that a man will take off from his wife's body on their first night together, the fabled *suhaag raat.*

NUMBER ONE

The national euphemism for urination, India's chief outdoor activity.

NUMBER TWO

The national euphemism for excretion of the more solid kind. India's other chief outdoor activity.

ONE TIGHT SLAP

The threat of which has subdued generations of young Indians who are rowdy in class. No one, however, can tell how a tight slap is worse than a loose slap.

PAGE 3

The page that is dedicated to society news and to the people who are famous for being famous.

For a deeper understanding of how India manages to take the worst ideas every other nation has and then succeeds in making them worse, this mnemonic verse should be of some assistance:

On page 3 in other countries, there is a show of tits.

On page 3 in India, there is a show of twits.

METAL TRUNKS

By which Indians transport much material. In smaller cities, the biscuit man still carries his wares in a tin trunk announcing, with no blushes, that everything has been made in pure ghee. This, like so many other accoutrements of Indian travel, seems to be passing into history and/into kitsch, which may be the postmodern version of history.

POST CARDS

The post card is the subaltern news service of India. It records the good, the bad and the ritualistic with equal space. And it is a holdover of the socialist subsidies of the country. According to the annual report of India Post, a post card costs the government an average of Rs 6.59 to print, to disseminate and to deliver and generates only 50 paise in revenue. However, printed postcards cost Rs 6.61 and bring in Rs 6, which is a little better. The competition post card, by which middle India votes for reality shows or tries to get on to game shows, costs Rs 4.43 and brings in a tidy Rs 10. Only, that was too high a price. The sales crashed as the television channels switched to short messaging services and to mobile phones.

India still writes post cards, and although that subsidy is not making India Post's profitability any easier, it's a subsidy worth keeping.

PRIVACY

Every Indian who returns from a protracted spell of living abroad brings home the notion that some things should be private. However, the returning Indian will ask invasive questions about other people's love lives ('So why hasn't your daughter got married? Some scandal?'), health ('Do you still get that herpes thing?'), body ('How come your son is so dark when you and your husband are so fair?'), money ('How much are you earning at your new job?'), while zealously protecting his right not to answer the same questions when they are asked of him.

QUIZZING

The middle-class boy's machismo quotient is judged by his ability to say what links Soviet Russia, the Congo, America, Egypt and China (Tintin's first five destinations) or Amalthea, Pasiphae and Himalia (three of Jupiter's 63 of satellites) or what's wrong with Donald Duck's name (he should be called Donald Drake).

RATION CARDS

The Public Distribution System by which the staples of life (wheat, rice, lentils, kerosene, sugar, cooking oil) get to the people has another function. It also throws up the ultimate proof of identity, residence, domicile, lineage—the ration card. In those Indian families that do not have passports, the ration card is treated as the household deity. In those Indian families that do have passports, the ration card is still treated as a minor deity, an older jealous god it would not be wise to displease, because no one is quite sure whether the passport is actually proof of anything but everyone is sure that if your name appears on the ration card, you have the right to be noticed, you have the right to be fed, and you have the right to live in the house mentioned on the card. (Never mind that the ration card is actually a booklet.)

REBIRTH

The Hindu way of giving everyone a second chance at life, except for those who have optimized this one.

The Bollywood way of reconciling irreconcilable differences of class and caste in romance.

SAFARI SUIT

The unofficial uniform of the Indian bureaucrat, the safari suit spells power in rural India as much as it spells a man who oils his hair, has *churan* after dinner, paan with his extracurricular delights and wants an imported car.

SHOUTING

What we use to demonstrate to ourselves and to others that we are having a good time.

What we do when we don't know what else to do.

What we do when placed on a panel on national television.

What we do when we are in restaurants and other public places where people might expect a little quiet.

What we do when we have mobile phones pressed to our ears.

What we do at concerts, plays, film shows.

What we do.

(This may explain our notion of fireworks—where the rest of the world prefers elegant patterns of light against the night sky, we prefer ugly exploding things we call atom bombs and rope bombs.)

STARDUST

A film magazine that invented gossip.

A film magazine that invented Hinglish.

A film magazine that invented Shobhaa De. Or vice versa.

STARING

Visitors are routinely shocked/horrified/ alarmed at the consistency and intensity of the Indian's gaze. However, if they take the trouble to watch the Indian in repose, it will be noted that he is staring fixedly at the ground, the tree in front of him, the sea, a flower, his companion's moustache, whatever comes in his way. This is a national habit.

SUHAAG RAAT

The first night of the married life of an Indian couple is called the suhaag raat. It is marked by high drama and celebrated in song, especially since it was often the first time the man and woman saw each other. (Or at least technically speaking it was.) And then they were supposed to sleep together, he was supposed to deflower her and she was supposed to bleed on the sheets, all this aided by a glass of milk. Talk about the fast forward button.

SAUNF

In the west, there is a tradition by which the peanuts on a bar are supposed to be the germ-filled and disease-inducing thing in the bar, the ground included, because you're not going to lick the ground. In India, this tradition is upheld in the tray of saunf or fennel seeds (or seeds of the *Foeniculum vulgare*), which is served after dinner in the lower class of restaurants. Into this tray, the bill is slipped. Into this tray, the coins that represent the tip are dropped. Into this tray, if it be a common tray at the cash counter, the hands of the multitude dip.

Meanwhile, saunf is supposed to help your digestion and freshen your breath.

STD

Just as the BSE refers to the Bombay Stock Exchange and not to Bovine Spongy Encephalitis, STD refers to Subscriber Trunk Dialling and not to Sexually Transmitted Diseases. Those we call venereal diseases or VD.

TAJ MAHAL

When a man marries a fourteen year old and she gives birth to almost as many children in as many years, she is likely to die. Most other men would sigh a bit and go off to find other young women to wear out before their time. The Mughal Emperor Shahjahan was different. He built a mausoleum to remind us all how much he loved his worn-out waif.

TALCUM POWDER

Also called powder or face powder. This is our cosmetic of choice, our deodorant of choice, our whitener of choice, and even a massage lubricant. (In Mumbai, it is possible to have a powder massage.) Most often to be seen in the creases of men's necks, a thin white line of hope left after the labours of the day.

TAPORI

The great unwashed of the city of Mumbai, specially a young cocky male member of that considerable number.

The language of the said great unwashed. This depersonalized and deodorized tapori is welcome in the air-conditioned boardrooms of the multinationals where it is now used to sell products that those who naturally speak tapori would never be able to afford.

THIRD DEGREE

Brutal interrogation methods in use by the police across the length and breadth of India. If you have not been subjected to them, it is only because you have been insulated by class or caste position. If you have, you might have third-degree burns on some parts of your body.

TONGUE-CLEANER

This is a narrow strip of plastic with which the fur that accumulates on the tongue, arising out of a troubled digestion, may be scraped off. Like so many Indian solutions, this focuses on the results rather than the causes.

TURBAN

At one point, you could tell where a man came from, what his caste was, whether he was in mourning or coming out of it and probably how many goats he had from his turban. Men who exchanged turbans were blood brothers. For a man to place his turban at your feet was for him to abase himself in front of you. In ancient India, so says turbansofindia.com, you could mortgage your turban. And so on. Only no one is going to wear them, except as fancy dress, in twenty-five years from now. Rajasthan may keep the turban alive but only because they know the value of a turban in the creation of the right mood for tourism.

UNDERWEAR (MEN)

We are a nation obsessed with underwear. Everywhere, you will see them hung out to dry—on balconies, terraces and potted plants. All over the countryside, you will see advertisements for various brands, ranging from the familiar (VIP, Rupa) to the bizarre (Dixcy underwear, Joker Cox shorts). Our television channels play endless advertisements of men going to work only in their underwear, ladies asking about the quality of the elastic while buying underwear, ageing action stars advising boys on vests, and even the occasional orang utan in tighty-whities.

Our relationship with hosiery dates back to the VIP underwear advertisements in which a man in a VIP Y-front and a dressing gown sent the bad guy flying while curving a protective arm around a woman in distress. This advertisement made VIP the chuddi of choice for the great Indian middle class when the men made the transition out of langoats and striped shorts and into black patches on the inner thigh. It took liberalization to bring us foreign names, vibrant colours, waistbands as fashion statements, misspelt names and a completely bizarre and irrelevant debate about boxers versus briefs.

We are also a nation that buys our underwear on the roads. Is there a middle-class woman anywhere else in the free world who would buy her panties in public view? Is there anywhere else in the world a man who will come to your home and measure you for a bra and then go away and stitch one up? Is there anywhere else in the world a programme that would ask you to guess what percentage of Indians walk around with holes in their underwear?

Meanwhile, just to prove that we carry our underwear fixation with us, the British now speak of chuddis quite casually after *Goodness Gracious Me* made 'Kiss my chuddis' a catchphrase.

UNDERWEAR (WOMEN)

The reason why tennis was such a big spectator sport on television in India.

VICCO TURMERIC AYURVEDIC CREAM

At one point in India's history, every middle-class school child knew three advertisement jingles by heart. The first one was for Lifebuoy. The second was for Vicco Vajradanti ('*Vajradanti, vajradanti, Vicco Vajradanti, toothpowder, toothpaste; Ayurvedic jadibootiyon se banaa sampoorna swadeshi, toothpowder, toothpaste; Vicco Vajradanti*') and the third was for Vicco Turmeric Ayurvedic Cream.

How deep the baritone with which the announcer began: *Kudrat jab meherbaan hokar, apni anmol khazaanon ka pata deti hai, to…* And so on.

Go on, sing along, you know you want to.

YES

This often means 'Yes'.

It also means 'No'.

It sometimes means 'I have no idea but my best guess is that you want to hear a "yes" so I will say that.'

The polite say that this uncertainty arises because Indians are trained to please their superiors and their elders and agree with them. The western visitor to India says it is because 'These guys shake their heads funny'. The rest think we're just liars or incompetent.

Is that the truth?

Yes.